Forms of Curriculum Inquiry

Edited by
Edmund C. Short

STATE UNIVERSITY OF NEW YORK PRESS

29.95

Published by
State University of New York Press, Albany

© 1991 State University of New York

For information, address State University of New York Press,
90 State Street, Suite 700, Albany, NY 12207

Production by Diane Ganeles
Marketing by Dana E. Yanulavich

Library of Congress Cataloging-in-Publication Data

Forms of curriculum inquiry / edited by Edmund C. Short.
        p.   cm. — (SUNY series, curriculum issues and inquiries)
      Includes bibliographical references.
      ISBN 0-7914-0648-2 (alk. paper). — ISBN 0-7914-0649-0 (alk. paper:
      pbk.)
      1. Curriculum planning—Research.   I. Short, Edmund C.
      II. Series: SUNY series in curriculum issues and inquiries.
      LB1570.F665   1991
      375′.001′072—dc20   90-40502
                                                                      CIP

10   9   8   7   6   5   4   3

SUNY Series, Curriculum Issues and Inquiries
——————— * ———————
Edmund C. Short, Editor

Forms of
Curriculum
Inquiry

To Dwayne Huebner
who first argued for multiple forms of curriculum inquiry

Contents

Preface

Upon reading Gareth Morgan's volume, *Beyond Method: Strategies for Social Research* (1983), I became convinced that a book surveying the variety of approaches being used in curriculum research was needed. Like Morgan's treatment of different ways of studying social organizations, I wanted this book on curriculum to reflect the diverse forms of inquiry that have developed in recent years to address new and different research questions in the field of curriculum studies. It was apparent to me that much significant work was being conducted in this field and that this was being accomplished largely through the use of a variety of research strategies and approaches seldom used in other branches of educational research. Not only did these varied forms of curriculum inquiry need to be recognized and articulated within the field of curriculum studies itself, but their viability also needed to be demonstrated and legitimated beyond curriculum studies to those who might be able to use them in similar or related fields of research.

It has taken longer to bring this book to press than anyone imagined when it was first conceived. I am pleased, nonetheless, with its final shape and substance now that it is completed. It provides a comprehensive, though not exhaustive, array of curriculum research methodologies characterized as different forms of inquiry. Researchers who are experienced in the use of each of these forms of inquiry describe their basic understanding of them and how they should be carried out. Standard disciplinary forms of inquiry, such as the philosophical, the historical, and the scientific, as well as more complex interdisciplinary forms, such as the critical, the deliberative, and the theoretical, are explained in relation to their appropriate use in addressing particular kinds of curriculum research questions.

Between the introductory essay and the closing reflections, seventeen different forms of curriculum inquiry are described. In each of these chapters, the authors explain the purposes and processes associated with conducting each of these forms of curriculum inquiry. They give an overview of the conceptual and procedural knowledge related to using these forms of inquiry and discuss their strengths and limitations as seen in particular examples. Bibliographies in each of the chapters cite particular curriculum studies and related methodological treatises relevant to the form of inquiry addressed by that chapter. Chapters are therefore relatively brief, yet they provide access to extensive knowledge elsewhere for readers who may wish to explore related sources.

This book not only surveys a wide range of different forms of curriculum inquiry; it also makes the case that multiple forms of inquiry are necessary if curriculum questions are to be adequately addressed. I have attempted to provide in the introductory essay some background for understanding this argument and for appreciating the development in recent years of curriculum inquiry as a field of study. For those who are entering this field for the first time, I have also tried to set the description of curriculum inquiry within a framework of fundamental ideas regarding inquiry generally and of educational and other practical research fields as well.

I wish to acknowledge the fine work of the contributing authors in the preparation and editing of their manuscripts for this book. It is they who deserve most of the credit for the high quality of the final product. Without their devoted efforts this book would never have been completed.

I also wish to acknowledge the help of all who have participated in reviewing various drafts of the manuscript for this book. They are too numerous to mention by name, but they constitute the core of scholars who make up the field of curriculum studies. I extend my gratitude to all of them.

————Edmund C. Short

Introduction: Understanding Curriculum Inquiry

——— Edmund C. Short

> Curriculum research involves establishing the aims or ends of ed-
> ucation and other aspects of schooling, clarifying the concepts central
> to the enterprise, working out what is logically required for organization
> and method by the nature of the enterprise, establishing insofar as we
> can what social, psychological, and administrative factors may have
> what effects on success at achieving our aims in practice, describing
> contingent and logical restraints and demands on procedures of imple-
> mentation and evaluation, and prescribing procedures for them. Each of
> these elements has to be approached in a different kind of way, yet each
> of these elements has to be given due attention if we are to make reason-
> able curriculum proposals. Curriculum research must therefore involve
> interrelationship (Barrow 1985: 36).

Those who are familiar with the real world of curriculum will find Barrow's characterization of curriculum research quite understandable and
credible. It implies, first of all, that curriculum research is related to a cluster
of practical activities focusing on conceiving, expressing, justifying and enacting educational programs. These curricular activities involve making
choices on a variety of issues which, when taken together, form both substantive and practical guidelines for governing these programs. If these
choices are to be informed choices, they must be made with full knowledge
of the relevant research that relates to such choices.

Besides implying that curriculum research is related directly to doing
practical curriculum activities, Barrow's statement also implies that doing
curriculum research is not the same thing as making practical curricular
choices. Curriculum research involves seeking and justifying the knowledge
that is relevant to the making of such choices. It is an enterprise that involves
undertaking formal inquiry to generate relevant knowledge. Curriculum activities and decision-making are, after all, matters which have been engaged
in repeatedly by many people in the past, and the attempt to learn something
useful about this practical enterprise through formal inquiry and study

1

seems to be a reasonable way of approaching these matters. The problem is to decide what curriculum research should be done and how to do it.

Barrow implies that no matter how interrelated the various facets of practical choice-making in curriculum may be and no matter how interrelated curriculum research needs to be with these practical curriculum choices, curriculum research must operate by theories and principles of procedure that are determined by the kind of research knowledge that is sought. Every research effort focuses on some particular knowledge need, on some particular research question, and not every research question can be approached in the same way. Barrow reminds us that different forms of inquiry are necessary to address different kinds of curriculum research questions. Indeed, curriculum research involves the use of multiple forms of inquiry.

In this introductory essay, I want to discuss the field of curriculum research as a whole, how it is similar to and how it is different from other fields of research, and why its methods of study have become more differentiated in recent years. This general understanding of the nature of curriculum research (I prefer to call it curriculum inquiry) will provide a useful frame of reference for the chapters that follow on various forms of curriculum inquiry. Since no previous book has attempted to describe the field of curriculum inquiry as a whole and the various forms of inquiry used within it, this particular formulation presented in this book must be considered the unique perspective of the editor and author of this introductory essay. Nevertheless, it is a perspective that attempts to reflect the way curriculum inquiry is rather than how I think it ought to be.

The Nature and Structure of Curriculum Inquiry

Curriculum inquiry is a species of educational research or inquiry. As such, it addresses particular kinds of educational research questions related to formulating curriculum policies, developing curriculum programs, and enacting these policies and programs. Curriculum inquiry involves identifying those curriculum questions that are amenable to inquiry, knowing what form of inquiry to use in attempting to answer those particular questions, and carrying out the appropriate processes of inquiry in order to obtain those answers.

To understand the nature and structure of curriculum inquiry, we need to understand its relation to inquiry in general, its structure, its relation to curriculum practice, its current status and problems, its special features as a field of practical inquiry, and the necessity of employing multiple forms of inquiry in addressing curriculum research questions. Each of these topics will be discussed in turn.

The General Nature of Inquiry

Inquiry is an intellectual activity in which we seek to find out something not yet known or clearly understood. Inquiry is prompted by the need to have reliable answers to certain perplexing questions. The need to have certain questions answered is an experience we all share; all of us engage regularly in some kind of inquiry. We may do so individually or in groups. We may do so formally or informally. We may discover that some questions we attempt to answer prove to be quite difficult to answer and that some are impossible to answer. The intent of inquiry, nevertheless, is clear: "Inquiry is an activity which produces knowledge" (Churchman 1971: 8).

Scholarly inquiry differs in function and approach from the more informal type of inquiry that we do in connection with our everyday activities. In many circumstances when we have questions for which we need answers, we turn to persons or sources that have the answers we need. We may assume that they are correct and trustworthy answers, try to understand them as best we can, and proceed to use them. So much of what we learn in school and in life involves this kind of informal inquiry that we may fail to realize that much of the knowledge we draw upon has its genesis in more formal scholarly inquiry. It is the function of this more formal kind of inquiry to provide reliable answers to new questions as they arise, questions that have never before been asked, or if they have been asked, have never been answered satisfactorily. Scholarly inquiry requires the use of painstaking and disciplined thought processes whereby answers to researchable questions can be established and verified until they can be taken with confidence as reliable by those who are not themselves involved in doing the necessary scholarly inquiry. The knowledge generated through scholarly inquiry and its various ways of knowing are of fundamental value for us to learn if we are to have access to trustworthy knowledge for use in our everyday activities and specialized pursuits (Eisner 1985b).

The problem of assessing the trustworthiness of scholarly knowledge is a persistent one for layman and scholar alike. Knowledge in most domains is not fixed once and for all. Certain questions are reopened from time to time because flaws are detected in the way answers were previously generated. How does anyone know whether those doing scholarly inquiry have conducted their inquiries appropriately and accurately and whether the answers to the questions posed are reasonably reliable? It helps to know something about the procedures and methods that are employed in formal inquiry and to be able to critically assess both the inquiry processes and the answers arrived at. Because there is considerable specialized knowledge and training involved in doing formal inquiry well, it is often difficult for the non-specialist to be knowledgeable enough about what is involved to be able to distinguish trustworthy inquiry from untrustworthy inquiry. Under these circumstances, it is particularly important that scholarly inquiry be done with as much skill and competence as possible so that the answers given to questions asked can be considered to be reasonably reliable.

Scholarly inquiry is a specialized intellectual activity in which relatively few people are engaged. We rely on these few people to engage in scholarly inquiry on behalf of the rest of us. They are expected to take the time and trouble necessary to do systematic inquiry and to check and recheck, individually and collectively, both their inquiry processes and their results. Many of these people are engaged in formal inquiry full-time, but for a great many others formal inquiry is only an occasional or part-time activity. Regardless of how much or how little formal inquiry they do, we expect them to be experts in this intellectual activity, to know how to do a particular kind of inquiry, and to be able to do it competently.

A system of training in doing a particular kind of research is usually prescribed and is undertaken by those who wish to become certified experts in a chosen field of inquiry. Some people, of course, master more than one mode of inquiry, but more often than not expertise is acquired in a single mode, or in a few related modes, because the complexities involved in learning to use them properly are often quite challenging. Experience in using a particular mode of inquiry is essential, and the more experience a person has in using a particular approach the more skill and competence that person is likely to develop. Unfortunately, after initial training is completed, there is seldom much quality control that can be exercised over the formal inquiry done by a particular individual, except as criticism may be extended by competent colleagues at scholarly meetings or through the screening of material presented for publication to refereed journals and book publishers. There are, admittedly, some persons who do scholarly inquiry that is somewhat weak, but there are many as well who do very high quality work.

Like scholarly inquiry in general, curriculum inquiry is a specialized field of research requiring trained experts who understand the nature and purpose of inquiry generally and are competent to conduct specialized research in curriculum by means of appropriate forms of inquiry. It will become clear from the chapters that follow that doing curriculum inquiry requires considerable knowledge and experience in selecting and carrying out accepted formal inquiry processes associated with any of these forms of inquiry.

The Structure of Inquiry

How is scholarly inquiry organized? Curriculum inquiry, or any field of formal inquiry, has an internal structure or organization that needs to be understood by all who engage in it or utilize its results. A field of inquiry is usually composed of several domains of inquiry, each of which may involve the use of several different forms of inquiry. In the long history of the development of scholarly inquiry, more and more differentiated fields of inquiry have been generated (King and Brownell 1966; Schwab 1978; Tykociner 1964). Today a wide array of distinct fields of inquiry exist. Some of these are referred to as *academic or basic disciplines* (Martin 1970; 1981; Phenix 1964a; 1964b; Schwab 1964). Formal inquiry in each of the academic disciplines, e.g., in physics, mathematics, music, or philosophy, addresses unique questions defined by the discipline itself without regard to the application or use of the answers to these questions outside the discipline. Indeed, much of the knowledge generated within a particular discipline cannot, by its very nature, be applied or used outside the context of that discipline. Those fields of inquiry having the explicit purpose of applying or using knowledge from the basic disciplines are usually referred to as *applied disciplines*. Such fields of inquiry as mineral economics, rural sociology, medical ethics, and geopolitics are included in this category (Cronbach and Suppes 1969; National Academy of Sciences 1977; Storer 1964; Tyler 1976).

Quite different from either the academic or the applied disciplines are those *practical fields of inquiry* that have developed in relation to some realm of practical human activity, such as criminal justice, law, medicine, education, electrical engineering, home economics, business, or greenhouse design. Each of these broadbased fields of practical inquiry may be further divided into narrower, more focused fields of inquiry. For example, education as a broad field of inquiry includes subdivisions devoted to inquiry related to teaching, administration, curriculum planning, and policy making, as well as to educational psychology, educational theory, comparative education, teaching methods in language for early childhood education, and a number of others. Several of these subdivisions correspond to particular subdivisions that exist within the realm of educational practice, but others do not seem to focus on any particular aspect of practice. The separation of a field of practical inquiry into a series of identifiable subdivisions usually results from conventional coalescence of research interests rather than from logical analysis or ease of accessibility for practitioners.

The field of curriculum inquiry, with which this book is primarily concerned, is itself gradually becoming further differentiated into a variety of inquiry domains and subdomains. There is, however, little consensus among those doing inquiry in the curriculum field about what these domains should be. A number of schemes have been used or advocated in the curriculum inquiry literature for structuring inquiry and the resulting curriculum knowledge (Rosales-Dordelly and Short 1985: 23–26; Short 1985). None of these has yet taken on conventional status. There is much overlapping among domains and much confusion about where to locate a particular topic of inquiry and related studies.

In fields of inquiry that are relatively new, like the field of curriculum inquiry, it can be expected that alternative schemes for organizing the field into fairly well-established domains of inquiry will compete with each other for some time before a dominant pattern emerges. The very fluidity of a field of practical activity such as curriculum practice may also contribute to the appearance in the field of curriculum inquiry of new and competing domains of inquiry. Standard questions and replicated studies are not as characteristic of practical fields of inquiry as may be true in the basic disciplines, and so, frequent changes in the way the structure of curriculum inquiry may be conceived is likely to occur. This whole matter of domain identity is of no great consequence unless its changing and multifarious character makes it difficult to locate related inquiry or inhibits the application and use of this inquiry. Nonetheless, it is well to know how a field of inquiry is structured and how to find one's way around in it.

All fields of practical inquiry, including curriculum inquiry, are in reality composite fields. Several domains of inquiry exist side-by-side within such a field of inquiry, each focusing on a different aspect of the practical activity toward which inquiry may be addressed (Freeman 1973). Each domain consists of a series of related topics and questions to be addressed (or already addressed) by formal inquiry processes, along with the answers to those questions, and the relevant sifted knowledge accumulated from all studies done within that domain.

Subdomains can also exist whenever distinguishable components become the focus of inquiry. For instance, if the curriculum development process is the focus of an entire domain of curriculum inquiry, subdomains devoted to questions about setting objectives, selecting content, organizing instruction, or evaluating a program may appropriately be among those embraced by the domain as a whole, and inquiry related to any one of these subdomains may be carried out whether inquiry in other subdomains occurs or not.

The process of identifying and establishing particular domains of inquiry in curriculum, or in any field of practical inquiry, is obviously not an entirely rational process; neither is it solely an arbitrary one. The questions and answers that are included within a given domain of inquiry necessarily relate to some aspect of concrete curriculum practice. The acts and events of practice, however construed or distinguished from one another, become the basis for whatever domains of curriculum inquiry are proposed.

The acts and events of curriculum practice occur as entities, as wholes. They cannot be divided arbitrarily into parts which correspond to some analytic scheme which may be possible to create mentally. To attempt to do so would distort the reality of these acts and events and substitute mental constructs for real ones. These acts and events come whole and must remain so if we are to deal with the reality as it presents itself to us and not deal merely with a thought or idea for which there is no corresponding reality. Domains of inquiry in practical fields such as curriculum must, therefore, be distinguished in ways that respect existing acts and events as entities or wholes rather than using analytic categories to distinguish them. If they are not distinguished in this way, inquiry may proceed on matters that exist in name only and do not relate to actual curriculum acts or events. Witness the difference between inquiry attempted on reading comprehension and on decoding individual words. Comprehension is a whole; decoding word-by-word may not be a necessary element of comprehension.

Here again a difference between basic disciplines and fields of practical inquiry is apparent. In many of the disciplines, at least some of the time, it is possible to ask and answer questions that relate solely to ideas and not to acts or events. In some cases, whole domains have arisen that have been distinguished from each other by analytic distinctions rather than actual ones. The domains of mathematical inquiry provide the best examples of this.

The problem of domain identity within the field of curriculum inquiry is one that cannot easily be resolved. This book does not attempt to resolve it. While it may be helpful to engage in critiques of existing domain distinctions and to offer alternative ones for consideration, it will no doubt require influences and actions other than scholarly ones for any one scheme to achieve widespread acceptance in the field of curriculum inquiry. There are some curriculum scholars who think no single scheme should become dominant because it might inhibit inquiry. There is some validity to this point of view.

In summary, all inquiries in the field of curriculum focus on certain aspects within particular domains of curriculum inquiry however they may be defined or distinguished. Understanding how these curriculum elements and domains may be structured is fundamental to designing and carrying out particular instances of curriculum inquiry.

The Relation of Inquiry to Practice

Consider the truism that before there is *inquiry*, there is *doing*, or at least the need to *do*. Action can be taken, and often is taken, before or without conducting formal or informal inquiry related to the action. This certainly has often been the case in much of curriculum practice. Nevertheless, the value of taking considered action, rather than acting before thinking carefully, is recognized as being quite desirable. The problem is to see just how action and inquiry may be most appropriately related.

The matter of the relationship between action and thought has been a perennial problem that has perplexed the best of scholars throughout human history (Gotshalk 1969; Hampshire 1982; McKeon 1954; Toulmin 1976). Should not thought be taken before acting or doing? If so, what kind of thought? How does one do the required thinking? And how does one use this when acting? These questions are the subject of much philosophical investigation; they remain largely open and unsettled.

Yet having inquiry of certain kinds available makes it possible for practitioners to do different things than they might do in the absence of such inquiry. Curriculum *inquiry* is assumed to have some requisite value for curriculum *action:* it has a practical purpose, to inform *curriculum action.* It is not an intellectual pursuit carried on for the sake of mere curiosity or for possible application to some other field, as is true of the academic disciplines in the sciences and the humanities. Curriculum inquiry exists only to help deal with an activity that must be done whenever people are to be educated in some organized way over time, that is, whenever curriculum must be developed and enacted.

Practical curriculum activity involves problems of decision and action, judgment and enactment. Curriculum inquiry involves answering questions for which definite answers can be obtained; it attempts to answer particular questions and to provide knowledge or understanding about them. Curriculum practice is action-oriented rather than inquiry-oriented. Getting something done is the essence of curriculum practice. As in all fields of practical activity, curriculum practice involves deciding what should be done to bring about a desired state of affairs, in this case toward an educative result through some curriculum processes, and then acting upon that decision. Curriculum inquiry, on the other hand, is a highly disciplined intellectual activity in which some formally justified logic of procedure is employed to obtain a confirmable answer to a researchable curriculum question that has been isolated for inquiry.

If we assume that curriculum practice is concerned with specifying, justifying, and enacting desired educative actions (what is to be taught, to which persons, under what rules of teaching, and how these shall be interrelated; Kliebard 1989), then the particular activities involved in doing curriculum practice can be (and have been) identified rather clearly through empirical investigation (Foshay 1980; Glatthorn 1987; Reid 1978; Vallance 1983). They tend to fall into domains of curriculum practice such as curriculum policy making and evaluation, curriculum program development, and curriculum change and enactment. Curriculum inquiry is concerned with answering specific questions related to any of these domains of curriculum practice about which knowledge and understanding is sought.

Until recently, most of the attention of practitioners and thoughtful academics in curriculum was devoted to the problems of doing curriculum;

their attention was directed largely to the activities associated with curriculum planning and designing. The emergence in the 1960s of a small cadre of research scholars in the field of curriculum marked the beginning of a self-conscious community of scholars who asked more fundamental questions about the whole enterprise than had previously been asked. No longer did it seem legitimate simply to pass along good practices and wisdom from those authorities who claimed wide experience in doing curriculum activity. Scholarly motives prompted the desire to qualify the sharing of this valuable experience with a degree of justification based on research and theory. The evolution of this expanded interest in curriculum research and inquiry has been traced elsewhere by Eisner (1985a), Schubert (1986), Short (1987), Short, Willis, and Schubert (1985), and Taylor (1979).

The number of research articles and books published in curriculum over the last twenty-five years suggests that curriculum practice should be benefiting tremendously from this increased research activity. Yet why curriculum knowledge is needed at all, let alone knowledge that is both useful and pluralistic in character and derivation, is for many curriculum practitioners (and for some curriculum scholars as well) problematic and not at all self-evident. Without an abundance of recognized and frequently drawn-upon curriculum knowledge, it is difficult to make a case for utilizing this sort of curriculum knowledge. In fact, it must be admitted that it is rare to find persons who are engaged in any domain of curriculum-related activity who deliberately and routinely seek out and utilize established curriculum knowledge.

Yet, the value of curriculum knowledge is much the same as the value of knowledge of any kind, and the case for generating it is no more difficult to justify than the case for any kind of knowledge. First of all, there is the argument from the negative: that knowledge is better than conjecture, half-truth, prejudice, superstition, and other undisciplined, uncritical thought forms. The history of the use of these other thought forms is so riddled with undesirable consequences that we should be drawn to a reliance upon those thought forms that have survived the careful and disciplined processes of formal inquiry and have thus achieved the status of "knowledge." We have enough trouble coping with life's activities when knowledge is the mainstay of our discourse; we have no reason to expect an advantage from drawing on less valid thought forms except when we have no disciplined knowledge available to us for our use. A second, more positive argument asserts that since knowledge is public, that is, since it is open to verification by all and is thus warranted by virtue of our common capacity to be persuaded by sound processes of reasoning and logical argument, knowledge is the vehicle par excellence by which we may communicate intelligibly with one another and solve problems of mutual concern with language that facilitates common understanding and efficient judgment. Without public knowledge, we languish in confusion and in aimless and unproductive discourse.

Still, it is not clear that the results of curriculum inquiry have deliberately and consistently been used in the doing of curriculum work (Short 1973: 283–284; Short, Willis, and Schubert 1985: 1–22, 66). There are several possible explanations for this state of affairs. Researchers may have addressed matters not considered useful or relevant to the actual doing of curriculum activities. Thus, research, even if available, may not seem credible. It may be too esoteric in its presentation. There may be reason to question the research methods employed, and consequently, confidence in results may be lacking. The scope and sophistication of inquiry required by the exigencies of practice may have escaped the research being done. These are empirical matters on which definitive information has not yet been collected. Just why this gap exists between curriculum research and practice needs to be more fully studied, and an analysis of its nature and dimensions needs to be more clearly understood before corrective action can be taken. If curriculum inquiry is to make a significant contribution to dealing with curriculum problems, it must be conducted with a clear understanding of what is relevant and how best to present its results. Congruence of intentionality between the researcher and the practitioners in the field of curriculum is the prime requisite for inquiry and practice to be meaningfully related.

Factors Affecting Quality and Status of Curriculum Inquiry

Regardless of the current status of curriculum research and its relevance to curriculum practice, the quality of inquiry in the field of curriculum depends upon the expertise with which it is conducted. Critics have suggested that inquiry in curriculum ranges broadly from rather poorly done work to quite sophisticated, expertly done studies (Rosales-Dordelly and Short 1985). That it is not uniformly of high quality should be of concern to everyone interested in curriculum research or practice.

Part of the disparity in the quality displayed among individual curriculum studies is due to the fact that there is no single, relatively cohesive method of research applicable to curriculum inquiry that can be mastered and then utilized routinely thereafter for all curriculum studies. A multiplicity of research approaches is possible and germane in curriculum inquiry. Curriculum researchers commonly learn to conduct a number of different types of research in the course of their careers without formal training or mentoring; as they attempt each new approach, they acquire the skills necessary to perform each of these types of research.

Curriculum researchers seldom have the luxury of being formally trained in each of these forms of inquiry. They find that the range and variety of curriculum research questions call for expertise in a variety of different forms of inquiry which they must acquire on their own initiative. No doubt these circumstances contribute to weaknesses noted from time-to-time in some curriculum research reports.

Features of Inquiry in a Practical Field

What are the particular activities involved in doing curriculum inquiry? How readily are they identifiable? The answers to these questions are not easy to provide. There is no single inquiry process that is associated with doing curriculum inquiry; a multiplicity of different inquiry processes can be identified for use in conducting curriculum inquiry. Not all of them are widely known, but they are available for use in answering various kinds of curriculum research questions. No one inquiry process is capable of addressing all questions so a number of different inquiry processes have been developed, each one suited to answering specific kinds of questions.

The primary purpose of this book is to acquaint readers with the activities involved in utilizing a wide variety of forms of inquiry related to the field of curriculum studies. These research approaches are, of course, not unique nor limited to studies in the curriculum field. They can be used in any kind of educational research field or in any field of practical research as well. Nevertheless, their use in curriculum is increasing, and the distinctions among them, as well as a clear grasp of the circumstances under which each may be appropriately utilized, are important to convey to all who would engage in curriculum inquiry or who wish to interpret reports of inquiry done by others.

How does inquiry related to a field of practical activity such as curriculum differ from inquiry related to a discipline? And why is a multiplicity of research approaches necessary rather than a single one?

First, in a field of practical activity, the problems are primarily related to doing something rather than to knowing something, as suggested earlier. Doing is best accomplished in the presence of knowing, but it is the taking of action that is the fundamental characteristic of all practical activity. Knowledge and understanding are instrumental to the action. Establishing knowledge claims by acceptable forms of reasoning is the purpose of an academic discipline. This is a rational intellectual process that ends there; disciplines do not concern themselves with knowledge use or application.

Second, practical activities involve people who do something in situations; what is done is the result of decisions by people. Either as groups or individuals, they take into account goals and purposes, possible actions for achieving them, and relevant knowledge, information, and values, and then make judgments on a course of action to be taken, following this up with the taking of action. The human element in a discipline is directed by the requirement to confirm knowledge assertions through intellectually verifiable means. In a practical activity the human element is directed by the requirements of personal or corporate commitments and responsibility, of making judgments and defending them in situations, and of acting. Because persons in relationships with other persons are central to practical activity, there is a wider range of human capacities involved than are involved in establishing and verifying knowledge claims in a discipline.

Third, all actions and events involving human beings occur as entities, as wholes. It is possible for intellectual convenience to analyze something or attend only to one part of a phenomenon at a time, but in the real world of human activity everything that is done occurs as wholes and must be recognized as such. If we impose an analysis or partial perception on what presents itself to us, we do not grasp the reality accurately. Wholes are often difficult to understand, but we must know when we are dealing with whole entities and when we are mentally separating parts of the whole for clearer analysis.

Each of the academic disciplines is constituted to examine one thing at a time, one limited question at a time, by a mode of inquiry capable of dealing only with that particular kind of question. There is no other way of doing inquiry successfully, given the limitations of mind, language, and reasoning. But we should not think we have knowledge of wholes as a result of this process. Every attempt to divide wholes into manageable researchable questions misses something, even if we try to synthesize all the answers to all the separate questions. (And how do we know we have identified *all* the right questions?) Of course, we cannot escape doing this in trying to understand wholes, but there is an inevitable discontinuity that results from trying to match up the results of research from all the different questions which were investigated by different forms of inquiry. Practical activity cannot proceed by this analytic and arbitrarily focused method of an academic discipline. We must act for good or ill in response to human beings and situations as wholes. Thus, in trying to do inquiry related to wholes, we face a most difficult task. If we are not to distort reality by resorting to the use of disciplinary forms of inquiry, how then are we to do inquiry on wholes? What kind of knowledge is going to be of most value in fields of practical activities like curriculum?

Research in curriculum, as in all fields of practical activity, must be multidisciplinary and transdisciplinary in nature. That is to say, we need to know everything about a whole that we can possibly know. If, for instance, we are planning curriculum and wish to know whether to formulate our plans around curriculum objectives or some other kind of conceptual organizer, we might turn to research that documents and interprets the experience of others in this regard, to scientific studies of what happens under various options, to historical studies that sum up the cumulative experience, to philosophical studies that critically examine this evidence in relation to various kinds of criteria, and to any other kind of research that may seem relevant. While these various pieces of knowledge will not fit together neatly into an integrated pattern or whole, it is not difficult to believe we would be in a better position to make our choice about organizing curriculum around objectives or something else if we had this wide range of knowledge available to us than if we did not have it. At the very least, knowledge from one or two perspectives alone would present too limited a picture of what we would like to know in order to make an informed decision. Even with all possible disciplinary approaches focused upon a single whole issue or possible action, we may feel at a loss in making such decisions. We may require some transdisciplinary perspective that helps us conceptualize and evaluate the very problem we are confronting in practice. Many of the policy- and action-oriented forms of inquiry provide assistance of this kind. For this reason, a practical field of activity is most closely linked to research through what has been called deliberative or action inquiry approaches that are characteristically transdisciplinary in nature. Curriculum inquiry, therefore, keeps central a focus upon the type of human decision and/or action being studied (Schubert 1980, 1986a; Strike 1979) while asking subsidiary questions and answering them by multiple forms of inquiry. It then uses this knowledge conjunctively in answering the ultimate question, "What is to be done step-by-step in order to bring about the desired curricular result?"

Multiple Forms of Inquiry

All fields of practical inquiry employ multiple forms of inquiry rather than a single form of inquiry to address their questions and obtain their answers. Unlike the basic and applied disciplines in which a particular form of disciplinary inquiry is used in each discipline, practical inquiry utilizes many different forms of inquiry. Many of the disciplinary forms of inquiry may be used in practical inquiry, but in addition, multidisciplinary and transdisciplinary forms of inquiry may also be used. And these multiple forms of inquiry are appropriate within several different domains of inquiry; seldom is a single form of inquiry identified with a particular domain of inquiry.

Why are multiple forms of inquiry necessary in fields of practical inquiry? It is because of the kind of the questions that are asked. Because many of the questions that give rise to inquiry in a realm of practical activity are holistic rather than analytic in character, most of the processes defined by the academic disciplines are not well suited for answering these kinds of questions. The disciplines require that questions be conceived and worded in a particular way such that they are amenable to the forms of inquiry associated with each discipline. This is well and good if the inquiry is being conducted for its own sake, that is, just to see what the answers to the questions are. But if there is a real-world imperative to have a particular practical question answered, rewording the question to fit the inquiry tools available is really not acceptable. One should search for approaches to inquiry other than these disciplinary ones and match the inquiry processes to the demands of the actual questions being asked (Dillon 1984).

The problem, of course, is whether we can identify alternative forms of inquiry that are appropriate for these more holistic questions that arise naturally in practice and whether we can distinguish the kinds of questions each is capable of addressing. It is largely to this problem, as it is represented in the field of curriculum inquiry, that this book is directed. We shall see that a number of forms of inquiry have been identified, formalized, and utilized in attempting to address different kinds of curriculum questions. The need is to disseminate these approaches more widely, to stimulate more scholars to use them in appropriate studies, and to clarify, extend, and critique our knowledge and use of them.

Curriculum Questions and Appropriate Forms of Inquiry

The attempt to identify and distinguish forms of inquiry, as well as any attempt to use them appropriately and accurately, presupposes a clear definition of the basic concept or entity to which the phrase, *forms of inquiry,* refers. A *form of inquiry* is a process designed to answer a certain class of previously unanswered questions. Any such process is comprised of a series of proven procedures for making and justifying knowledge claims or obtaining answers to such questions that are congruent with some theory of inquiry (Dewey 1938; Hamlyn 1970). A form of inquiry is often thought of, loosely, as a method of research in which established procedures are followed and from which conclusions inexorably follow. This mistaken notion overlooks the fact that procedures cannot be separated from a theory of inquiry that gives them meaning and purpose and a clear rationale (Buchler 1961). In fact, an accurate interpretation of a theory of inquiry may allow for some flexibility in procedures rather than a rigid adherence to a fixed pattern of procedures.

It has been demonstrated that a single theory of inquiry and an associated logic of procedure cannot suffice to answer all questions that may arise in formal inquiry (King and Brownell 1966). The very differences inherent in different kinds of questions require that they be addressed differently. For example, a question about what constituted the common branches of learning in the curriculum of nineteenth-century grammar schools in the United States requires obtaining data and drawing conclusions about that data in ways quite different from what is required by a question about how a particular set of teachers interprets their participation (or lack of participation) in curriculum policy making decisions at the local school district level. The first question is historical in its focus, and the canons of historical inquiry apply. The second question is phenomenological in type and requires the use of interpretive forms of inquiry. The processes designed to answer these two different kinds of questions call for different procedures, different data-gathering techniques, different methods of analysis, different logic or reasoning processes to establish justifiable knowledge claims, etc. — in short, two separate and distinct forms of formal inquiry.

Classifying and labeling various forms of inquiry is hardly a science with formal rules and procedures. Nevertheless, scholars have done some comparative analysis and systematization of various forms of inquiry (Phenix 1964a; Phenix 1964b; Schwab 1978; Tykociner 1966). The most commonly distinguished forms of inquiry, such as the scientific, the artistic, or the philosophical, are familiar enough to us, but each of these is not really as singular as might be supposed. They each represent, in actuality, several related forms of inquiry. For instance, within the empirical/theoretical sciences there are forms of inquiry ranging from the analytic-classificatory procedures of biology and zoology to the hypothetical-deductive procedures of theoretical physics and chemistry. These and other related ones are all clearly classified as scientific forms of inquiry. They may be distinguished, for instance, from artistic forms of inquiry, such as the non-discursive presentation of an aesthetic idea or feeling through music or art and the discursive presentation of human character and ideals through dramatic fiction or biography. Each of these sets of related forms of inquiry is distinguished from the other, and from all other forms of inquiry, by the type of questions they are able to address and the characteristic way they go about establishing answers to them.

Listed below are the forms of inquiry that are described in this book. Each is discussed by its respective author or authors in terms of its intended purpose, the classes of questions it is capable of addressing, the theories of inquiry it can employ, and the logic of procedure it requires to generate and substantiate the knowledge claims it yields. Certain of these forms of inquiry are the conventional disciplinary forms of inquiry. Others toward the end of the list are multidisciplinary or transdisciplinary in character, and are well-suited to the kinds of holistic questions posed in curriculum. While some of these may be less familiar to curriculum scholars than most of the conventional disciplinary ones, they have existed (under some name) for a very long time and have been widely utilized in numerous studies in various

fields of research, including education (Bredo and Feinberg 1982; Kockelmans 1979).

Analytic	Hermeneutic
Ampliative	Theoretical
Speculative	Normative
Historical	Critical
Scientific	Evaluative
Ethnographic	Integrative
Narrative	Deliberative
Aesthetic	Action
Phenomenological	

Questions that arise in the field of curriculum inquiry are answerable
by using any or all of these forms of inquiry. These questions range quite
widely in subject matter and focus, and thus no single form of inquiry is
characteristically employed in answering them. The most common types of
questions asked in curriculum inquiry, however, are those which require
multidisciplinary or transdisciplinary forms of inquiry, such as the theoretical, the normative, the critical, the evaluative, the integrative, the deliberative, and the action forms of inquiry. This is the case because of the nature
of curriculum activity itself, the kind of knowledge required in the course of
doing curriculum activity, and the type of inquiry questions formulated to
obtain this kind of knowledge.

No definitive taxonomy of research questions needing answers has
been devised in the field of curriculum inquiry. However desirable such a
taxonomy might appear to be to some curriculum researchers, the task
would be nearly impossible to complete. New questions are always being
identified that had not been thought of before, and circumstances of practice
change rapidly enough that some old questions no longer seem relevant.
What can be done, however, is to identify some typical questions or classes
of questions that are capable of being addressed by the forms of inquiry
available to us. If certain classes of questions arise that are not amenable to
the forms of inquiry we have at hand, some new forms of inquiry would obviously have to be devised to deal with them.

To illustrate the categorical differences among curriculum research
questions that exist in relation to the various forms of inquiry described in
this book, some typical questions are given in Figure 1 for each of these seventeen forms of curriculum inquiry. By comparing and contrasting these
questions, differences in the purposes and procedures of the various forms
of curriculum inquiry will become apparent, and some sense of the appropriateness of a given form of inquiry for addressing certain kinds of questions may be gained.

Figure 1
Typical Questions Dealt with by Various Forms of Inquiry

Analytical   To what does the term "curriculum" ordinarily refer?

What concept might serve to guide curriculum practice better than "educational objectives?"

Ampliative   What assumptions and norms are implicit in the arguments presented in support of a particular educational program and how appropriate are they?

What alternative rationales would be more appropriate and why?

Speculative   What personally synthesized knowledge and experience can I usefully convey to others about the curriculum planning process (or about needed changes in school programs)?

What warning or guidance can I offer about current trends in curriculum theory (or school curriculum practice)?

Historical   What were the common factors supporting the passage in 36 state legislatures between 1983 and 1986 of increased curriculum requirements and standards for high school graduation?

How (and in what political context) were the processes of curriculum decision-making carried out at City Center Magnet School between 1968 and 1973?

Scientific   How many schools use the curriculum model employed in John Dewey's Laboratory School at the University of Chicago?

Is "expanding environments" the most common scheme used in grades 1–3 social studies throughout the U.S. for organizing curriculum units?

Ethnographic   What elements constitute or influence curriculum decision-making at district or state levels?

What factors in the processes of curriculum planning improve or inhibit teachers' abilities to take part in curriculum development?

Narrative   What historically (autobiographically) can I reconstruct about the meaning I have ascribed to my teachers' or courses' influence on my career choice?

Have I changed my views as a music teacher over the last 25 years about what's important to teach in the music curriculum and why?

Aesthetic   How can the impact of the curriculum experienced by Mrs. Smith's class be characterized qualitatively?

What are the salient qualities of text materials in company X's packaged reading program?

Phenomenological   What does the pupil perceive and feel about being placed half day in a separate vocational school program and half day in a comprehensive school program?

Is the development of a new health program in District One perceived differently by a committee person who is a teacher, a curriculum coordinator, or an administrator?

Hermeneutic   What does the phrase "I hated school" really mean in a journal written by a dropout from Jefferson High?

What does Mr. Jones, tenth-grade science teacher, mean when he says, "Curriculum evaluation in this school is like trying to shoe a horse on the freeway."

What was meant by the term "a curriculum branch," used in late nineteenth-century curriculum literature?

Theoretical   How shall statements relating structural elements, normative perspectives, and action guidelines best be formulated to convey the overall conceptual scheme posited for a specific curriculum?

Is the concept "curriculum design" a valid and efficacious one for grasping and communicating the idea of organizing all aspects of a curriculum into a workable whole (including normative, practical, and structural dimensions)?

Normative   On what premises can a curriculum be created?

What systematic justification can be offered for a proposed curriculum?

Critical   What contradictions and inconsistencies exist between fundamental norms (e.g., equal access to knowledge, intellectual freedom, human dignity) and existing curriculum decisions and practices?

How clear is the link between rhetoric and action regarding "no bias" (sexual, economic, ideological) in curriculum and its enactment?

Evaluative   Does the "post-holing" method of content selection in history contribute to stated objectives better than the chronological coverage method?

Is curriculum enactment generally enhanced or inhibited by the use of a curriculum guide by teachers?

Integrative   Do the available empirical studies on how curriculum change occurs in schools indicate any congruence (or ambiguity) in theoretical understanding or in hypotheses for further investigation?

Does the explanation of case studies on the use of various types of curriculum development strategies give evidence of which strategy is most effective?

Deliberative   Should we change our curriculum policies or guidelines (e.g., with respect to goals, content, curriculum organization and resource allocations)?

What is the best course of action to accomplish the desired ends?

Action   What shall be done at this step to align our actions with the ultimate goal?

What adjustment in the next step is necessary as a result of what happened after the last step?

By making an overall examination of the forms of inquiry and illustrative curriculum questions in Figure 1, a number of insights may be drawn regarding curriculum inquiry. First, it would appear that a wider and more varied range of questions can be asked and answered within this field of inquiry than many of us have previously realized (Kimpston and Rogers 1986; Posner 1989). The differentiation of the many different forms of inquiry makes it possible to conceive of a variety of specific questions that correspond to the function and processes of the different forms of inquiry—questions that might not otherwise have come to mind. The scope of substantive matters that even these illustrative questions encompass suggests that the domains of knowledge that are relevant to curriculum activity may be more numerous than many scholars have previously realized. While the variety of available forms of inquiry in no way defines the number or substance of these domains of curriculum knowledge, nevertheless, their availability for use in curriculum research can stimulate scholars to deal with more questions relevant to practice than could have been accommodated by a narrower range of inquiry forms and processes.

Second, those questions cited toward the end of the list—ones related to action, deliberative, integrative, evaluative, critical, normative, and theoretical inquiry—seem to be the kinds that resemble most closely those questions confronted in the day-to-day work of ordinary curriculum practice. The questions amenable to earlier forms of inquiry on the list are narrower and less easily related to the holistic problems of practice than are those associated with the complex, multidisciplinary or transdisciplinary forms of inquiry toward the end of the list. This suggests that, if the problems of curriculum practice are going to be informed by formal inquiry, the most desirable and useful kinds of inquiry to be attempted would be those involving these latter types of questions and forms of inquiry.

For example, theoretical knowledge can assist with the problem of conceiving, structuring, and expressing the constitutive elements or form of a usable curriculum; theoretical inquiry yields theoretical knowledge. Normative knowledge can assist with the problem of determining the preferred norms and values that shall govern the substance of the curriculum; normative inquiry yields normative knowledge. Critical knowledge can assist with the problem of determining discrepancies between curricular ideals and practices and what could bring them more into alignment; critical inquiry yields critical knowledge. Evaluative knowledge can assist with the problem of determining what curricular norms and practices are being appropriately or inappropriately enacted; evaluative inquiry yields evaluative knowledge. Integrative knowledge can assist with the problem of determining what is known from research or experience that is relevant to making curriculum decisions and taking curriculum actions; integrative inquiry yields integrative knowledge. Deliberative knowledge can assist with the problem of determining a course of action that integrates preferred form and substance, norms and practices, into a unified and workable plan of action; deliberative inquiry yields deliberative knowledge. Action knowledge can assist with the problem of determining how best to enact a chosen plan of action, step-by-step over time, until the state-of-affairs anticipated by the plan is ever-more-closely approximated; action inquiry yields action knowledge.

Knowledge generated by the less immediately practice-oriented forms of inquiry farther up the list can, of course, be sought when relevant as a part of the process of generating answers to the holistic questions of practice by means of the more strictly practice-oriented forms of inquiry toward the end of the list. This insight, incidentally, implies that whenever we have relied on a single dominant form of inquiry in curriculum research, or even on a few of the rather limited forms of inquiry, we have unfortunately restricted the applicability of our work to curriculum practice. The identification of deliberative, action, critical inquiry, etc., as being the forms of inquiry closest to being able to inform practical curriculum activity should not blind us, however, to the contribution that the other forms of inquiry can make to these types of inquiry and to the body of knowledge in specific domains of inquiry that may be utilized long after it has been generated.

Third, the questions toward the end of the list should remind us that practitioners may in many cases be the most appropriate persons to conduct much of the inquiry in a practical field such as curriculum. Because they are already immersed in and familiar with actual curriculum settings, they are in an excellent position to appreciate and to articulate the need for certain kinds of practical knowledge and then to carry out appropriate inquiry to obtain that knowledge. It is also evident from those questions toward the end of the list that much of the knowledge obtainable by the more practical, interdisciplinary forms of inquiry is situation-specific. Outside researchers coming into a specific situation to do practical curriculum inquiry may find it considerably more difficult to grasp the existing research opportunities and constraints than would those who are intimately connected with that setting. It is, therefore, imperative to equip practitioner-researchers with the knowledge and skills associated with doing practical inquiry in one or more of its practice-oriented forms of inquiry.

Finally, it should be noted that the forms of inquiry identified in this list and described in this book are not all of the existing ones that might be utilized nor are they as finely distinguished as to type as might be possible. For instance, within scientific forms of inquiry, political inquiry or sociological inquiry or "natural history" inquiry might well have been included. Within deliberative inquiry, particular forms of inquiry might have been designated differently, as, for example, policy inquiry, development inquiry, or implementation inquiry or perhaps deliberative inquiry of the evaluative, prescriptive, or enactive types. Interpretive forms of inquiry are among the least clearly differentiated from each other. It is true that phenomenological, narrative, and hermeneutic inquiry overlap in some fashion. Researchers frequently use what they call the interpretive sociology approach, the psychoanalytic approach, symbolic interactionism, human science, linguistic analysis, the subject dialectic method, the autobiographic method, and other forms of interpretive inquiry (Polkinghorne 1983). These examples of alternative ways of classifying and labeling various forms of inquiry should warn us against believing that the seventeen forms of inquiry presented in this book are the only ones or the preferred ones. They simply represent ones for which these writers could develop authentic statements on how to conduct particular types of curriculum inquiry as they understand them after years of experience using them.

The chapters that follow will demonstrate the basic thesis of this introduction to curriculum inquiry, its nature, questions, and forms of inquiry: that an appropriate form of curriculum inquiry must be selected to match the particular type of curriculum research question being studied. If the correct match is not made, successful inquiry will be thwarted. If an attempt is made to try to answer a particular type of curriculum research question and the form of inquiry selected is not one designed for that type of question, the most diligent application of that research procedure will not generate an adequate answer to it. On the other hand, many ill-formulated questions can be reformulated in a way that one of the available forms of inquiry can successfully address. As in any sound inquiry, time spent in properly formulating a research question and in determining what method is appropriate for addressing that question will be time well spent. Then utilizing the guidelines stipulated by the authors in this book for properly conducting inquiry of the type selected should yield the knowledge desired.

References

Barrow, R. (1985). The paradigm to end paradigms: Reorienting curriculum research for the secondary school. In G. Milburn and R. Enns (Eds.), *Alternative research perspectives: The secondary school curriculum. Curriculum Canada VI* (pp. 21–38). Vancouver: Center for the Study of Curriculum and Instruction, University of British Columbia.

Bredo, E., and Feinberg, W. (Eds.) (1982). *Knowledge and values in social and educational research.* Philadelphia: Temple University Press.

Buchler, J. (1961). *The concept of method.* New York: Columbia University Press.

Churchman, C. W. (1971). *The design of inquiring systems.* New York: Basic Books.

Cronbach, L. J., and Suppes, P. (Eds.) (1969). *Research for tomorrow's schools: Disciplined inquiry for education.* New York: Macmillan.

Dewey, J. (1938). *Logic: The theory of inquiry.* New York: Holt, Rinehart and Winston.

Dillon, J. T. (1984). The classification of research questions. *Review of Educational Research, 54,* 327–361.

Eisner, E. W. (1985a). The curriculum field today: Where we are, where we were, and where we are going. In *The educational imagination,* 2d ed. (pp. 1–24). New York: Macmillan.

Eisner, E. W. (Ed.) (1985b). *Learning and teaching the ways of knowing.* Eighty-fourth yearbook of the National Society for the Study of Education, Part II. Chicago: The University of Chicago Press.

Foshay, A. W. (Ed.) (1980). *Considered action for curriculum improvement.* Alexandria, VA: Association for Supervision and Curriculum Development.

Freeman, F. N. (1973). Controlling concepts in educational research. In H. S. Broudy, Ennis, R. H., and Krimmerman, L. I. (Eds.), *Philosophy of educational research* (pp. 70–78). New York: John Wiley & Sons.

Glatthorn, A. A. (1987). *Curriculum leadership.* Glenview, IL: Scott, Foresman.

Gotshalk, D. W. (1969). *The structure of awareness.* Urbana, IL: University of Illinois Press.

Hamlyn, D. W. (1970). *The theory of knowledge.* London: Macmillan Press Ltd.

Hampshire, S. (1982). *Thought and action,* new edition. London: Chotto & Windus.

Kimpston, R. D., and Rogers, K. B. (1986). A framework for curriculum research. *Curriculum inquiry, 16,* 463–474.

King, A. R., Jr., and Brownell, J. A. (1966). A unity in diversities: The pluralism of the modern realm of knowledge. In *The curriculum and the disciplines of knowledge: A Theory of curriculum practice* (pp. 37–66). New York: John Wiley & Sons. (Reprinted, 1976, Huntington, NY: Robert E. Krieger Publishing Company).

Kliebard, H. M. (1989). Problems of definition of curriculum. *Journal of Curriculum and Supervision, 5,* 1–4.

Kockelmans, J. J. (Ed.) (1979). *Interdisciplinarity and higher education.* University Park, PA: The Pennsylvania State University Press.

McKeon, R. (1954). *Thought, action, and passion.* Chicago: The University of Chicago Press.

Martin, J. R. (1970). The disciplines and the curriculum. In J. R. Martin (Ed.), *Readings in the philosophy of education: A study of curriculum* (pp. 65–86). Boston: Allyn & Bacon.

———. (1981). The forms of knowledge theory. In J. F. Soltis (Ed.), *Philosophy and education* (pp. 37–59). Eightieth yearbook of the National Society for the Study of Education, Part I. Chicago: The University of Chicago Press.

Morgan, G. (Ed.) (1983). *Beyond method: Strategies for social research.* Beverly Hills: Sage.

National Academy of Sciences. (1977). *Fundamental research and the process of education.* Washington, D.C.: U.S. Government Printing Office (017–080–01795–4).

Phenix, P. H. (1964a). The architectonics of knowledge. In S. Elam (Ed.), *Education and the structure of knowledge* (pp. 44–62). Chicago: Rand McNally.

———. (1964b). *Realms of meaning.* New York: McGraw-Hill Book Co.

Polkinghorne, D. (1983). Existential-phenomenological and hermeneutic systems. In *Methodology for the human sciences: Systems of Inquiry* (pp. 201–240). Albany: State University of New York Press.

Posner, G. J. (1989). Making sense of diversity: The current state of curriculum research. *Journal of Curriculum and Supervision, 4,* 340–361.

Reid, W. A. (1978). *Thinking about the curriculum: The nature and treatment of curriculum problems.* Boston: Routledge & Kegan Paul.

Rosales-Dordelly, C. L., and Short, E. C. (1985). Studies of existing curriculum knowledge. In *Curriculum professors' specialized knowledge* (pp. 20–27). Lanham, MD: University Press of America.

Schubert, W. H. (1980). Recalibrating educational research: Toward a focus on practice. *Educational Researcher, 9*(1), 17–24, 31.

———. (1986a). Curriculum research controversy: A special case of a general problem. *Journal of Curriculum and Supervision, 1,* 132–147.

———. (1986). Portrayal: The curriculum field. Paradigms in curriculum. In *Curriculum: Perspective, paradigm, and possibility.* (pp. 25–53 and pp. 169–187). New York: Macmillan.

Schwab, J. J. (1964). Problems, topics, and issues: The structure of the disciplines. In S. Elam (Ed.), *Education and the structure of knowledge* (pp. 4–42). Chicago: Rand McNally.

———. (1978). Education and the structure of the disciplines. In I. Westbury and N. J. Wilkof (Eds.), *Science, curriculum, and liberal education: Selected essays by Joseph J. Schwab* (pp. 229–272). Chicago: The University of Chicago Press.

Short, E. C. (1973). Knowledge production and utilization in curriculum. *Review of Educational Research, 43,* 237–301.

———. (1985). Organizing what we know about curriculum. *Curriculum Inquiry, 15,* 237–243.

———. (1987). Curriculum research in retrospect. Paper given at the meeting of the Society for the Study of Curriculum History. (ERIC Document Reproduction Service No. ED 282 919).

Short, E. C., Willis, G. H., and Schubert, W. H. (1985). *Toward excellence in curriculum inquiry.* State College, PA: Nittany Press.

Storer, N. W. (1964). *Basic and applied research: The conflict between means and ends in science.* Cambridge: Harvard University Press.

Strike, K. A. (1979). An epistemology of practical research. *Educational Research, 8*(1), 10–16.

Taylor, P. H. (1979). Curriculum studies in retrospect and prospect. In P. H. Taylor (Ed.), *New directions in curriculum studies* (pp. ix–xii). Philadelphia: The Falmer Press.

Toulmin, S. (1976). *Knowing and acting.* New York: Macmillan.

Tykociner, J. T. (1964). Zetetics and the areas of knowledge. In S. Elam (Ed.), *Education and the structure of knowledge.* Chicago: Rand McNally.

———. (1966). *Outline of zetetics: A study of research and artistic activity.* Urbana, IL: Electrical Engineering Department, University of Illinois. ERIC: SP030 305.

Tyler, R. W. (1976). Definitions of research and development. In R. W. Tyler (Ed.), *Prospects for research and development in education* (pp. 1–16). Berkeley, CA: McCutchan.

Vallance, E. (1983). Curriculum as a field of practice. In F. W. English (Ed.), *Fundamental curriculum decisions* (pp. 154–164). Alexandria, VA: Association for Supervision and Curriculum Development.

1

Philosophical Inquiry: Conceptual Analysis

—————— Jerrold R. Coombs and
Le Roi B. Daniels

Analytic philosophical inquiry cannot be identified with any specifiable methodology. Rather it comprises a diverse set of analytic questions, techniques, and procedures. What distinguishes it from other kinds of inquiry is its purpose or point. Basically, analytic philosophical inquiry aims at understanding and improving the sets of concepts or conceptual structures in terms of which we interpret experience, express purposes, frame problems, and conduct inquiries. It is an important part of all curriculum research because the conceptual structures we possess determine the kinds of curriculum policies we can entertain and the kinds of empirical and normative research questions we regard as significant. If our conceptual structures lack logical coherence, blur important distinctions, or create useless dichotomies, or if we understand them so poorly that we are unable to translate them adequately into research instruments and policy prescriptions, curricular policies and research studies will fail to be fruitful.

Within curriculum studies there are a number of important tasks that can be adequately accomplished only by the use of some form of analytic philosophical inquiry. Three kinds of inquiry are especially significant. For ease of reference we call these "concept interpretation," "conception development," and "conceptual structure assessment." Concept interpretation inquiry (CI) seeks to provide adequate concrete interpretations of the concepts we use to formulate curricular studies and programs. To be useful our statements of fundamental curricular aims, goals, and principles must be translated into less abstract terms. Fruitful curricular development and evaluation requires, for example, that we acquire a clearer understanding of what such concepts as *critical thinking, creativity* and *literacy* imply in terms of fairly concrete attainments. It requires as well that we acquire a better understanding of the way in which the achievements implied by such terms are related to one another. What, for example, are the relationships among such things as appreciation, understanding, and sensitivity?

Conception development (CD) is inquiry designed to develop and defend a conception or conceptual structure. We engage in such inquiry when we attempt to develop and justify a defensible view of what citizenship education, liberal education or intellectual autonomy consists in. Conceptual structure assessment (CSA) aims at determining the adequacy of conceptual structures we have built explicitly to frame curriculum inquiries and programs. These include such things as the taxonomies of educational objectives devised by Bloom, Krathwohl and their associates, conceptions of educational growth, liberal education and multicultural education, and distinctions such as that between teaching content and teaching processes or skills.

This chapter provides an account of the essential features of each of these types of analytic inquiry and some guidelines for conducting them. Success in these inquiries requires the use of a variety of techniques of analysis. The more important techniques are described as part of our explication of the various kinds of inquiry. To lend concreteness to our account, we have provided several very brief examples of analysis in our discussion of the assessment of conceptual structures. This account is not meant to be adequate for someone wanting to attain operational competence in analytic techniques, nor should it foster the impression that knowledge of techniques is sufficient for fruitful philosophical inquiry. One also needs considerable background knowledge of analytic concepts and distinctions philosophers have developed, and the kind of sensitivity and good judgment that one is likely to acquire only by working with someone who has been trained in philosophy.[1]

Concept Interpretation (CI)

Concept interpretation inquiry attempts to provide an adequate account of the potential range of reference of some term in ordinary language. Curriculum researchers engage in CI whenever they do such things as construct observation instruments or assessment instruments for curriculum evaluation or research. When, for example, we devise a measure of creativity, respect for law, or racial tolerance, we are interpreting a concept. We also interpret these concepts when we analyze them into component abilities and dispositions for the purpose of designing curricula to teach them. Arriving at a defensible concrete interpretation of a term requires a sound understanding of its use or meaning in ordinary language.

Unfortunately, educational researchers, curriculum developers, and social scientists often propose interpretations without attempting to understand fully the use or meaning of the concepts they are interpreting. The prevailing perception, that one need merely define one's terms in such a way as to minimize vagueness, is clearly mistaken. All of our important educational purposes, problems and issues are formulated in the concepts of ordinary language. If curricular research and policy are to be of any use in solving our problems and achieving our purposes, they must be based on adequate interpretations of these concepts, i.e., interpretations that are both accurate and sufficiently rich to capture the complexity of the concepts, not on stipulative definitions which may fail to capture important aspects of their meaning. Research based on stipulated definitions runs the risk of being trivial or irrelevant. If, for example, researchers operationally define *creativity* without conducting a careful conceptual analysis to ensure that their definition captures what we ordinarily mean by creativity, neither they nor we can know whether they have found out anything of importance to persons concerned with developing creativity as we normally understand it. It is worth noting also that no explicit interpretation is likely to capture the full meaning of a concept. Prudence dictates that we try to understand as far as possible the strengths and limitations of the interpretations we adopt.

The mode of analysis by which we come to a sound understanding of the ordinary meaning of a concept or set of related concepts is called "conceptual analysis." Conceptual analysis[2] attempts to provide an explicit and perspicuous account of the meaning of a concept by clearly detailing its relationships to other concepts and its role in our social practices—including our judgments about the world. It does not attempt to change our concepts, but to understand them. Since our concepts are embodied in our language, the techniques of conceptual analysis are techniques for closely examining the meanings of terms.[3] We analyze the concept of *learning,* for example, by examining carefully how competent language users use the term *learn* and its cognates. Our aim is not to produce a simple or concise definition of *learn* but to make clear what role the term plays in our linguistic and social practices. Conceptual analysis has been used to good effect in CI inquiries by a number of persons. Good exemplars in the field of curriculum are Komisar's study (1961) of the concept of *need,* Scheffler's analysis (1965) of *knowledge,* Martin's analysis (1970) of *explaining* and *understanding,* and Peters's analysis (1974) of *character.*

Although techniques of conceptual analysis are varied, all involve consideration of what competent language users would or would not say in various carefully identified circumstances. The "data" for a conceptual analysis of the concept of *discipline,* for example, are cases in which we normally would use the term *discipline,* cases in which we ordinarily would not use it, and cases where we are uncertain whether or not it is appropriate to use it. If a CI inquiry is to have any point, there must be some genuine problem or puzzle the interpretation is needed to resolve. This problem gives direction to the conceptual analysis because it determines what relations between the target concept and other concepts need to be investigated and thus the kinds of cases (examples of use) that need to be examined. An interpretation of the concept of *discipline,* for example, could be needed to answer at least two different questions: 1) What are the implications of accepting (or rejecting) the view that the content of school curricula should be drawn from the disciplines? and 2) Should we accept an interpretation of the concept of *discipline* that identifies operant conditioning as a way of promoting discipline in the classroom? The sorts of cases we examine will be determined by which question we want to answer.

Because conceptual analysis takes a variety of forms, it is difficult to formulate prescriptions for conducting this sort of study. The closest approximations we can give are suggestions concerning things it is very often useful or important to do in a conceptual analysis, and pitfalls to be avoided. These we will call "guidelines." Where appropriate we will illustrate them by noting how they would inform an analysis of the concept of *discipline.*

Guideline 1. Not all concept interpretations need involve the same depth of analysis. Extensive analysis is required only when the concept is complex or difficult to grasp. And it is worth doing in depth only when conducting fruitful research or establishing responsible policy depends on having an accurate interpretation of the concept.

Guideline 2. Early in the analysis it is important to identify the range of sentence contexts in which the term is ordinarily used. In analyzing *discipline,* for example, we find that the various sentences in which the term is used can be reduced to four kinds of sentence contexts represented by the following sentence schemas: 1) X is disciplining Y, 2) X has discipline, 3) X is a disciplined Z, and 3) X is a discipline. The appropriate unit of analysis generally is the use of the term in a particular kind of sentence context. Failure to analyze the term's use in clearly identified sentence contexts could result in a confused and fruitless inquiry. When the term means somewhat different things in different sentence contexts, cases drawn from different contexts may support conflicting conclusions. Moreover, the term's use in some contexts may be completely irrelevant to the problem that motivates the analysis.

Guideline 3. There is a strong tendency to suppose that every term is used to describe some object, state of affairs, or relationship. It is important to consider the possibility that the term being analyzed has a different kind of use — that it is used, for example, to: formulate slogans, recommend courses of action, ascribe responsibility, make commitments, or express a metaphor. In analyzing *discipline,* for example, we might consider the possibility that saying "X is a discipline" is a way of ascribing special status to some field of study, rather than a way of describing some feature or features of it.

Guideline 4. It is important to study, compare, and contrast a variety of cases where it is clearly appropriate to use the term, cases where it is clearly not appropriate to use the term, and cases where we are uncertain whether or not it is appropriate to use the term. The point is to try to understand as precisely and as fully as possible what it is about each case that makes the use of the term appropriate, inappropriate or uncertain. Thus, in analyzing the term *discipline,* one would study a variety of cases in which it is appropriate and inappropriate to say things like "X is disciplining Y," "X failed to discipline Y," or "X needs to discipline Y." It is also useful to compare and contrast cases of the concept being analyzed with cases of other closely related concepts. In analyzing the concept of *discipline,* for example, it is desirable to consider how it relates to concepts, such as *control, order, management, direction, rule enforcement, training* and *punishment.* It is important, then, to ask questions such as: "Is it possible to have a case in which X disciplines Y but does not control Y?" "Are there cases in which X is controlling Y but is not disciplining Y?" This study of cases forms the basis for generating a set of hypotheses about the rules or criteria we follow in using the term *discipline* in the sentence context "X is disciplining Y."

Guideline 5. In so far as possible one should avoid considering cases within the context of education, because our intuitions about what competent language users would say in such cases may be colored by long exposure to special uses of the term by educational theorists or social scientists. For example, many educators have come to use the notions of *classroom control* and *classroom discipline* interchangeably. But our analysis is meant to find out whether or not, in our ordinary way of thinking and talking about the world, controlling people really is equivalent to disciplining them. If we do use cases from the educational context, it is a good idea to find out if our judgments about them are confirmed by competent language users untainted by "educationese." Indeed, it is always a good idea to check our judgments against those of other competent language users. For such checks to be valid, however, it is necessary that the cases be fully and carefully described. When cases are poorly described, judgments may differ simply because the judgers are implicitly filling in missing parts of the case in different ways.

Guideline 6. Because it is not always possible to identify clear sets of necessary and sufficient conditions for using a term, we should resist the tendency to suppose that our conclusions or hypotheses must be claims about necessary and sufficient conditions. Hypotheses may be of four kinds: 1) Whenever the sentence schema is correctly used, condition N is present (we will call this an N hypothesis). N may be a disjunctive set of conditions rather than a single condition, i.e., we may hypothesize that either N^1, N^2 or N^3 must be present for the schema to be correctly used. 2) Typically, when the sentence schema is correctly used, condition T is present

(T hypothesis). 3) The greater the amount or degree of condition V, the more appropriate it is to use the schema (V hypothesis). 4) The sentence schema is correctly used whenever conditions S are present (S hypothesis).

Guideline 7. When one has arrived at tentative conclusions, it is important to test these hypotheses by making a careful search for counter-examples, and to revise them appropriately to take account of the counter-examples.

To find a counter-example to an N hypothesis we try to think of a case, or we ask others to try to think of a case, to which the sentence schema applies even though condition N is absent. Suppose we were to hypothesize that it is appropriate to say "X is disciplining Y" only when X has legitimate authority over Y. A counter-example would be a case in which X has no authority over Y but we would nonetheless say "X is disciplining Y."

T hypotheses are not susceptible to test by a single counter-example. If we find a variety of important cases where the schema clearly applies, but T is absent, we must conclude that hypothesis T is false. On the other hand, a T hypothesis is supported if the cases in which T is lacking are either relatively unimportant given our interests or are mainly ones where the absence of T makes us either reluctant to apply the schema or uncertain about whether or not it applies. Suppose we were to hypothesize that typically when it is appropriate to say "X is disciplining Y," X is punishing Y. To test this hypothesis we need to try to think of a number of significant cases where X is not punishing Y, yet we would not hesitate to say "X is disciplining Y."

Testing a V hypothesis involves trying to think of a set of cases each having differing amounts or degrees of V but where we think it equally appropriate to use the term in each case. Suppose we were to hypothesize that the more difficult it is to attain proficiency in an area of study the more appropriate it is to say of the area "It is a discipline." To test this hypothesis we would have to try to identify a number of areas of study that vary in difficulty but about which we are equally willing to say "X is a discipline."

Counter-examples to an S hypothesis are cases in which it is inappropriate to use the relevant sentence schema even though conditions S are present. Suppose we were to hypothesize that it is appropriate to say "X is disciplining Y" whenever X has legitimate authority to control Y's behavior and X is punishing Y in order to get him to behave as X wants. To test this hypothesis we need to try to think of a case having all of these features but about which we would not say "X is disciplining Y."

Guideline 8. The proper response to finding a valid counter-example is not necessarily to reject the hypothesis altogether. Where possible one should strive to modify or restate the hypothesis so as to preserve its truth. After all, our initial attempt to describe or characterize a criterion of use may be only a rough approximation of a criterion we actually do follow. It is also useful to consider the possibility that the hypothesis has been disconfirmed because it is of the wrong type. For example, we may have formulated the hypothesis as an N hypothesis when it should have been formulated as a T or a V hypothesis.

Conception Development (CD)

Conceptions are developed by modifying or reconstructing aspects of our existing conceptual structures, i.e., sets of interrelated concepts. New conceptions are developed to allow us to accomplish tasks for which our present concepts appear to be inadequate. They may be constructed to serve one or more of several different kinds of purposes. Some are designed to make vague concepts more precise and thus more useable in guiding curricular development. Paul Hirst (1974), for example, developed a conception of liberal education to make this notoriously vague ideal more precise.[4] Conceptions are also constructed to specify descriptive criteria for applying value terms. One may want, for example, to develop a conception of indoctrination that specifies criteria for identifying cases of indoctrination. Finally, conceptions are developed to clearly differentiate the constituents of some abstract concept and thus provide a fruitful categorization of a related set of phenomena. Robert Ennis (1979), for example, developed a conception of critical thinking which identifies the various proficiencies and tendencies that are implicit in being a critical thinker. Conceptions are not always developed by philosophers. In constructing their taxonomy of cognitive educational objectives (1956), Bloom and his associates developed a conception of cognitive achievement.

Although there are no standard procedures for carrying out conception development (CD), the following guidelines provide suggestions we believe are generally useful.

Guideline 1. It is necessary to be clear what job we want the conception to do — what problem or problems it should help us solve, for the use we expect to make of the conception determines the nature of the conceptual reconstruction undertaken. Some philosophers go so far as to explicitly formulate a set of criteria stating what problems and issues the conception must help us resolve.[5]

Guideline 2. If the conception is to be useful for anything, it must preserve the core meaning of the original concepts in terms of which we have come to understand and articulate our educational purposes, concerns, problems and questions. It will not do, for example, to develop a conception of critical thinking that fails to capture most of what persons who regard critical thinking as a crucially important educational goal mean by the term. Thus an important part of any CD is the analytic task of discovering the meanings persons attach to the concept or set of concepts the conception is meant to reshape or replace.

When the concept to be reshaped is an ordinary language concept such as indoctrination, we can gain a better understanding of its meaning through conceptual analysis. When the concept is a technical or semi-technical concept such as *critical thinking, moral education,* or *liberal education,* a different mode of analysis is called for. We need to find out what the various users of the technical concepts mean by them. The results of this sort of analysis, which we shall call technical use analysis, is not an account of the meaning of the technical term, but an account of the range of diverse and sometimes conflicting meanings it has for educational theorists and researchers.

Essentially a technical use analysis has the same point as conceptual analysis — understanding the term's use or meaning. The difference is that the primary data to be analyzed are uses of the term by various theorists, researchers and program developers. If a definition or other explicit account of the meaning of the technical term is available, it will provide good initial hypotheses about the meaning of the term. It should not be regarded as authoritative, however, because educational theorists and researchers often give very inaccurate accounts of how their own technical terms are being used. Other data one should look at include: states of affairs or activities the term is used to characterize, implications seen as following from sentences containing the term, conditions thought to confirm or disconfirm such sentences, and justifications that are given for regarding the phenomena or states of affairs identified by the term as important, or desirable.

Guideline 3. When the technical term contains several words as does the term *liberal education,* conceptual analysis of the constituent words may provide grounds for determining what aspects of the meanings currently given to the term are most central. The ordinary meanings of the constituent words may provide insight into the fundamental purposes that gave rise to the technical term. Thus, analysis of the terms *liberal* and *education* might help us to understand what significant interest is served by adding the notion of *liberal* to our concept of *education.*

Guideline 4. In some cases one or more educational theorists may already have developed a conception to give precision, concreteness, or depth to the ordinary language or semi-technical terms around which we propose to develop a conception. For example, Ennis (1979) and others have constructed conceptions of critical thinking. Assessment of the strengths and weaknesses of existing conceptions may be a useful preliminary to developing a new one. How one makes such assessments is the subject of the next section, Conceptual Structure Assessment.

Guideline 5. Providing good reasons for thinking that the new conception is better than the concept or set of concepts it is meant to replace is an essential part of conception construction. In addition to capturing the core meaning of the concepts it is meant to replace, the new conception must be potentially more fruitful in guiding our thinking about curricular research, policy or program development. It might have such potential because: it is less vague, it gives salience to a more significant range of distinctions and relationships, it does away with dichotomies that misrepresent experience, or it systematically organizes a set of concepts that were previously only loosely related.

Conceptual Structure Assessment (CSA)

The purpose of conceptual structure assessment (CSA) is not simply to understand the conceptual structure underlying a theory, model, argument or research program, but to determine its adequacy for use in curriculum research and development. Basically, such assessments are comparative. We want to find out whether or not the conceptual structure is an improvement over our "pretheoretical" ways of thinking about our tasks, activities, and problems, or over competing conceptual structures. Good examples of this sort of inquiry are Strike's analysis (1974) of behaviorist theories of learning, Coombs's analysis (1986) of theories of multicultural education, and Tom's analysis (1984) of the theory of teaching implicit in the "process-product" program of research on teaching.

Guideline 1. It is always desirable to consider the morality of viewing the world as the structure would have us view it. We want to ask questions such as the following. Would adopting the structure subtly change our views about how persons should be treated or about their rights and obligations? Does it obliterate distinctions important to treating persons justly and with respect, or make distinctions that will encourage or facilitate unjust treatment of persons?

Generally we tend to assume that our conceptual structures are morally neutral technical tools. This assumption is often false. For example, the conceptual structure associated with operant conditioning, which has been widely adopted as a way of thinking about classroom instruction and discipline, invites us to think of children, not as autonomous moral agents, but as objects to be manipulated by conditioning techniques. For educators to be justified in adopting such a morally hazardous conceptual structure, it would have to be significantly more fruitful for achieving our educational purposes than our ordinary ways of viewing these activities.

Guideline 2. Since a worthwhile conceptual structure must be useful in achieving our educational purposes, it is important to analyze the extent to which the structure permits us to describe and formulate questions about educational purposes and problems we ordinarily take to be significant. Conceptual analysis often plays an important role in performing this task. Suppose we were assessing a conceptual structure which views educational objectives as behaviors students will exhibit as the result of teaching. We would need to consider the extent to which the objectives we ordinarily take to be important can be adequately expressed as behaviors.

An objective ordinarily taken to be of fundamental importance is that students come to know that something is the case. Obviously, "X knows that Y is the case" is not a description of behaviors. Can it be accurately translated into descriptions of sets of behaviors? Conceptual analysis is needed to answer this question. Philosophers who have done such analyses generally agree that the phrase has three primary implications: 1) X believes that Y, 2) Y is the case, and 3) X has adequate reasons for believing Y to be the case, the import of which she appreciates. This seems to be getting us further from behavioral description rather than closer to it, but perhaps it is plausible that "X believes that Y" can be accurately translated into a description of X's behaviors. Thus, we need further conceptual analysis of the concept of *belief*. Under what conditions is it appropriate to say "X believes that Y"? When, for example, would we say "X believes that Ottawa is the capital of Canada"? There seem to be several kinds of circumstances in which it would be appropriate to say this: 1) X says "Ottawa is the capital," understanding the meaning of her words and intending to inform us. 2) X buys a ticket for Ottawa when she wants to visit the capital. While both of these cases involve behavior on the part of X, the behavior by itself is insufficient for ascribing the belief. X's saying "Ottawa is the capital of Canada" does not imply the belief if X does not know what those words mean or if she thinks Toronto is the capital but wants to deceive us. Similarly, X's buying a ticket to Ottawa does not indicate a belief that Ottawa is the capital independently of X's intending to visit the capital. The belief that Ottawa is the capital of Canada does not appear to be translatable into any finite set of behaviors or even into a determinate set of dispositions to behave. How one who believes that Ottawa is the capital of Canada will behave is determined by her individual wants, purposes, and other beliefs. *Belief* is an "intentional" concept; it cannot be explicated adequately without reference to intentions. So far no philosopher has succeeded in finding a way of reducing intentional concepts to behavioral ones.

This analysis of "X knows that Y" could be pushed much further. But if "X believes that Y" cannot be given an accurate behavioral interpretation, it is unlikely the other aspects of this objective can. We must conclude that the behavioral objectives conceptual structure does not allow us to express one of our most basic educational objectives. This surely must count heavily against its being regarded as an adequate way of thinking about educational programs.

Guideline 3. A conceptual structure is unlikely to be as fruitful in helping us to achieve our purposes as its competitors if it postulates or implies mysterious or empirically problematic powers or processes. Thus, assessment should strive to identify the extent to which the powers or processes implied by the structure are justified. This, too, is a task that requires conceptual analysis.

One popular conception of critical thinking suggests that being good at thinking is basically a matter of having a set of thinking skills or being skilled at a set of thinking processes. Usually it is assumed that one becomes better at these processes by practicing them. The processes typically identified include such things as classifying, hypothesizing, inferring, observing, and the like. Since we do not observe these processes, they are presumably covert mental processes.

Are we justified in supposing there are such processes? To answer this question we need to analyze how present tense, action words such as *classifying* and *inferring* are used, and what their use implies about the existence of processes. Let us begin by considering present tense action words that have no flavor of the mental. Do we imply that X is engaging in a specific kind of physical activity or process and that the same kind of physical activity or process is being engaged in whenever it is appropriate to say "X is playing," "X is practicing" or "X is winning"? Gilbert Ryle (1962) pointed out many years ago that words such as *playing, practicing,* and *winning* are not used to denote specific physical activities. *Playing* may refer to such diverse activities as engaging in a tennis match, giving a performance on the piano and "playing house." *Practicing* can refer to any activity that may be engaged in for the purpose of getting better at it. *Winning,* as Ryle also points out, does not refer to any activity at all. Rather it is used to refer to achievements, and these may be the upshots of such diverse activities as betting, racing, or playing chess.

There would seem to be no good reason for supposing that "ing" words which seem to refer to mental processes actually do so. If this supposition is to be supported, therefore, we need additional conceptual or empirical grounds. Are such grounds available? There is not space here to consider the case for all of the presumed mental processes, but we can consider two which are somewhat representative—classifying and inferring. Let us begin by taking seriously the suggestion that classifying and inferring do denote specific mental processes, and ask what implications follow from this. If the implications are false or improbable, we are warranted in supposing that these terms do not actually denote mental processes. If classifying and inferring are specific mental processes, it follows that having learned to classify or infer in one sort of case, one should be better able to classify or draw appropriate inferences in other sorts of cases. These implications are clearly false. A child may have learned to classify buttons but be completely incapable of classifying theories. Moreover, additional practice at classifying buttons is not likely to improve her ability to classify theories. Similarly, one who has learned to draw appropriate inferences from statements like "It is raining" may be incapable of drawing any inference at all from "The square of the hypotenuse of a right triangle is equal to the sum of the squares of its sides." We must conclude that there are good grounds for rejecting the claim that classifying and inferring denote specific mental processes in which one acquires skill through practice.

Guideline 4. If a conceptual structure is to be fruitful, it must be coherent, i.e., free of inconsistencies, contradictions, and terms having no sensible interpretation within the structure. Thus a search for these various kinds of incoherence is an important part of CSA. Such a search involves drawing out the implications of the structure and considering the extent to which the truth of some of its implications is incompatible with or casts doubt on the truth of others.

This aspect of assessment can be aptly illustrated by reference to Bloom's taxonomy of cognitive educational objectives. It is a central tenet of this taxonomy that the objectives it classifies are related such that attainments at the higher level are in some way dependent upon or include prior attainments at the lower level. The lowest level of achievement, knowledge of specifics, is defined as

> The recall of specific and isolable bits of information. The emphasis is on symbols with concrete referents. This material, which is at a very low level of abstraction, may be thought of as the elements from which more complex and abstract forms of knowledge are built (Bloom et al. 1956:201).

This conception of cognitive achievement is basically incoherent. If what a person recalls is to be meaningful to her, she must already possess certain concepts. Without the relevant concepts, nothing could count as a bit of information. The incoherence in this conception stems from the fact that recall of specifics cannot be given any satisfactory meaning within the theory. If what is recalled is meaningless, it cannot serve as a building block for abstract and complex forms of knowledge. On the other hand, if what is recalled is meaningful, the person doing the recalling must already have concepts, and having concepts would seem to be a matter of having and applying semantic rules. Thus, the recaller must already possess at least some of the more abstract sorts of knowledge that presumably are dependent on recollection.

This is neither a minor nor a benign incoherence. It betrays a very fundamental deficiency in the conception of cognitive achievement contained in the taxonomy. This conceptual structure does not permit us to give any intelligible account of the most basic cognitive achievement of all, namely the acquisition of concepts. Although there is not space to pursue the issue here, we believe that no "building block" conception of cognitive achievement can give an adequate account of concept learning. If we are right about this, the conceptual structure underlying Bloom's taxonomy is fundamentally misguided.

In some cases assessing the internal coherence of a conceptual structure may involve the use of argument analysis. We shall not attempt any explication of argument analysis here. There is a large and very accessible literature on this topic for curriculum inquirers who are not already familiar with the techniques and standards of this sort of analysis.[6] Generally speaking, argument analysis seeks to understand the structure of an argument; identify its presuppositions, implications, and any gaps it may have; and assess its validity or strength.

Notes

1. Although it is useful for all researchers to understand the nature and significance of analytic philosophical inquiry, it seems reasonable to suppose that curricular research will be most fruitful when it is conducted by research teams which include persons trained in philosophical analysis.

2. It should be noted that philosophers have undertaken a considerable number of different kinds of activities under the name of conceptual analysis. We are using the term in a fairly restricted sense to refer to what many people have called "ordinary language analysis." Although most philosophical study incorporates some analysis of this sort, it is exemplified most purely in the works of J. L. Austin, Gilbert Ryle, and Ludwig Wittgenstein.

3. Philosophers often suggest that the point of conceptual analysis is to *clarify* concepts. This way of talking is dangerously ambiguous, for it may be taken to suggest that such analysis is meant to make vague or "fuzzy" concepts precise. Such is not the case. Analysis aims at clarity only in the sense of making clear the nature of the concept. If it is a vague concept, analysis seeks an accurate and instructive portrayal of the nature of the vagueness.

4. It should be noted that Hirst does not explicitly acknowledge in this essay that he is building a conception of liberal education.

5. See for example Gerald Dworkin's criteria for a conception of *autonomy* (Dworkin 1988:7–12).

6. One of the better texts dealing with argument analysis is by Scriven (1976).

References

Editor's Note: In this list of References, as well as in the reference lists in subsequent chapters, references are coded in the following way:

o   for examples of curriculum studies using the form of inquiry discussed in the chapter;

+   for works on the nature of this form of inquiry in curriculum studies; and

√   for works on the nature of this form of inquiry from more general sources.

√   Austin, J. L. (1961). A plea for excuses. In J. O. Urmson and G. W. Warnock (Eds.), *Philosophical papers.* Oxford: Clarendon Press.

+   Barrow, R. (1990). The role of conceptual analysis in curriculum inquiry: A holistic approach. *Journal of Curriculum and Supervision, 5,* 269–278.

√   Black, M. (1949). *Language and Philosophy.* Ithaca, NY: Cornell University Press.

o   Bloom, B. S., Englehart, M. D., Furst, E. J., Hill, W. H., and Krathwohl, D. R. (1956). *Taxonomy of educational objectives: Handbook I, the cognitive domain.* New York: David McKay.

√   Coombs, J. R. (1986). Multicultural education and social justice. *International Yearbook of Adult Education, 14,* 1–13.

o   Daniels, L. B., and Coombs, J. R. (1982). The concept of curriculum. In D. B. Cockrane and M. Schiralli (Eds.), *Philosophy of education: Canadian perspectives.* Don Mills, Ontario: Collier Macmillan, Canada.

√   Dworkin, G. (1988). *The theory and practice of autonomy.* Cambridge: Cambridge University Press.

o   Ennis, R. H. (1979). A conception of rational thinking. In J. R. Coombs (Ed.), *Philosophy of education 1978.* Normal, IL: Philosophy of Education Society.

o   Flinders, D. J., Noddings, N., and Thornton, S. J. (1986). The null curriculum: Its theoretical basis and practical implications. *Curriculum Inquiry, 16,* 33–42.

√   Green, T. E. (1971). *The activities of teaching.* New York: McGraw-Hill.

√ Hall, R. (1963). Excluders. In C. Caton (Ed.), *Philosophy and ordinary language.* Urbana, IL: University of Illinois Press.

○ Hirst, P. H. (1974). Liberal education and the nature of knowledge. In *Knowledge and the curriculum.* London: Routledge & Kegan Paul.

○ Johnson, M. (1967). Definitions and models in curriculum theory. *Educational Theory, 17,* 127–140.

○ Komisar, B. P. (1961). Needs and the needs curriculum. In B. O. Smith and R. H. Ennis (Eds.), *Language and concepts in education.* Chicago: Rand McNally.

√ Komisar, B. P. and McClellan, J. E. (1961). The logic of slogans. In B. O. Smith and R. H. Ennis (Eds.), *Language and concepts in education.* Chicago: Rand McNally.

√ Leiser, B. M. (1969). *Custom, law, and morality.* Garden City, NY: Anchor Books.

○ Martin, J. R. (1970). *Explaining, understanding, and teaching.* New York: McGraw-Hill.

○ Peters, R. S. (1974). *Psychology and ethical development.* London: Allen & Unwin.

√ Ryle, G. (1962). *The concept of mind.* New York: Barnes and Noble.

√ Scheffler, I. (1960). *The language of education.* Springfield, IL: Charles C. Thomas.

○ ———. (1965). *Conditions of knowledge.* Chicago: Scott Foresman.

√ Scriven, M. (1976). *Reasoning.* New York: McGraw-Hill.

√ Soltis, J. F. (1978). *An introduction to the analysis of educational concepts,* 2d ed. Reading, MA: Addison Wesley.

√ Strike, K. A. (1974). On the expressive potential of behaviorist language. *American Educational Research Journal, 11,* 103–120.

√ Tom, A. R. (1984). *Teaching as a Moral Craft.* New York: Longman.

√ Wilson, J. (1963). *Thinking with concepts.* Cambridge: Cambridge University Press.

√ Wittgenstein, L. (1961). *Tractatus Logico-Philosophicus.* London: Routledge & Kegan Paul.

2

Philosophical Inquiry: Ampliative Criticism

——— *Nelson L. Haggerson*

Arguments and justifications for, and critiques of, curricular policies, practices, changes, and research results are often examined by the process of "critical philosophical inquiry." This chapter includes explications, explanations, and discussions of the roots, purposes, and outcomes of this process, as well as the manners in which it is done. Exemplars are used to assist in understanding critical philosophical inquiry.

Roots of Critical Philosophical Inquiry in Curriculum Studies

Critical philosophical inquiry in curriculum studies is not merely a matter of curriculum theory or practice. Nor is it the sole domain of philosophy of education or of the social sciences. It uses all of these bases of inquiry, but it has its deepest roots in philosophy, in reflective thinking, critical analysis. Philosopher Max H. Fisch describes philosophy as the "critic of institutions." By institution, he means

> any provision or arrangement of means or conditions for subsequent activity, additional to or in modification of the means or conditions that are already present prior to the institution, whether present in nature prior to all institutions or present in nature only as modified by previous institutions (Fisch 1956:15).

Following this definition, schools and curriculum both are institutions, as are policies, conventions, and customs surrounding them. Each is peculiar in having its own values, rationale, and even rationality. Such educational institutions will be the foci of the critical inquiries described in this chapter.

The search for those rationales, ways of reasoning, guiding values — norms which govern thoughts and actions (in philosophy) — is what Will

(1988) terms reflective philosophical governance in practice. When that search is carried out through educational philosophy and curriculum philosophy, both being special cases of philosophy, it is called critical philosophical inquiry or educational criticism. (Criticism and critical philosophical inquiry are considered synonymous throughout the remainder of this chapter.)

Educational criticism has often taken what has been referred to as a "reasoned" approach. This consists of construing a set of "universal" norms or principles which we allege should guide curriculum development, curriculum inquiry, and curriculum reform and applying those norms as criteria for judging the effectiveness or appropriateness of the curriculum. This form of criticism is called "deduction." Rational, reasonable, logical, generalizable, and algorithmic are other terms used to describe such inquiries or criticisms.

There are at least four manifestations of deduction used in critical philosophical inquiry: One manifestation is called syllogistic reasoning. It was used in its purist form in philosophical criticism of educational institutions by Mortimer Adler and Robert Hutchins. For instance, in putting forth his philosophy of education, Adler used the following syllogism:

> Major premise: Every human capacity can be determined by habits which are good by conformity to the natural tendency of the power being habituated.
>
> Minor premise: All individual men have the same natural powers or capacities.
>
> Conclusion: All men are capable of having the same good habits (Haggerson 1960:107).

From this syllogistic conclusion Adler argues that education should be the process of developing good habits, that since good habits are the same for all humans, education (curriculum) should be the same for all humans. From this he issues a call for a compulsory curriculum for all students, a curriculum that is absolute and universal, and he is critical of curriculum and educational practice and policy that do not follow his orientation.

Others, such as White (1984), less oriented to syllogistic reasoning, yet philosophically sophisticated, argue for "compulsion" in the curriculum for moral and safety reasons. Still others, such as those proposing the *A Nation at Risk* report, deduce the need for certain kinds of compulsory curriculum from political, economic, or social conditions. Their approach is often called a "reasoned" or "rational" approach to curriculum development and criticism. If practice does not follow their line of reasoning, they find it lacking.

A third basis for deduction is often referred to as "logico-deductive." This approach finds its roots in the formal study of Logic, and is found, among other places, in philosophy of science literature. However, it also finds its way into curriculum development and criticism when focusing on such notions as, "everything that exists is measurable." Curricularists deduce from that assumption that all aspects of schooling should be both measurable and measured, and that measurement is the prime factor in producing data for policy formulation and curricular decisions. The logic of measurement is basic for criticism from this orientation.

Still another basis for deduction is what might be called the empirical/statistical. Carefully controlled, statistically significant, experimental, sometimes referred to as empirical studies, allow for what Lincoln and Guba (1985) call "scientific generalizations." From those generalizations curricularists deduce that all of a population to which the generalizations apply should have a similar treatment. They attempt to apply the generalizations as bases for policy and other curricular decisions and criticism.

These deductive approaches in philosophy (Will 1988), educational philosophy (Haggerson 1960), policy development (Wise 1977), and curriculum research (Macmillan and Garrison 1984), when used solely as the governance procedures for criticism, have been found wanting.

On the other hand, criticism has been based on "induction" processes, too. Intuition, custom, habit, myth, insight, common sense — all are terms which occur when referring to induction. They provide a different location for the norms governing criticism, critical philosophical inquiry. The principles (if that is not a contradiction of terms) of induction are, in Pascal's terms:

> scarcely seen; they are felt rather than seen; there is the greatest difficulty in making them felt by those who do not of themselves perceive them. These principles are so fine and so numerous that a very delicate and very clear sense is needed to perceive them, and to judge rightly and justly when they are perceived, without for the most part being able to demonstrate them in order as in mathematics; because the principles are not known to us in the same way, and because it would be an endless matter to undertake it. We see the matter at once, at one glance, and not by a process of reasoning, at least to a certain degree (Will 1988:184)[1].

In terms of induction being a basis for criticism, the question becomes, "Can one learn this knowledge, this intuitive, mythic ... knowledge" as a basis of either criticism, development, or reform? The answer to that question, according to Will as he quotes both Murphy and Wittgenstein, is:

> Yes; some can. Not, however, by taking a course in it, but through "experience." Can someone else be a man's teacher in this? Certainly. From

time to time he gives him the right tip. This is what "learning" and
"teaching" are like here. What one acquires here is not a technique; one
learns correct judgments. There are also rules, but they do not form a
system, and only experienced people can apply them right. Unlike cal-
culation rules . . . (Will 1988:185)[2].

Will (1988) prefers the term "ampliative" to that of induction as the descriptor of the intuitive source of critical norms. An aspect of the ampliative,
not previously discussed, is that of "going beyond" the norms which seem
to be governing institutions, imagining and proposing alternatives. Fisch
agrees and states that:

> We cannot adequately criticize institutions without conceiving alterna-
> tives. For purposes of criticism, the scope of an institution includes that
> to which, taken as a whole, an imagined alternative whole is preferred
> which is like the given whole in some respects and unlike it in others
> (Fisch 1956:50).

The norms, both deductive and ampliative, are found governing
thoughts and actions among practitioners and also among critics. So it may
be said that the critic's search for the norms governing certain institutions,
and, at the same time, their criticism is governed by deductive and/or ampliative norms in the process we are calling critical philosophical inquiry.
And what purpose does this critical philosophical inquiry serve?

> The conception of reflective philosophical governance as one particular
> species of a wide array of social processes helps to regularize and make
> understandable the employment of widely varied and context-relevant
> considerations in the actual practice of assessing, confirming, revising,
> and reconstructing norms of thought and action. Reflective philosophi-
> cal governance appears widely and in a variety of forms in all those do-
> mains of human activity— science, law, morals, and the rest—**includ-
> ing education and curriculum** (emphasis added) — in which those
> engaged in the activities, and particularly those leaders who naturally
> play strong roles in their guidance, are, as a necessary part of their par-
> ticipation in these activities, engaged in the critical scrutiny and gover-
> nance of implicated norms (Will 1988:12)[3].

This means that not only do we find the norms governing institutions in
our inquiries into the institutions, we also find the criteria to criticize their
effects, effectiveness, goodness, and appropriateness in the situation. It also
means that those curriculum developers, critics, administrators, and teachers who are active in curriculum studies and development need to be critics
of their own institutions. In order to adequately comprehend their institu-

tions, competent critics "need to command the apparatus and techniques of comprehension" (Fisch 1956:50). This calls for curricularists not to give away their critical powers to the scientists and social scientists, rather to seek their help while becoming more effective critical philosophical inquirers.

Critical philosophical inquiry in curriculum, then, has roots in philosophy in general. The mission of criticism is a given: It gives meaning to institutions, brings their norms of governance to consciousness and finds criteria by which to make judgments of goodness, effectiveness, appropriateness, effect, and the like. The search for the norms governing institutions is only part of the critical process; the other part is to imagine and articulate alternatives. While some forms of criticism, i.e., deduction, are concerned with absolutes, universals, and applications; other forms, i.e., ampliative, are concerned with histories (Tanner 1982), contexts, specifics, contingencies, and constructions. In this chapter it is argued that the latter are presently more appropriate for the practices of curriculum, curriculum development, and curriculum inquiry.

The next section of the chapter includes a discussion of purposes of critical philosophical inquiry as it is appropriate for curriculum.

Purposes of Critical Philosophical Inquiry in Curriculum Studies

We now go beyond the roots of critical philosophical inquiry to its purposes in curriculum.

Paul Hirst (1974), in his collection of philosophical papers entitled *Knowledge and the Curriculum,* makes a strong case for the purpose of critical philosophical inquiry being **clarification, understanding, and elucidation.** He argues that we can plan and implement good curriculum only if we have a clear notion of where we are going. Furthermore, without a clear notion of curriculum aims or objectives, there is little hope of planning appropriate means to carry out those aims:

> What we need above all in curriculum planning is a much more profound grasp of the nature of the objectives of the exercise and their logical interrelations. If we can get the ends clearer, maybe we can plan more effective means (Hirst 1974:29).

Hirst, then, spends the remainder of the book in an effort to clarify aspects of curriculum. His chapters, among others, on "The nature and structure of curriculum objectives," "Liberal education and the nature of knowledge," "Realms of meaning and forms of knowledge," "Language and

thought," "Curriculum integration," "The two-cultures, science and moral
education," and "Morals, religion and the maintained school," provide exemplars of the process construed to clarify, elucidate, and lead to understanding.

Immediately after the Russians launched Sputnik, there was a rash of
criticism of schools and their curricula. Being a high school principal at the
time, I felt bewildered as to the nature and meaning of the criticism. After all,
our students seemed to be doing moderately well, we seemed to live in a
good, relatively crime free community where there was little unemployment
and unrest. What was the meaning of all this criticism? I was driven to attempt to find out, so I went back to graduate school and studied philosophy
of education as a main focus of my doctoral work. My major research project
was one of critical philosophical inquiry. My goal was, at first, to understand
the nature of the criticism. I did an analytic study (Haggerson 1960) of the
basic tenets of several philosophic world views, criticized each from the other's world view. Criticism was inevitable, because the governing norms of
each world view were, at a philosophical level, irreconcilable. I then criticized my own school curriculum from each point of view. I came to realize
that criticism was inevitable, and that when coming from a systematically
explicated world view the direction of the criticism was predictable. It was
only a brief jump to realizing that in order to understand criticism in general,
I had to find the norms, hidden or manifest, psychological or philosophical,
vicious or well-meaning from which the criticism emanated. **A purpose of
critical philosophical inquiry is to enhance understanding.**

But awareness and understanding are not enough. As Fisch (1956) said,
"We cannot adequately criticize institutions without conceiving alternatives." In his famous "The Practical: A Language for Curriculum," Schwab
(1978) first criticized the inadequacies of the theories upon which much of
the post-Sputnik curriculum reform was based. The foci of those criticisms
were the incompetencies of scope, abstraction, and multiplicity of the theories which were used to undergird the vast curriculum reform movement.
He then proposed what he called "The Practical: A Language for Curriculum." Rather than calling the practical an inductive approach as contrasted
to the deductive approach he was criticizing, he named his approach "deliberative." He says:

> It is neither deductive nor inductive. It is deliberative. It cannot be in-
> ductive because the target of the method is not a generalization or ex-
> planation, but a decision about action in a concrete situation. . . . It can-
> not be deductive because it deals with the concrete case and not
> abstractions from cases, and the concrete case cannot be settled by
> mere application of a principle, for almost every concrete case falls un-

der two or more principles, and is not, therefore, a complete instance of either principle. . . . Deliberation is complex and arduous. It treats both ends and means and must treat them as mutually determining one another. . . . It must try to identify the desiderata in the case. It must generate alternative solutions . . . (Schwab 1978:318).

In the deliberative processes proposed by Schwab (1978), just as the ampliative processes suggested by Will (1988), inhere the **purpose of going beyond, of imagining and proposing alternatives** to that which is critiqued as inadequate.

Oberg (1982) asserts that the ultimate purpose of educational criticism, critical philosophical inquiry, is **improvement of educational practice.** That purpose could well encompass the work of Schwab (1978) and Will (1988) when applied to curriculum. It also implies that **evaluation,** that is, assessing the effectiveness, appropriateness, or the goodness of a reform or practice by using appropriate criteria, is a part of the inquiry process. Educational improvement as a result of critical philosophical inquiry also calls for the inquiry to include recommendations or at least discussion of implications of the findings of the inquiry for improvement of practice.

Wise (1977) provides an example of a critical philosophical inquiry which ends with a discussion section entitled "Toward more effective educational policy making." In his analysis, "Why Educational Policies often Fail: The Hyperrationalization Hypothesis," Wise argues that hyperrationalization, excessive prescription, procedural complexity, inappropriate solutions, wishful thinking, excessive dependence on management systems, all contribute to the failure of educational reform, the inability to formulate effective educational policy. The basic reason for the failure is that there is a "disjuncture between the rational model (resulting from these forms of hyperrationalization) and school reality." Curriculum and instruction, personnel and teaching, administration and the legislature are all actually only "loosely coupled." "Hyperrationalization is, then, the perceived antidote to loose coupling which is reality; that it does not work should not surprise us" (Wise 1977:54).

To bring about improvement in educational practice, Wise suggests more effective educational policy making. Such policies would depend upon drawing a distinction between rationalization and hyperrationalization which would sensitize us to distinguish between proper and excessive rationalization of curriculum. But, most importantly:

the idea of hyperrationalization underscores the need for a new paradigm for thinking about the schools. **Educational policies fail because they are premised on the idea that the school is a rational**

> **organization — like a factory — which can be managed and im-**
> **proved by rational management procedure. Indeed, much of the**
> **collective effort of policy makers, researchers, and administra-**
> **tors is aimed at making school reality conform to the rational**
> **model. We then bemoan that the schools fail to conform to the**
> **model. It just may be that we need a new paradigm** (emphasis
> added) (Wise 1977:57).

Interestingly enough, the present cry for restructuring in education is based
on the same kinds of analyses and similar recommendations.

Critical philosophical inquiry, then, has as its mission: clarification,
elucidation, enhancing understanding, comprehension, providing alternatives, going beyond, leading to rationality as opposed to hyperrationalization, justifying curriculum policy recommendations, and ultimately improving educational practice, including curriculum. The outcomes of critical
philosophical inquiry most often appear in the form of a critique, often published in scholarly journals. They may serve as working papers with recommendations for policy formation or change, or they may serve as heuristics for bringing about changes in thoughts and/or actions. In what manners
do we carry out those missions?

A Manner of Doing Critical Philosophical Inquiry

In previous sections of the chapter, it was established that "going beyond" understanding and awareness of issues is an essential aspect of critical philosophical inquiry. Will (1988) used the term "ampliative" to describe and give credence to this approach. Current critics (Macmillan and
Garrison 1984) using the ampliative rationale have referred to Thomas
Kuhn's *The Structure of Scientific Revolutions,* 1962, as providing a theoretical base for their "going beyond" efforts. They use "The New Philosophy of
Science" as the descriptor of their critical philosophical inquiry activities,
purportedly because the focus of their current critique is "process-product
research on teaching" which is assumedly scientific.

> The most important feature of the new philosophy of science is that at-
> tention is focused not on observation statements, theories, and gener-
> alizations, but rather on 'paradigms,' 'research programmes,' or 're-
> search traditions' . . . A research tradition is a set of general assumptions
> about the **entities** and **processes** in a domain of study and about the
> **appropriate methods** to be used for investigating the problems and
> constructing the theories in that domain (italics added) (Macmillan and
> Garrison 1984:16).

Having established the "ampliative," and now "new philosophy of science" as essential aspects of critical philosophical inquiry, we now move from the theoretical frames of reference to criticism of curriculum institutions using examples found in the literature. Macmillan and Garrison (1984) suggest three major tasks, with numerous sub-tasks, which philosophical critics use in doing criticism in the ampliative, "new philosophy of science" tradition.

The first task is **to explicate the basic methodological and ontological assumptions of the tradition they are examining.** An example of this explication of basic assumptions process is found in an article entitled "Reconceptualizing Inquiry in Curriculum: Using Multiple Research Paradigms to Enhance the Study of Curriculum (Haggerson 1988), in which I have critiqued four research paradigms for inquiry in curriculum. I first explicated the basic assumptions undergirding each paradigm regarding the source of the research problem, the role of the researcher, methods and modes of research, research objects/subjects, and research goals. The assumptions about the role of the researcher in each paradigm, for instance, are markedly different. In the explication process, I used the metaphor of the stream to enhance understanding the differences. In the paradigm which I call "rational/theoretical," the researcher is on the edge of the stream using all sorts of measurement instruments and logical constructs to describe, measure, and predict the flow of the stream (curriculum). A major assumption is that of objectivity. The researcher is objective, uses valid and reliable instruments for measurement, and does not make a difference in the stream itself. In the "mythological/practical" paradigm, the researcher is in a boat in the stream. The researcher is a participant observer and does not assume the norm of objectivity, rather that of subjectivity. That assumption of subjectivity and its implications is insightfully addressed by Peshkin:

> It is no more useful for researchers to acknowledge simply that subjectivity is an invariable component of their research than it is for them to assert that their ideal is to achieve objectivity. Acknowledgments and assertions are not sufficient. Beginning with the premise that subjectivity is inevitable, I argue that researchers should systematically seek out their own subjectivity, not retrospectively when the data have been collected and the analysis is complete, but while their research is actively in progress. The purpose of doing so is to enable researchers to be aware of how their subjectivity may be shaping their inquiry and its outcomes (Peshkin 1988:17).

Explicating these assumptions leads to the realization of the basic and profound differences in the different paradigms. It is a necessary part of critical philosophical inquiry.

A sub-task of the explication or assumption process is that of informing that explication by use of appropriate literature and personal experience. In the "evolutionary/transformational" research paradigm (Haggerson 1988) where the self is the focus of the inquiry, the researcher is the stream. Erick Jantsch in *Design for Evolution: Self-Organization and Planning in the Life of Human Sciences* (1975), my own training and experience with Gestalt therapy, and my studies in Tarthang Tulku's *Time, Space and Knowledge* (1977), helped me name and recognize the assumptions underlying the researcher as the stream.

In the "normative/critical" research paradigm, the researcher has been the stream, is now on the other edge of the stream, drying off, and identifying and explicating the "hidden curriculum (forces)" in the stream for the purposes of both consciousness raising and emancipation. Identifying, informing and explicating these assumptions leads to further ontological, epistemological, and methodological discussion.

The second task of the critical philosophical inquirer in this manner of criticism is **one of comparison** (Macmillan and Garrison 1984). No theory or research tradition grew up or exists in a vacuum. In order to better understand the different traditions and determine their usefulness in curriculum inquiry and the improvement of educational practice, we need to compare their traditions, their histories, methods, desired outcomes, their assumptions, and their communities of scholars. The use of the stream metaphor was one means of comparison.

In comparing the "rational/theoretical" paradigm with the "mythological/practical" paradigm regarding research goals, I (Haggerson 1988) discussed the concepts of "generalization" and "naturalistic generalization." In the former case, the goal is to generalize research findings to a larger population or to predict the effects of a certain treatment in similar situations. In order to make such generalizations and predictions, as many variables as possible must be controlled, sampling must meet rigorous criteria, and the like. In the latter case, the "naturalistic generalization" (Stake and Trumbull 1982) is an insight that the reader or consumer of the research gets from the research and which elicits vicarious experiences in the minds of the consumer. It only applies to larger populations if in the mind and experience of the reader there are connections with a larger population. The naturalistic generalization does not depend upon the same set of assumptions or controls as does the so-called scientific generalization (Lincoln and Guba 1985) as explicated in the "rational/theoretical" paradigm. To fail to compare the two paradigms in multiple ways is to lead to misunderstandings and erroneous conclusions.

The critical philosophical inquirer, in order to assist in improving educational practice, including curriculum, uses various norms in the comparison process. For instance, can the "rational/theoretical" paradigm solve all of the important problems in curriculum? Or, as Wise (1977) asks, "Do we need a new paradigm?" A similar question is, "At what rate is the tradition or paradigm solving the problems?" These questions and others may be subsumed under the inquirer's third task of **determining what Laudan calls the "progressiveness" of the research tradition.** Progressiveness is the ability of a paradigm or tradition "to answer the questions or solve the problems that are crucial in its domain of investigation" (Macmillan and Garrison 1984:16). James Macdonald, the focus of my investigation of using multiple paradigms to enhance the study of curriculum (Haggerson 1988), found the "rational/theoretical" tradition to be totally inadequate for investigating and understanding the domain of curriculum as he described it. In other words, the "rational/theoretical" paradigm was not sufficiently progressive. I argued for three different research paradigms which would be useful for studying Macdonald's domain of curriculum.

Other curricularists, too, have found that inquiry based totally on empirical assumptions and practices have not answered some of the most crucial problems in education. There are conceptual problems which also need to be solved. The empirical aspect of the "rational/theoretical" paradigm is not progressive enough to solve both kinds of problems. In answer to this anomaly, the American Educational Research Association, which long gave priority to the empirical, has expanded its recognition of conceptual research to the extent that it now accepts dissertations with either empirical or conceptual emphasis for prize consideration. As a matter of fact, Sarah Lightfoot's *The Good High School: Portraits of Character and Culture* won the 1984 American Educational Research Association Award. Her research clearly fits in the "mythological/practical" research paradigm which was described earlier. Other examples of the empirical/conceptual dichotomy are found in Pinar's (1988) *Contemporary Curriculum Discourses,* where he sketches the history of several who have recently protested the lack of progressiveness in the traditional rational/theoretical/empirical research paradigm for curriculum studies and gives exemplars of their dissent.

In summary, the major tasks for the critical philosophical inquirer suggested by Macmillan and Garrison (1984) include: explication of the basic methodological and ontological assumptions underlying the research tradition being examined, comparison of multiple research traditions for addressing the problem at hand, and determining the efficacy of the most appropriate tradition or paradigm by applying the criterion of progressiveness; that is, does the paradigm answer the questions or solve the crucial problems in the domain of investigation?

This discussion of Macmillan and Garrison's (1984) critiques highlights some theoretical and practical aspects of "a manner of doing critical philosophical inquiry." Examples of other critiques are given to enhance understanding of the process. Notice that the foci of the inquiries are written texts, texts of thoughts and actions in curriculum studies. The purpose of criticizing those texts is to bring clarification and understanding of their meaning to the readers, the policy makers, the educational reformers; to explicate and justify alternative positions, and to contribute to improvement of educational practice. It should be clear that critical philosophical inquiry is in Hirst's words:

> A distinctive type of higher order pursuit, primarily an analytical pursuit, with the ambition of understanding the concepts used in all other forms of lower-order knowledge and awareness. Philosophy [critical philosophical inquiry] (interpretation mine) is a second-order area of knowledge, concerned above all with the necessary features of our primary forms of understanding and awareness in the sciences, in morals, in history, and the like. Philosophical questions are not about, say, particular facts or moral judgments, but about what we mean by facts, what we mean by moral judgments, how these fundamental elements in our understanding relate to each other, and so on (Hirst 1974:2).

That critical philosophical inquiry is ampliative in nature, that it calls for going beyond deduction, also implies that it is analogical rather than algorithmic in methodology. There is no algorithm (formula) which directs the inquiry, but there are analogies (resemblances) which allow somewhat different approaches to be useful and to accomplish similar purposes. For instance, Oberg (1982) in critiquing Eisner's *The Educational Imagination* has approached her task in manner quite differently from that used by Macmillan and Garrison (1984) in their critique of Gage's "product-process research on teaching," and yet, she has disclosed meanings, penetrated the meanings behind terms, suggested alternatives, and, in terms of "naturalistic generalizations," she has vicariously experienced beyond the words of Eisner's book. Oberg, guided by the perspective of what she called an "Ordinary Reasonable Educator (modeled on the "Ordinary Man of legal discourse, which refers to the average right-thinking person"), forged "an image of educational criticism as a mode of deliberative activity" as she addressed Eisner's book. The questions which gave direction to her reflection were:

> (1) What is the conception of intentionality which underlies the planning and doing of those educational activities which foster ineffable qualities in learners [the ones proposed by Eisner]? (2) What is the conception of judgment that complements this conception of intentionality and underlies the activity of the educational critic? (3) What is the con-

ception of focus and purpose that underlies the practice of educational criticism as a form of educational evaluation? (4) What is the conception of the nature of educational practice and the improvement of practice that underlies the suggestion to use educational criticism as a form of educational evaluation? (5) What is the conception of the nature of educational inquiry which underlies the practice of educational criticism (Oberg 1982:385–386)?

Oberg is a critical philosophical inquirer criticizing the work of Eisner, itself a proposal that art criticism be used in the service of education. She has used her perception of the norms which govern educational practitioners as criteria with which to criticize Eisner's imagined norms. Her conclusion is that "Eisner has created an image of educational practice which is greater than the sum of its parts, and in the process he has sparked the imagination" (Oberg 1982:404). Her deliberate critical activity resembles the deliberative nature of the "practical curriculum" proposed by Schwab (1978) and referred to earlier in this chapter.

Norms of Caution for Critical Philosophical Inquirers

The over-arching precaution for critical philosophical inquirers is that their reflective deliberations should also be self-critical. Attending to the following questions will help in this self-reflective process:

1. Does the critic understand the positions of both the object of the criticism and the source of critical standards? This implies knowledge of not only the original work being critiqued, but also the researcher's or practitioner's own comments about the work and related literature. It also implies knowledge of and clear explication of the critical standards, norms, or criteria upon which judgment is made (Macmillan and Garrison 1984).

2. Does the critic address the internal logic of the object, the generalizations, the applications, the conclusions, and does the critic clearly articulate what is being addressed?

3. Is the criticism fair? Does it do injustice to the object? Or does it try to degrade the work? Does the critic act responsibly (Macmillan and Garrison 1984)?

4. Are the biases of the critic made known, considered when conclusions are drawn, recommendations made (Peshkin 1988)? Does the critic realize that even the selection of passages for critique is interpretive?

5. Does the critic listen to and read responses to the criticism? It is enlightening to read "letters to the editor" over a series of interchanges to see the shifts in view, to become conscious of hidden norms, nuances, and the like?

6. Does the critic become critical of her/his own work over the years? Many years later I did an aesthetic self-study entitled "Reconceptualizing Professional Literature: An Aesthetic Self Study (Haggerson 1986b), in which, with fifteen years additional experience and feedback from others, I discovered both the frailty and the power of the pieces criticized. Sometimes it takes several years before the results of cogent criticism is accounted for in practice. In studying the current criticism of curriculum, it is essential to refer to earlier reform movement criticism lest we continue to "invent the wheel."

7. Is the criticism palatable to the reader, the researcher, the composer of the object of criticism (Macmillan and Garrison 1984)? If one goal of critical philosophical inquiry is to improve educational practice, then the criticism itself must be palatable.

8. Are the basic assumptions of the object elucidated?

9. Are insidious comparisons made?

10. Is the purpose of the criticism articulated. Is the purpose fulfilled?

11. Since critical philosophic inquiry is a secondary-order area of knowledge (Hirst 1974), is it used to help clarify and understand lower-order knowledge? Aoki (1983) is highly critical of "secondary order curriculum world" criteria used to criticize "first order curriculum world" phenomena. Or, put in another way:

12. Does the critic use the appropriate critical standard? For instance, Aoki (1983) criticizes those who use rational/theoretical (Haggerson 1988) critical standards to criticize the curriculum which he insists is situational/interpretative. He calls for interpretative standards instead.

13. Is the criticism deliberative rather than entirely deductive or inductive? Schwab (1978) insists that both deductive and inductive research norms have been found wanting in curriculum studies. He builds a case for using deliberative, practical, critical standards for criticizing curriculum studies and practices.

The critical standards for self-reflection can be summarized as: informed, fair, responsible, usable, palatable, provocative, situational, and historical. If the criticism meets these standards, the critic is more likely to accomplish the purposes of good critical philosophical inquiry.

Who Are the Critical Philosophical Inquirers? What Do They Critique? Where Do They Publish Their Criticisms?

There is surely no definitive answer to these questions, but a sampling might be instructive. The entries in the references (marked "○") contain answers to the questions in the section heading for those whose works were studied in the preparation of this chapter.

While these exemplars do not provide a model or an algorithm for critical philosophical inquiry, they may provide the "tip" which will enhance both understanding and use of the critical process. Those whose works are highlighted here and/or referenced in the text of the chapter are considered critical philosophical inquirers. There is no single guru to whom all critical inquirers pay deference, yet there does seem to be a "community of scholars" who are writing and thinking in a similar vein. Of course, there are many others whose works are not mentioned in this chapter. The journals and publishers cited here are among those who publish such critiques. There are other journals and publishers, too. While the journals and books referred to here are published in England, Canada, and the United States, recent experiences in Australia indicate that critical philosophical inquiry is also popular there. Study of philosophical and scientific literature will, of course, lead to many areas of the world in which such inquiry is rooted and practiced. The credentials of the critics seem to include: broad experience and knowledge, deliberative minds, self-reflective attitudes and habits, a willingness to make judgments based on careful argument, a passion for ideas, and a commitment to the progress of the institutions they criticize.

Notes

1. Reprinted from *Beyond Deduction: Ampliative Aspects of Philosophical Reflection* with the permission of the publisher, Routledge, Chapman & Hall.

2. Ibid.

3. Ibid.

References

(Symbols preceding entries are explained on page 40)

+ Aoki, T. T. (1983). Towards a dialectic between the conceptual world and the living world: Transcending instrumentalism in curriculum orientation. *Journal of Curriculum Theorizing, 5*(4), 4–21.

√ Fisch, M. H. (1956). The critic of institutions. *Proceedings and Addresses of the American Philosophical Association, 29,* 42–56.

√ Garrison, J. W., and Macmillan, C. J. B. (1984). A philosophical critique of process-product research on teaching. *Educational Theory, 34,* 255–278.

o Gordon, D. (1982). The concept of the hidden curriculum. *Journal of Philosophy of Education, 16,* 187–198.

o ———. (1983). Rules and the effectiveness of the hidden curriculum. *Journal of Philosophy of Education, 17,* 207–218.

√ Green, T. (1980). Extended review (Review of Peter Wood's *The Divided School*). *British Journal of Sociology of Education. 1,* 121–128.

o Haggerson, N. L. (1960). *A philosophic approach to criticism of schools.* Unpublished dissertation, Claremont Graduate School.

+ ———. (1986a). Research and the researcher: Multiple research paradigms for inquiry in healthcare education. *Amercian Society for Healthcare Education and Training Journal, 1,* 16–29.

+ ———. (1986b). Reconceptualizing professional literature: An aesthetic self-study. *Journal of Curriculum Theorizing, 6*(4), 74–97.

+ ———. (1988). Reconceptualizing inquiry in curriculum: Using multiple research paradigms to enhance the study of curriculum. *Journal of Curriculum Theorizing, 8,* 81–102.

o Hirst, P. H. (1974). *Knowledge and the curriculum: A collection of philosophic papers.* Boston: Routledge and Kegan Paul.

√ Lincoln, Y., and Guba, E. (1985). *Naturalistic inquiry.* Beverly Hills: Sage.

o Lister, I., Green, M., and Bernbaum, G. (1980). Review symposium (reviews of Michael W. Apple's *Ideology and Curriculum*). *British Journal of Sociology of Education, 1,* 111–119.

√ Macmillan, C. J. B., and Garrison, J. W. (1984). Using the "new philosophy of science" in criticizing current research traditions in education. *Educational Researcher, 13*(10), 15–21.

o Martin, J. R. (1976). What should we do with a hidden curriculum when we find one? *Curriculum Inquiry, 6,* 135–151.

o Oberg, A. A. (1982). Book review: Imaging educational criticism (review of *The Educational Imagination* by Elliot Eisner). *Curriculum Inquiry, 12,* 385–404.

√ Peshkin, A. (1988). In search of subjectivity — One's own. *Educational Researcher, 17*(7), 17–22.

○ Pinar, W. F. (1988). Preface. In W. F. Pinar (Ed.), *Contemporary Curriculum Discourses* (pp. 1–10). Scottsdale, AZ.: Gorsuch Scarisbrick.

○ Reid, W. A. (1979). Schools, teachers, and curriculum change: The moral dimension of theory-building. *Educational Theory, 29,* 325–336.

○ Schwab, J. (1978). The practical: A language for curriculum. In I. Westbury and N. J. Wilkof (Eds.), *Joseph J. Schwab: Science, curriculum, and liberal education* (pp. 287–321). Chicago: University of Chicago Press.

○ Soltis, J. (1979). Review and response: Knowledge and the curriculum (review of Paul Hirst's *Knowledge and the Curriculum*). *Teachers College Record, 80,* 771–778.

√ Stake, R., and Trumbull, D. (1982). Naturalistic generalizations. In M. V. Belok and N. Haggerson (Eds.), *Naturalistic research paradigms: Theory and practice* (pp. 1–12). Meerut, India: ANU Books.

+ Tanner, L. N. (1982). Observation: Curriculum history as usable knowledge. *Curriculum Inquiry, 12,* 405–411.

○ Tyrrell, R. W. (1974). An appraisal of the Tyler rationale. *School Review, 83,* 151–162.

○ Walker, D. F. (1975). Straining to lift ourselves: A critique of the foundations of the curriculum field. *Curriculum Theory Network, 5,* 3–25.

○ White, J. (1984). Compulsion and the curriculum. *British Journal of Educational Studies, 33,* 148–156.

√ Will, F. L. (1988). *Beyond deduction: Ampliative aspects of philosophical reflection.* New York: Routledge.

○ Wise, A. E. (1977). Why educational policies often fail: The hyperrationalization hypothesis. *Journal of Curriculum Studies, 9,* 43–57.

3

Philosophical Inquiry:
The Speculative Essay

——— *William H. Schubert*

To claim that the philosophical essay can be a form of curriculum inquiry requires the characterization of the essay as a form of rhetoric embodying speculative or personal knowledge. The *Oxford English Dictionary* defines the essay quite broadly as, "A composition of moderate length on any particular subject, or branch of a subject; originally implying want of a finish, 'an irregular undigested piece' ... but now said of a composition more or less elaborate in style, though limited in range" (p. 294). *Webster's Third New International Dictionary* differentiates only between the essay and the dissertation or thesis, characterizing an essay as:

> An analytic, interpretive, or critical literary composition usually much shorter and less systematic and formal than a dissertation or thesis and usually dealing with its subject from a limited often personal point of view ... something resembling or suggesting such a composition, especially in its presentation of an extended analytic, interpretive, or critical view of something (p. 777).

It is intriguing to reflect on the lack of definitional precision associated with the term *essay*. The idea has broadened and deepened over the centuries to incorporate more and more variations (Birkett 1967).

One can readily see the rhetorical characteristics of the philosophical essay in curriculum articles found often in contemporary professional and scholarly journals in education. The writer often makes a personal statement, asserts some knowledge with conviction, treats a variety of different topics, develops an argument shorter than a thesis, and frequently writes in an informal style. The curriculum scholar often strives to convert the reader or at least to persuade; a central mission of much curriculum writing is to convert or persuade. I also contend that the philosophical essay has been a major form of curriculum inquiry throughout the history of curriculum studies.

Curriculum Inquiry as the Written Essay

The roots of twentieth century curriculum writing can be traced rather directly back to the fifteenth century. We find essays by Aenea Silvio, Martin Luther, and Desiderius Erasmus; at least some of their writings could now be classified as essays according to the loosely knit criteria for essays today. In the next century we find Montaigne, followed by Bacon, and Descartes, whose *Discourse on Method* is surely an essay with curriculum overtones. The period that Robert Ulich (1954) marks as "The Development of Modern Education" includes selections by Johann Amos Comenius, Sr. William Petty, John Locke, Jean Jacques Rousseau, Benjamin Franklin, Thomas Jefferson, Johann Heinrich Pestalozzi, Johann Friedrich Herbart, Wilhelm Froebel, Ralph Waldo Emerson, and John Dewey. Although some of their writings were extensive, they often wrote in a fashion that could be called the essay. Curiously, their longer works are more of the thesis variety, but even these when excerpted in anthologies seem to hold together exceptionally well in smaller units. Others could only be called essays, e.g., Pestalozzi's "The Evening Hour of a Hermit" (1912), Dewey's "My Pedagogic Creed" (1897) and his later autobiographical essay, "From Absolutism to Experimentalism" (1930). Similarly, though labeled "talks" and talks they were as delivered, William James's *Talks to Teachers* (1958) are undeniably essays.

As important and revealing as these authors are, they are still precursors to the curriculum literature that became a distinct subfield of educational inquiry at the beginning of the twentieth century (Schubert 1980). The first well-known curriculum essays were by Dewey: *The School and Society* (1900) and *The Child and Curriculum* (1902). Clearly, Dewey's central mission was to integrate misguided dualisms; such integration can be seen more clearly if in Dewey's titles one reads *is* as interchangeable with *and*.[1] This is symbolic of Dewey's persuasive rhetoric.

Perhaps the educational writer with the greatest gift for the essay form approaching the elegance of a Montaigne or Emerson is Alfred North Whitehead. His "Aims of Education" (1929) and other essays in the book by the same name are stylistic masterpieces. Similarly, though with rougher edges but perhaps greater philosophic penetration and incisive wit, we cannot omit Boyd H. Bode from a list of exemplars. Each chapter in Bode's *Modern Educational Theories* (1927) is an essay, and the essays in the first half of the book focus on curriculum. In fact, it seems that many of the most widely cited curriculum writings are essays.

In a 1982 study of curriculum authors whose works had been most influential in shaping the thought of prominent contemporary curriculum scholars (Schubert, Posner, and Schubert 1982), 42 respondents listed the following authors five or more times: Ralph W. Tyler, Elliot W. Eisner, Joseph J. Schwab, John Dewey, Hollis L. Caswell, John I. Goodlad, Dwayne Huebner, Hilda Taba, Michael W. Apple, L. Thomas Hopkins, Herbert Kliebard, and William F. Pinar. Of these twelve, in considering their nonbook-length writings, I would agree that at least eight (Eisner, Schwab, Dewey, Huebner, Apple, Hopkins, Kliebard, and Pinar) write principally in the essay form.

When asked to list influential educational writers who did not primarily write about curriculum, their answers were very wide-ranging, except in the case of Dewey who was selected by twenty-four of the forty-two respondents. Others selected four or more times were: Harry S. Broudy, Arthur Combs, George S. Counts, Lawrence A. Cremin, Maxine Greene, Plato, Carl Rogers, and Alfred North Whitehead. Clearly, a great deal of the writing of Broudy, Combs, Greene, and Whitehead must be considered essays.

Finally, as the questionnaire was becoming progressively more concrete, respondents were asked to identify books and articles most influential to curriculum thought, novices, administrators and supervisors, and for scholarly use by professors. Considering the philosophical essay as a form of inquiry, it makes sense to focus on the first and last categories: curriculum thought and scholarly use. However, when one reflects on the hope that inquiry will affect practice, the other two categories are also relevant. Therefore, by combining all four ratings, the ten most influential articles are:

> Cronbach, L. J. (1963). "Course Improvement through Evaluation."
>
> Dewey, J. (1897). "My Pedagogic Creed."
>
> Eisner, E. W. (1969). "Instructional and Expressive Objectives."
>
> Huebner, D. (1966). "Curriculum Language and Classroom Meanings."
>
> Kliebard, H. M. (1970). "The Tyler Rationale."
>
> Macdonald, J. B. (1977). "Curriculum Theory."
>
> Schwab, J. J. (1969). "The Practical: A Language for Curriculum."
>
> Schwab, J. J. (1973). "The Practical 3: Translation into Curriculum."
>
> Vallance, E. (1974). "Hiding the Hidden Curriculum."
>
> Whitehead, A. N. (1929). "The Aims of Education."

All of these articles are essays. They are shorter than theses; they are persuasive philosophical pieces that use analytic, interpretive, and/or critical literary style rather than rigorous data-based or other highly rule-bound systematic forms of inquiry. Stylistically, some are more personal expressions than others; nevertheless, as personal expressions, they would qualify by most contemporary definitions as philosophical essays.

An excellent example of a systematic analysis of the literature is provided by Rosales-Dordelly and Short (1985). Thirty-six salient bibliographic references (books and articles) were circulated through a questionnaire to prominent curriculum scholars to ascertain their familiarity with and use of these references. I would classify nineteen of the thirty-six references as utilizing the essay form. This, of course, does not mean that the sources were entirely essays. In fact most of the sources used other forms of curriculum inquiry (e.g., hermeneutic, analytic, empirical, critical, normative) simultaneous with the essay form.

Another empirical strategy for identifying essays in curriculum literature is to survey collections of articles available in anthologies. I have surveyed several of these sets of readings, including the following: Caswell and Campbell (1937); Alcorn and Linley (1959); Hass and Wiles (1965); Hass, Wiles, and Bondi (1970); Short and Marconnit (1968); Martin (1970); Levit (1971); Van Til (1972 and 1974); Pinar (1975); Taylor and Tye (1975); Orlosky and Smith (1978); Bellack and Kliebard (1977); Gress and Purpel (1978); Hass (1974, 1977, 1980, 1983); Giroux, Penna, and Pinar (1981). While my survey of these sources was informal, I conservatively estimate that one-third of the articles included are philosophical essays. I suspect that a systematic analysis using criterial characteristics as set forth above would identify as essays nearly half of the articles included in these books of readings. I further suggest that these articles are included in books of readings because editors feel that they are among the best or more influential pieces. However, the status of the essay as a form of curriculum literature could be realized more fully if the content of anthologies were systematically analyzed relative to criteria for essays. The same might be done for articles in prominent curriculum journals, such as *Curriculum Inquiry, The Journal of Curriculum Theorizing, The Journal of Curriculum and Supervision, Educational Leadership, Teaching Education, Curriculum Perspectives, Journal of Curriculum Studies, Curriculum and Teaching,* and *Curriculum.*

It is important to identify two caveats in concluding this section. One is that it is clearly only the most influential pieces of curriculum literature that are represented in anthologies and studies noted above; therefore, it may be concluded that while the essay is prevalent among the most significant curriculum writings, it is not representative. Even if this is the case, as I suspect it is, I feel certain that the philosophical essay is prevalent among the most widely used curriculum literature for good reason. It can provide integrative, imaginative, and speculative leaps of interpretation that are still soundly grounded in a variety of other research traditions. Metaphorically, it is a kind of meta-analysis or research synthesis that uses the informed and insightful scholar (rather than a set of statistical rules) as the instrument for synthesis and illumination.

Thus, the speculative essay as a form of inquiry yields insight only as great as that mustered by its author. In many cases, however, giving free reign to the insightful imagination is the best way to advance knowledge. Clearly, it can bring the quality of insight and understanding that has been called *paradigmatic*. In view of this, the speculative essay has at least as much potential as possibility for misuse. Indeed, this tempers the first caveat greatly.

The second caveat relates to the fact that the idea of the essay over the centuries has expanded so greatly. For example, Winchester and Weathers (1968) refer to both "the formal essay" and "the personal essay." The latter refers to a variety of writings in popular media, such as magazines and newspapers. If the essay refers to almost any kind of writing that is shorter than the systematic thesis or dissertation or formal research study, does it lose its meaning due to the fact that it can encompass such variety? To this caveat, I suggest that much of the essay's strength lies in the fact that it defies classification. Defying classification, however, does not mean that it defies characterization. Characterization is more situationally specific and deals with qualities rather than pervasive generalization. This leads directly from our discussion of exemplars to a consideration of qualities and characteristics of essays that can inform those who wish to contribute to curriculum knowledge through the essay form of inquiry.

Characteristics of the Essay Form of Curriculum Inquiry

Essayist Sir William Cornwallis (in his *Essayes* of 1600 – 1601) said, "I profess not method, neither will I chain myself to the head of my chapters" (Reaske 1969:444). Cornwallis provides a prime example of a widespread viewpoint among essayists and those who comment on essays, that the glory of the essay resides in its eschewing of rules. It is, as it were, a search for a way to reflect about an issue of significance to the writer—and potentially to the reader. It is a form of writing quite unlike the research report which summarizes the product of empirical inquiry. In contrast, the essay lets the reader travel the undulating trek of thought and feeling that the essayist travels. This, of course, means that every essay will be of a different method; in fact, the essay symbolizes the essayist in search of method. It might even be said that the essay is an inside look at curriculum; it is a record of the author speculating or theorizing. No formula can teach such method. It must evolve for the time being, within a given context and moment of history in the lived experience of the writer and the issue being discussed.

This is not to say that there are no standards of quality for the essay as a form of curriculum inquiry. One might, for example turn to *referential adequacy* and *structural corroboration* which Elliot Eisner (1985:241 – 245) characterizes as standards for educational criticism patterned after art criticism. Prerequisite to both is the necessity that the writer be a connoisseur of the topic about which he or she is writing. Although Eisner's points are directed to criticism as a form of educational evaluation, the prerequisites of connoisseurship, of referential adequacy, and of structural corroboration stem from a long tradition of standards in the arts. Applied to the essay, readers would want to sense that the essayist knew and loved the topic under inquiry. There must be no doubt in the reader's mind about the essayist's expertise on and experience with the subject discussed. For example, there is no doubt that Bernard Shaw's (1923) commentary on "The Nibelung's Ring" by Wagner is the work of a connoisseur. Similarly, the reader of a curriculum essay must be convinced that the reading is a journey with one who has experienced the terrain and knows it well. The standard of referential adequacy helps to judge the author's interpretation as the reader checks to see if critical observations are grounded in the situation or issue that the author discusses. If so, the essayist's rendition may become a means for readers (perhaps less qualified connoisseurs or at least different connoisseurs) to see the issue or situation in a new light. Structural corroboration refers to a continuous inquiry by the reader as to whether the different parts of the essay fit together. The internal fit of an essay, however, should not be expected to be as cohesive as more refined forms of art. Montaigne, for instance, likened his essays to "a poetical kind of march, by friskes, skips, and jumps" (in Reaske 1969:444 [translated by John Florio, 1603]).

One must remember that the essay is a portrayal of the author's way of reflecting. It is, thus, a form of philosophical inquiry put into writing. As such, each essay might be considered a thread in the fabric of Dewey's idea of logic, as developed in *Logic: The Theory of Inquiry* (1938). To the great consternation of fellow logicians (of symbolic, syllogistic, and propositional persuasions alike), Dewey suggested that a meaningful conceptualization of logic could be built from the study of the way people actually reflect on problems. This surely involves scientific problem solving, but much more as well. The essay, an art form with solidly ethical purpose on many occasions, might well reveal a more pluralistic epistemology than Dewey's scientific method which dominated the *Logic*. Dewey, however, offers in several of his books of essays more than a beginning of such latitude: in *Art as Experience* (1934b) he presents expressive thought; in *The Public and Its Problems* (1927) he points to the necessity of genuinely democratic communities; and in *A Common Faith* (1934a) he offers his treatment of reverie.[2]

Thus, building from Dewey, who had perhaps greater impact on curriculum thought than any other scholar, we can envision essays that portray curriculum issues addressed through reverie, artistic expressiveness, democratic discourse, and practical scientific problem solving. It is intriguing to compare these qualities with Dwayne Huebner's (1966) call for new languages for curriculum that illuminate dimensions of classroom meaning, transcending the usual technical and scientific languages. It is interesting to observe the mutual relevance of Dewey's logic of practical problem solving and Huebner's scientific language, of Dewey's democratic community and Huebner's political language, of Dewey's expressive thought and Huebner's aesthetic language, and of Dewey's reverie and Huebner's ethical language. All of these postures of inquiry[3] are means to become emancipated from the fetters of the positivist, technical, and managerial inquiry that too often dominate curriculum thought and practice. It is in the most neglected languages of aesthetic and ethical inquiry that Huebner sees the greatest potential for more comprehensive, penetrating, and flexible[4] insight into curricular phenomenon. The inanity of the monocular managerial approach to curriculum is vividly portrayed by Huebner (1966):

> Think of it—there standing before the educator is a being partially hidden in the cloud of unknowing. For centuries the poet has sung of his near infinitudes; the theologian has preached of his depravity and hinted at his participation in the divine; the philosopher has struggled to encompass him in his systems, only to have him repeatedly escape; the novelist and dramatist have captured his fleeting moments in never-to-be-forgotten aesthetic forms; and the man [sic] engaged in curriculum has the temerity to reduce this being to a single term — "learner" (p. 10).

Herein Huebner has exposed the epitome of simplistic solutions to extraordinarily complex curriculum problems. How is it that educators unwittingly can be so certain about solutions to curriculum problems, when those very problems are embedded within a context of uncertainty amid the most profound questions that beset humankind? It is telling that Huebner chooses to inquire about such matters by using the essay form. Much of Dewey's writing noted above is of the essay variety. In fact, I contend that the most penetrating contributions to curriculum thought have been presented in the essay form. Indeed, it may be no coincidence that the philosophical essay has been selected among rhetorical forms to deal with curriculum issues precisely because an essayist may write by interacting with a complex and ever-changing situation. Moreover, the essayist has the latitude to continuously reshape the inquiry to relate ideas to the character of audiences addressed. Christopher Reaske refers to Joseph Addison's comments in the *Spectator* in 1711 on this very matter;

> Joseph Addison, as "the spectator" commended his essays to various classes of readers and stated that the purpose of his essays was "to en-

liven morality with wit, and to temper wit with morality." He added, "It was said of Socrates that he brought philosophy down from heaven, to inhabit among men; and I shall be ambitious to have it said of me, that I have brought philosophy out of the closets and libraries, schools and colleges, to dwell in clubs and assemblies, at tea-tables, and coffee-houses. (Reaske 1969:444; excerpts from Addison in *Spectator, 10,* 1711).

Despite Addison's limitation of public to elite publics, I suggest that when taken into the curriculum realm, it causes one to reflect on the centrality of the public space[5] to curriculum concerns. A public space essentially refers to a community of growth through liberating dialogue and open communication. If the essay is a form of writing that relates to the public space, and if curriculum (especially that preparing for universal education) represents a striving to build a public space, then it would seem that there exists a compatibility of substantive concern and form of expression in the joining of curriculum and essay. Thus, a rationale for the essay as a form of curriculum inquiry resides in both the subject matter and method of inquiry that address curricular matters.

Advice to Those Who Wish to Use the Essay as a Form of Curriculum Inquiry

What then do we say to someone who wants to do philosophical curriculum inquiry using the essay form? To provide a recipe is clearly out of the question. By its very nature there could not and should not be a how-to manual of instruction on constructing curricular essays. I do, however, wish to suggest five phases of preparation, the order of which is not as important as their presence in the life-world of the curriculum essayist.

1. The first phase of preparation is to acquire experience with the phenomenon under inquiry. The would-be essayist on curricular issues must become a connoisseur of curriculum issues. This might mean immersing oneself for a period of time in schools or other curricular settings. Or it might mean conscientious and sustained reflection on the experience of being a teacher, a student, a parent, a curriculum leader, etc.

2. A second phase is simply to have something important to say about curriculum matters. Most issues that relate to crucial curriculum issues deal with such questions as: What is worth knowing and experiencing? Why is the latter worthwhile? How can someone be helped to learn and experience that which is worthwhile? How can we recognize the growth of worthwhile knowledge and experience in others and in ourselves? How can we distin-

guish between worthwhile knowledge and experience and sham? How can the perpetuation of sham, wittingly or not, be exposed and replaced with worth? Surely, such questions are illustrative, not inclusive, but curriculum inquirers would do well to heed one or more of them and to make them central to their inquiry. To have all of the skillful form of the essayist but nothing to say is probably worse than having something worthwhile to say and lack of the skills to express it.

3. The third phase is to immerse oneself in the essay form by reading the giants of that genre. Here, I recommend reading widely works of the great originators of the essay whose balance of substance and style is exemplary, and as well those moderns who are equally talented and insightful, and whose work can be found in both literary journals and high calibre popular periodicals. One should pay careful attention to the details of form and how they relate to the substance discussed and to the intended audience. One should not prepare to parrot these exemplars, but to let their work fashion a repertoire that stimulates the clarity, pursuit of meaning, imagination, and integrity of direction that informs one's work.

There are numerous anthologies of exemplary essays to begin the process of developing a repertoire. Werner Taylor's (1932) *Types and Times of Essays*, John L. Stewart's (1952) *The Essay: A Critical Anthology*, Christopher R. Reaske's (1969) *Seven Essayists: Varieties of Excellence in English Prose*, and Burgess Johnson's (1970) *Essaying the Essay* are prime exemplars. Reading essays and commentary about them in these books will lead to related sources, all of which provide a context that elicits what Schwab (1971) has called *eclectic arts*.

The essayist, among all inquirers, is eclectic. The problem he or she unearths gains meaning when related to extant knowledge — the first art of eclectic. It is obvious, however, that neither personal experience nor perspectives from the best liberal education fits precisely to interpret and explain a given problem encountered. Thus, the inquirer must tailor, adapt, and combine extant knowledge to fit the problem under inquiry — the second art of eclectic. This weaving and re-weaving is at the heart of the essayist's art. Finally, the essayist realizes that even tailoring, adapting, and combining have their limitations. Existing knowledge simply does not speak to the needs of a great many issues. Needed is speculative or "imaginative projection as a method of curriculum invention" (Schubert 1975) or "the anticipatory generation of alternatives," as Schwab describes the third eclectic art (Schwab 1973). This is the essay's strength. It is not just a way of writing or a mode of expressing that which is already known.

For the essayist, writing is a special way of thinking. It is a method of inquiry, one that allows the reader to follow along the often convoluted journey that leads to greater illumination. Perhaps traveling such a journey allows the reader to embark on his or her own byways and even pursue other journeys at the same time. In a sense, then, the essay is a process of inquiry that transcends the problem of reducing human experience to an objectified commodity, a snare of all formal systems of inquiry.[6] The essay, a fluid and less formal form, retains the vitality of lived experience by creating method of inquiry within its presentation. Perhaps, too, it is not mere coincidence that both the essay, as a form of inquiry, and curriculum are often described by journey metaphors.

4. The fourth phase that enables one to pursue curriculum issues using the essay form of inquiry is to become immersed in the works of a variety of writers who have made important contributions to curriculum thought through their essays.[7] The variety can be perceived by thinking again of Huebner's categories of curriculum language. When I think of the aesthetic, writings of Maxine Greene, Madeleine Grumet, George Willis, and Thomas Barone come to mind. The ethical language invokes works by James B. Macdonald, Dwayne Huebner, Max van Manen, and Valerie Suransky. Political essays on curriculum often depict the pervasive impact of ideology, and I think of Michael W. Apple, Henry A. Giroux, and Paulo Freire. This is certainly not to pigeonhole any of the above authors in the associated category alone. There is a real sense in which each of them deals with all of Huebner's categories and more in integrated fashion. Thinking of integrative essays that draw from a variety of fields to produce curriculum insights today, I think of Harry Broudy, Philip Phenix, Louise Berman, Philip Jackson, Herbert Kliebard, A. W. Foshay, O. L. Davis, Elliot Eisner, Joseph J. Schwab, Decker Walker, Daniel Tanner, Laurel Tanner, Elizabeth Vallance, Ralph Tyler, William Pinar, Landon Beyer, and numerous others. In past literature one could readily turn to essays by John Dewey, William C. Bagley, Aflred North Whitehead, Boyd Bode, George Counts, Harold Rugg, William Kilpatrick, Paul Goodman, L. Thomas Hopkins, and many more.

Clearly the literature that such an array of authors turns to is as diverse as their philosophical and ideological persuasions. Nevertheless, all of these writers use the essay extensively in their curriculum inquiries, a use that merely symbolizes the expanding use of essays today in curriculum literature. One symbol of increased recognition of the essay is the appearance in the Spring 1985 issue of *The Journal of Curriculum Theorizing*, 6 (1), of a new title, "Essays," to refer to the major articles. More systematic empirical evidence can be found in the research of Dillon (1985), who analyzed and categorized 171 articles in six major curriculum journals during 1981. Methodologically, 70% of the articles were conceptual or rhetorical while only 30% were empirical studies. Moreover, 46% of solutions to problems discussed in the articles were classified as notional (dealing with definition, conception, and perspective) as contrasted with factual and material solutions. This emphasis on the conceptual, rhetorical, and notional weighs heavy in favor of the philosophical essay as a form of curriculum inquiry in wide use.

5. The fifth phase is to practice. I think, here, of Mark Twain's alleged advice to a would-be author. He told him to devote three solid years to writing as much as he could and encouraged him to send it all with haste to publishers everywhere. If at the end of three years he did not receive payment for his writing, he should seek another kind of employment.

The overall advice is (1) to write from experience for which one is a connoisseur; (2) to write from commitment to ideas to which one is deeply committed; (3) to immerse oneself in the general masters of the essay form; (4) to immerse oneself in the abundance of essays on curriculum; and (5) to write a great deal. The five phases are not necessarily presented in a recommended sequence. In fact, it would be likely that all might be done simultaneously.

The Unwritten Essay as Curriculum Inquiry

It may indeed seem strange to refer to an unwritten essay. I recall a short play by William Saroyan on public television in the early 1970s; perhaps it was an adaptation of a short story. In any event, its main character was a young man who spoke frequently about the unwritten novels on which he was working. I think we all work on unwritten stories and essays. These are the reflections that abound through our lives. Donald Schön (1983), for instance, tells us much about the way professionals think in action. But why limit it to professionals? All persons have stories; they "write" essays about their impressions of life. Their thoughts and feelings are their unwritten essays.

Perhaps, it is the unwritten essays that we need to study—the essays of teachers, curriculum leaders, and even students, in addition to those of curriculum scholars. Such essays are embedded in the lived experience of all persons. As such they are undistilled, "undigested" (to return to Dr. Johnson's phase). They have not been segmented into brittle categories; they are etched in the protoplasm of those who created them.

Such inquiry by teachers, students, curriculum leaders, and scholars (by us all) somehow seems to conjoin all inquiry forms into one which superimposes each form upon the other. Through unwritten personal reflection, each person writes hermeneutically upon the text of his or her lived experience. Acting in the continuous problem solving mode, each person acts as an action researcher in the tradition of John Dewey, Stephen Corey, and others, and according to the practical inquiry of Schwab. In the privacy of one's life, one tends to believe in the situational nature of subject matter and search more for insights than timeless generalizations or laws. Our search is an interactive epistemology. We learn from living in the circumstances inquired about, and the end of our inquiry in ordinary action is increased capacity to act and decide with moral defensibility. Like the educational critic, we strive to be connoisseurs of our situations and fashion reviews of our endeavors. Like the critical theorist we strive for emancipation from ideological and epistemological constraint in an effort to write justice and fairness into our lives. With the positivist we search for data that enhance our position. Analytic philosophy helps us clarify our expressions, and normative philosophy gives credence to our sense of direction and purpose.

Thus, our everyday experience bespeaks a continuous editing of the unwritten essays that we are. We write ourselves through the reflectivity of many different forms of inquiry, sometimes simultaneously. Moreover, the essay that we each are writes indelible essays on the world through the continuous flow of consequences of our being. Just as the beginning of writing was a mark, leading to hieroglyphics and cuneiform, our unwritten essays become written most profoundly as our mark on the world.

If every essayist, including the curriculum essayist and the writer of unwritten essays, would heed the advice of Arthur Christopher Benson in "The Art of the Essayist," I doubt that the worth of the essay (written and unwritten) as a form of curriculum inquiry could be defensibly questioned:

> We may follow any mood, we may look at life in fifty different ways— the only thing we must not do is despise or deride, out of ignorance or prejudice, the influences which affect others; because the essence of all experience is that we should perceive something which we do not begin by knowing, and learn that life has a fullness and a richness in all sorts of diverse ways which we do not at first even dream of suspecting.
>
> The essayist, then, is . . . an interpreter of life, a critic of life. He does not see life as the historian, or as the philosopher, or as the poet, or as the novelist, and yet he has a touch of all these. He is not concerned with discovering the theory of it all, or by fitting the various parts of it into each other. He works [by] . . . observing, recording, interpreting, just as things strike him, and letting his fancy play over their beauty and significance; the end of it all being this: that he is deeply concerned with the charm and quality of things, and desires to put it all in the clearest and gentlest light, so that at least he may make others love life a little better, and prepare them for its infinite variety and alike for its joyful and mournful surprises (in Taylor 1932:12).

If essays on curriculum even approximate these ideals, they illuminate. Is any purpose of inquiry more worthwhile than illumination? I think not.

And is inquiry that contributes to the love of life not providing more than expected? The best essays on curriculum both illuminate and contribute to a fullness of vision and imagination that enables one to lead a better life. Such an orientation is not only a boon to inquiry, but serves as a model of what curriculum itself might be.

Notes

1. I wish to thank Charles Smith, doctoral student at the University of Illinois at Chicago, for facilitating this insight, Fall 1985.

2. I wish to thank Joe Burnett, University of Illinois at Urbana-Champaign, for drawing my attention to Dewey's emphasis on expressive thought and reverie, June 1985.

3. I acknowledge Thomas P. Thomas, doctoral student at the University of Illinois at Chicago for his use of the term *inquiry postures* in a course paper, May 1986.

4. Philip G. Smith refers to *comprehensive, penetrating,* and *flexible* as criteria for certain philosophical ideas. Classnotes at Indiana University, 1966.

5. Maxine Greene (1988) has impressed me with her frequent use of "public space," drawing upon work by Hannah Arendt and John Dewey, among others.

6. This is drawn from a point argued cogently by Ann Lynn Lopez Schubert in "Curriculum and Policy Analysis" (1981).

7. An overview of the work of a number of these essayists is found in Schubert (1986).

References

(Symbols preceding entries are explained on page 40)

o Alcorn, M.D., and Linley, J. M. (Eds.) (1959). *Issues in curriculum development.* New York: Harcourt Brace & World.

o Bellack, A. A., and Kliebard, H. (Eds.) (1977). *Curriculum and evaluation.* Berkeley, CA: McCutchan.

√ Birkett, W. N. (1967). Essay. In *Encyclopaedia Britannica* (Vol. 8) (pp. 713 – 714). Chicago: Encyclopaedia Britannica, Inc.

o Bode, B. H. (1927). *Modern educational theories.* New York: Macmillan.

o Caswell, H. L. and Campbell, D. S. (Eds.) (1937). *Readings in curriculum development.* New York: American Book Company.

o Cronbach, L. J. (1963). Course improvement through evaluation. *Teachers College Record, 64,* 672–683.

o Dewey, J. (1897). My pedagogic creed. *The School Journal, 54*(3), 77–80.

o ———. (1900). *The school and society.* Chicago: University of Chicago Press.

o ———. (1902). *The child and the curriculum.* Chicago: University of Chicago Press.

o ———. (1927). *The public and its problems.* New York: Henry Holt.

o ———. (1930). From absolutism to experimentalism. In G. P. Adams and W. P. Montague (Eds.), *Contemporary American philosophy* (pp. 13–27). New York: Macmillan.

o ———. (1934a). *A common faith.* New Haven, CT: Yale University Press.

o ———. (1934b). *Art as experience.* New York: Minton, Balch & Co.

√ ———. (1938). *Logic, the theory of inquiry.* New York: Henry Holt.

+ Dillon, J. T. (1985). The problems/methods/solutions of curriculum inquiry. *Journal of Curriculum and Supervision, 1*(1), 18–26.

o Eisner, E. W. (1969). instructional and expressive objectives: Their formulation and use in curriculum. In W. J. Popham (Ed.), *AERA monograph on curriculum evaluation: Instructional objectives* (pp. 1–18). Chicago: Rand McNally.

+ ———. (1985). *The educational imagination: On the design and evaluation of school programs.* New York: Macmillan. (1st ed., 1979).

o Giroux, H. A., Penna, A. N., and Pinar, W. F. (Eds.) (1981). *Curriculum and instruction.* Berkeley, CA: McCutchan.

o Greene, M. (1988). *The dialectic of freedom.* New York: Teachers College Press.

o Gress, J. R., and Purpel, D. E. (Eds.) (1978). *Curriculum: An introduction to the field.* Berkeley, CA: McCutchan.

o Hass, G., and Wiles, K. (Eds.) (1965). *Readings in curriculum.* Boston, MA: Allyn and Bacon.

o Hass, G., Wiles, K., and Bondi, J. (Eds.) (1970). *Readings in curriculum.* Boston, MA: Allyn and Bacon.

o Hass, G. (Ed.) (1983). *Curriculum planning: A new approach.* Boston, MA: Allyn and Bacon. (Previous editions 1980, 1977, 1974).

o+ Huebner, D. (1966). Curricular language and classroom meanings. In J. B. Macdonald and R. R. Leeper (Eds.), *Language and meaning* (pp. 8–26). Washington, D.C.: Association for Supervision and Curriculum Development.

o James, W. (1958). *Talks to teachers.* New York: W. W. Norton (first published in 1899).

√ Johnson, B. (1970). *Essaying the essay.* Freeport, NY: Books for Libraries Press.

o Kliebard, H. M. (1970). Reappraisal: The Tyler rationale. *School Review, 78,* 259–272.

o Levit, M. (Ed.) (1971). *Curriculum: Readings in the philosophy of education.* Urbana, IL: University of Illinois Press.

o Macdonald, J. B. (1971). Curriculum theory. *Journal of Educational Research, 64*(5), 196–200.

o Martin, J. R. (Ed.) (1970). *Readings in the philosophy of education: A study of the curriculum.* Boston, MA: Allyn and Bacon.

o Orlosky, D. E., and Smith, B. O. (Eds.) (1978). *Curriculum development: Issues and insights.* Chicago, IL: Rand McNally College Publishing Company.

o Pestalozzi, J. H. (1912). *Educational writings.* New York: Longmans, Green, and Company. (Edited by J. A. Green with F. A. Colie).

o Pinar, W. F. (Ed.) (1975). *Curriculum theorizing: The reconceptualists.* Berkeley, CA: McCutchan.

√ Reaske, C. R. (Ed.) (1969). *Seven essayists.* Glenview, IL: Scott, Foresman.

+ Rosales-Dordelly, C. L., and Short, E. C. (1985). *Curriculum professors' specialized knowledge.* Lanham, MD: University Press of America.

√ Schön, D. A. (1983). *The reflective practitioner: How professionals think in action.* New York: Basic Books.

+ Schubert, A. L. (1981). Curriculum and policy analysis. A paper presented at *The Journal of Curriculum Theorizing* Conference, Airlie, VA.

+ Schubert, W. H. (1975). *Imaginative projection: A method of curriculum invention.* Unpublished doctoral dissertation, University of Illinois, Urbana-Champaign.

o ———. (1980). *Curriculum books: The first eighty years.* Lanham, MD: University Press of America.

+ ———. (1986). *Curriculum: Perspective, paradigm, and possibility.* New York: Macmillan.

+   Schubert, W. H., and Posner, G. J. (1980). Origins of the curriculum field based on a study of mentor-student relationships. *The Journal of Curriculum Theorizing, 2*(2), 37–67.

o   Schubert, W. H., Posner, G. J., and Schubert, A. L. (1982, March). Professional preferences of curriculum scholars: A genealogical study. A paper presented at the Annual Meeting of the American Educational Research Association, New York.

o   Schwab, J. J. (1969). The practical: A language for curriculum. *School Review, 78,* 1–23.

+   ———. (1971). The practical: Arts of eclectic. *School Review, 79,* 493–542.

o+ ———. (1973). The practical 3: Translation into curriculum. *School Review, 81,* 501–522.

o   Shaw, G. B. (1923). *The perfect Wagerite: A commentary on the Niblung's ring.* London: Constable & Company.

o   Short, E. C., and Marconnit, G. D. (eds.) (1968). *Contemporary thought on public school curriculum.* Dubuque, IA: William C. Brown.

√   Stewart, J. L. (Ed.) (1952). *The essay: A critical anthology.* New York: Prentice-Hall.

o   Taylor, P. H., and Tye, K. A. (Eds.) (1975). *Curriculum, school, and society: An introduction to curriculum studies.* Atlantic Highlands, NJ: Humanities Press.

√   Taylor, W. (Ed.) (1932). *Types and times in the essay.* New York: Harper and Brothers.

o   Ulich, R. (Ed.) (1954). *Three thousand years of educational wisdom.* Cambridge, MA: Harvard University Press.

o   Vallance, E. (1974). Hiding the hidden curriculum. *Curriculum Theory Network, 4*(1).

o   Van Til, W. (Ed.) (1972). *Curriculum: Quest for relevance.* Boston, MA: Houghton Mifflin.

o   ———. (Ed.) (1974). *Curriculum: Quest for relevance.* Boston, MA: Houghton Mifflin.

o   Whitehead, A. N. (1929). *The aims of education and other essays.* New York: Macmillan.

√   Winchester, O., and Weathers, W. (1968). *The prevalent forms of prose.* New York: Houghton Mifflin.

4

Historical Inquiry:
Telling Real Stories

——— *O. L. Davis, Jr.*

A story about curriculum?

When did you last hear a story about curriculum? A real story set in an understandable time, maybe just recently in a nearby school or, maybe, one which took place many years ago in a distant place? A story which relates the actions of fully-dimensioned people, individuals with names, ones with ideas and passions and concerns? A story which in its telling, unfolds meanings or a story which you must probe for meanings? A story that . . .

Probably, you have heard few real curriculum stories, robust, fully fleshed out stories. As likely, you have not read them either. The simple fact is that stories about curriculum have enjoyed an uncertain reputation within both curriculum practice and scholarship.

The curriculum field, from its beginnings earlier in this century, has honored its history by neglect. It emerged as a separate specialty of practice from early educational empiricism (psychology) which even now emphasizes description and experimentation in the present rather than according special note to the past. Only slowly has the curriculum field developed a culture in which some want to know about its origins, practices, people, and paths, its ideas and assumptions. Almost reluctantly, the field appears to recognize the need to foster the study of curriculum history, the telling of curriculum stories. This realization may be reluctant and fainthearted at times; even so, it is present.

While neglecting its history, the curriculum field has not been unaware of its past. Its asserted ahistoricism (Kliebard 1968; Bellack 1969) helped dramatize and legitimate the need for a self-conscious curriculum history, but the claim was overstated. The curriculum field consistently has employed history in its proposals and justifications (Hazlett 1979). To be sure, most of this use has been slighting and self-serving. Its most grievous mischief persists in two special ways. History, or, more properly, the "past" or "old," commonly has been positioned as a rhetorical foil for proposals of the moment. As such, the past has been intended to be seen as inadequate, and it usually has been so understood. Second, anecdote or ambiguous reference has been converted into an insufficient sense of history. Therefore, the general need to study curriculum history, to prepare (write) and to hear (and read) curriculum stories, must be joined with the commitment to develop a richer and more adequate historiography for the field.

But do curriculum stories exist to be told and to be heard or read? To be talked about and wondered with? To inform the proposals and decisions of practice? Not to be only decorations to conversations or as trophies for a career?

As in so much of scholarship, both a simple "yes" and "no" must be the response to this reasonable question. Some curriculum stories exist. Most stories, however, exist in fragments and wonder and await their construction and telling. Therefore, opportunities for fruitful inquiry into curriculum history may be unmatched with any in other areas of curriculum study.

Telling Stories: Narrative and Interpretations

Always, story has been crucial to history. The story transports incidents and interpretations through time against the fabric of context. The narrative of history originally was a verbal rendering, but has come to be mainly one to be read. That the forms have changed has not altered the centrality of narrative, the story.

The historical narrative, like all good stories, enables coherence to emerge from chaos. Its details add texture and vividness and tones to the characters and settings and actions. As contrasted to the "thinness" of journalistic accounts, stories of history are "thick." They enable the reader or hearer "to be there" with the narrator, to approximate the intimacy of witness to the actual events. And the historical narrative does more. It provides a structure, while differing from that of the actual events, which offers meaningful understandings. In these narratives, individuals and their actions are known in company with their perceptions and motivations and the times and the world in which they lived.

Telling stories illuminates previously inadequate understanding. Stories also constitute reminders of what is known. They can never prove the correctness of this knowledge even though a dominant cultural empiricism tends to confer this power on them. Increased light, especially in long darkened spaces of experience, reveals that which has been obscured or hidden. These told stories require an investment by their hearers/readers. Understanding is the yield of the active engagement of mind with the narrations and their meanings.

History well told is a rendering which is as faithful as possible to available evidence. Yet, special confidence and hope are embedded in the historical dialogue between narrator and hearer/reader. Based on the uncomplicated awareness that all the facts about the past can never be available, a confident hope exists for the discovery of new evidence by which a freshened, revised history may be fashioned. Even without new evidence, more lively renderings are expected.

Also, history is an artful engagement of mind with the past of life. The resultant story has always been accorded a special literary status. Some history, to be sure, is more artful, is better literature than other history. Nevertheless, a basic expectation of history is not only that it informs, but that its meanings are carried by an enriched and enlivened narration.

Interpretation offered within a told story certainly may not be interpretation accepted by the hearer/reader. Nonetheless, without interpretation, an asserted history fails. Interpretive themes not only aid the telling of the story, they provide a structure for meanings illuminated by the story. A special hallmark of competent history is the story's dominance of explicit interpretations. Clearly, when a narrator's proffered interpretations are only illustrated by story elements, the possibilities for history have been transformed into ideological justifications. Interpretation offered, while essential to history, recognizes other interpretative possibilities even if they are contested. Indeed, this struggle of interpretations within the narrative, rather than marring the story, likely adds credibility to it.

History, thus, does not serve up meanings ready to be grasped and used. Its meanings are revealed to be the objects of thought, deliberation, and wonder, the intimations of meanings still to be made.

Curriculum history, whose subject is the practical field of curriculum, nevertheless is a member of the family of historical studies (Kliebard and Franklin 1983; Kaestle 1988). Thus, the told stories of curriculum history are guided by the same historiographic canons that apply generally. Historians have written often about the guiding principles of the field (Nevins 1938; Carr 1962; Gottschalk 1969; Marius 1989). Selected writings about the discipline and exemplars of historical scholarship serve as happy companions both to the inquiry and to the writing of curriculum history. As an invitation to the exacting canons of historical inquiry, several guidelines are suggested for research and writing of curriculum history.[1]

1. *Authority.* The curriculum story told is supported by and traceable to valid historical evidence. Primary sources are employed whenever possible. Failure to use primary sources or to employ sources not easily accessible is acknowledged, and justifications for these actions are offered. Methods of inquiry (e.g., oral history, corroborating evidence) are noted and the particularly relevant work of other historians is not ignored.

2. *Interpretation.* The narrative offers mindful interpretations of the curriculum story within the appropriate contexts. Further, possible interpretations may exist as a part of narrative structure (e.g., themes) and, also, as elements of description (e.g., motives attributed by colleagues). Historical knowledge is neither eliminated, muted, nor given undue emphasis because of parochial pressures. Issues that are controversial or which may be difficult to understand are treated accurately and sensitively.

3. *Significance.* Major turning points, events, and people in the curriculum story are treated in-depth sufficient to the development both of their importance to the story and its interpretations and of a realistic portrayal of the times. Significance may be asserted, but it is also developed.

4. *Context.* Presentism is avoided. Contemporary interpretations and judgments of curriculum practice and issues are not imposed upon events, individuals, and actions of the past. Curriculum ideas, practices, proposals, terms, and quotations are embedded clearly in the social, intellectual, and educational history contexts of time and place. Explicit orientation to time is obvious regardless of the narrative structure employed in telling the curriculum story.

5. *Representativeness.* Simplism and stereotypes are avoided. A full sense of identity is sought. The curriculum story is not romanticized.

6. *Perspective.* Curriculum proposals, developments, deliberations, appraisals, and consequences are presented evenly. Multiple perspectives emphasize both continuity and change over time. Curriculum history is offered as a special human story within a chronology, rather than as an inevitable progression of events.

7. *Style.* The curriculum narrative is well told, is well written. Artful, its writing aspires to recognition as graceful literary expression. Its minimum level of style is not ponderous, stuffy, or boring. Readers and listeners should find the told story stimulating and interesting, even compelling.

These guidelines for curriculum history inquiry are reminders during work in progress. They neither select a subject for a story nor determine its contents. These story elements are choices of the curriculum historian, the teller of stories, the inquirer into the curriculum past.

Telling Stories: Prospects for Curriculum History

Curriculum history has prospered especially during the past decade (Davis 1989). Quite likely, more curriculum stories have been written during that period than any previous one. To recognize the vigor of the current enterprise, however, should not close off recognition of some valuable work accomplished earlier. Two conclusions seem obvious. More curriculum history research is needed. Many significant stories remain to be told and to be retold. Indeed, the need for added historical light probably will not be met even with a much energized commitment and the addition of new scholars to the field. An abundant harvest of scholarship seems to be a certain prospect for curriculum history.

The intellectual history of the curriculum field has become a particularly productive arena for inquiry. Herbert Kliebard's studies (Kliebard 1986), in particular, have rendered more intelligible the spate of proposals and counterproposals and commission reports throughout the past century. In no small measure because of his work, the prospects for additional study of the intellectual history of the field seem more promising than they did only a few years ago. Other scholars, among them Barry Franklin (1986), continue this exploration of ideas and add impressive meanings to the general understanding of the field. Especially significant, in this regard, has been the expanded attention to historical interpretations in synoptic curriculum textbooks (Tanner and Tanner 1980; Schubert 1986) which afford students their initial acquaintance with curriculum practice and thought.

To extend this excellent tradition clearly is worthy. Additionally, a number of wonderments await attention. Mention of several illustrate the prospects for inquiry. How have specific curriculum proposals been accepted and rejected? For example, over the first decade after the issuance of the *Cardinal Principles* report, what offerings, other than history, were changed and how were they changed in particular schools to reflect the report's positions? How was the report used to legitimate new proposals and to justify new practices? And is a pattern or path of change and justification discernible in regions and types of schools across the nation? Another example: What curriculum myths have been invoked by curriculum workers to define their practice and professional lives and have thus guided their practice and contemplation of it? And another: At particular times and for particular events (e.g., post-WWI commodity crash, anticipation of U.S. involvement in the 1930s European war, awareness of high rejection rate of WWII draftees on the basis of physical fitness), how have rhetorics of crisis fueled proposals and debates and changes, if any, in curriculum practices? The reservoir of such important questions seems inexhaustible. Another reality is also recognizable. Implicit in questions such as these is the necessity to employ concepts from sociology, rhetoric, linguistics, journalism, and other fields along with contextual historical knowledge and procedures.

The practice of the curriculum field continues to suffer inattention from historical inquiry. Too commonly, prominent rhetoric of the times has been taken to represent common practices in the schools. Such conclusion is conspicuous error. The mischief brewed has not been restricted to popular critics like Admiral Rickover and Arthur Bestor; it also has characterized much comment of teachers and administrators. The simple fact is that few stories are available of curriculum practice in particular schools undertaken by particular individuals during particular times (Mayhew and Edwards 1936; Collings 1923; Washburne and Marland 1963; James 1987). To be sure, anecdotes may exist and, in some situations, a too feeble folklore exists. Without doubt, the need for study of curriculum practice is impressive. Several examples illustrate the prominent possibilities.

Although the famous Denver curriculum revision program is acknowledged, its told stories do not do justice to this major school initiative (Peltier 1967; Cuban 1984: 67–75). Moreover, the reported actions of Superintendent Jesse Newlon and A. Threlkeld, the Assistant Superintendent, seem more inferred than documented. On the other hand, the activities of L. Thomas Hopkins and W. D. Armentrout, the general consultants to the program, are not understood and, in fact, have been omitted from most renderings. Likewise, the role of local research studies relating to the curriculum revision and the activities of outside consultants for curriculum specialties (e.g., Ernest Horn) are unknown.

For almost half a century, the Horace Mann-Lincoln Institute for School Experimentation of Teachers College, Columbia University, has conducted research studies in cooperation with local schools. One project in Springfield, Missouri, among many Institute programs, offers another example of the fruitful prospects for curriculum history research (Foshay and Wann 1954). What were the politics of selection of the action research project? How did the faculty and community power groups understand this research focus and expenditures for it in the context of concerns about other issues at this time? To ask research questions like these does not damage the project's reputation. Rather, the project is honored by returning to it and its context for retrospective, historical attention.

The curriculums of the nation's laboratory schools are another example of inadequate historical knowledge. These schools, in the main, were established as "model training" or "demonstration" schools and were converted to "laboratory schools," at least in name, during the transformation of normal schools into multi-purpose colleges and universities. That these laboratory schools, even those considered among the best, for example, at Teachers College and The Ohio State University, served curriculum innovation poorly has been a general judgment. In most cases, the generalization exists apart from particular stories.

The curriculum development accompanying introduction of a major project in a school provides a final example. What was the nature and continuity of local curriculum development related to implementation of AAAS SCIENCE in Doss Elementary School and in other Austin, Texas, public schools? This science program, highly touted and impressively supported at first, has disappeared from both the school's and the district's science offerings. The story of "what happened?" needs to be told.

Histories of courses and studies of lives are two other areas which deserve much increased attention. Although the history of school textbooks offers important information about the histories of courses of study (Carpenter 1963; Neitz 1961; Elson 1964), the still secret gardens of the courses merit specific and sustained inquiry. Recent studies (Goodson 1987; Popkewitz 1987) call attention to both the needs and possibilities of mindful research into the history of the course of study. Biographical renderings of the lives of significant curriculum workers, already seen as reasonable dissertation projects, should become increasingly attractive to senior scholars as well.

These several examples only hint at the possibilities for curriculum history research. Productive agendas for inquiry will emerge for each investigator as questions of wonder and interpretation yield mute responses.

Telling Stories: Toward Strengthened Curriculum History

Curriculum history inquiry should be enhanced by improvements in three areas of historiographic labor. Other areas could be named, but these three seem to be especially promising within a reasonable future.

Without question, a serious impediment to penetrating historical studies is the continuing paucity of collections of primary curriculum documents and records (Davis 1976). This condition not only holds for inquiries about events and persons of times long past; it is as true for studies investigating even recent curriculum practices. Two circumstances appear to explain this poverty of resources.

The documents of the curriculum field are seen mainly as ones serving the moment. Routinely discarded are superceded curriculum guides, notes and minutes of curriculum committee deliberations, memoranda and letters, personal diaries, notes for or manuscripts of presentations by visiting consultants and sub-groups, records of in-service meetings, even lists (and copies) of textbooks and ancillary curriculum materials, course descriptions, records of classroom visitations, pupil essays and logs, teacher lesson plans, personnel records. All these and many more constitute cabinets full of files, all potentially valuable to one who would tell a curriculum story. Such records, on the other hand, occupy space needed for the flood of paper that will wash through a school during the next round of curriculum work. Some of the records, to be sure, are shrouded by regulations of privacy and may not be viewed by unauthorized persons under legal penalty. Thus, most school records are purged routinely and are consigned to the rubbish bin.

Schools and district offices have never been mandated to maintain archives and, likely, never will be so charged. The "paper trail" for curriculum history, in most cases, simply does not exist.

The absolute need for curriculum history archives is uncontested. Several efforts to collect curriculum history materials during the past decade or so have enjoyed reasonable success (Davis and Mehaffy 1989). Oral history interviews have been collected. The personal papers of some prominent curriculum workers have been assembled. Special collections (e.g., photographs of individuals in the field) have continued. Unpublished conference addresses and papers presented at and official records of a very few (and, typically, small) scholarly societies have been accessed. These collections, however, suffer from serious funding and administrative neglect and exist more by an individual commitment and local sufferance than from mindful scholarly policy.

More adequate archival collections of curriculum documents must become available for study. Collection simply must continue for curriculum history inquiry to prosper. Under current circumstances, contributions of documents and research notes and papers from those work to tell curriculum stories that will add materially to a legacy for future scholarship. Also, collection and accession should be a prominent element of several graduate programs which encourage curriculum history scholarship. Archives of social and intellectual history, especially those of universities and state historical societies, should be petitioned to expand their province to include records relating to educational history.

Handicapped by a relative scarcity of primary sources, curriculum history inquiry must persist. Additional stories still can be researched and more ably written. Resourcefulness and enthusiasm can match the excitement and wonder of questions without ready or satisfying answers. Continuing to inquire about the past in the curriculum field is a simple but important contribution to strengthening curriculum history inquiry. Presentation and continued lively discussion of told curriculum stories at professional meetings emphasizing curriculum practice as well as at sessions of specialist societies can extend the attractiveness of curriculum history within the field. Publication of these told stories in an expanded number of journals can be expected. Book publication of curriculum history appears to be a growth industry.

The continued incorporation of a robust history in the teaching and pursuit of curriculum studies generally seems to constitute another significant assist to curriculum history inquiry. Each curriculum scholar and course need only acknowledge the viable importance of told curriculum stories for curriculum history to gain impressively. A special seminar for advanced students might be a sufficient introduction to the exciting study of curriculum history.

Some curriculum stories already are known and can be shared in professional discourse. Others wait to be told and preserved in writing. Just imagine . . .

At the next professional curriculum meeting you attend or the next curriculum course you engage, you may be prompted to ask, "Could you tell us the story of . . . ?" One day, sooner than might be hoped—at a conversation in the lounge or at a conference, in a curriculum deliberation at school, in a staff development session or a university curriculum course, someone could begin, "Have you heard . . . ?" and continue by narrating a substantive curriculum story. Or refer you to a recent curriculum history article. Maybe, even, you may think that the story is too fragile, that a better story is possible, and you decide to look into the matter yourself. Whatever the scenario, welcome to curriculum history, to the telling of the stories of our professional practice.

Note

1. Gerald Ponder and I developed these formulations for use in an evaluation project. As stated here, the guidelines are adapted from those included in the project report (Davis et al. 1986). These guidelines have been found helpful by graduate students as they engage in curriculum history research.

References

(Symbols preceding entries are explained on page 40)

○ Bellack, A. A. (1969). History of curriculum thought and practice. *Review of Educational Research, 39,* 283–292.

○ Carpenter, C. H. (1963). *History of American textbooks.* Philadelphia: University of Pennsylvania Press.

√ Carr, E. H. (1962). *What is history?* New York: Alfred A. Knopf.

○ Collings, Ellsworth. (1923). *An experiment with a project curriculum.* New York: Macmillan.

○ Cuban, L. (1984). *How teachers taught: Constancy and change in American classrooms 1890–1980.* New York: Longman.

86 O. L. Davis, Jr.

+ Davis, O. L., Jr. (1976). Epilogue: Invitation to curriculum history. In O. L. Davis, Jr. (Ed.), *Perspectives on curriculum development 1776–1976* (pp. 257–259). Washington, D.C.: Association for Supervision and Curriculum Development.

+ Davis, O. L., Jr., et al. (1986). *Looking at history* (pp. 14–15). Washington, D.C.: People for the American Way.

+ Davis, O. L., Jr. (1989). Opening the door to surprise: The next decade of curriculum history studies. In C. Kridel (Ed.), *Curriculum History* (pp. 2–13). Lanham, MD: University Press of America.

+ Davis, O. L., Jr., and Mehaffy, G. L. (1989). An elusive quarry: On the trail of curriculum history. In C. Kridel (Ed.), *Curriculum history* (pp. 40–47). Lanham, MD: University Press of America.

o Elson, R. M. (1964). *Guardians of tradition: American schoolbooks of the nineteenth century.* Lincoln: University of Nebraska Press.

o Foshay, A. W., and Wann, K. W. (1954). *Children's social values.* New York: Bureau of Publications, Teachers College, Columbia University.

o Franklin, B. M. (1986). *Building the American curriculum: The school curriculum and the search for social control.* Philadelphia: The Falmer Press.

o Goodson, I. (Ed.) (1987). *International perspectives in curriculum history.* Dover, NH: Croom Helm.

√ Gottschalk, L. (1969). *Understanding history: A primer of the historical method,* 2nd Ed. New York: Alfred A. Knopf.

+ Hazlett, J. S. (1979). Conceptions of curriculum history. *Curriculum Inquiry, 9,* 129–135.

o James, T. (1987). *Exile within: The schooling of Japanese-Americans 1942–1945.* Cambridge, MA: Harvard University Press.

√ Kaestle, C. F. (1988). Recent methodological developments in the history of American education. In R. M. Jaeger (Ed.), *Complementary methods for research in education* (pp. 61–73). Washington, D.C.: American Educational Research Association.

o Kliebard, H. M. (1968). The curriculum field in retrospect. In P. W. F. Witt (Ed.), *Technology and the curriculum* (pp. 69–84). New York: Teachers College Press.

+ Kliebard, H. M., and Franklin, B. M. (1983). The course of the course of study: History of curriculum. In J. H. Best (Ed.), *Historical Inquiry in Education* (pp. 138–157). Washington, D.C.: American Educational Research Association.

○ Kliebard, H. M. (1986). *The struggle for the American curriculum 1893 – 1958.* Boston: Routledge & Kegan Paul.

○ Kridel, C. (1989). *Curriculum history.* Lanham, MD: University Press of America.

√ Marius, R. (1989). *A short guide to writing about history.* Glenview, IL: Scott, Foresman.

○ Mayhew, K. C., and Edwards, A. C. (1936). *The Dewey School.* New York: D. Appleton-Century Co.

○ Neitz, J. A. (1961). *Old textbooks.* Pittsburgh: University of Pittsburgh Press.

√ Nevins, A. (1938). *The gateway to history.* New York: D. Appleton-Century Co.

○ Peltier, G. L. (1967). Teacher participation in curriculum revision: An historical case study. *History of Education Quarterly, 7,* 209–219.

○ Popkewitz, T. S. (Ed.) (1987). *The formation of school subjects: The struggle for creating an American institution.* Philadelphia: The Falmer Press.

○ Schubert, W. H. (1986). *Curriculum: Perspective, paradigm, and possibility.* New York: Macmillan.

○ Tanner, D., and Tanner, L. N. (1980). *Curriculum development: Theory and practice,* 2d ed. New York: Macmillan.

○ ———. (1990). *History of the school curriculum.* New York: Macmillan.

○ Washburne, C. W., and Marland, S. P. Jr. (1963). *Winnetka: The history and significance of an educational experiment.* Englewood Cliffs, NJ: Prentice-Hall.

5

Scientific Inquiry:
Explanations and Limits

——— *Arthur W. Foshay*

When James B. Conant (1947) proposed a course on science as a part of the general education of undergraduate students, he did two things that mark great teachers. He put science in the largest human context he could imagine, and he proposed that students learn by doing — that is, that they undertake the basic experiments that define parts of contemporary physical science, thus learning something about what it is to think like a scientist. On this latter point, Conant (supported, I have found, by Popper, Nagel, and by Bridgman, whom he cites) disposes of the notion of a "scientific method." "The scientific method, as far as it is a method, is nothing more than doing one's damndest with one's mind, no holds barred. What primarily distinguishes science from other intellectual enterprises is not the method but the subject matter" (Conant 1947:115, note).

When we consider a scientific approach to the curriculum, therefore, we must begin, not with science, but with curriculum.

The curriculum, as a field for study and action, consists of three main dimensions: purpose, substance, and practice (Foshay 1987; 1988). That is, we intend to accomplish something (a purpose), by offering some experiences (the substance), and by fitting the learning method to actual students (educational practice). Study of the curriculum consists of dealing with the manifold interactions among these three dimensions, as well as studying the nature of each part. However, it is in the interaction, not in the parts separately, that the curriculum exists.

The basic curriculum problem, therefore, is this: how do purpose, substance (or content), and practice interact? A complete map of the field would be enormously complex. Differing specifics can be included in such a map. My version would include a theoretical 145,000 such interactions (Foshay 1987; 1988).

This complexity is ordinarily ignored by curriculum developers and their critics, who choose to emphasize one or two aspects of the whole as if they were the whole. This taking a part to be the whole I have called the great educational synecdoche, as when SAT scores are taken to indicate the quality of a school or school system, or gaps in the knowledge of the facts of geography or U.S. history are taken as an indictment of public education — or any other unhappy fact, taken out of its context, as having meaning.

Science involves facts, of course — observed phenomena. But science deals with explanations — the *why* of things — not inert facts, which, as Whitehead (1957:1–2) said so long ago, are the curse of mankind. If the purpose of systematic curriculum inquiry is to discover why things are — the meanings — then we must begin by acknowledging that *all facts about the curriculum derive their meanings from their contexts.* "Scientific" curriculum studies therefore consist of facts-in-context. The broader the context, the more profound the meanings.

As Conant pointed out, there is no single "scientific method." Ultimately, there are as many methods as there are problems. Dewey, in *How We Think* (1933), indicated that any thinking involves the analysis of something taken to be puzzling (his "disequilibrium"), and attempts to verify one's opinions about how the puzzle may be solved or "equilibrium" restored. Such a meta-method, however, doesn't suit any problem in particular. As a colleague in bacteriology at Ohio State once pointed out to several of us, Dewey's "complete act of thought" does not describe the way he did his work. Why? Because experiments in bacteriology are plagued by legions of unknown variables. It takes enormous effort, and intellectual acrobatics, to find relatively certain explanations in that field.

The problem the bacteriologists face should sound familiar to the curriculum researcher. The complexity of the field and the fact that most of what affects the results of our efforts to teach is beyond our knowledge or control forces us to rely, not on certainties, but on frequently weak probabilities and logical consistencies.

Certain things follow from this inherent weakness — weakness, that is, from the point of view of physical science. One consequence of the nature of the field is that we cannot often claim to have found cause-and-effect relationships. What we can find, it is worth repeating, are probabilities that are often weak. Another thing that follows is this: almost always, when we single out a factor and try to study its effect on student achievement, we find that the effect is negligible. Sometimes, we find an effect that seems to teachers to be simply implausible, and they ignore the research. That has been the sad fate of the research of more than a half century that shows that ability grouping, *by itself,* has no effect on the achievement of individual students, or that other finding that differences in class size between about 10 and 40 students are not related to achievement. Reducing class size from 30 to 18, if this research is correct, would have no perceptible effect on achievement.

Of course not. Factors like ability grouping and class size, out of context, couldn't affect anything. But if these factors are coupled with other contextual factors, such as reconceived subject matter or a broadening of school purposes to include more than the strictly intellectual—and if these other elements are also measured—there may well be unanticipated effects.

I have said much of context. One way to become aware of the context of the curriculum is to consider the various forms curriculum research takes.

As Best and Kahn (1989:24) point out, there are three basic approaches to understanding educational phenomena: the historical (what *was*), the descriptive (what *is*), and the experimental (what *might be*).

Fortunately, the curriculum is beginning to attend to its brief history as a self-conscious field. Its roots go back for centuries, even millennia, of course, and the deep past lives in the present, as does the more recent past. As is true of all history, all of the facts are never in, and one cannot know the possible importance of what is missing. What remains from the past, however, explains some of the present. The historical fact that in ancient times the teachers were among the prophets, and in later times, in the clergy, helps us to understand the extraordinarily virtuous behavior expected of teachers now. It also helps us to understand why the public expects textbooks to deal only with self-evident, non-controversial truth. "Treasure the doubt" is inscribed in stone on the facade of the former University School building at Ohio State. The people of Columbus don't believe that schools should teach such a value, because the ancient history of education lives among them. The questioning tradition of the nineteenth-century university, which is reflected in the slogan, has always been in conflict with the history of education. Conservatives of both the present century and the nineteenth century have, therefore, always distrusted the university academics, and have actively attacked teachers in the lower schools for dealing with matters that question any aspect of the political, not to mention the religious or economic traditions. The history of education has its effect on educational inquiry: some is permitted, some is not.

Descriptive-analytical research does not have the appeal that experimental research has, but it may well be that it is the best now possible in the curriculum field. Like meteorologists, we in education don't control most of what we deal with. Like the weatherman, we can forecast only short-term phenomena, and even these uncertainly. Unlike the meteorologists, however, we have done only little in the way of close observation of educational endeavors. Typically, we observe only gross phenomena — dropouts, teen pregnancy, and such sensational tragedies, or total achievement test scores on SATs, or other such coarse surveys. What we have done very little of so far is what in medicine would be called studies of clinical practice. To be sure, there has been a revival of interest in teaching methods, and there have been some systematic observations of teaching, but lacking has been close observation of individual students. It is because of this gap in the data that we have only correlations with gross achievement scores and other coarse data, plus a limited amount of anecdotal material to work with.

It is significant that the public, including the journalists and many teachers, believe anecdotal material more than they do logico-deductive, quantitative data. There are many examples of this. Silberman's *Crisis in the Classroom,* which is no more than anecdotal journalism, had the effect of causing several hundred "open classroom" school buildings to be constructed (at considerable cost in public funds), and these buildings have failed to function as designed. *Why Johnny Can't Read,* though its author had obtained a doctorate at Teachers College with Irving Lorge, one of the most respected and rigorous of researchers, entered the language because of its clever title. The fact that its author misrepresented his sources went unnoticed.

The response of the curriculum professionals to the barrage of name-calling and vilifying has been defensive. We can do much better. We can learn from the effectiveness of this material to do better research. This can be done, not by imitating the polemicists, but by recognizing that these attacks are popular because they offer recognizable slices of life. They are not abstract, like a correlation or a regression analysis. They are concrete, like a child saying something clever and childlike, or someone unable to fill out a job application.

By comparison, the data of curriculum research are inert — lifeless. A factor analysis does not portray a student in triumph or despair.

The difficulty with lifelike, or living, data is that they, too, are hard to believe. Such data are "soft"; they lack rigor; they can easily mislead people into overgeneralizations — and they have.

Only recently has this problem been faced squarely. Emerging now is a field currently called qualitative research, which seeks to bring systematic analysis to bear on live data such as interviews, anecdotal records, informal writing, motion pictures and sound recordings, direct observation, and other such fugitive materials.

Qualitative (or naturalistic) research has a background at least a half century old. Child study, widely practiced during the thirties and forties, was carried out in school settings by teachers and others. Researchers gathered just such "natural" data and formalized it in case studies. These studies mounted into a substantial research literature that continues to be consulted. The data were solid. Late in the thirties, A. T. Jersild published an article on classroom observation, in which he detailed how observers could train themselves until their records were comparable, and how they might use time samples to make their data uniform (Jersild and Meigs 1939). Many people were trained to carry on what was called by Herbert Stolz "systematic, incidental observation." Content analysis of written materials, now greatly facilitated by computerized document searches, was refined during World War II as one of the means of propaganda analysis. Interestingly, content analysis first appeared as a form of literary criticism. In addition, operations research was devised by the near-genius head of the Bureau of Indian Affairs in the U.S. government, John Collier.

Translated into cooperative action research, operations research had a brief flurry in education during the early fifties under the leadership of Stephen M. Corey (1953). It has recently been revived in England (Somekh et al. 1987; Winter 1987).

The almost universal difficulty with research on the curriculum has been that the important findings will not hold still. They are influenced by surrounding social factors that change their significance. For example, the work on the "project method" done during the twenties was important in its time, and it had a substantially liberalizing effect on classroom practice. Now, sixty years later, the approach itself has come under fire because the times have changed. The approach is as valid now as it was then, but it no longer fits what we ask of the schools. In any case, the approach was put forth on the basis, not of research as that term is usually understood, but on the basis of William Heard Kilpatrick's eloquence. The findings that have stood up through the decades have been of limited importance for actual school practice, and some, such as the vocabulary studies of the twenties, had an effect on textbooks now called into question by Chall and others (Chall 1967; Chall et al. 1977). The findings held because of the rigor of the inquiry supporting them.

That is the apparent trade-off: rigor for significance and actual usefulness in classrooms as they really are.

What kinds of studies seem to carry enduring significance? Here are two examples: *surveys of school achievement* and *experimental studies.*

Surveys of school achievement have had a significant effect on school policy and practice ever since Horace Mann reported the appalling results of such a survey to his New England School Committee. The results of such surveys are often misinterpreted, but they need not be. They have served the useful purpose of calling attention to a problem. What they fail to do is to analyze the problem closely enough to suggest approaches to its solution. At present, the distressing results of such surveys do little more than to erode public confidence in the schools and to have a demoralizing effect on the education professionals.

Some experimental studies have made permanent contributions. Ever since Ebbinghaus found that his memory improved if what was to be memorized made sense, we have sought to make school learning "meaningful."

Ever since the Lewin, Lippitt, and White studies of classroom atmosphere (Lippitt 1940), we have sought to make school a participatory, not an authoritarian and forbidding place. The experiment with the project method has not led to universal use of that approach but it did emphasize the importance of linking otherwise disparate school subjects and of seeking connections between school subjects and out-of-school life. While the experiments with the learning of skills have had only a limited effect on school practice, they have had a very much larger effect on the training of adults in industry and in the military.

There have, of course, been many experimental studies of significance to education. However, the most influential of them have been concerned with finance, school organization, the political setting in which the schools function, and the like. They have had little to do with the purposes, substance, and practice of education itself—the curriculum.

What are the chances that a more rigorous, therefore more effective, kind of inquiry can be conducted on the actual curriculum? It has been pointed out that the curriculum field is exceedingly complex. Experience in other fields, equally complex, offers some encouragement.

For example, if the curriculum field is complex, it is not more so than is the human mind. Psychiatrists have for generations confronted this ill-understood entity with impressive results. Psychotherapy not only often succeeds, but as a field sheds light on human behavior generally.

Another highly complex field is society itself—cultural anthropology. Margaret Mead and other anthropologists opened the field to the general public generations ago.

Other complex fields can be mentioned: meteorology (already mentioned), astronomy, theology, and history. One need not be wholly stopped by complexity and lack of detailed knowledge.

In none of these fields is the inquirer able to control what is examined. What holds the fields together is not controlled experiments or a "double blind" design. What holds them together is theory which makes it possible to interpret such information as is available. The data themselves are not always quantitative. They are more like case studies than they are like any other form of inquiry.

In the case of curriculum research, such theories as we have had have led to action. The theory of a unified curriculum, according to which the barriers between the various school subjects would be removed, has led to such approaches to general education as the "broad fields" concept, which has led to the development of the social studies, language arts, and general science. The theory that learning consists of personal experience led to the emphasis on "hands on" approaches in the classroom, greatly supplementing the formerly exclusive reliance on vicarious experience with textbooks and other purely verbal learning.

Much of the difficulty with current efforts to reform the schools arises from the failure to connect the criteria of success with the theory underlying educational efforts. Listing the presidents of the United States in order, for example, has little to do with authentic U.S. history, though one who has studied the subject may well be able to list the presidents. We need bottom lines to assess the consequences of our educational efforts, but what is taken as a "bottom line" must represent authentic achievement, actual achievement, not some indirect indicator of it. As things stand, many of the instruments used to evaluate schools have the same relationship with authentic education that a barometer has with the weather, or a fever thermometer has with a disease, or gasoline consumption has with the market value of an automobile. It is misleading to confuse the measuring instrument with the thing measured.

As has been implied here, one difficulty with the instruments now in use is their limited capacity to identify the "fine grained" aspects of curriculum problems. Surveys can only indicate that something is true in a general sense—that an unanalyzed something is wrong, or is going well. They lack diagnostic power.

But there is another difficulty, more fundamental. It arises from the unpredictability of the context within which curriculum efforts are made. There is no way to predict what local events will influence the flow of curriculum actions at any level, from the nation to the individual student. This being the case, there is no way to know enough to make predictions confidently.

The fundamental difficulty is that curriculum researchers continue to think in linear terms. It is as if they were trying to debug a machine. As the mathematicians now working on chaos theory point out, Newton's theory that the universe is a vast machine, to be understood through greater and greater understanding of its parts and interactions, does not in fact describe how the universe behaves. Much of it is in fact random, turbulent. While the turbulence may take place within limits, the smaller events within the turbulent area cannot be predicted. That's why the weather cannot be predicted beyond the very short range. That's why the movements of drops of water flowing down a stream cannot be predicted, either. The model of turbulence fits the reality of the curriculum much better than does the concept of it as a machine. While curriculum events can be understood in mechanical terms in the very short run in a known situation, even within a single classroom, or within the life of a single individual, too much enters into the flow of events to make longer term predictions possible. The familiar "input-process-output" model of education doesn't fit the reality.

What, then, would be an appropriate strategy for curriculum research? Without abandoning what has been learned from the familiar statistical strategies, the curriculum researcher must make use of them within a context that allows for turbulence, randomness, or the mathematician's chaos.

There are examples available of this approach. One of them, in England, is the keeping of records of all kinds, including unverified anecdotes, samples of students' work, and other attempts to make the data of evaluation studies identical with what is evaluated. Instead of relying entirely on indicators, such as short-answer tests, supplement them with controlled samples of the behavior sought. Instead of judging writing by the student's ability to detect a grammatical flaw in a passage given as a test item, cause the students actually to write. Instead of taking the ability to recall facts in history as an indicator of a knowledge of history, ask students to interpret historical facts as they appear in their original form. Instead of asking students to detect misspelled words (which is really proofreading), ask them to spell.

An interesting example of the use of systematic study to explain complicated human behavior appeared in the 1957 ASCD *Yearbook* (Miles and Corey 1957). Matthew Miles, at that time a research assistant in the Horace Mann-Lincoln Institute at Teachers College, Columbia University, was a participant-observer in a week-long institute at East Lansing, in which the forty-three participants considered the possibilities of cooperative curriculum research at the school level. Parts of the week went well, parts went poorly. The data gathered included post-meeting evaluations by the participants, interviews, tape-recorded discussions, pre- and post-inventories of attitudes, skills, and ability to influence others, and a great deal of annotated observation of the various groups that functioned within the institute. Miles' attempt was not to predict, but to describe in depth what happened. The data are incomplete, but they are far richer than those usually gathered about learning situations. It is interesting that they do not include tests of achievement. The participants knew what they had learned. What was important was whether they wanted more such institutes to be undertaken.

More recently, Harold Berlak, Fred Newman, and others have developed somewhat similar ways of assessing educational achievement (in manuscript as this is written; not yet ready for citation). A flurry of articles is appearing attacking "scientism" in curricular studies.

Some of the most influential curriculum studies have been of the kind discussed here. In the classic *An Experiment with a Project Curriculum*, Collings assessed the consequences of Kilpatrick's proposal in a one-room school (Collings 1923). Could the results of the study be generalized? Strictly speaking, which is to say speaking linearly, no. But the study was alive and the ideas promising, so it was influential in its time. Fawcett's *The Nature of Proof* (1938), could have transformed the teaching of geometry, but the idea remains at the frontier of mathematics education. The Hartshorne and May's *Studies in Deceit* (1928) and the Smith and Tyler *Appraising and Reporting Student Progress* (1942) opened the way to some new approaches to gathering information about what were widely thought of as "intangibles," and A. T. Jersild made direct use of psychiatric data in his *In Search of Self* (1952).

These old studies are rich in implications for curriculum research approaches and techniques. However, the most influential studies now continue to present slices of life, not abstractions from it. The most common approaches to the current curriculum problems recognize (though not explicitly) the randomness of curriculum events.

In general, the approach to curriculum inquiry that seems promising now takes advantage of techniques for describing reality that now exist, but the approach would be comprehensive, not linear. It would be realistic, not abstract. It would present recognizable cases, not only mass data. In the degree that these conditions are met, and curriculum researchers abandon their attempts to act like analysts of a machine, we can have hope.

References

(Symbols preceding entries are explained on page 40)

√ Best, J. W., and Kahn, J. V. (1989). *Research in education,* 6th Ed. Englewood Cliffs, NJ: Prentice-Hall.

○ Chall, J. S. (1967). *Learning to read: The great debate.* New York: McGraw-Hill.

○ Chall, J. S., Conard, S. S., and Harris, S. (1977). *An analysis of textbooks in relation to declining SAT scores.* New York: College Entrance Examination Board.

○ Collings, E. (1923). *An experiment with a project curriculum.* New York: Macmillan.

√ Conant, J. B. (1947). *On understanding science.* New Haven, CT: Yale University Press.

+ Corey, S. M. (1953). *Action research to improve school practices.* New York: Bureau of Publications, Teachers College, Columbia University.

√ Cronbach, L. J., and Suppes, P. (1969). *Research for tomorrow's schools: Disciplined inquiry for education.* New York: Macmillan.

√ Dewey, J. (1933). *How we think.* Boston: D.C. Heath.

○ Fawcett, H. (1938). *The nature of proof.* The Thirteenth Yearbook of the National Council of Teachers of Mathematics. New York: Bureau of Publication, Teachers College, Columbia University.

+ Foshay, A. W. (1987). The curriculum matrix. *The Educational Forum, 51,* 341–353.

+ ———. (1988). The curriculum matrix — some further thoughts. *Thresholds in Education, 14,* 8–10.

o Fraley, A. (1981). *Schooling and innovation.* New York: Tyler Gibson.

+ Goodlad, J. I., and Associates (1979). *Curriculum inquiry: The study of curriculum practice.* New York: McGraw-Hill.

o Hartshorne, H., and May, M. A. (1928). *Studies in deceit.* Book one: General methods and results. New York: Macmillan.

√ Jaeger, R. M. (Ed.) (1988). *Complementary methods for research in education.* Washington, D.C.: American Educational Research Association.

+ Jenkins, D. (1985). Curriculum research. In T. Husen and T. N. Postlethwaite (Eds.), *The International Encyclopedia of Education* (pp. 1257–1263). London: Pergamon.

o Jersild, A. T. (1952). *In search of self.* New York: Bureau of Publications, Teachers College, Columbia University.

√ Jersild, A. T., and Meigs, M. F. (1939). Direct observation as a research method. *Review of Educational Research, 9,* 472–482; 597–599.

+ Kimpston, R. D., and Rogers, K. B. (1986). A framework for curriculum research. *Curriculum Inquiry, 16,* 463–474.

+ Klein, M. F., Tye, K. A., and Wright, J. E. (1979). A study of schooling: Curriculum. *Phi Delta Kappan, 61,* 244–248.

o Lippitt, R. (1940). An experimental study of the effect of democratic and authoritarian group atmospheres. Studies of topological and vector psychology. *University of Iowa Studies in Child Welfare, 16*(3), 43–195.

o Miles, M. B., and Corey, S. M. (1957). The first cooperative curriculum research institute. In *Research for curriculum improvement.* 1957 Yearbook of the Association for Supervision and Curriculum Development (pp. 305–348). Washington, D.C.: The Association.

√ Nagel, E. (1979). *The structure of science.* Indianapolis: Hackett.

√ Phillips, D. C. (1985). On what scientists know, and how they know it. In E. W. Eisner (Ed.), *Learning and teaching the ways of knowing.* 84th Yearbook of the National Society for the Study of Education, Part II (pp. 37–59). Chicago: University of Chicago Press.

+ Posner, G. J. (1989). Making sense of diversity: The current state of curriculum research. *Journal of Curriculum and Supervision, 4,* 340–361.

o Smith, E. R., and Tyler, R. W. (1942). *Appraising and recording student progress.* New York: Harper.

+ Somekh, B., Norman, A., Shannon, B., and Abbott, B. (Eds.) (1987). *Action research in development.* Cambridge, England: Cambridge Institute of Education, Classroom Action Research Network. Bulletin No. 8.

+ Stenhouse, L. (1975). *An introduction to curriculum research and development.* New York: Holmes & Meier.

+ Walker, D. (1973). What curriculum research? *Journal of Curriculum Studies, 5,* 58–72.

+ ———. (1976). Toward comprehension of curricular realities. *Review of Research in Education, 4,* 268–308.

√ Whitehead, A. N. (1957). *The aims of education and other essays.* New York: The Free Press. (Originally published in 1929).

√ Winter, R. (1987). *Action-research and the nature of social inquiry.* Aldershot, Hants, England: Gower.

6

Ethnographic Inquiry: Understanding Culture and Experience

——— *Valerie J. Janesick*

Ethnographic techniques have a long and dependable history in the social sciences. We have the disciplines of anthropology and sociology to thank for this and the relentless spirit driving researchers to understand and explain a given culture or group. In my own experience, I use the following definition for ethnography that is a combination of many definitions found in many texts over the years and which describes exactly what I do in my own ethnographic studies. Ethnography is the work of describing and explaining a given culture at a particular point in time. For purposes of this chapter, culture is defined as the acquired knowledge that people use to interpret experience and generate social behavior (Spradley 1979). It is no surprise, then, that curriculum researchers have discovered the wonderful fit between many questions in our field and the techniques of the ethnographer.

We are fortunate in educational research to have in the last ten years a number of excellent methods textbooks describing much of the theory, technique, and practice of ethnographic inquiry (Bogdan and Biklen 1982; Fetterman 1989; Goetz and LeCompte 1984; Lincoln and Guba 1985; Spindler 1982). Furthermore, textbooks in the field of anthropology, such as Spradley's (1979, 1980), offer a great deal to enhance the written record as far as methodology is concerned. In addition, many completed ethnographies or components of ethnographies are in print in journal and textbook format. These will be discussed later in the chapter as examples of completed and illustrative works in the arena of curriculum.

The Kinds of Questions We Ask

It is not by accident that there is a heightened interest in research questions which lend themselves to ethnographic techniques and analysis. Historically the twentieth century gave us a heritage which is reflective of today's milieu in the arena of research approaches. On the one hand we have the "scientific curriculum makers" and the "progressive, democratic, problem solving experientialists" on the other (Schubert 1986). At present, researchers are debating the merits of traditional "post-positivistic approaches and naturalistic ones" (Lincoln and Guba 1985) in much the same way people in curriculum have done since the 1920s.

The debate in and of itself causes us to reflect on our own work and clarify our own thinking and behavior regarding what we do and why we do it. Questions which are suited to ethnographic inquiry have long been the questions of many curriculum researchers and theorists:

1. Questions of the quality of a given curriculum, innovation, or program;

2. Questions regarding meaning or interpretation about some component of curriculum;

3. Questions which relate to curriculum in terms of its sociolinguistic aspects;

4. Questions related to the whole system as in a classroom, school, school district, etc.;

5. Questions regarding the political, economic, or sociophychological aspects of curriculum;

6. Questions regarding the hidden curriculum;

7. Questions pertaining to the social context of curriculum;

8. Questions pertaining to teachers' implicit theories about teaching and curriculum.

This list is not meant to be exhaustive but serves to illustrate the basic areas where research has been completed in the field of curriculum and which has employed ethnographic techniques, due to, among other things, the suitability of the technique and the question.

Distinguishing Characteristics of Ethnographic Inquiry

Once we acknowledge the types of questions typically suited to ethnographic method and vice versa, we are forced to delineate the distinguishing characteristics of ethnographic techniques. This is for the purpose of clarity and to avoid confusion in the vast arena of different forms of inquiry.

Based upon the extensive volume of literature which describes and explains any given culture, these distinguishing characteristics emerge for consideration:

1. Ethnographic work is wholistic. It looks at the larger picture, the whole picture, and begins with that type of outlook.

2. Ethnographic work looks at relationships within a system or culture.

3. Ethnographic work is personal, face to face, and immediate.

4. Ethnographic work is focused on understanding a given social setting not necessarily making predictions about that setting.

5. Ethnographic work demands that the researcher stay in the setting over time.

6. Ethnographic work demands time in analysis equal to the time in the field.

7. Ethnographic work demands that the researcher develop a model of what occurred in the social setting.

8. Ethnographic work requires the researcher to become the research instrument. This requires the ability to observe behavior and sharpen the skills necessary for observation and face to face interview.

9. Ethnographic work is usually published in book or monograph format. New journals are emerging like the *International Journal of Qualitative Studies in Education* which will publish ethnographic studies. Consistently, journals like *Curriculum Inquiry* and *Harvard Education Review* have always published ethnographic work, as well as *Anthropology and Education Quarterly.*

Furthermore, it may be helpful to put this in perspective in terms of what *does not* constitute ethnographic work. A researcher who merely works in a naturalistic setting is not necessarily doing ethnographic research. For example, a person who enters the field with pre-coded categories and a checklist waiting to check off a particular behavior, is not doing ethnographic work. It is important to realize that working in the field, in and of itself, does not constitute ethnographic research.

Similarly, researchers who call their work ethnographic because they somehow describe their work in cultural terms do not necessarily meet the standards of ethnographic work. Researchers in all fields need to be aware of the various canons, rules, and techniques of any given methodology.

Ethnographic Methods

Since the 1800s,[1] when anthropologists first codified their rules for observing other cultures, researchers who do ethnography have relied principally on observation, participant observation, and interview as the cornerstone of ethnography. The discipline of working on a daily basis over long periods of time in a social setting usually unfamiliar to the researcher evolved into the extensive, fully documented method we are now able to use in our work as curriculum researchers.

Observation and Its Many Faces

The most useful breakdown of types of observation has been described by Spradley (1980). He talks about:

1. Descriptive Observations

2. Focused Observations

3. Selective Observations

These can be viewed as sub-categories of observation and provide a way to view observation in relationship to questions asked by the researchers. As Spradley (1980:73) puts it, "the basic unit of all ethnographic inquiry is the *question — observation.*" In brief, any observation the researcher makes is influenced by the kinds of questions asked by the researcher in a particular social setting.

These three types of observations are exactly what classic ethnographers have been doing in the field. Descriptive observation, for example, includes observation in the social setting in which the researcher describes as much of the behavior as possible. As Spradley (1980) puts it, the researcher responds to the general question, "What is going on here?"

A focused observation is exactly that. The researcher focuses on a particular part of the day, setting, or social interaction and describes in detail exactly what is going on with the particular people in the study, in their own milieu. For example, when Cusick (1983) describes tracking students and how this affects poor, black students in a biracial urban school, he uses both descriptive observations and focused observations. In the course of the study, he found out that attendance was a critical factor in determining effects on students, through descriptive observations. Next, he asked questions which allowed for focused observations in the area of attendance and what resulted from getting students to come to class.

Selective observations are used by the researcher to pinpoint exactly what needs to be documented regarding some component of the social setting. To continue with Cusick (1983), once he found out about teachers' views on attendance, he was able to selectively look for and document those instances of behavior which supported or disconfirmed the teachers' views on attendance. All three types of observations enable the researcher to come to terms with key elements which define the world of those under study and to probe deeply into the critical issues.

Types of Participation in the Observation

The level of involvement by the researcher in any ethnographic study varies, in terms of participation. Some researchers are completely and actively involved in a study. Some are passive participants or even non-participatory. A passive participant observer is at the scene recording the behaviors of the participants in the study but does not take part in the events or does not interact with participants. In any given study, the researcher may assume a participation level which varies depending on the circumstances. For example, Janesick (1982a) observed a teacher in his sixth grade classroom as an active participant in all aspects except for actually teaching in the class. However, when she accompanied that teacher to district meetings, she was a passive participant, taking on a role as a spectator and not commenting on the activities of the meeting.

It is possible to see this as a continuum:

Total Participation	Mid-Range Participation	Passive Participation	Non-Participation w/no Involvement

Whatever level of participation selected by the researcher must be explained and described in field notes. In traditional field note format, the researcher documents the behavior under study on the scene with the field notes as the written record of what occurred. It is a good rule of thumb to include the following:

a. Date, time, place, participants

b. Some type of page numbering system

c. Some code for identifying the time sequence of the study

d. Some portion of the field note page itself which is blank allowing for the researcher's own thoughts on the behavior under study.

Figure 1 shows an example of such a format.

Figure 1

SAMPLE FIELD NOTES: QUAKERS STUDY

March 8, 1981
Quaker Meeting
"A" Street Building

11:05 a.m. – 12:15 p.m.
Carol Alaska (observer), John and
Jane Doe, Kay Smith, other adult
and children members of the meeting

My goal today is to find out more about the children's program. What a difference a week makes! I feel comfortable coming here, I know where things are, I know who some of the people are, and I know what to expect.

I arrived at the meeting room approximately 10 minutes before it was scheduled to begin. Saw John was there so I sat next to him. He introduced me to his wife, Jane. We chatted about school for a few minutes while Jane introduced herself to a new arrival. She took her name and mine to be included on the mailing list. People gradually filed into room. I asked John if his wife taught the children's group. He said no, that she ran the displaced homemaker's program in Schenectady. I asked them if they could introduce me to the person teaching the children as I am very anxious to learn more about the children's program. Jane offered to take me down to meet the teacher and ask her if I could observe the class.

I followed Jane to the first floor and entered a room very similar to the upstairs meeting room.

The researcher should try to capture as much of the behavior of the participants in the words of the participants. If a researcher is unable to take notes in the setting for any reason, the researcher needs to immediately sit down after leaving the field and write down all recollections of what took place. For example, when Janesick (1982a) was attending an art teachers' meeting with the sixth grade teacher she studied, she was unable to take notes due to the obtrusiveness of taking notes in that setting. Immediately, upon returning from that meeting she wrote down what took place with the notation that the notes were written after returning from the field setting.

Usually, field researchers type their notes after a day's work. This helps the researcher in reflecting on what took place and allows the researcher to remain close to the data. Furthermore, in a study which takes place over time, say six months to a year, if field notes are not immediately typed, there is a danger of being unable to read them later due to shorthand or abbreviations. It has always been a good practice to type field notes each day and type the notes over in clear English sentences. Many researchers use their own shorthand to expedite the description. This must be rewritten if for no other reason than for clarity for your outside reader. An outside reader is a person who is chosen to read notes and interview transcripts as part of a system of checks and balances in field research.[2] There are mounds of typewritten pages in an ethnographic study from field notes. The more creative and sensible the researcher is in codifying the data, the easier it is for the researcher to analyze those mounds of data. In the Janesick (1982a) study, for example, there were over 1,200 pages of typed field notes. The researcher codified those pages by setting, time, and social interaction. For example, field notes which had to do with teacher student interaction in the class were flagged with blue paper and identified by page number and day of the week, like 21/M for p. 21 on Monday, etc. This device of creating a system early in the study saves hours of labor in the analysis stage.

Ethnographic Interviews

In addition to observation and participation observation, ethnographic interviewing is a major and symbiotic technique. Spradley (1979) has devoted an entire book to the ethnographic interview. The main components include:

1. Greetings

2. Explaining the project

3. Asking descriptive, structural, and/or contrast questions

4. Restating the participants' responses to double check on data

5. Creating hypothetical questions when needed, and

6. Taking leave and/or setting up the next interview.

Another text which is valuable for curriculum researchers to study is Mishler's (1986) which proposes that interviewing is a type of discourse, jointly shaped by asking and answering questions. The main component of ethnographic interviews are questions.

Descriptive, Structural, and Contrast Questions

Spradley (1979) has described at length the nature of descriptive, structural, and contrast questions. Nonetheless, a brief definition of each is in order.

1. Descriptive questions include
   a. Grand Tour Questions
   b. Mini-Tour Questions
   c. Example Questions
   d. Experience Questions
   e. Native-language Questions

2. Structural questions are those which can be repeated to discover the structures or components of any given social behavior.

3. Contrast questions are those used by the researcher to compare and contrast differences in any category of social behavior.

Some examples of these questions are:

1. *Descriptive*
   a. A grand tour question would be broad in scope and would allow the participant to describe a great deal. For example, "Tell me about a typical teaching day for you in your classroom."
   b. A mini-tour question is a follow-up usually to some response from a grand tour question. Let us imagine that the teacher responds to describing a typical teaching day and mentioned that "planning time" has a great deal to do with a typical day. A mini-tour follow-up question could take this form: "Tell me how you use planning time in a typical day in your classroom."
   c. Example questions are those which need clarification. For example, let's assume the teacher in describing a typical day, said that other teachers in the school are helpful in encouraging a sense of professionalism. An example question could be, "Can you give me an example of how another teacher in school encouraged professionalism?"
   d. Experience questions are simply questions which bring out the non-routine aspects of life. For example, let us suppose the researcher asks this teacher, "You've mentioned how many things you love about teaching and that you once worked as acting principal. How would you describe that experience? What can you tell me about your reactions to being principal for three days?"
   e. A native language question allows the participant to let the researcher know what a particular term means. For example, if the participant uses a term which the researcher is unsure about in terms of its meaning, the researcher may simply say, "How would you define XXXXXXXXXXX?" The researcher may also ask the participant to give examples of the term and its use.

2. *Structural Questions*

An example of a structural question could be the following: "You mentioned that planning is complicated and takes a good deal of time. Are there stages of planning or types of activities you can identify as part of planning?" Another possibility could be: "You mentioned that you had a few problems with the principal. What would you describe as the cause of those problems?"

3. *Contrast Questions*

Contrast questions usually ask for differences or contrasts within or between some category of behavior. For example, the researcher might ask the participant the following question: "You mentioned that there is a big difference between an excellent principal and one who just shows up for work everyday. What do you see as the differences between these two?"

To summarize, ethnographic interviewing relies on questions which are descriptive, structural, and contrasting in nature. The researcher needs to know how and when to use these questions to elicit information from the participant in the participant's own words. The researcher usually records on tape the process of interviewing and ought to transcribe the tape immediately. It is usually the case that one hour of taped interview is equal to twenty pages of typed data. When transcribing tapes, many ethnographers delete "ums" — "ahs" and the like and note when they have done so. Furthermore, if something is repeated over and over again, many researchers transcribe the information once and note the number of times the information was repeated. In addition, most ethnographers take field notes during the interview even while a tape recording is being made. This allows the ethnographer to document any non-verbal behavior or outside behavior which takes place. For example, another person may enter the room and interrupt the interview. This should be documented. In any event, the ethnographic interview allows the researcher to establish an ethnographic record of the culture or group under study. As a researcher stays in the field, the researcher becomes more skilled as an interviewer and establishes a close connection with the data as it unfolds. Usually, the researcher takes field notes during the interview to complement the verbatim-taped transcript. Often researchers document non-verbal expressions and any related notes to themselves during the interview. In other words, even though a tape is running and a transcript will be made, it is helpful if the researcher still takes field notes during the interview.

Examples of Ethnographic Studies:
Implications for Curriculum Researchers

The following completed ethnographic studies are excellent examples of major works related to our field. These have been chosen for the following reasons:

1. Each study meets the basic requirements of ethnographic methodology

2. Each researcher spent a year or more in the field

3. Each study was published in book form

4. Each study includes a description of the exact techniques employed

5. Each study was conducted by an experienced and credible ethnographic researcher, and

6. Each study carries implications for some aspect of curriculum development, improvement, theory, and/or practice.

One of the important texts which deals with curriculum development, improvement, and practice is Philip Cusick's (1983) *The Egalitarian Ideal and the American High School.* Cusick undertook three studies that bear upon our understanding of curriculum in this multicultural society of ours. The data in his book are taken from three high schools—two of them urban and biracial, one all white and suburban. Cusick pointed out that, while there are differences among the three, all three share a similar structure as embedded in a strong "commitment to an American version of the egalitarian ideal, that is, to provide each student with an opportunity for social, political, and economic equality" (1983:1). These particular schools were studied in the early 1970s, a time characterized by white flight from the inner cities and a time of outspoken black militancy. Two of the schools under study were changing from predominantly white to predominantly black. In the districts where both schools were located, litigation was underway with the Civil Rights Commission regarding integration.

Cusick identified biracialism as the strongest contributor to the creation of conflicts among students. They did not openly riot, but they did fight frequently, and they remained isolated, black from white. He argued that the isolation was a result of the formal structure of the school, which was designed to "keep the lid on":

The total organization was gearing up to prevent the potential conflict among students from developing into violence. "Keeping the lid on" de-

voured all the excess energy that might have been used for pursuing
other ends. Biracialism . . . dominated everything else in the school
(1983:23).

Cusick designed his studies of the biracial schools to pursue the question: What do black and white students do together, and how does this affect
the school? What he found was that blacks and whites did very little together:

> Biracialism was too sensitive an issue to talk about rationally in either
> of our urban schools. One could not even publicly discuss its potentially
> good effects such as increasing racial tolerance and mutual understand-
> ing. Its ill effects of increasing tension and occasions for violence were
> treated, but as part of the general problem of attendance or discipline
> (1983:104–105).

Cusick found teachers and students unwilling to talk about race. Cusick
related this fact to the standards set in the schools regarding attendance and
discipline. He found the school to be obligated to the egalitarian ideal to
such an extent that the schools needed to demonstrate that they could maintain order. This meant maintaining order among many who "would prefer
not to come to school" (1983:109). Cusick argued that the very legitimacy of
the schools rests with its obligation to preserve the egalitarian ideal. In fact,
black students' chances for political, social, and economic equality are improved by virtue of attending classes and attending those classes in a "disciplined" fashion. This research directly relates to curriculum issues in the
area of biracialism and the curriculum. The author describes his interview
and observation techniques and offers curriculum researchers much to
work with and translate into practice.

Educating Minorities from Generation to Generation:
Curriculum Reformation

John Ogbu (1974) was intrigued by the question, "Why is it that some
children, especially minority children, do so badly in school?" He went to
Stockton, California, in 1968 and spent 21 months studying that community,
which had a high proportion of school failure among blacks and Mexican-
Americans. In his book, *The Next Generation: An Ethnography of Education
in an Urban Neighborhood,* Ogbu focused on the beliefs, behaviors, and
functions of education in that neighborhood, which he called "Burgher-
side." Originally from Nigeria, Ogbu completed this study as his doctoral
dissertation at the University of California at Berkeley. Unfamiliar with the
American education system, he set out to study;

> ... how the people in Stockton ... conceptualize their educational sys-
> tem and their place in it and how these conceptualizations influence the
> way they behave within the institution. I feel that understanding this
> would throw some light on ... why they (minorities) have such a high
> proportion of failure (1974:15).

After months of observation, interviews, and reviewing documents,
Ogbu carefully analyzed the data and offered an eloquent and provocative
explanation of school failure as a historical adaptation to unequal opportunity. He probed the combination of forces that created and sustain the pattern of failure, including:

1. Social stratification

2. Myths and stereotypes that support the system

3. The behaviors and beliefs about school of local teachers and administrators

4. The attitudes of ghetto residents toward competition with members
of the dominant whites

5. The exclusion of minorities from the rewards of education.

In the end, he concluded that most remedial programs are not effective
because they treat the symptoms rather than the causes of the problem.
Worse, he sees this cycle repeating itself in "the next generation."

Ogbu takes issues with existing theories that attempt to explain school
failure for minorities through factors such as cultural deprivation, inferiority
of schools attended, or genetic inferiority. He takes all of these theorists to
task for not studying this problem with any sense of history.

> ... the inadequacy of these theories is their essentially ahistorical ap-
> proach to a problem that has its roots in history (1974:254).

A fundamental historical factor in school failure of blacks and other
subordinate minorities, Ogbu explained, is the basis of their association
with the dominant group and the adaptation they have made to the institutions of American society because of their real and historical experiences in
these institutions. He argued in his final chapter that the initial association
of subordinate minorities such as blacks was not voluntary. Furthermore, it
was not motivated by the drive for economic self-improvement, as in the
case of other immigrant minorities such as the Japanese and Koreans.

What is even more striking is that historically, after emancipation,
blacks were led to believe that they would receive equal treatment with

whites in education and the benefits of education. In practice they have systematically been denied this equal treatment. Historically, blacks have been given both inferior educations and inferior rewards for education. They often have been denied the opportunity of getting good jobs and good wages. Ogbu's argument rests on these historical factors, which ultimately led to blacks adapting to these factors by reducing their efforts in school tasks. This, of course, meant that they would eventually have fewer rewards in the workplace, thus perpetuating the cycle that restricts success and advancement. Ogbu supports his detailed analysis with evidence from the statements and actions of the "Burghersiders" in his book. In conclusion, he described three ways in which adaptation to school failure is maintained:

1. There is a "lag" in efforts to achieve stated educational goals. For example, absenteeism is high, and some students do not try to make it academically.

2. Teachers behave in a way that indicates they do not understand subordinate minorities' educational problems.

3. The school system insists on defining educational problems in psychological and clinical terms.

In general, Ogbu's study shows us that the egalitarian ideal, or "equal educational opportunity," refers to (a) equal favorable learning conditions for all children, and (b) the equal enjoyment of benefits or rewards of education by individuals according to their educational achievement. When these two meanings begin to be realized and make sense to minorities, then and only then will some change take place. This study is powerful and instructive. It leaves the reader with a realistic explanation for school failure among subordinate minority groups. It also makes us question the entire curriculum in its present structure. It raises questions about teaching in our multicultural society.

Another long-term ethnographic study has much to say regarding education, race, and curriculum. Janet Ward Schofield (1982), assisted by a team of researchers, spent nearly seven years researching and writing *Black and White in School: Trust, Tension, or Tolerance?* This book reports the study of Wexler Middle School, situated in a large industrial northeastern city. Schofield focused on beliefs and behaviors related to the dynamics of racial interaction. She looked at individual classrooms and the relationship of the classroom to the policies of the school board and the city. This is a careful study of the role of race and social class in a desegregated middle school—a model school created with high hopes, good intentions, superb facilities, and staff and community support. Even with this, the school was soon diverted from its stated original goals and objectives. Schofield explained the political trade-offs involved in integration, class politics, and racial politics. The main message of the book is straightforward: Local political realities determined the future of the school.

Schofield studied teachers, administrators, students, and other related personnel through observations and interviews. Her findings are grouped by major categories relating to students and teachers. As for the teachers, Schofield found their main orientation to be one of "academics: first, last, and only." In fact, academics were so heavily stressed that other goals, such as social goals, were virtually excluded. At the same time, the school was highly publicized as one fostering positive interracial relations. Other beliefs of teachers included the notion that black and white relations will occur and develop naturally rather than through planned or forced activities. Schofield labeled this the "natural progression assumption."

Teachers also tended toward what Rist (1974) has called "the colorblind view of interracial schooling" — a view that sees interracial education as a vehicle for success in a middle-class world. In this context, it is amost inappropriate to bring up the topic of race. If one does so, it implies racism or prejudice or both. All these beliefs of teachers, along with the belief that the individual classroom is a world in itself, contributed to the development of a strong norm or taboo. This taboo discouraged teachers and students from making direct reference to or even discussing the fact that, in most cases, blacks and whites in this country are distinct social groups (Schofield 1982:55).

Given this ideology of the teachers, it is not surprising to find black and white students separate and unequal. Schofield is masterful in her analysis of the achievement gap, classroom policies and desegregation, and racial stereotypes in relationship to the achievement gap. She probes into the student's social interaction by analyzing the patterns of interaction between male and female groups and goes still further by analyzing race and romance and fears between both groups. Schofield did find that as students progressed through Wexler over a three-year period, they found ways to work with each other, although both groups held traditional racial stereotypes of each other as well. Most of Wexler's staff held a traditional assimilationist perspective (1982:219): Integration will be achieved when blacks are assimilated into white culture in terms of behavior, economic status, education, and access to the rewards of education and other social institutions. This is a widely held belief, as other researchers have documented (Rist 1978; Willie 1973). Schofield concluded by arguing that

> . . . rather than creating problems, sensitivity to and careful analysis of underlying racial tensions can help schools to avoid exacerbating such

tensions and to better meet the needs of all their constituents (1982:222).

Curriculum researchers can benefit from these three works since they address fundamental issues in our field and provide rich descriptions of the social and cultural environment, methods used in the study, and conclusions for school practice. Each ethnographic study also poses questions for further research.

The Golden Rules for Ethnographers

Ethnographic inquiry offers the curriculum researcher the opportunity to describe and explain some of the most pressing questions of our field in any given social context related to curriculum. The techniques and prototype studies described in this chapter provide useful examples to follow in curriculum research. In summary, I offer eight golden rules for ethnographers which have emerged from my own experience as an ethnographic researcher:

1. *Try not to study your own group*

The reasons for this rule are obvious but one thing you should remember about fieldwork; your work may someday return to haunt you. Also, if you are a member of a group you may be so close to it that you may miss much of the nuance of the social dynamics and critical factors that outsiders pick up on more readily. That is why the classic models of anthropological fieldwork and sociological participant observation always require that you study a culture of which you are not a member. You may have familiarity with a culture. For example, you were once a teacher and plan to do a study of teacher effectiveness. Yet, if you are too close to the inner workings of a group, you jeopardize your validity as a field researcher.

2. *Be sure to have an outside reader of your field notes and interview transcripts*

This technique used by Malinowski, Margaret Mead, Gregory Bateson, and others assures that validity checks are made on types of questions asked and types of data collected.

3. *Try not to design a study to prove something*

Ethnographers enter the field with the purpose of understanding the social structure of the group, not to prove one thing or another. Of course, you have many hypotheses to test, but the crusader attitude or evangelical spirit is out of place in the field.

4. *Time in the field equals time in analysis*

If you collect data for a year, you should use a year for analysis. Typically, ethnographic work is reported in book length or monograph format due to the mass of data which is collected and the complexity of analysis in portraying the social world.

5. *Always develop a model of what occurred in the study*

In this type of research, theory is constructed by being grounded in the data. The researcher develops a model of the social world based on the meaning given to that world by its members. In other words, theory comes from the actual case.

6. *Always look for negative evidence or points of tension and conflict*

This technique is from sociology, tried and tested over time.

7. *Remember the trade-offs in ethnographic work*

a. Time: If you are worried about time, don't do an ethnographic study. These studies take more time usually because it is not always possible to predict social factors in the real world. For example, what if your key participant is in an accident and is hospitalized for three weeks? Do you put the study on hold? Do you continue with other alternatives?

b. Money: It is very costly to study a social group for a year. For example, a student who recently completed an ethnographic interview study of PL 94–142 implementation in four school districts spent nearly $1,500.00 on typing and transcription of interview costs for his dissertation. He absorbed all travel costs in addition to that.

8. *Try to keep an ethnographic journal*

This technique evolved for me because I initially wanted students to practice writing and reflection on the process of their individual studies. A designated writing time is suggested each day so that researcher puts in writing, all the thoughts of the day related to the design, implementation, problems and joys of the study. By keeping a written record of each step and corresponding reflections, the researcher keeps track of how the study developed and this often is valuable during final analysis of the data. In addition, the researcher gets into the habit of writing at a level deeper than the descriptive level. This technique has been used by many anthropologists in their field diaries. The term ethnographic journal is used because it documents the role of the researcher in a disciplined, reflective, and interpretive way.

Notes

1. In 1800, the French philosopher, Joseph Marie Degenerando, wrote the first field research guide titled, "Considerations on Various Methods to follow in the Observation of Savage People." This field guide listed all sorts of observational and interview techniques. In the nineteenth century Franz Boas developed the technique of historical reconstruction by interviewing people about the past. In the twentieth century Bronislaw Malinowski and his students developed the technique of participant observation. The reader should consult the *Handbook of Social and Cultural Anthropology*, edited by John Honegimann (1977), for the history of these techniques and the method itself.

2. I learned to use the outside reader in my own research from Philip A. Cusick while assisting him in teaching a class on ethnographic methods. In talking to other ethnographic researchers, I found that they do the same thing. Each year in my own class in Qualitative Research Methods, I teach my own students to use an outside reader. I have been searching the literature to find out its origin and I have read that Malinowski definitely had colleagues check his notes.

References

(Symbols preceding entries are explained on page 40)

√ Bogdan, R. C., and Biklen, S. K. (1982). *Qualitative research for education*. Boston: Allyn & Bacon.

○ Cusick, P. A. (1973). *Inside high school*. New York: Holt, Rinehart and Winston.

○ ———. (1983). *The egalitarian ideal and the American high school*. New York: Longman.

√ Erickson, F. (1977). Some approaches to inquiry in school-community ethnography. *Anthropology & Education Quarterly, 7*(2), 58–69.

√ ———. (1986). Qualitative methods in research on teaching. In M. C. Wittrock (Ed.), *Handbook of research on teaching*, 3rd ed. (pp. 119–161). New York: Macmillan.

√ Fetterman, D. M. (1989). *Ethnography: step-by-step*. Newbury Park, CA: Sage.

√ Glaser, B., and Strauss, A. (1967). *The discovery of grounded theory: Strategies for qualitative research*. Chicago: Aldine.

√ Goetz, J. P., and LeCompte, M. D. (1984). *Ethnography and qualitative design in educational research.* New York: Academic Press.

√ Green, J., and Wallatt, C. (1981). *Ethnography and language in educational settings.* Norwood, New Jersey: Ablex.

○ Guthrie, G. P. (1985). *A school divided: An ethnography of bi-lingual education in a Chinese community.* Hillsdale, NJ: Erlbaum Associates.

○ Heath, S. B. (1983). *Ways with words.* New York: Cambridge University Press.

√ Honegimann, J. (Ed.) (1977). *Handbook of social and cultural anthropology.* Chapel Hill: University of North Carolina at Chapel Hill.

○ Janesick, V. J. (1979). An ethnographic study of a teacher's classroom perspective. Research Series No. 33. East Lansing, Michigan: Michigan State University, Institute for Research on Teaching.

○ ———. (1982a). Of snakes and circles: Making sense of classroom group processes through a case study. *Curriculum Inquiry, 12,* 161–185.

+ ———. (1982b). Constructing grounded theory: Reflections on a case study of a professor of architectural design. *Studies in Art Education, 24,* 16–24.

√ ———. (1983). Reflections on teaching ethnographic research methods. *Anthropology & Education Quarterly, 14,* 198–202.

○ ———. (1985). Ethnographic research in education: A case study of the Fillmore Arts Center. *Educational Horizons, 63,* 142–145.

○ ———. (1988). Our multicultural society. In E. L. Meyen & T. M. Skrtic (Eds.)., *Exceptional children and youth: An introduction,* 3rd Ed. (pp. 519–535). Denver, CO: Love.

○ Lightfoot, S. L. (1983). *The good high school.* New York: Basic Books.

√ Lincoln, Y. S., and Guba, E. (1985). *Naturalistic inquiry.* Beverly Hills, CA: Sage.

√ Mishler, E. G. (1986). *Research interviewing: Context and narrative.* Cambridge, MA: Harvard University Press.

○ Ogbu, J. (1974). *The next generation: An ethnography of education in an urban neighborhood.* New York: Academic Press.

○ Rist, R. (1974). Race, policy, and schooling. *Society, 12,* 59–63.

○ ———. (1978). *The invisible children.* Cambridge, MA: Harvard University Press.

○ Schofield, J. W. (1982). *Black and white in school: Trust, tension, or tolerance?* New York: Praeger.

+ Schubert, W. H. (1986). *Curriculum: Perspective, paradigm, and possibility.* New York: MacMillan.

√ Smith, L. M. (1978). An evolving logic of participant observation, educational ethnography, and other ease studies. *Review of Research in Education, 6,* 316–377.

o Smith, L. M., and Geoffrey, W. (1968). *The complexities of an urban classroom.* New York: Holt, Rinehart and Winston.

√ Spindler, G. (1982). *Doing the ethnography of schooling: Educational anthropology in action.* Prospect Heights, IL: Waveland Press.

√ Spradley, J. P. (1979). *The ethnographic interview.* New York: Holt, Rinehart and Winston.

√ ———. (1980). *Participant observation.* New York: Holt, Rinehart and Winston.

o Willie, C. (1973). *Race mixing in public schools.* New York: Praeger.

√ Wolcott, H. F. (1975). Criteria for an ethnographic approach to research in schools. *Human Organization, 34,* 111–128.

o ———. (1973). *The man in the principal's office: An ethnography.* New York: Holt, Rinehart and Winston.

7

Narrative Inquiry:
Storied Experience
——— *F. Michael Connelly and D. Jean Clandinin*

It is equally correct to say "inquiry into narrative" as it is "narrative inquiry." By this we mean that narrative is both phenomenon and method. Narrative names the structured quality of experience to be studied, and it names the patterns of inquiry for its study. To preserve this distinction we use the reasonably well established device of calling the phenomenon "story" and the inquiry "narrative." Thus, we say that people by nature lead storied lives and tell stories of those lives, while narrative researchers describe such lives, collect stories of them, and write narratives of experience.

Perhaps because it focuses on human experience, perhaps because it is a fundamental structure of human experience, and perhaps because it has a holistic quality, narrative is exploding into other disciplines. Narrative is a way of characterizing the phenomena of human experience and its study which is appropriate to many social science fields. The entire field of study is commonly referred to as "narratology," a term which cuts across such areas as literary theory, history, anthropology, drama, art, film, theology, philosophy, psychology, linguistics, education, and even aspects of evolutionary biological science. One of the best introductions to the scope of this literature is Mitchell's (1981) *On Narrative.*

Narrative has a long history in literature where literary theory is the principal intellectual resource (e.g., Kermode 1967; Hardy 1968; Frye 1957; Scholes and Kellogg 1966; Booth 1961, 1979). The fact that a story is inherently temporal means that history (especially White 1973, 1981) and the philosophy of history (especially Ricoeur 1984, 1985, 1988; Carr 1986), which are essentially the study of time, have a special role to play in shaping narrative studies in the social sciences. Therapeutic fields are making significant contributions (see especially Spence 1982; Schafer 1976, 1981). Narrative has only recently been discovered in psychology although Polkinghorne (1988) claims that closely related inquiries were part of the field at the turn of the century but disappeared after the second world war when they were suffocated by physical science paradigms. Bruner (1986) and Sarbin (1986) are frequently cited psychology sources. Among the most fundamental and educationally suggestive works on the nature of narrative knowledge is Johnson's philosophical study of bodily knowledge and language (1981, 1987, 1989 in press, and Lakoff and Johnson, 1980). Because education is ultimately a moral and spiritual pursuit, MacIntyre's narrative ethical theory (1966, 1981) and Crites' theological writing on narrative (1971, 1975, 1986) are especially useful for educational purposes.

The first broadly conceived methodologically oriented book on the use of narrative in the social sciences came out of the therapeutic fields, Polkinghorne's *Narrative Knowing and the Human Sciences* (1988). This book was preceded by Mishler's more narrowly focused *Research Interviewing: Context and Narrative* (1986). Van Maanen's (1988) *Tales of the Field* gives a critical introduction to the ethnography of storytelling both as subject matter and as ethnographers written form. Reason and Hawkins (1988) wrote a chapter titled "Storytelling as inquiry." Undoubtedly others will follow.

Related Educational Studies

Most educational studies of narrative have counterparts in the social sciences. Polkinghorne's (1988: 101–105) history of "individual psychology" from the mid-1800s describes narrative-related studies which have educational counterparts. Case history, biography, life history, life-span development, Freudian psychoanalysis and organizational consultation are discussed. The focus of Polkinghorne's review is on an individual's psychology considered over a span of time.

Narrative inquiry may also be sociologically concerned with groups and the formation of community (see especially Carr's 1986 narrative treatment of community). Goodson's (1988) historical discussion of teachers' life histories and studies of curriculum in schooling gives a sociologically oriented account of life history in sociology, anthropology, and educational studies. Goodson sees autobiography as a version of life history. However, given recent educational developments in works such as Sikes, Measors and Woods' (1985) *Teacher Careers,* Ball and Goodson's (1985) *Teachers Lives and Careers* and Huberman's (1988) *Teacher Careers and Social Improvement* in which the focus is on professionalism, it would appear reasonable to maintain a distinction between biography/autobiography and life history. Goodson assigns to the 'Chicago school' the main influence on life history work through sociologists such as Park and Becker. Polkinghorne emphasizes Mead's (also Chicago school) philosophical theories of symbolic interaction.

Berk (1980), in a discussion of the history of the uses of autobiography/ biography in education, states that autobiography was one of the first methodologies for the study of education. Shifting inquiry from the question "What does it mean for a person to be educated?" to "How are people, in general, educated?" appears to have led to the demise of autobiography/ biography in educational studies. This decline paralleled the decline of the study of the individual in psychology as described by Polkinghorne. Recently, Pinar and Grumet (see, for example, Pinar's 1988 *Contemporary Curriculum Discourses* and Grumet's 1988 *Bitter Milk: Women and Teaching*), developed an autobiographical tradition in educational studies.

Three closely related lines of inquiry focus specifically on story: oral history and folklore, children's storytelling, and the uses of story in preschool and school language experiences. Dorson (1976) distinguishes between oral history and oral literature; a distinction with promise in sorting out the character and origins of professional folk knowledge of teaching. Dorson names a wide range of phenomena for narrative inquiry which suggest educational inquiry possibilities such as material culture, custom, arts, epics, ballads, proverbs, romances, riddles, poems, recollections, and myths. Myths, Dorson notes, are the storied structures which stand behind folklore and oral history, an observation which links narrative to the theory of myth. (See, for example, Frye's 1988 *On Education*.) The best known educational use of oral history in North America is the Foxfire project (Wigginton 1985, 1989).

Applebee's (1978) work is a resource on children's storytelling and children's expectations of story from teachers, texts and others. Sutton-Smith's (1986) review of this literature distinguishes between structuralist approaches, which rely on 'schema' and other cognition theory terms (e.g., Mandler 1984, Schank and Abelson 1977), and meaning in a hermeneutic tradition (e.g., Gadamer 1982; Erwin-Tripp and Mitchell-Kernan 1977; McDowell 1979). A curricular version of this literature is Egan's (1986) suggestion that school subject matter be organized in story form. He suggests a model that "encourages us to see lessons or units as good stories to be told rather than sets of objectives to be obtained" (p. 2).

Applebee's work is an outgrowth of the uses of story in language instruction: a line of enquiry sometimes referred to as the work of "The Cambridge group." Much of this work has a curriculum development/teaching method focus (e.g., Britton 1970) but there are also theoretical (e.g., Britton 1971; Rosen 1986) and research traditions (e.g., Applebee described above; Wells 1986; Bissex and Bullock 1987). Lightfoot and Martin's (1988) book in honor of Britton gives an introduction to this literature. Recently this work has begun to establish a counterpart in studies of adult language and second language learning (Enns-Connolly 1985, in press; Cumming 1988;

Vechter 1987; Conle 1989; Allen 1989; Bell in press). In our work on curriculum, we see teachers' narratives as metaphors for teaching-learning relationships. In understanding ourselves and our students educationally, we need an understanding of people with a narrative of life experiences. Life's narratives are the context for making meaning of school situations. This narrative view of curriculum is echoed in the work of language researchers (Calkins 1983) and general studies of curriculum (Lightfoot and Martin 1988).

Because of its focus on experience and the qualities of life and education, narrative is situated in a matrix of qualitative research. Eisner's (1988) review of the educational study of experience implicitly aligns narrative with qualitatively oriented educational researchers working with experiential philosophy, psychology, critical theory, curriculum studies, and anthropology. Elbaz's (1988) review of teacher thinking studies created a profile of the most closely related narrative family members. One way she constructs the family is to review studies of "the personal" to show how these studies have an affinity with narrative. Another entry point for Elbaz is "voice" which, for her, and for us (Clandinin 1988), aligns narrative with feminist studies (e.g., Personal Narratives Group 1989). Elbaz's principal concern is with "story." Using a distinction between story as "primarily a methodological device" versus story as "methodology itself," she aligns narrative with many educational studies which, while specific researchers may not be conscious of using narrative, report data either in story form or use participant stories as raw data. On this basis, for Elbaz, works such as Shulman's (1987) research on expert teachers, Schön's (1987, in press) reflective practice, Reid's (1988) policy analysis, Munby's (1986) study of teachers' metaphors, and Lincoln and Guba's (1981) naturalistic approach to evaluation qualify as narratively related work.

There is a collection of educational literature which is narrative in quality but which is not found in review documents where it might reasonably appear (e.g., Wittrock 1986). We call this literature "Teachers' Stories and Stories of Teachers." This name refers to first and second hand accounts of individual teachers, students, classrooms and schools written by teachers and others. Some illustrations of "teachers' stories" are Coles' (1989) *The Call of Stories;* Barzun's (1944) *Teacher in America;* Rieff's (1972) *Fellow Teachers;* Booth's (1988) *The Vocation of a Teacher;* Natkins (1986) *Our Last Term: A Teachers Diary;* Paley's (1981) *Wally's Stories: Conversations in the Kindergarten,* and (1986) *Mollie is Three: Growing Up in School;* Calkin's (1983) *Lessons From a Child;* Stedman's (1982) *The Tidy House;* Armstrong's (1980), *Closely Observed Children;* Dennison's (1969) *The Lives of Children;* Rowland (1984), *The Enquiring Classroom;* and, Meek et al's (1983), *Achieving Literacy.* Examples of "stories of teachers" are Yonemura's (1986) *A Teacher At Work;* Bullough's (1989) *First-Year Teacher;* selected chapters in Lightfoot and Martin's (1988) *The Word for Teaching is Learning;* several chapters in Graff and Warner's (1989) *The Origins of Literary Studies in America;* Smith et al's *Trilogy* (1986, 1987, 1988) *Anatomy of Educational Innovations;* Kilbourn's (in press) *Oliver and Taylor;* Ryan's (1970) *Don't Smile Until Christmas;* and Shulman and Colbert's (1988), *Mentor Teacher Casebook.* Jackson's (1968) *Life in Classrooms* plays an especially generative role with respect to the literature of "teachers' stories and stories of teachers."

We intend this overview of narrative and storytelling approaches in and out of education to help locate narrative in an historical intellectual context. On the one hand, narrative inquiry may be traced to Aristotle's *Poetics* and Augustine's *Confessions* (see Ricoeur's, 1984, use of these two sources to link time and narrative) and may be seen to have various adaptations and applications in a diversity of areas including education. Dewey's (e.g., 1916, 1934, 1938a, 1938b) work on time, space, experience and sociality is also central. On the other hand, there is a newness to 'narratology' as it has developed in the social sciences, including education.

In the remainder of this chapter we explore methodological issues of narrative inquiry under the headings of Beginning the Story, Living the Story, Writing the Narrative, Risks, Dangers and Abuses of Narrative, and Selecting Stories to Construct and Reconstruct Narrative Plots. The educational importance of this line of work is that it brings theoretical ideas about the nature of human life as lived to bear on educational experience as lived.

Beginning the Story: The Process of Narrative Inquiry

Many accounts of qualitative inquiry give a description of the negotiation of entry into the field situation. Negotiating entry is commonly seen as an ethical matter framed in terms of principles which establish responsibilities for both researchers and practitioners. However, another way of understanding the process as an ethical matter is to see it as a negotiation of a shared narrative unity. We wrote about it in the following way:

> We have shown how successful negotiation and the application of principles do not guarantee a fruitful study. The reason, of course, is that collaborative research constitutes a relationship. In everyday life, the idea of friendship implies a sharing, an interpenetration of two or more persons' spheres of experience. Mere contact is acquaintanceship, not friendship. The same may be said for collaborative research which requires a close relationship akin to friendship. Relationships are joined, as MacIntyre (1981) implies, by the narrative unities of our lives (Clandinin and Connelly 1988: 281).

This understanding of the negotiation of entry highlights the way narrative inquiry occurs within relationships among researchers and practitioners, constructed as a caring community. When both researchers and practitioners tell stories of the research relationship, they have the possibility of being stories of empowerment. Noddings (1986: 510) remarks that in research on teaching "too little attention is presently given to matters of community and collegiality and that such research should be construed as research for teaching." She emphasizes the collaborative nature of the research process as one in which all participants see themselves as participants in the community which has value for both researcher and practitioner, theory and practice.

Hogan (1988: 12) writes about the research relationship in a similar way. "Empowering relationships develop over time and it takes time for participants to recognize the value that the relationship holds. Empowering relationships involve feelings of 'connectedness' that are developed in situations of equality, caring and mutual purpose and intention." Hogan highlights several important issues in the research relationship: the equality between participants, the caring situation and the feelings of connectedness. A sense of equality between participants is particularly important in narrative inquiry. However, in researcher/practitioner relationships where practitioners have long been silenced through being used as objects for study, we are faced with a dilemma. Practitioners have experienced themselves as without voice in the research process and may find it difficult to feel empowered to tell their stories. They have been made to feel less than equal. Noddings is helpful in thinking through this dilemma for narrative inquiry. She writes:

> . . . we approach our goal by living with those whom we teach in a caring community, through modeling, dialogue, practice and confirmation. Again, we see how unfamiliar this language has become (1986: 502).

In this quotation, Noddings is speaking of the teaching/learning relationship but what she says has significance for thinking about researcher/practitioner relationships as well. She draws attention to the ways we situate ourselves in relation to the persons with whom we work, to the ways in which we practice in a collaborative way, to the ways all participants model, in their practices, a valuing and confirmation of each other. What Hogan and Noddings highlight is the importance of time, relationship, space and voice necessary for establishing the collaborative relationship, a relationship in which both researchers and practitioners have voice in Britzman's (in press) sense. She writes:

> Voice is meaning that resides in the individual and enables that individual to participate in a community . . . The struggle for voice begins when

a person attempts to communicate meaning to someone else. Finding the words, speaking for oneself, and feeling heard by others are all a part of this process . . . Voice suggests relationships: the individual's relationship to the meaning of her/his experience and hence, to language, and the individual's relationship to the other, since understanding is a social process.

In beginning the process of narrative inquiry it is particularly important that all participants have voice within the relationship. It implies, as Elbow (1986) notes, that we play the "believing game," a way of working within a relationship which calls upon connected knowing in which the knower is personally attached to the known (Elbow 1986). Distance or separation does not characterize connected knowing. The believing game is a way of knowing which involves a process of self-insertion in the other's story as a way of coming to know the other's story and as giving the other voice. Elbow emphasizes the collaborative nature of the believing game when he writes "the believing game . . . is essentially cooperative or collaborative. The central event is the act of affirming or entering into someone's thinking or perceiving." (Elbow 1986: 289).

In narrative inquiry it is important that the researcher listen first to the practitioner's story, that it is the practitioner who first tells his/her story. This does not mean that the researcher is silenced in the process of narrative inquiry. It does mean that the practitioner, who has long been silenced in the research relationship, is given the time and space to tell her/his story so that it too gains the authority and validity that the research story has long had. Coles (1989: 22) makes a similar point when he writes, "But on that fast-darkening winter afternoon, I was urged to let each patient be a teacher: hearing themselves teach you, through their narration, the patients will learn the lessons a good instructor learns only when he becomes a willing student, eager to be taught." Narrative inquiry is, however, a process of collaboration involving mutual storytelling and restorying as the research proceeds. In the process of beginning to live the shared story of narrative inquiry, the researcher needs to be aware of constructing a relationship in which both voices are heard. The above description emphasizes the importance of the mutual construction of the research relationship, a relationship in which both practitioners and researchers feel cared for and have a voice with which to tell their stories.

Living the Story: Continuing the Process of Narrative Inquiry

What should be clear from the above description is an understanding of the process as one in which we are continually trying to give an account of the multiple levels (which are temporally continuous and socially interactive) at which the inquiry proceeds. The central task is evident when it is grasped that a person is both living their stories in an ongoing experiential text and telling their stories in words as they reflect upon life and explain themselves to others. For the researcher, this is a portion of the complexity of narrative since a life is also a matter of growth toward an imagined future and, therefore, involves retelling stories and attempts at reliving stories. A person is, at once, then, engaged in living, telling, retelling, and reliving stories.

Seeing and describing story in the everyday actions of teachers, students, administrators, and others requires a subtle twist of mind on behalf of the enquirer. It is in the tellings and retellings that entanglements become acute, for it is here that temporal and social/cultural horizons are set and reset. How far of a probe into the participants' past and future is far enough? Which community spheres should be probed and to what social depth should the inquiry proceed? When one engages in narrative inquiry the process becomes even more complex for, as researchers, we become part of the process. The two narratives of participant and researcher become, in part, a shared narrative construction and reconstruction through the inquiry.

Narrative inquiry in the social sciences is a form of empirical narrative in which empirical data is central to the work. The inevitable interpretation that occurs, something which is embedded even in the data collection process, does not make narrative into fiction even though the language of narrative inquiry is heavily laced with terms derived from literary criticism of fiction. A number of different methods of data collection are possible as the researcher and practitioner work together in a collaborative relationship. Data can be in the form of field notes of the shared experience, journal records, interview transcripts, others' observations, storytelling, letter writing, autobiographical writing, documents such as class plans and newsletters and writing such as rules, principles, pictures, metaphors and personal philosophies. In our later discussion of plot and scene, the importance of the narrative whole is made clear. The sense of the whole is built from a rich data source with a focus on the concrete particularities of life which create powerful narrative tellings. In the following we draw small excerpts from several narrative studies. These excerpts are illustrative of the variety of narrative data sources and ways of collecting narrative data.

Field Notes of Shared Experience

Field records collected through participant observation in a shared practical setting is one of the primary tools of narrative inquiry work. There are numerous narrative studies (Clandinin 1986, 1989; Hoffman 1988; Kroma 1983) which make use of field notes. An example of field notes taken from a narrative study with an intern teacher, is given below.

Marie sent them off to get started in the haunted house. She gave the other children their choice of centers and then they walked over and watched the students at the haunted house. They had built a haunted house with the large blocks. They had made a number of masks that they moved up and down. The walls moved which they said was the Poltergeist. They showed this for two or three minutes and the other students clapped. Then they went off to their centers and the children at the block center continued to work on their haunted house (Notes to file, October 22, 1985). (Clandinin and Connelly 1988).

These notes are a small fragment of the notes used in a narrative study which explored the ways in which the intern teacher (Marie) constructed and reconstructed her ideas of what it meant to teach using themes in a primary classroom setting. The researcher participated in the situation with the children and the intern teacher and in recording the field notes. The researcher's notes are an active recording of her construction of classroom events. We term this "active recording" to suggest the ways in which we see the researcher as both expressing her personal practical knowing in her work with the children and the intern teacher and also to highlight that the notes are an active reconstruction of the events rather than a passive recording which would suggest that the events could be recorded without the researcher's interpretation.

Journal Records

Journals made by participants in the practical setting are another source of data in narrative inquiry. Journal records can be made by both participants, researcher and/or practitioner. The following journal excerpt is taken from Davies (1988). Davies, a teacher, has kept a journal of her ongoing classroom practice for a number of years as a participant in a teacher researcher group. In the following journal excerpt she writes about her experiences with one of her student's journals in which Lisa, the student, figures out her writing.

This episode with Lisa makes me realize that we're still moving forward in the "gains" of this experience. I've been wondering about when the natural "peak" will occur, the moment when I feel we've gone as far as we can without the downslide effect—the loss of momentum. I just have to watch for the natural ending. I see time as so critical. Kids need and get the time with each other—kid to kid time responding is so important —they make their connections just as we make ours in the research group.

In this journal entry, Davies is trying to make sense of her work with the children in her classroom as they work in their journals. But she is also trying to understand the parallels between her experiences of learning through participating in the teacher researcher group with the work that is going on with the children in her classroom.

Interviews

Another data collection tool in narrative inquiry is the unstructured interview. Interviews are conducted between researcher and participant, transcripts made, and these discussions are available for further discussion and become part of the ongoing narrative record. There are many examples of interviews in narrative inquiry. Mishler (1986) has completed the most comprehensive study of interview in narrative inquiry. We have chosen to highlight a sample of interview from the work of Enns-Connolly (1985). The following excerpt is taken from her case study with a language student in her exploration of the process of translation.

> Brian, Student: The situation about which he was talking I've thought about a lot
>
> Esther, Researcher: Mhmmm.
>
> B: mainly because, um, I've often been concerned that my own political beliefs might lead me in certain situations into a similar kind of thing.
>
> E: Yeah, that's interesting because um you're thinking of it politically — as a political — as a consequence of politics which um, well this background — do you recall the background of this particular author? Like I'm sure that's probably a real factor in, in his writing. He's writing immediately after the Second World War after coming back from Russia and his war experiences and everything, and uh — For me, though, I don't know — I guess that just for me it's not political — I'm not focussing on the fact that it's the consequences of a political situation, but I'm focussing on the whole idea of a human being being alone and probing into himself and coming to terms with himself, and I see it more as somebody in the face of death. Like, for me death was really — like the presence of impending death was a really big thing that I was concerned about and I saw him as a person in the face of death and trying to — as reacting to impending death.
>
> B: I saw him as a person who was just desperately trying to survive. Not survive in the face of death, but survive in the face of his own, his own capacity to break down mentally, I guess.
>
> (Enns-Connolly 1985: 38–39)

What Enns-Connolly explores in her work with the German student are the ways in which translator's personal practical knowledge is shaped by and shapes the translation. The above interview segment is one in which both participants come to understand narratively the ways in which their narrative experiences shape their translation of a particular text.

Storytelling

There are many powerful examples of the uses of individual's lived stories as data sources in narrative inquiry. These are as diverse as Paley's (1981, 1986) work with children's stories to Smith et al's (1986, 1987) Kensington Revisited project. The following is an example of a story drawn from Clandinin and Connelly's (in press) work with a school principal, Phil. Phil told the following story of his experiences as a child as a way of explaining one of his actions as principal at Bay Street School.

> He had been sent to school in short pants. He and another boy in short pants were caught by older students who put them in a blanket. Phil had escaped while the other boy was trapped. He went home saying he was never going to go back to that school again. He said he understood about being a member of a minority group but he said he didn't look like a minority. He said you understood if you've had the experience (notes to File, April 15, 1981).

This story is part of Phil's storying and restorying of the ways in which he administers an inner-city school. Many stories are told by participants in a narrative inquiry as they describe their work and explain their actions. The tendency to explain through stories can easily be misinterpreted as establishing causal links in narrative inquiry. We later discuss this matter under the heading of the "illusion of causality" in narrative studies.

Letter Writing

Letter writing, a way of engaging in written dialogue between researcher and participants, is another data source in narrative inquiry. For many narrativists, letter writing is a way of offering and responding to tentative narrative interpretations (Clandinin 1986). The following, another way of thinking about letter writing, occurs within the narrative study of a group of practitioners. The practitioners are exploring the ways in which they work with children in language arts. The following example is taken from Davies (1988), one of the teacher researchers.

> I really realized just how important written response is to all of us in the research group. That made me think of the same thing for kids, which is what I'm doing now with their logs/journals of thinking. I have a reason to do these journals and that acts to focus my teaching and their learning. I really see the value, it's a lifelong one, for them as well as me.

Another participant in the group responds to Davies' comment in the following way in a written response similar to a response to a letter.

> The notion of trusted friends has been built in your classroom since the beginning of the year. These journals are part of your evolving curriculum and as such they come into the curriculum at exactly the right time for the children to make the best possible use of them. They are working so well because they are a natural outgrowth of everything that has gone before. These kids are so open, so trusting, so sensitive, so caring, so everything! The usual kid school journals are an activity that the teacher comes up with to address some part of the mandated curriculum. Kids treat the activity like any of the regular sorts of assignment — for the teacher. This latest 'chapter,' the journal writing, really highlights the similarities between our group and what goes on in your classroom — the empowerment, validation, voice, sense of community, caring, connectedness are all there.

The exchange is drawn from a two-year study that is looking narratively at teachers' experiences with writing and the ways in which their ways of knowing are expressed in their classroom practices.

Autobiographical and Biographical Writing

Another data source in narrative inquiry is autobiographical and biographical writing. Autobiographical writing sometimes appears in stories that teachers tell or in more focused autobiographical writing. We see an example of such writing in Conle's (1989) work.

> To mind comes the image of a young teenager standing by a row of windows in a classroom which has become more spacious by open folding doors which usually separate it from the adjoining room. It is gym period in a small Ontario high school in the mid 50's and two grade 10 classes are enjoying a break in routine, a snowball dance. It started with one couple who then each asked a partner and so on. The girl by the window has been waiting. No one asked her yet. The crowd around her is getting smaller and smaller. Finally she is the only one left. She stays until the bell rings and everyone files out. "Perhaps no one noticed," she thinks but a friend remarks, "Oh, you didn't dance!"
>
> I have never forgotten the incident. Many years later a colleague and I talked about it in a discussion about my early years in Canada as an immigrant teenager. We wondered how those early experiences might have shaped my interest in teaching English as a second language? What did I remember of this episode and why did I remember it at all? (Conle 1989: 8).

What Conle draws attention to is the ways in which her experience shapes her interest in, and ways of constructing, particular research and teaching interests. Other research references to autobiographical/biographical writing as a data source for narrative inquiry, are for example, Rose (1983), on the parallel lives in the marriages of well known Victorian writers, Grumet (1988), on women's experiences, and Pinar (1988), Olney (1980), and Gunn (1982) on method.

Other Narrative Data Sources

There are other data sources which narrative inquirers use. Documents such as class plans and newsletters (Clandinin 1986), writing such as rules and principles (Elbaz 1983), picturing (Cole 1986), metaphors (Lakoff and Johnson 1980) and personal philosophies (Kroma 1983) are all possible data sources for narrative inquiry. See Connelly and Clandinin (1988) for a more extended discussion of these various resources.

Writing the Narrative

At the completion of a narrative study, it is often not clear when the writing of the study began. There is frequently a sense that writing began during the opening negotiations with participants or even earlier as ideas for the study were first formulated. Material written throughout the course of the inquiry often appears as major pieces of the final document. It is common, for instance, for collaborative documents such as letters to be included as part of the text. Material written for different purposes such as conference presentations may become part of the final document. There may be a moment when one says "I have completed my data collection and will now write the narrative," but even then narrative methodologies often require further discussion with participants such that data is collected until the final document is completed. Enns-Connolly's (1985) letters to her student in German language is an example where data collection and writing were shared through final drafts, thesis hearing and subsequent publication. It is not at all clear when the writing begins.

It is important, therefore, for narrative researchers to be conscious of the end as the inquiry begins. The various matters we describe below are, of course, most evident in one's writing. But if these matters have not been attended to from the outset, the writing will be much more difficult.

What Makes a "Good" Narrative?: Beyond Reliability, Validity and Generalizability

Van Maanen (1988: xi) writes that reliability and validity are overrated criteria while "apparency" and "verisimilitude" are underrated criteria. The sense that the mainstay criteria of social science research are overrated is shared by Guba and Lincoln (1989) who reject the utility of the idea of generalization and argue that it "be given up as a goal of inquiry" and replaced by "transferability." Van Maanen, in discussing the origin of his book, writes that "the manuscript I imagined would reflect the quirky and unpredictable moments of my own history in the field and likely spoof some of the maxims of the trade. The intent was to be less instructive than amusing. Along the way, however, things grew more serious" (1988: xi–xii). This is a telling remark coming as it does as a story in a researcher's own narrative of inquiry. It is a helpful reminder to those who pursue narrative studies that they need to be prepared to "follow their nose" and, after-the-fact, reconstruct their narrative of inquiry. For this reason books such as Elbaz's (1983) *Teacher Thinking* and Clandinin's (1986) *Classroom Practice* end with reflective chapters which function as another kind of methods chapter. What are some of these "more serious" matters that guide the narrative writer in the creation of documents with a measure of "verisimilitude?"

Like other qualitative methods, narrative relies on criteria other than validity, reliability, and generalizability. It is important not to squeeze the language of narrative criteria into a language created for other forms of research. The language and criteria for the conduct of narrative inquiry are under development in the research community. We think a variety of criteria, some appropriate to some circumstances and some to others, will eventually be the agreed upon norm. It is currently the case that each inquirer must search for, and defend, the criteria that best apply to his or her work. We have already identified "apparency," "verisimilitude" and "transferability" as possible criteria. In the following paragraphs we identify additional criterion terms being proposed and used.

An excellent place to begin is with Crites' (1986: 168) cautionary phrase "the illusion of causality." He refers to the "topsy-turvy hermeneutic principle" in which a sequence of events looked at backwards has the appearance of causal necessity and, looked at forward, has the sense of a teleological, intentional, pull of the future. Thus, examined temporally, backward or forward, events tend to appear deterministically related. Because every narrativist has either recorded classroom and other events in temporal sequence (field notes, for example) or has solicited memory records, which are clearly dated (stories, autobiographical writing, for example), and intentional expectations (goals, lesson plans, purposes, time lines, for example), which often tend to be associated with temporal targets, the "illusion" can become a powerful interpretive force for the writer. Adopting what might be called "the principle of time defeasability," time may be modified to suit the story told. We make use of this notion in graduate classes, for example, in which students are often encouraged to write their own narrative by beginning with present values, beliefs and actions and then to move to their childhood or early schooling experiences. Narrative writers frequently move back and forward several times in a single document as various threads are narrated. Chatman (1981) makes use of temporal "defeasability" in his distinction between "storied-time" and "discourse-time." This is a distinction between events-as-lived and events-as-told, a distinction central to the writing of good narratives and for avoiding the "illusion of causality."

If not causality, what then? Narrative explanation derives from the whole. We noted above that narrative inquiry was driven by a sense of the whole and it is this sense which needs to drive the writing (and reading) of narrative. Narratives are not adequately written according to a model of cause and effect but according to the explanations gleaned from the overall narrative or, as Polkinghorne (1988: 116) says, on "change from 'beginning' to 'end.' " When done properly one does not feel lost in minutia but always has a sense of the whole. But this presents a dilemma in the writing since one needs to get down to concrete experiential detail. How to adjudicate between the whole and the detail at each moment of the writing is a difficult task for the writer of narrative.

One may fulfill these criterial conditions and still wonder if the narrative is a "good" one. Crites (1986) writes that a good narrative constitutes an "invitation" to participate, a notion similar to Guba and Lincoln's (1989) and our own (Connelly 1978) idea that case studies may be read, and lived, vicariously by others. Peshkin (1985: 280) notes something similar when he writes, "When I disclose what I have seen, my results invite other researchers to look where I did and see what I saw. My ideas are candidates for others to entertain, not necessarily as truth, let alone Truth, but as positions about the nature and meaning of a phenomenon that may fit their sensibility and shape their thinking about their own inquiries." On the grounds suggested by these authors, the narrative writer has an available test, that is, to have another participant read the account and to respond to such questions as "What do you make of it for your teaching (or other) situation?" This allows a researcher to assess the invitational quality of a manuscript already established as logically sound.

What are some of the marks of an explanatory, invitational, narrative? Tannen (1988) suggests that a reader of a story connects with it by recognizing particulars, by imagining the scenes in which the particulars could occur, and by reconstructing them from remembered associations with similar particulars. It is the particular and not the general that triggers emotion and moves people and gives rise to what Rosen (1988: 81) calls "authenticity." This theme is picked up as integral to plot and scene in the next section.

Robinson and Hawpe (1986: 111 – 125) in asking the question "What constitutes narrative thinking?" identify three useful writing criteria: "economy," "selectivity," and "familiarity." With these criteria they argue that stories stand between the general and the particular mediating the generic demands of science with the personal, practical, concrete demands of living. Stories function as arguments in which we learn something essentially human by understanding an actual life or community as lived. The narrative inquirer undertakes this mediation from beginning to end and embodies these dimensions as best he/she can in the written narrative.

Spence (1982: 31) writes that "narrative truth" consists of "continuity," "closure," "aesthetic finality" and a sense of "conviction." These are qualities associated both with fictional literature and with "something well done." They are life criieria. In our studies we use the notions of "adequacy" (borrowed from Schwab 1964) and "plausibility." A "plausible" account is one that tends to "ring true." It is an account of which one might say "I can see that happening." Thus, while fantasy may be an invitational element in fictional narrative, plausibility exerts firmer tugs in empirical narratives.

We can understand the narrative writer's task if we examine significant events in our lives in terms of the criteria here described. Life, like the narrative writer's task, is a dialectical balancing act in which one strives for various perfections, always falling short, yet sometimes achieving a liveable harmony of competing narrative threads and criteria.

Structuring the Narrative: Scene and Plot

Welty (1979: 163) remarks that time and place are the two points of reference by which the novel grasps experience. This is no less true for the writing of empirical narratives. Time and place become written constructions in the form of plot and scene respectively. Time and place, plot and scene, work together to create the experiential quality of narrative. They are not, in themselves, the interpretive nor the conceptual side. Nor are they on the side of narrative criticism. They are the thing itself.

Scene: Place is where the action occurs, where characters are formed and live out their stories and where cultural and social context play constraining and enabling roles. Welty writes the following on the construction of scene:

> Place has surface, which will take the imprint of man — his hand, his foot, his mind; it can be tamed, domesticated. It has shape, size, boundaries; man can measure himself against them. It has atmosphere and temperature, change of light and show of season, qualities to which man spontaneously responds. Place has always nursed, nourished and instructed man; he in turn can rule it and ruin it, take it and lose it, suffer if he is exiled from it, and after living on it he goes to it in his grave. It is the stuff of fiction, as close to our living lives as the earth we can pick up and rub between our fingers, something we can feel and smell (Welty 1979: 163).

It may be that place and scene (more than time and plot) is the more difficult construction for narrativist researchers. Documents frequently contain brief character sketches and brief descriptions of classrooms, principal's offices and the like. Setting these scenes in interesting relief is a puzzling writing task since these matters are "as close to our living lives as the earth we can pick up and rub between our fingers" and depend, therefore, on writing talents for making the plain and prosaic, interesting and invitational.

It is less customary to set the scene in physical terms than in character terms. To describe seating arrangements, pictures and layouts on classroom walls in a way that helps tell the narrative and enhance its explanatory capability is no easy task. The necessary field records for the construction of scene are often missing at the time of writing since one tends, during data collection, to focus on people rather than things.

Character and physical environment need, in the writing of narrative, to work in harmony with a third feature of scene, namely, context. Context may consist of other characters and physical environments other than the classroom. For instance, department heads, principals, school and community all bear on a classroom scene and need, depending on the inquiry, to be described. Setting the context of scene may be more troublesome to the writer than the other two features because context is "out of sight" and requires active searches during data collection. Nevertheless, difficult as it may be to write scenes composed of character, physical environment and context, they are essential to narrative and are "as informing as an old gossip" (Welty 1979: 163).

Plot: Time is essential to plot. If it were not that time is insubstantial one might say that time is the substance of plot. Welty develops this point in a metaphorical way. She says that "many of our proverbs are little nut shells to pack the meat of time in" (1979: 164) and proceeds to give incipient plot examples such as "pride goeth before destruction" and "he that diggeth a pit shall fall into it." These temporal constructions which she calls "ingots of time" are also "ingots of plot" (1979: 164). They are both story containers and conveyors of stories, expressions that "speak of life-in-the-movement" with a beginning and an end. They mark what Kermode (1967) calls the tick-tock structure of story. With the addition of the middle, a basic explanatory plot structure of beginning, middle and end is in place.

From the point of view of plot, the central structure of time is past-present-future. This commonsense way of thinking about time is informative of the temporal orientation taken in various lines of narrative and narratively oriented work. For example, narrative data sources may be classified according to their relative emphasis on the past, present and future. Story telling and autobiography, for instance, tend to be located in the past; picturing and interviewing tend to be located in the present; and letter writing, journals and participant observation tend to be located in the future. From the point of view of the narrative writer, then, different kinds of data tend to strengthen these different temporal locales.

In addition to these methodological consequences of the three-part structure of time, Carr (1986) relates the structure to three critical dimensions of human experience—significance, value, intention—and, therefore, of narrative writing. In general terms, the past conveys significance, the present conveys values, and the future conveys intention. Narrative explanation and, therefore, narrative meaning consists of significance, value, and intention. By virtue of being related to the structure of time, these three dimensions of meaning help a writer structure plots in which explanation and meaning themselves may be said to have a temporal structure. Furthermore, this structure helps convey a sense of purpose on the writing as one deals with various temporal data and fits them into past, present, or future oriented parts of the narrative.

We use an adaptation of this temporal plot structure as a device to initiate data collection. The device is based on White's (1981) distinction between annals, chronicles, and narratives in the narrative study of history. Annals are a dated record of events in which there is no apparent connection between the events. A person might, for example, simply search their memory for important life events with no particular interpretive agenda in mind. As events emerge their date of occurrence is recorded and the event described. The same may happen in the ongoing record of participant observation where one may have no clear idea of the meaning of the events described but in which one makes dated records nonetheless.

Chronicles have somewhat the character of Welty's "ingots of time and plot" in which events are clearly linked as, for example, a series of events from one's elementary school years or, perhaps, a series of events from one's years as a sports fan, or from a marriage, or during the time of a particular government with a particular educational policy and so forth. While it is clear that the events in a chronology are linked, the meaning of the events, and the plot which gives the explanatory structure for linking the events, is unstated. It is these matters which, when added to the chronology, make it a narrative. There is, of course, no clear separation of each of these ways of linking events. Nevertheless, the distinction is a useful one both in data collection and in the writing of the narrative.

In our own work, especially in teaching but also in research, instead of asking people at the outset to write a narrative we encourage them to write a chronology. We avoid asking people to begin by writing biographies and autobiographies for the same reason. People beginning to explore the writing of their own narrative, or that of another, often find the chronology to be a manageable task whereas the writing of a full fledged autobiography or narrative, when one stresses plot, meaning, interpretation and explanation, can be baffling and discouraging. Looked at from another point of view, many amateur biographies are often more akin to chronologies than narratives. The linking themes that transform the annal into a chronology are often mistaken for an account of plot and meaning. In the end, of course, it is of no real theoretical significance what the writing is called since all chronicles are incipient narratives and all narratives reduce to chronicles as one pursues the narrative, remembers and reconstructs new events, and creates further meaning. For inquiry, the point is that a heartfelt record of events in one's life, or research account of a life, does not guarantee significance, meaning, and purpose.

The creation of further meaning, which might be called "the restorying quality of narrative," is one of the most difficult of all to capture in writing. A written document appears to stand still; the narrative appears finished. It has been written, characters' lives constructed, social histories recorded, meaning expressed for all to see. Yet, anyone who has written a narrative knows that it, like life, is a continual unfolding where the narrative insights of today are the chronological events of tomorrow. Such writers know in advance that the task of conveying a sense that the narrative is unfinished and that stories will be retold and lives relived in new ways is likely to be completed in less than satisfactory ways. Furthermore, even when the writer is personally satisfied with the result he or she needs always to remember that readers may freeze the narrative with the result that the restorying life quality intended by the writer may become fixed as a print portrait by the reader.

Multiple "I's" in Narrative Inquiry

In an earlier section, we wrote about the multiple levels at which narrative inquiry proceeds. We described each participant, researcher, and teacher, as engaged in living, telling, retelling, and reliving their stories as the narrative inquiry proceeds.

Part of the difficulty in writing narrative is in finding ways to understand and portray the complexity of the ongoing stories being told and retold in the inquiry. We are, as researchers and teachers, still telling in our practices our ongoing life stories as they are lived, told, re-lived and re-told. We restory earlier experiences as we reflect on later experiences so the stories and their meaning shift and change over time. As we engage in a reflective research process, our stories are often restoried and changed as we as teacher and/or researcher "give back" to each other ways of seeing our stories. I tell you a researcher's story. You tell me what you heard and what it meant to you. I hadn't thought of it this way, am transformed in some important way, and tell the story differently the next time I encounter an interested listener or talk again with my participant.

As researchers writing narratively, we have come to understand part of this complexity as a problem in multiple "I's." We become "plurivocal" (Barnieh 1989) in writing narratively. The "I" can speak as researcher, teacher, woman, commentator, research participant, narrative critic, and as theory builder. And yet in living the narrative inquiry process, we are one person. We are also one in the writing. But in the writing of narrative, it becomes important to sort out whose voice is the dominant one when we write "I."

Peshkin addresses an aspect of this problem in writing about the researcher's personal qualities elicited in the research process. While Peshkin's reference is to the data collection process, his comments are also helpful in thinking about the writing of narrative.

> Thus fieldworkers each bring to their sites at least two selves — the human self that we generally are in everyday situations, and the research self that we fashion for our particular research situations . . . participant observation, especially within one's own culture, is emphatically first person singular. The human I is there, the I that is present under many of the same political, economic, and social circumstances as when one is being routinely human and not a researcher . . . Behind this I are one's multiple personal dispositions . . . that may be engaged by the realities of the field situation. Because of the unknown and the unexpected aspects of the research field, we do not know which of our dispositions will be engaged (Peshkin 1985: 270).

While in this quotation Peshkin addresses a dual "I," researcher and person, he suggests that the issue of multiple "I's" in writing narrative is more complex. There are more "I's" than person and researcher within each research participant. Peshkin acknowledges what he calls the personal dispositions as drawn out by the situation. In narrative inquiry we see that the practices drawn out in the research situation are lodged in our personal knowledge of the world. One of our tasks in writing narrative accounts is to convey a sense of the complexity of all of the "I's" all of the ways each of us have of knowing.

We are, in narrative inquiry, constructing narratives at several levels. At one level it is the personal narratives and the jointly shared and constructed narratives that are told in the research writing. But narrative researchers are compelled to move beyond the telling of the lived story to tell the research story. We see in Clandinin's (1986) work her story with Stephanie and Aileen as well as a research story of a way of understanding classroom practice as an expression of teacher images. In Enns-Connolly's (1985) work there is her story with Brian as well as a story of understanding the translation process as an expression of the personal practical knowledge of the translator as it is drawn forth in the experience of reading the text. This telling of the research story requires another voice of researcher, another "I."

In this latter endeavor we make our place and our voice as researcher central. We understand this as a moving out of the collaborative relationship to a relationship where we speak more clearly with the researcher "I." In the process of living the narrative inquiry, the place and voice of researcher and teacher become less role defined. Our concern is to have a place for the voice of each participant. The question of who is researcher and who is teacher becomes less the question as we concern ourselves with questions of collaboration, trust, and relationship as we live, story, and restory our collaborative research life. But in the process of writing the research story, the thread of the research inquiry becomes part of the researcher's purpose. In some ways the researcher moves out of the lived story to tell with another "I," another kind of story.

Risks, Dangers and Abuses of Narrative

The central value of narrative inquiry is its quality as subject matter. Narrative and life go together and so the principal attraction of narrative as method is its capacity to render life experiences, both personal and social, in relevant and meaningful ways. But this same capacity is a two-edged inquiry sword. Falsehood may be substituted for meaning and narrative truth by using the same criteria that give rise to significance, value, and intention. Not only may one "fake the data" and write a fiction but one may also use the data to tell a deception as easily as a truth.

In this section we do not give a complete listing of possible deceptions nor a list of devices for revealing unintentional and intentional deceptions. Rather, we simply remind potential narrative inquirers to listen closely to their critics. Our view is that every criticism is valid to some degree and contains the seed of an important point.

Take, for example, one of the central tenets of narrative, that is, the intersubjective quality of the inquiry. To dismiss criticisms of the personal and interpersonal in inquiry is to risk the dangers of narcisissm and solipsism. Narrative inquirers need to respond to critics either at the level of principle or with respect to a particular writing. It is too easy to become committed to the whole, the narrative plot, and to one's own role in the inquiry and to lose sight of the various fine lines that one treads in the writing of a narrative.

One of the "multiple I's" is that of narrative critic. Empirical narrativists cannot, as Welty claims fictional writers can, avoid the task of criticism. She writes that "story writing and critical analysis are indeed separate gifts, like spelling and playing the flute, and the same writer proficient in both is doubly endowed. But even he can't rise and do both at the same time" (1979: 107). Empirical narrativists cannot follow this dictum but must find ways of becoming "I, the critic." To accomplish this, Dalley (in press) is experimenting with different tenses, uses of pronoun and text structure in an autobiographical study of bilingualism.

A particular danger in narrative is what we have called "the Hollywood plot," the plot where everything works out well in the end. "Wellness" may be a thorough and unbending censure, such as is sometimes found in critical ethnographies, or a distillation of drops of honey, such as is sometimes found in program evaluations and implementations. Spence (1986) calls this process "narrative smoothing." It is a process that goes on all the time in narrative both during data collection and writing. The problem, therefore, is a judicial one in which the "smoothing" contained in the plot is properly balanced with what is obscured in the smoothing for narrative purposes. To acknowledge narrative smoothing is to open another door for the reader. Kermode (1981) calls the hidden matters "narrative secrets" to which a careful reader will attend. Unlike the case in fiction, which is Kermode's topic, the empirical narrativist helps her reader by self-consciously discussing the selections made, the possible alternative stories and other limitations seen from the vantage point of "I the critic."

Selecting Stories to Construct and Reconstruct Narrative Plots

Because collaboration occurs from beginning to end in narrative inquiry, plot outlines are continually revised as consultation takes place over written materials and as further data are collected to develop points of importance in the revised story. In long-term studies the written stories, and the books and papers in which they appear, may be constructed and reconstructed with different participants depending on the particular inquiry at hand. Our work in Bay Street School is illustrative. There are many computer disks of field records and interview transcripts. There are, as well, file cabinets full of memoranda, school, board of education and government documents, and newspaper clippings. It is obvious that only a small portion of it may be used in a paper, report or even a book. We cannot summarize in formats that condense the volume in a way that data tables condense survey results. Since we know that a sense of the entire inquiry is useful context for readers, a descriptive overview is required. A "narrative sketch," something like a character sketch except that it applies to the overall inquiry, is useful. It is primarily a chronicle of the inquiry. Like the notes playgoers receive as they are escorted to their seats, it has broad descriptions of scene and plot and a number of subsketches of key characters, spaces and major events that figure in the narrative. A narrative sketch, might be called an "ingot of time."

In selecting how to use the data, there are choices of form and substance. Choices of substance relate to the purposes of the inquiry which, at the time of writing, may have evolved from the purposes originally conceived for the project and in terms of which much of the data was collected. Once again our work at Bay Street School is illustrative. The original purpose defined in our National Institute of Education grant proposal was to better understand policy utilization from participants' points of view. The current purpose is to understand, through narrative, something of a school's cultural folk models (see Johnson 1987) and to link these to participants' personal knowledge and to the policy and community context. Thus, data collected and, therefore, shaped by one purpose is to be used for another. Our first task is to satisfy ourselves that the data is suitable to our new purpose.

The broad outlines of plot are contained in statements of narrative purpose. Which records are most telling? No matter how familiar they are with their data, narrative writers need to search their memories, both human and computer, for significant events preparatory to writing in much the same way that individuals search their memories and files for important life events in preparation for writing a biography. If one has worked as a team the process is richer since events can be brought to mind, discussed, and refreshed in detail with reference to field records.

Practical considerations of space and imagined audience eventually determine the quantity of data contained in the written narrative. Some narrative researchers deal with detailed accounts of experience while others prefer theory and abstraction. As noted earlier, both are important and a balance needs to be struck.

Another influence on the selection of data used in the final document is the form of the narrative. Eisner (1982) has stressed the need to experiment with "forms of representation." Narratives may be written in a demonstration mode or in an inductive mode, the former adopting more standard social scientific forms and the latter opening up possibilities imagined by Eisner. In the demonstrative mode, data tend not to speak for themselves but, instead, to be used in exemplary ways to illustrate the thoughts of the narrative writer. In an inductive mode, data more clearly tell their own story. It is in this latter mode that researchers such as Beattie (in press) and Mullen (in press) are experimenting with different literary forms.

Our final section refers again to the restorying quality of narrative. Once a writer selects events it is possible to do at least three very different things with them. The first which we have termed "broadening" occurs when we generalize. An event recalled will be used in a chronicle or insipient narrative to make a general comment about a person's character, values, or way of life or, perhaps, about the social and intellectual climate of the times. These generalizations appear as character and social descriptions, longhand answers to the questions "What sort of person are you?" or "What kind of society is it?". While these are interesting questions, they are not, as stated, narrative ones. A useful rule of thumb is to avoid making such generalizations and to concentrate on the event, in a process we have termed "burrowing." We focus on the event's emotional, moral, and aesthetic qualities; ask why the event is associated with these feelings and what their origins might be. We imagine this to be somewhat like Schafer's (1981) narrative therapy. This way of approaching the event is aimed at reconstructing a story of the event from the point of view of the person at the time the event occurred. The third thing to do with the story follows from this. The person returns to present and future considerations and asks what the meaning of the event is for them and how they might create a new story of self which changes the meaning of the event, its description, and its significance for the larger life story the person may be trying to live. These questions often emerge at the point of writing, after the data were collected. Thus, whether one feels that the appropriate task is "broadening," "burrowing," restorying, or all three, additional data collection is a likely possibility during the latter stages of writing. In long-term studies, where the inquiry purpose has evolved, as it has in our Bay Street work, and where some participants may have retired or moved to other positions, maintaining collaboration on the construction and reconstruction of plots may become a task requiring special ingenuity.

This observation brings us to our final point on narrative inquiry which is that it is common in collaborative ventures to either work with participants throughout the writing, in which case records of the work itself constitute data, or to bring written documents back to participants for final discussions. Thus, the process of writing the inquiry and the process of living the inquiry are coincident activities tending, perhaps, to shift one way or the other and always to work in tandem.

A version of this chapter appears under the title, "Stories of Experience and Narrative Inquiry," in *Educational Researcher, 19*(5), 2–14. Copyright 1990 by the American Educational Research Association. Adapted by permission of the publisher.

References

(Symbols preceding entries are explained on page 40)

○ Allen, J. P. B. (1989). Instructional models. Volume 9, *Annual Review of Applied Linguistics,* Cambridge University Press.

√ Applebee, A. N. (1978). *The child's concept of story: Ages two to seventeen.* Chicago: The University of Chicago Press.

○ Armstrong, M. (1980). *Closely observed children: Diary of a primary classroom.* London: Writers and Readers.

○ Ball, S. J., and I. F. Goodson. (1985). *Teachers' lives and careers.* London: The Falmer Press.

√ Barnieh, Z. (1989). *Understanding playwriting for children.* University of Calgary.

○ Barzun, J. (1944). *Teacher in America.* New York: University Press of America.

○ Beattie, M. (ongoing). *Teacher planning and inquiry as curriculum development.* Unpublished doctoral dissertation, University of Toronto. Toronto.

○ Bell, J. (ongoing). *Narrative self-study: The acquisition of literacy in a second language.* Unpublished doctoral dissertation, University of Toronto. Toronto.

○ Berk, L. (1980). Education in lives: Biographic narrative in the study of educational outcomes. *The Journal of Curriculum Theorizing, 2*(2), 88–153.

○ Bissex, G., and R. Bullock (Eds.). (1987). *Seeing for ourselves: Case-study research by teachers of writing.* London: Heinemann Educational Books.

√ Booth, W. C. (1961). *The rhetoric of fiction* (2nd ed.). Chicago: The University of Chicago Press.

√ ———. (1979). *Critical understanding.* Chicago: The University of Chicago Press.

○ ———. (1988). *The vocation of a teacher: Rhetorical occasions 1967–1988.* Chicago: The University of Chicago Press.

○ Britton, J. (1970). *Language and learning.* London: Allen Lane.

√ ———. (1971). *Introduction to A. R. Luria, speech and the development of mental processes in the child.* London: Penguin.

○+ Britzman, D. (1989). Who has the floor: Curriculum, teaching, and the English student teacher's struggle for voice. *Curriculum Inquiry, 19*(2), 143–162.

146   *F. Michael Connelly and D. Jean Clandinin*

√   Bruner, J. (1986). *Actual minds, possible worlds.* Massachusetts: Harvard University Press.

o   Bullough, R. V. Jr. (1989). *First-year teacher: A case study.* New York: Teachers College Press.

o   Calkins, L. M. (1983). *Lessons from a child: On the teaching and learning of writing.* Melbourne: Heinemann Educational Books.

√   Carr, D. (1986). *Time, narrative, and history.* Bloomington: Indiana University Press.

√   Chatman, S. (1981). What novels can do that films can't (and vice versa). In W. J. T. Mitchell (Ed.), *On Narrative.* Chicago: University of Chicago Press.

o   Clandinin, D. J. (1986). *Classroom practices: Teacher images in action.* London: The Falmer Press.

+   ———. (1988). Understanding research on teaching as feminist research. Paper presented at the annual meeting of the Canadian Society for the Study of Education, Windsor, Ontario.

o   ———. (1989). Developing rhythm in teaching: The narrative study of a beginning teacher's personal practical knowledge of classrooms. *Curriculum Inquiry, 19*(2), 121–141.

o+ Clandinin, D. J., and F. M. Connelly. (1988). Narrative, experience, and the study of curriculum. (Working Paper).

+   ———. (1988). Studying teachers' knowledge of classrooms: Collaborative research, ethics, and the negotiation of narrative. *The Journal of Educational Thought, 22*(2A), 269–282.

o+ ———. (in press). Narrative and story in practice and research. In D. Schön (Ed.), *Case studies in reflective practice.* New York: Teachers College Press.

o   Cole, A. L. (1986). *Teachers' spontaneous adaptations: A mutual interpretation.* Unpublished doctoral dissertation, University of Toronto. Toronto.

o   Coles, R. (1989). *The call of stories: Teaching and the moral imagination.* Boston: Houghton Mifflin.

o   Conle, C. (1989). *Stories toward an interpretive thesis.* Ontario Institute for Studies in Education, Toronto.

+   Connelly, F. M. (1978). How shall we publish case studies of curriculum development? *Curriculum Inquiry, 8*(1), 78–82.

o+ Connelly, F. M., and D. J. Clandinin. (1988). *Teachers as curriculum planners: Narratives of experience.* New York and London: Teachers College Press.

√ Crites, S. (1971). The narrative quality of experience. *Journal of the American Academy of Religion, 39*(3), 391–411.

√ ———. (1975). Angels we have heard. In James B. Wiggins (Ed.), *Religion as Story* (pp. 23–63). Lanham: University Press of America.

√ ———. (1986). Storytime: Recollecting the past and projecting the future. In Theodore R. Sarbin (Ed.), *The Storied Nature of Human Conduct* (pp. 152–1973). New York: Praeger.

○ Cumming, A. (1988). The orchestration of ESL performance. University of British Columbia. Working Paper.

○ Dalley, P. (ongoing). *Mes langues, mes couleurs: A question of identity.* Unpublished master's thesis, University of Toronto. Toronto.

○ Davies, A. (1988). *Two caring communities: A story of connected empowerment and voice.* Unpublished Manuscript, University of Calgary.

○ Dennison, G. (1969). *The lives of children.* New York: Vintage Books.

√ Dewey, J. (1916). *Democracy and education.* New York: Macmillan.

√ ———. (1934). *Art as experience.* New York: Capricorn Books.

√ ———. (1938a). *Experience and education.* New York: Collier Books.

√ ———. (1938b). *Logic: The theory of inquiry.* New York: Henry Holt and Company.

√ Dorson, R. M. (1976). *Folklore and fakelore: Essays toward a discipline of folk-studies.* Cambridge, Mass.: Harvard University Press.

+ Egan, K. (1986). *Teaching as story telling.* London, Ontario: The Althouse Press, Faculty of Education, The University of Western Ontario.

+ Eisner, E. W. (1982). *Cognition and curriculum: A basis for deciding what to teach.* New York: Longman.

+ ———. (1988, June/July). The primacy of experience and the politics of method. *Educational Researcher,* pp. 15–20.

+ ———. (In Press). *The enlightened eye: On doing qualitative inquiry.* New York: Macmillan.

○ Elbaz, F. (1983). *Teacher thinking: A study of practical knowledge.* London: Croom Helm.

○+ ———. (1988, September). Knowledge and discourse: The evolution of research on teacher thinking. Paper presented at the Conference of the International Study Association on Teacher Thinking meeting of the University of Nottingham, England.

o+ Elbow, P. (1986). *Embracing contraries: Explorations in teaching and learning.* Oxford: Oxford University Press.

o Enns-Connolly, E. (1985). *Translation as interpretive act: A narrative study of translation in university-level foreign language teaching.* Unpublished doctoral dissertation, University of Toronto, Toronto.

o ———. (In Press). Translation and the translator: A narrative study of personal practical knowledge in the construction of meaning. *Curriculum Inquiry.*

√ Erwin-Tripp, S., and C. Mitchell-Kernan. (1977). *Child discourse.* New York: Academic Press.

√ Frye, N. (1957). *Anatomy of criticism.* Princeton, N.J.: Princeton University Press.

√ ———. (1988). *On education.* Markham, Ontario: Fitzhenry & Whiteside.

√ Gadamer, H. G. (1982). *Truth & method.* New York: Crossroad.

o Goodson, I. (1988). Teachers' life histories and studies of curriculum and schooling. In Ivor F. Goodson (Ed.), *The Making of Curriculum: Collected Essays.* London & Philadelphia: The Falmer Press.

o Graff, G., and M. Warner (Eds.). (1989). *The origins of literacy studies in America: A documentary anthology.* New York: Rutledge, Chapman and Hall.

o Grumet, M. R. (1988). *Bitter milk: Women and teaching.* University of Massachusetts Press.

√ Guba, E. G., and Y. S. Lincoln. (1989). *Personal communication.* Beverly Hills, CA: Sage.

√ Gunn, J. V. (1982). *Autobiography: Toward a poetics of experience.* Philadelphia: University of Pennsylvania Press.

√ Hardy, B. (1968). Towards a poetics of fiction: An approach through narrative. *Novel, 2,* 5–14.

o Hoffman, L. (1988). *Teacher personal practical knowledge in the curriculum of a Christian school.* Unpublished master's thesis, University of Calgary. Calgary.

o Hogan, P. (1988). *Empowerment and voice: One teacher's story.* Unpublished Manuscript, University of Calgary.

o Huberman, M. (1988). Teacher careers and social improvement. *Journal of Curriculum Studies, 20*(2), 119–132.

o Jackson, P. W. (1968). *Life in classrooms.* Chicago: Holt, Rinehart & Winston.

√ Johnson, M. (Ed.). (1981). *Philosophical perspectives on metaphor.* Minneapolis: University of Minneapolis Press.

√   ———. (1987). *The body in the mind: The bodily basis of meaning, imagination, and reason.* Chicago: The University of Chicago Press.

√   ———. (1989). Embodied knowledge. *Curriculum Inquiry, 19*(4), 361–377.

√   Kermode, F. (1967). *The sense of an ending: Studies in the theory of fiction.* London: Oxford University Press.

√   ———. (1981). Secrets and narrative sequence. In W. J. T. Mitchell (Ed.), *On Narrative* (pp. 79–97). Chicago: The University of Chicago Press.

○   Kilbourn, B. (In Press). *Oliver and Taylor: Learning the art of constructive feedback in teaching.* New York: Teachers College Press.

○   Kroma, S. (1983). *Personal practical knowledge of language in teaching.* Unpublished doctoral dissertation, University of Toronto, Toronto.

√   Lakoff, G., and M. Johnson. (1980). *Metaphors we live by.* University of Chicago Press.

○+ Lightfoot, M., and N. Martin (Eds.). (1988). *The word for teaching is learning: Essays for James Britton.* Portsmouth, NH: Boynton/Cook.

√   Lincoln, Y. S., and E. G. Guba. (1985). *Naturalistic inquiry.* Beverly Hills, CA: Sage.

√   MacIntyre, A. (1966). *A short history of ethics.* New York: Macmillan.

√   ———. (1981). *After virtue: A study in moral theory.* Notre Dame, Indiana: University of Notre Dame Press.

√   Mandler, J. M. (1984). *Stories, scripts and scenes: Aspects of schema theory.* Hillsdale, N.J.: Lawrence Erlbaum.

√   McDowell, J. (1979). *Children's riddling.* Bloomington, IN: University of Indiana Press.

○   Meek, M., S. Armstrong, V. Austerfield, J. Graham, and E. Placetter. (1983). *Achieving literacy: Longitudinal studies of adolescents learning to read.* London: Routledge and Kegan Paul.

√   Mishler, E. G. (1986). *Research interviewing: Context and narrative.* Cambridge, Mass.: Harvard University Press.

√   Mitchell, W. J. T. (Ed.). (1981). *On narrative.* Chicago: The University of Chicago Press.

○   Mullen, C. (In Progress). *The self I dream: A narrative reconstruction of a personal mythology.* Unpublished master's thesis, University of Toronto. Toronto.

○   Munby, H. (1986). Metaphor in the thinking of teachers: An exploratory study. *Journal of Curriculum Studies, 18,* 197–209.

o Natkins, L. G. (1986). *Our last term: A teachers diary.* Lanham, MD: University Press of America.

+ Noddings, N. (1986). Fidelity in teaching, teacher education, and research for teaching. *Harvard Educational Review, 56*(4), 496–510.

√ Olney, J. (Ed.). (1980). *Autobiography: Essays theoretical and critical.* Princeton, New Jersey: Princeton University Press.

o Paley, V. G. (1981). *Wally's stories: Conversations in the kindergarten.* Cambridge, Mass.: Harvard University Press.

o ———. (1986). *Mollie is three: Growing up in school.* Chicago: The University of Chicago Press.

√ Personal Narratives Group. (1989). *Interpreting women's lives.* Bloomington: Indiana University Press.

√ Peshkin, A. (1985). Virtuous subjectivity: In the participant-observer's eyes. In D. Berg, and K. Smith (Eds.), *Exploring Clinical Methods for Social Research.* Beverly Hills: Sage.

o+ Pinar, W. F. (1988). "Whole, bright, deep with understanding": Issues in qualitative research and autobiographical method. In William F. Pinar (Ed.), *Contemporary Curriculum Discourses* (pp. 135–153). Scottsdale, Arizona: Gorsuch Scarisbrick.

√ Polkinghorne, D. E. (1988). *Narrative knowing and the human sciences.* New York: State University of New York Press.

√ Reason, P., and P. Hawkins. (1988). Storytelling as inquiry. In Peter Reason (Ed.), *Human Inquiry in Action: Developments in New Paradigm Research* (pp. 79–101). Beverly Hills: Sage Publications.

√ Reid, W. A. (1988). Institutions and practices: Professional education reports and the language of reform. *Educational Researcher, 17,* 10–15.

√ Ricoeur, P. (1984). *Time and narrative: Vol. I.* Chicago: The University of Chicago Press.

√ ———. (1985). *Time and narrative: Vol. II.* Chicago: The University of Chicago Press.

√ ———. (1988). *Time and narrative: Vol. III.* Chicago: The University of Chicago Press.

o Rieff, P. (1972). *Fellow teachers: Of culture and its second death.* Chicago: The University of Chicago Press.

√ Robinson, J. A. and L. Hawpe. (1986). Narrative thinking as a heuristic process. In Theodore R. Sarbin (Ed.), *Narrative Psychology* (pp. 111–125). New York: Praeger.

√ Rose, P. (1983). *Parallel lives*. New York: Vintage Books.

√ Rosen, H. (1986). The importance of story. *Language Arts, 63*(3), 226–237.

√ ———. (1988). The autobiographical impulse. In Deborah Tannen (Ed.), *Linguistics in Context: Connecting Observation and Understanding*. Norwood, NJ: Ablex Publishing Corp.

○ Rowland, S. (1984). *The enquiring classroom*. London: The Falmer Press.

○ Ryan, K. (1970). *Don't smile until Christmas: Accounts of the first year of teaching*. Chicago: The University of Chicago Press.

√ Sarbin, T. R. (Ed.). (1986). *Narrative psychology: The storied nature of human conduct*. New York: Praeger.

√ Schafer, R. (1976). *A new language for psychoanalysis*. New Haven and London: Yale University Press.

√ ———. (1981). Narration in the psychoanalytic dialogue. In Mitchell, W. J. T. (Ed.), *On Narrative* (pp. 25–50). Chicago: The University of Chicago Press.

√ Schank, R. C., and R. P. Abelson. (1977). *Scripts, plans, goals and understanding: An inquiry into human knowledge structures*. Hillsdale, N.J.: Lawrence Erlbaum Associates.

√ Scholes, R., and R. Kellogg. (1966). *The nature of narrative*. Oxford: Oxford University Press.

√ Schön, D. (1987). *Educating the reflective practitioner*. San Francisco: Jossey-Bass.

√ Schön, D. (Ed.). (In Press). *Case studies in reflective practice*. New York: Teachers College Press.

√ Schwab, J. J. (1964). The structure of the disciplines: Meanings and significances. In G. W. Ford, and L. Pugno (Eds.), *The Structure of Knowledge and the Curriculum* (pp. 1–30). Chicago: Rand McNally.

○ Shulman, J. H., and J. A. Colbert. (1988). *Mentor teacher casebook*. American Association of Colleges for Teacher Education. ERIC Clearing House on Teacher Education.

√ Shulman, L. S. (1987). Knowledge and teaching: Foundations of the new reform. *Harvard Educational Review, 57*(1), 1–22.

○ Sikes, P. J., L. Measor, and P. Woods. (1985). *Teacher careers: crises and continuities*. London: The Falmer Press.

○ Smith, L. M., P. F. Kleine, J. P. Prunty, and D. C. Dwyer. (1986). *Book 1 of the triology: A mid to long-term re-study and reconstrual. Educational innovators: Then and now*. Philadelphia: The Falmer Press.

152 F. Michael Connelly and D. Jean Clandinin

○ ———. (1987). *Book 2 of the triology ... A mid to long-term re-study and re-construal. The fate of an inner-city school.* Philadelphia: The Falmer Press.

○ ———. (1988). *Book 3 of the triology: Anatomy of educational innovation: A mid to long-term re-study and reconstrual. Innovation and change in schooling: History, politics, and agency.* Philadelphia: The Falmer Press.

√ Spence, D. P. (1982). *Narrative truth and historical method.* New York & London: W. W. Norton & Company.

√ ———. (1986). Narrative smoothing and clinical wisdom. In Theodore R. Sarbin (Ed.), *Narrative Psychology: The Storied Nature of Human Conduct* (pp. 211–232). New York: Praeger Special Studies.

○ Steedman, C. (1982). *The tidy house.* London: Virago Press.

√ Sutton-Smith, B. (1986). Children's fiction making. In Theodore R. Sarbin (Ed.), *Narrative Psychology: The Storied Nature of Human Conduct* (pp. 67–90). New York: Praeger.

√ Tannen, D. (1988). Hearing voices in conversation, fiction, and mixed genres. In Deborah Tannen (Ed.), *Linguistics in Context: Connecting Observation and Understanding.* Norwood, NJ: Ablex Publishing Corp.

√ Van Maanen, J. (1988). *Tales of the field: On writing ethnography.* Chicago: The University of Chicago Press.

○ Vechter, A. R. (1987). *Je suis la langue: An alternative approach to second language curriculum.* Unpublished doctoral dissertation, University of Toronto. Toronto.

√ Wells, G. (1986). *The meaning makers.* Portsmouth, NH: Heinemann Educational Books Inc.

√ Welty, E. (1979). *The eye of the story: Selected essays and reviews.* New York: Vintage Books.

√ White, H. (1973). *Metahistory: The historical imagination in nineteenth-century Europe.* Baltimore: The Johns Hopkins University Press.

√ ———. (1981). The value of narrativity in the representation of reality. In W. J. T. Mitchell (Ed.), *On Narrative* (pp. 1–23). Chicago: The University of Chicago Press.

○ Wigginton, E. (1985). *Sometimes a shining moment: The foxfire experience.* New York: Doubleday.

○ ———. (1989). Foxfire grows up. *Harvard Educational Review, 59*(1), 24–49.

√ Wittrock, M. C. (Ed.). (1986). *Handbook of research on teaching* (3rd ed.). A project of the American Educational Research Association. New York: Macmillan Publishing Co.

√ Woods, P. (1985). Sociology, ethnology and teacher practice. *Teaching and Teacher Education, 1*(1), 51–62.

○ Yonemura, M. V. (1986). *A teacher at work: Professional development and the early childhood educator.* New York: Teachers College Press.

8

Aesthetic Inquiry:
Art Criticism

——— Elizabeth Vallance

The movement to establish both the legitimacy of and some standards for various kinds of "qualitative" inquiry in educational research is now two decades old, and to a large extent it has succeeded. In the years since the mid-1960s, when some of the most articulate arguments for qualitative research in education were first being formulated, some forms of qualitative research have become an established part of the repertoire. Ethnographic modes of research, for example, are an accepted approach to studying classroom dynamics, and references to the anthropologist Clifford Geertz's (1973) concept of "thick description" in educational research studies no longer surprise us. As the drive for strictly "scientific" replicable studies in education has relaxed somewhat, and as educators have come to appreciate the value of close understandings of unique (and non-replicable) phenomena, naturalistic and other qualitative approaches to research have come into their own as legitimate and valuable ways of understanding the processes and effects of schooling.

Aesthetic inquiry, as one mode of qualitative inquiry that probably risks the charge of "softness" more than most, poses special problems for a handbook on forms of curriculum inquiry. In 1929, John Dewey struggled with the problem of defining a science of education and developed instead an articulate argument for studying education through a synthesis of perspectives drawn from other social sciences. The "sources of a science of education" (Dewey 1929) proved to be chiefly other disciplines (psychology, sociology, and others) which themselves must regularly be defended as "sciences" and offer an only slightly longer experience in exploring the rules of human behavior. The identification of education as a "social science"—explicitly so in the organizational structure of many institutions of higher education—both accords it a legitimacy borrowed from the social sciences and raises the same doubts among both humanists and "hard" scientists that these professions traditionally have about the social sciences themselves. Aesthetic inquiry, as a means of understanding educational phenomena, works alongside and against this tradition that seeks scientific principles to guide the policies and practices that affect schooling.

It may be that much of even the most traditional experimental research in curriculum studies is filtered somewhere in the researchers' thinking through a "qualitative" understanding of the thing being studied. There are indeed common wisdoms, mythologies, and uncodifiable truths that seem to guide much of teaching and much of our understanding of the schooling process: "teacher warmth," visible as it is as a contributer to effective teaching, is hard to quantify and harder still to impart to prospective teachers; the impossibility (and now finally the undesirability) of "teacher-proof" curricula reminded us of the limits to efforts to systematize the variables in the complex thing called schooling. To accept such limits is tacitly to accept the principles that underlie much of qualitative inquiry — principles that acknowledge the uniqueness, the contextual basis, the difficulty of completely controlling for the many complex contributors to the schooling experience in any given setting. And while we need not enthusiastically embrace "qualitative inquiry" as such in admitting these limitations, it seems fair to argue that the basic principles of qualitative inquiry are applied more often than we think by researchers seeking to understand schooling from more traditional perspectives.

Qualitative inquiry, and aesthetic inquiry especially, draws on the kinds of sensitivities and questions that educators and others tacitly or explicitly use in many settings. We apply principles of aesthetic inquiry more or less consistently and more or less usefully depending on our background, many times a day in real life and many times a day in the course of studying curriculum problems. It is always there. The question here is to identify its component parts, make them accessible to educational researchers in a practical and even "generalizable" way, and introduce them into the repertoire of curriculum inquiry. Our task here is to demystify the general concept of aesthetic inquiry and make it available to researchers sensitive to the qualities of schooling it addresses. Aesthetic inquiry can be valuable either as the guiding methodological approach to the study of a problem in curriculum or as a secondary/complementary perspective shaping the interpretation of information gathered by other means.

The pages that follow offer some definitions of aesthetic inquiry as well as some guidelines — guidelines both for undertaking one approach to aesthetic inquiry and for applying its perspectives to the interpretation of other curriculum studies.

Some Traditions of Aesthetic Inquiry

If education (or curriculum studies) is not in itself clearly a "science" with laws of its own, then we can accept that it may also be at least partly an

"art," a set of practices guided by individual judgment and contextual decisions not subject to prior control. Education happens in classrooms in ways
we can never fully predict, and it depends on many variables educators can
never fully control—even including whether the students are well nourished
or have access to books in their homes. Given that many educational decisions must be made spontaneously and must reflect the sensitivities and
predispositions of teachers, any efforts to systematize the variables in education will be limited by those uncontrollable factors. And given this, it follows that research efforts in education (including curriculum studies) must
reflect a perspective that admits this state of affairs and is willing to work
with it.

This line of thought roughly characterizes the attitudes that engendered
a spate of studies in the mid to late 1960s arguing against the prevailing conception of educational research as strictly quantifiable and controllable. A
few representative studies merit mention here. John Mann's several articles
(1966, 1968, 1969) questioning the bases of curriculum research and especially the metaphors guiding curriculum research were among the first of
these. Dwayne Huebner's (1966) study of the kinds of language and metaphors that can shape our understanding of education argued for metaphors
of aesthetics and ethics, to balance the traditional emphases on technical,
scientific, and political understandings of schooling. Maxine Greene's
(1967, 1968) philosophical/humanistic perspective on educational problems worked on some of the same arguments. Elliot Eisner's arguments for
aesthetic inquiry originated in some earlier arguments on the dangers of the
quantifiable behavioral-objectives emphasis that was emerging about the
same time (1967, 1969) and have taken clear shape in recent years (1977,
1985). The tradition of educational ethnography, not as new as aesthetic inquiry, has also demonstrated to curriculum researchers an alternative perspective for studying schooling and classrooms (Waller 1932; Jackson 1966;
McCutcheon 1979; Ross 1981, 1984). Walker's (1971) "naturalistic model for
curriculum development" codified some principles of a "naturalistic" approach to understanding the curriculum change process and introduced a
term that has since become a regular part of the repertoire.

Aesthetic inquiry as a regular tool for understanding curricular problems has been developed by a number of investigators, including chiefly Eisner (1977, 1985) and some of his students and others (Barone 1980, 1983;
Munby 1979; Vallance 1977). Various methods of qualitative inquiry have
been applied in a number of illustrative studies and under a variety of rubrics: Eisner focuses on the qualities and applications of "connoisseurship,"
Vallance attempts to draw direct parallels between art criticism techniques
and curriculum evaluation, and Barone's work has emphasized a kind of
aesthetic inquiry that is closer to literary criticism and journalistic inquiry,
as does Kelly's (1975) approach. No researchers to my knowledge call their

own approach specifically "aesthetic inquiry," yet it is possible to distinguish some elements common to all their work and to identify the chief characteristics of a general mode of inquiry that we can call "aesthetic." All purport to examine the educational event — a classroom setting, a moment of teaching, a set of curriculum materials — as a unique event analogous to a non-replicable work of art. All refer at least tacitly to the investigator's aesthetic response to the event.

The nature of the aesthetic response itself is a topic addressed by generations of aestheticians. The reader is referred to the works of Beardsley (1966, 1970), Bullough (1957), Dewey (1958), Eisner (1972), Langer (1951, 1957), Meager (1963), Osborne (1955), Pepper (1945), Rader (1960), Rosenberg (1966), Smith (1966), Sparshott (1966), Stolnitz (1970), Tomas (1963), Weitz (1966); these classic works on aesthetics outline the nature of the aesthetic response and attempt to identify the responsibilities and capabilities of the field of aesthetics and art criticism.

The basic argument runs like this: Our interactions with the world are guided by a number of needs and predispositions, many of which are extremely practical and are themselves shaped by our needs to make instantaneous decisions to get us through the day with some progress toward whatever goals we may have had in mind. Thus, we react to situations and other stimuli according to our practical needs at the time: we judge an umbrella in a shop according to whether or not it collapses small enough to fit in a briefcase, has a strap for easy hanging when not in use, is of a color suitable to our general wardrobe or color preferences; we appreciate the community garbage truck when it is doing its duty collecting refuse and keeping our neighborhood presentable; we may value an old family rocking chair for its comfort and its sentimental value. Reactions such as these are based on practical assessments of the objects (or situations) in question and they are necessary judgments. But from time to time, even in the course of the most humdrum errands or routine, we will be struck by a novel and unexpected view of these common objects — we will see them, in Bullough's (1957) terms, "from the reverse," from a perspective reflecting a kind of psychological distance that allows us to react not to their practical value but to the visual impact they may make on us. Thus, a bright yellow umbrella held by a lone pedestrian waiting for a bus may strike us as a welcome gleam of color in a rainy grey street, and be noticed for that reason alone. A child's broken rocking horse, rescued by the sanitation workers and hanging on the outside of the garbage truck, may form a brief but memorable image as the truck turns a corner. A rearrangement of a room may place the old familiar rocker in a position that causes us suddenly to enjoy its curves in the afternoon light and to appreciate its appearance as well as its proven comfort.

Such reactions are, essentially, aesthetic reactions. They may or may not influence subsequent practical decisions, but the point is that they *need not* immediately shape our decisions: appreciating the yellow flash of color on a rainy day has a value in itself, and we needn't rush out to buy an identical umbrella for that moment to have had some value for us. The aesthetic response in each example given above has provided, in effect, a moment of repose, a break from our normal practical way of valuing our environment, a chance to be impressed or amused by seeing things in a new way. There is often an "Aha!" quality to the aesthetic response, a quality of delighted and unexpected insight that is its own reward. Most importantly, the aesthetic response provides us with a bank of images, memories, flavorful qualities that we draw on from time to time. As we "bracket" our everyday experience (Dewey 1958), placing temporary fleeting frames around parts of it to isolate images or feelings or sounds and make them accessible to this aesthetic response, we create a store of memorable moments that tacitly shape our future responses. Our having once noticed a brightly colored umbrella one long-ago rainy day may shape our reaction to a painting of a crowd of umbrellas in a city park; our having noticed at last the pleasing curves of the old family rocker may help us one day to notice a similar one amidst the jumble of an antique store's collection; and so on. Aesthetic responses at their most natural are spontaneous, unplanned, usually enjoyable, and they invariably offer us an unexpected new perspective on something we already know.

What has all this to do with aesthetic inquiry in curriculum studies? A great deal, in fact, although the examples cited above illustrate fairly clearly the difficulties we could encounter in trying to codify aesthetic inquiry: how could we possibly know in advance that seeing an umbrella on a rainy day might lift our spirits for a moment, and especially how (or why) would we train someone to be receptive to such images and to find a way to make them professionally useful later? This is essentially the problem facing us in aesthetic inquiry: since the qualities to which we might respond in any curriculum materials are not always knowable in advance, by what methods of study and preparation can we ensure that the researcher will know what to look for and how to capture what he/she has found? Most importantly, why try? The specific relevance of the aesthetic response (and of systematic inquiry into it) for the field of curriculum studies is addressed in the following section.

Definitions and Principles of Aesthetic Inquiry in Curriculum Studies

What, then, is "aesthetic inquiry" and what is its relevance to curriculum studies? Aesthetic inquiry is the systematic inquiry into the aesthetic qualities of any given curricular situation: we may want to study the aesthetic qualities (positive or negative) of a textbook series, or of a series of deliberations and discussions leading to curriculum change, of a given teacher's classroom, or of a full degree sequence that we may be planning to alter. In each case, aesthetic inquiry will focus on certain qualities and principles that shape our reaction to the situation; it will seek to identify patterns, balances or imbalances, rhythms, discordant notes, any experiential qualities that color our judgment of the situation. In many cases these qualities will not be the qualities we may *think* are important to the curriculum decision: a racist tone or a sexist bias may color our reactions to a textbook more than its readability level or the fact that it covers all the topics we hope to cover in a course. The important point is that aesthetic inquiry into a curriculum problem must above all leave us free to *respond to qualities that may take us by surprise;* our response to these qualities will be helped and shaped by our training and experience in seeing these qualities.

The aesthetic response is often spontaneous, but it is rarely random; art critics and students of art history spend long years learning to "see" works of art, and their response to a painting is shaped by this experience. A first-time viewer of an exhibition of abstract painting may have quite a different reaction to the work, and while the critic's response is not necessarily "right," it will be more defensible because the critic has built up a repertoire of other references and of language by which to explain his or her reaction. The task of training in aesthetic inquiry is to provide the researcher with a set of principles and experiences that will shape reactions to curriculum problems and stimulate intelligent discussion about them.

Definitions

Aesthetic inquiry is perhaps a misleading term. By its semantic construction it may imply that the inquiry process itself has some aesthetic qualities, and while that may well be true, the discussion here does not concern itself with that. Indeed, it is important to alert the reader that "aesthetic" inquiry may have all the hallmarks of drudgery of any other kind of educational research: it is methodical, it requires extensive record-keeping and comparison, it demands its own kind of corroboration techniques, it takes a lot of time, it is hard work and not necessarily the aesthetically pleasing experience that we might hope. Aesthetic inquiry is the systematic inquiry into the tacit, hidden, "underside" of a curricular situation; it seeks to identify the experiential qualities that color the situation and govern our reaction to it, and once identified, to present them in a way that helps others to see them and thus to understand the curricular problem more fully. Thus two things need to be said by way of qualification: 1) aesthetic inquiry has the same *purposes* as traditional experimental research: it seeks to help the researcher — and others — to see the qualities of a curriculum that help account for students' *and* educators' reactions to it; 2) But aesthetic inquiry in today's educational climate is *neither necessary nor sufficient;* it is, however, highly *desirable.* Just as our pleased reaction to the yellow umbrella is not necessary (the umbrella would be there whether we enjoyed it or not), the education community *can* still do without aesthetic inquiry and would probably not much bemoan its absence. One reason aesthetic inquiry is not essential is that it is clearly not efficient for practical decision-making purposes. The same is true of art criticism. A critic may rave about a certain traveling art exhibition, but if the practical and quantifiable information about the exhibition does not fit our museum's needs, we may not be able to act on her judgments: we may not have the gallery space or the security provisions that the sponsor requires to host the exhibit. Likewise, the aesthetic qualities of a curriculum may be stunning in some sense, but budget constraints or political pressures may keep us from acting on them. Thus the information made available through aesthetic inquiry, while immensely valuable and contributing to informed decisions, is not enough; other, more mechanical and logistical, information must also go into any decision. Educational researchers adopting aesthetic inquiry methods must be sensitive to this "fringe" quality of the approach; aesthetic inquiry works best by complementing traditional inquiry results with portrayals of other qualities that also help us to understand the situation.

The chief *difference* between aesthetic and traditional/experimental research modes is in their relationship to means-end thinking. The causal relationships sought by traditional research efforts are replicable, generalizable, and verifiable; traditional research seeks rules of cause and effect, rules that enable us to understand, predict, and ultimately control events: "x kind of curriculum, under y conditions, can be expected to produce z results." Aesthetic inquiry does not go that far. It seeks to help us see the special qualities of a particular curriculum (or curriculum problem), chiefly for the purposes of understanding that curriculum better. Aesthetic inquiry, like art criticism, serves an evaluative purpose by enabling us to see why we (or the students) react as we do. In this sense it illuminates in ways that may help us to make practical decisions about the curriculum — we may elect not to change the cheerful tone of a textbook if it seems that that tone governs children's positive response to it. But we are not able to generalize from one piece of aesthetic inquiry about a curriculum to other curricula. Just as brilliant red works well in a Matisse painting but might destroy the effect of an Impressionist work, so the effect qualities of one curriculum may not be transferable to another. Aesthetic inquiry does not partake of the means-ends thinking that governs the search for causality in traditional research. It rarely helps us to predict our reactions to *other* curricular events, focusing instead on the particular. It is partly this abstention from seeking generalizable rules that contributes to its maverick identity within educational research circles.

An analogy may help to clarify: the researcher using aesthetic inquiry methods works something like an art critic works. The art critic, steeped in the artistic traditions of a particular period or style, speaks as something of an expert on that body of work and works as a kind of translator or bridge to a public which is less fully informed. The critic, in Max Kozloff's (1968) terms, "renders" the work of art into a language accessible to the public, pointing out visual patterns, color schemes, techniques, etc., that account for his own informed reaction to the work. This information, available to the general viewer, helps that viewer identify the elements he or she could be reacting to, the aesthetic qualities of the painting that can dominate the aesthetic response to it. In similar fashion, aesthetic inquiry in curriculum studies seeks to identify the salient qualities of a curriculum and render them accessible to others who may need to make practical decisions about it. Aesthetic inquiry, like art criticism, helps others to see and understand the curriculum in a new way.

General principles

Any of a number of different sets of general principles may guide aesthetic inquiry. The easiest way to think about this is to imagine the analogs between the world of art and the world of schooling. The arts include the plastic visual arts which in turn include painting, sculpture, photography, textiles, "earth art," and others. The arts also include drama, opera, dance, symphonic music, chamber music, and other dynamic "live" arts. Each art form has evolved its own tradition of criticism: generally drama critics do not review musical performances, and dance critics do not review straight drama. Generally art critics work within their own traditions and in turn contribute to the repertoire of references, vocabulary, comparisons, and other tools available to other critics within the same art form.

This chapter does not address all possible forms of aesthetic inquiry in curriculum. It bypasses, for example, a possibly useful comparison between curriculum in use in the classroom and drama criticism. Instead, it offers by way of example a close examination of *one* approach to aesthetic inquiry (inquiry drawn from the principles of the criticism of painting and other plastic arts) applied to *one* kind of educational event (the assessment of curriculum materials). For the sake of convenience I shall be referring to this process as "art criticism," but the reader should be mindful of the selective focus. My emphasis on criticism of the visual plastic arts is for quite practical reasons: it is the area of the arts with which I am most familiar. My orientation is highly visual: I am a photographer, I have studied the history of painting extensively, and I've maintained an active interest in the visual arts and the literature associated with them. In addition, however, an art-criticism approach to curriculum has a certain practical value itself: many curriculum decisions are made on the basis of the examination of the materials themselves as static textbooks not observed in use in a classroom and not necessarily accompanied by evaluative data on their effectiveness. To the extent that teachers and other educators must select materials such as textbooks, workbooks, science kits, art materials, magazine articles, or any others strictly on the basis of the teachers' own immediate reactions to them while sitting at a desk (or standing at a convention book-display booth), careful scrutiny of the materials *as* static works of art is justifiable.

A number of principles clarify the analogy between the work of art and a set of curriculum materials and as such strengthen the case for applying art-criticism techniques to curriculum decisions. These general principles shape our understanding of the curriculum as an artifact; they form the underlying theme of the aesthetic inquiry into any set of curriculum materials. The principles describing a curriculum as an artifact analogous to a work of art include these:

> 1. Both a curriculum and a work of art are *products* of human construction; they are "artifactual."
>
> 2. Both are means of *communication* between the originators (developer or artist) and an audience (students or museum-goers).
>
> 3. Both are *transformations* of the knowledge of the originator into a form that is accessible to the audience: Susanne Langer (1951, 1957) views art as a transformation of non-discursive knowledge into a physical medium, and the curriculum can be seen as a transformation of a content expert's knowledge into a form accessible to young children.
>
> 4. Both are the products of a *problem-solving* process: Ecker's (1963) description of artistic work as a series of meeting and resolving problems of form and expression has a clear parallel in the kinds of deliberations engaged in by curriculists (see Walker 1971).
>
> 5. Both depend for their meaning on an encounter with an *audience:* both provide situations in which the audience's response is invited and demanded.
>
> 6. Both provide sets of "brackets" or *boundaries* to the audience's experience: both curricula and works of art present selections from the total realm of experience, shaped in a way that structures the viewer's perceptions. Both do this deliberately.

7. When they succeed in capturing the attention of an audience, both can provide strong *reactions*. Neither is often received neutrally.

8. Both can be placed within a *tradition* of history and style change; both are partners in an ongoing development of style and a cumulation of tradition. Any curriculum or work of art can be superseded in style by something more "modern" or more "innovative."

9. Both *invite criticism* and assessment.

One example may illustrate some of the principles above: both Picasso's "Guernica" and my seventh-grade Virginia history textbook were created by someone to communicate the "author's" knowledge about a certain subject to others who may not yet know it. Both reflect decisions shaping the choices of what is included, excluded, and how the parts are arranged (composition, chapter sequence). Both were created to be seen by others and to provoke a reaction, and neither can be received "neutrally": "Guernica" provokes a wrenching reaction to the human suffering of war, and the textbook (I clearly recall, as a Northerner in a Virginia school) provoked substantial anger at its allowing only one sentence on Abraham Lincoln. Both are best understood as products of their time and as contributions to a history of style, and the reactions to both today are probably quite different from the reactions evoked at the time. Both invite criticism and assessment — "Guernica" by every viewer who reacts to it, the textbook by the teachers using it, and the students subjected to it.

How can we best *do* aesthetic inquiry of curriculum materials? To adopt the principles sketched above is to accept the possibility of critiquing a set of curriculum materials as an artifact. But criticizing a textbook as a static work of art invites us to apply a number of techniques and principles of criticism of the visual arts. These techniques are drawn from examples of art criticism — critics reviewing individual painting or exhibits — and they reflect description techniques that are particularly effective in providing the kinds of vivid descriptions by which art critics communicate the qualities of a painting that most affect the viewer.

An "art criticism" of curriculum materials seeks chiefly to *portray* the curriculum in terms that communicate their aesthetic impact to the viewer. It seeks to provide information that complements the information available from traditional evaluations or from the standard "factual" descriptions of age level, number of pages, cost, topics covered, etc., provided by publishers and clearinghouses of curriculum materials. Thus the result of an aesthetic-inquiry study will be "data" in the form of an account of the materials' aesthetic impact on the informed critic and, by implication, on the teacher and student who would eventually use the materials in the classroom.

As an example of what "criticism" or "critical description" can mean, we will consider two selections, from a piece of art criticism and from a piece of curriculum criticism:

On Matisse's "The Red Studio"

The composition of forms assumes ... (an) elliptical shape around a central void. This circular sensation is reinforced by Matisse's arabesque, the coiling line of the vine flaring out from the green vase and the twist of the wicker chair. The off-center green vase is the nearest thing to a vertical axis around which objects (images in Matisse's own paintings) glide in a circular movement. Red from floor to ceiling, the room is at once flat—a marked plane surface—and deep. It is a room. A room in which Matisse, and we the spectators, reign calmly from a central, invisible position. The wheel of space, carefully punctuated with forms that in their similitudes echo and re-echo, turns and creates a totality ... It becomes the universe, the one-world perceived first in its mysterious harmony and only later as a subject (Ashton 1969:17).

On a college-level TV courses entitled "The Great Plains Experience": ... after this carefully documented introduction to what was adapted to, the theme of adaptation takes on a stronger momentum. The course materials move us through a television segment, readings, and activities on human perceptions that the various Indian tribes made to this land. The moving television program on the Lakota is a poetic study of a tribe. It manages to make the case study representative of something grander. The momentum is slowed periodically when we dive deep into particulars, as in the details of the explorers' trips or in case studies of Indian tribes. The audio-tutorial exercise on Indian art is vivid, alive, concerned, and quite detailed. The Broad Sweep of History that opened the course might be more fun, more pulsating, more inviting than some of the closer looks, but these details are gripping if we let ourselves be reached by them ...

The tension in these materials is between the dynamism and drama of the broad sweep, grand patterns, and conclusions, on the one hand, and the slower-moving, methodical, and sometimes dry examination of facts, on the other hand. It can be bewildering. We can easily lose the forest for the trees. We want to rise from the bottom of the river and ride along on top for a while, enjoying the view. We do, from time to time. It is a constant to and fro, and since there is no one around to talk to about this course (perhaps the professor is on lunch break at his WATS extension), we are very much at the mercy of the materials. Because they are all we have, and they clearly seem to know what they're doing (the study guide spent 17 pages telling us just that), we return to them (Vallance 1977:100). (Quotation is from *Curriculum Inquiry*, published and copyrighted by John Wiley & Sons.)

Both pieces of criticism reflect techniques of observation and description drawn from the following:

1. *Selective emphasis:* few critics attempt to address every aspect of a painting. Instead, they focus on one or two salient features, those qualities that especially color the reaction to the work. In one case it may be the use of the color red, in another the effect of a strong circular composition, or the accessibly chatty tone adopted by the author of a textbook.

2. *Simile and metaphor:* Vivid critical description relies heavily on comparisons to other features of our experience or to images evoked by the work. Connections to both the critic's and the reader's experience can make the criticism more accessible and more understandable.

3. *Incidental comparison:* A passing reference (sparing us an exhaustive comparison) to similar works in the same tradition can clarify the work's impact on the critic. An art critic might compare a new painting unfavorably to the greater energy of the artist's earlier works; a curriculum critic may suggest that a new basic reader smacks of Dick & Jane in its repetition and stiltedness. Through incidental comparison the reader shares the repertoire of references to other works in the same tradition.

4. *Implied technique:* A critic may tacitly suggest how that work may have been created—more for the sake of communicating its appearance than as an accurate statement of the technique actually used. Thus, an art critic may refer to the "overexposure" of a photograph to describe a paleness and lack of detail in an image; the illustrations in a textbook may *seem* to have been chosen randomly though that is an inference. Language implying certain techniques is used extensively by art critics; it can be valuable in communicating the salient qualities of curriculum materials.

5. *Implied movement:* Art critics are notorious for the colorful verbs they use, and for seeing action that, of course, can't be present in a static piece: "colors straining to merge," shadows "creeping," and other such phrases communicate the visual dynamism of a static piece. Curriculum critics can do the same: the story of the War of 1812 may "leap from event to event with no clear theme" or "flow smoothly" from the biographies presented earlier. Techniques communicating a sense of "implied movement" can be effective particularly in critiquing materials whose dominant quality has to do with direction, energy, or timing.

6. *Redundant adjectives:* Art critics are notorious too for their flowery language that dwells on the particular. A "milky, pearly, opalescent sky" may seem an overdone way of describing an overcast sky, but its effect is important: it allows the reader to linger on one detail, to be aware of why the sky may be so important to a particular painting. It invites re-

flection. Likewise curriculum materials may invite comment on their "turgid, dull, painful prose" if that quality contributed strongly to the critic's reaction to the materials. Lingering on qualitative details is not something that traditional educational research encourages us to do; this quality of aesthetic criticism invites just that.

In these — and surely in other — techniques by which art critics examine and convey their understanding of works of art, they provide insights and judgments not available in promotional literature on an art exhibit or in the technical information of cost, size, security requirements any gallery director would need in order to decide to host the exhibition. Likewise, the same techniques applied to any analysis of curriculum materials will yield qualitative information quite different from the technical and practical information that may be available from prior evaluations, publishers' brochures, or even content analyses of the textbooks: a text might well give girls and boys equal time in illustrations and *still* be aesthetically deadening. The aesthetic information yielded by an aesthetic analysis of a curriculum complements other data in a way that enriches our understanding and informs our decisions.

Criteria and Comment

It remains to be asked how we know a piece of aesthetic criticism is exemplary and how we know when it is weak. The criteria of excellence in traditional educational research are well established in the terminology we use: traditional experimental educational research seeks certain standards of reliability, verifiability, validity, replicability, generalizability, and so forth — all referring to tests of variable control and methodological consistency. The same standards cannot be applied to aesthetic inquiry: we do not expect any two art critics to see the same things in an art exhibition and indeed would feel cheated if they did — we expect different critics to produce different insights and to help us see the event in as many informative ways as possible. Indeed, we often seek out different and conflicting reviews of a new film, both in deciding whether to bother seeing it and in sorting out our own reactions after seeing it. We expect art criticism to diverge to some extent. In that respect it differs enormously from traditional educational research paradigms.

But there is a canon of consistency that *is* applied to art criticism and it applies as well to curriculum criticism. Stephen Pepper (1945) refers to it as *"structural corroboration."* Structural corroboration is best understood in contradistinction to multiplicative corrobation that characterizes scientific research: multiplicative corroboration depends on multiple (and identical) measurements for corroborating the researcher's perceptions and is the basis of the standard of replicability. An experiment that is not replicable lacks multiplicative corroboration, and its conclusions as a result are suspect at best. By contrast, structural corroboration requires that the structure of evidence and observation clearly support the interpretation offered; it is applied in cases such as criminal law, where the act in question cannot be repeated but must be interpreted and the evidence presented in a way that persuades a jury of one interpretation over another. Mystery novels rely on the pattern of structurally corroborable evidence they develop. Likewise, a piece of art criticism or of curriculum criticism must be structurally corroborated to be effective — the critic's selection of focus and use of metaphor and other techniques should hang together in a coherent argument that the reader can test his/her own perceptions against. The reader's test of the criticism against his/her own experience of the work (or of the curriculum) is in turn a test of it *referential adequacy* — the criticism must tell "the truth" in its account of the work, should describe it well enough that a reader encountering the work later will recognize it from the critic's rendering of it. A criticism of a textbook that portrays jarring psychedelic colors as "pastel candy-colored drawings" is not referentially adequate and loses considerable power as a result.

The development of aesthetic criticisms of curriculum that are both structurally corroborated and referentially adequate is not easy. These two tests put the brakes on any critic's tendency to wax poetic for the sake of pretty language; they demand an accuracy as stringent as the accuracy imposed by canons of replicability and validity. The two criteria of structural corroboration and referential adequacy keep the curriculum critic honest.

At least three other criteria of excellence are worth noting here: (1) A piece of aesthetic inquiry, to be really effective in conveying the salient qualities of a curriculum, needs to be presented in *fresh jargon-free language*. If qualitative inquiry is to free us at all from the limitations of traditional research, it must be able to speak in a fresh new voice that itself acknowledges this freedom. Art critics, of course, have their own jargon; so will curriculum critics; the point is that it must be a jargon closer to ordinary language — closer to the ultimate users' own way of describing the impact of curriculum materials—than to the dry and unevocative language of statistical research; (2) Aesthetic inquiry demands *good writing*. The best art critics write exceptionally well; they are lucid, persuasive, fun to read. Curriculum criticism should do the same if it is to inform us in ways that traditional research cannot do. Turgid dry criticism cannot effectively provide the vivid fresh perspective on practical curriculum situations that aesthetic inquiry seeks to provide; (3) Aesthetic inquiry demands that the researcher have *both the large perspective of the big picture and a sensitivity to the telling detail.* A piece of aesthetic criticism is most effective when the judgments it suggests are placed in an appropriate context: red is wonderful in Matisse largely by virtue of the artist's audacious use of other bright colors, and "Guernica" is best understood in the context of the Spanish Civil War and Picasso's involvement in it. The telling details of a set of curriculum materials are best assessed in the context of the whole and indeed of the place of those materials in the entire school curriculum. Unlike an experiment which can isolate the variables and study them virtually in isolation, trusting the tradition of research in that field to be able to judge their importance, the aesthetic researcher is responsible to context because criticism is in part a matter of context and perspective. Thus, effective aesthetically-based research will be thorough, balanced, and set in a context that the author makes clear.

The above discussion outlines the basics of only one approach to aesthetic inquiry—the aesthetic criticism of educational materials. Other principles and techniques of aesthetic inquiry will emerge from other artistic traditions and from the need to understand other qualities of the curriculum besides its immediate aesthetic impact as a static artifact.

The point is, however, that aesthetic inquiry itself encourages an exploration of those qualities of a curriculum — of curriculum materials or of a curriculum decision demanding resolution — that most directly shape the critic's (and by implication the users') reactions to it. Aesthetic inquiry offers a perspective on curriculum research that traditional research methods assiduously avoid. In every case it offers a perspective that at best complements the perceptions of the situation gleaned from other sources; it cannot suffice as the sole basis of judgment or decision. But aesthetic inquiry can assist educators in seeing more clearly what they are dealing with—seeing what they may really be reacting to and why, and providing a basis on which to compare alternatives. Aesthetic inquiry can be a powerful tool for curriculum studies. Much has been learned about this methodological approach in recent years, and those of us involved in this approach to understanding curriculum problems look forward to the insights that continuing research will shed on this connection between the arts and education.

References

(Symbols preceding entries are explained on page 40)

√ Ashton, D. (1969). *A reading of modern art.* Cleveland: Press of Case Western Reserve University.

+ Barone, T. E. (1980). Effectively critiquing the experienced curriculum: Clues from the New Journalism. *Curriculum Inquiry, 10,* 29–53.

o ———. (1983). Things of use and things of beauty. *Daedalus, 112*(3), 1–28.

√ Beardsley, M. C. (1966). Aesthetics and criticism. In R. A. Smith (Ed.), *Aesthetics and criticism in art education.* Chicago: Rand McNally.

√ ———. (1970). The aesthetic point of view. In H. E. Kiefer and M. K. Munitz (Eds.), *Perspectives in education, religion, and the arts.* Albany: State University of New York Press.

√ Bullough, E. (1957). Psychical distance as a factor in art and an aesthetic principle. In *Aesthetics: Lectures and essays.* Stanford: Stanford University Press.

√ Dewey, J. (1929). *The sources of a science of education.* New York: Liveright.

√ ———. (1958). *Art as experience.* New York: Capricorn Books, Putnam's. (Original 1934).

√ Ecker, D. W. (1963). The artistic process as qualitative problem-solving. *Journal of Aesthetic and Art Criticism, 21,* 283–290.

+ Eisner, E. W. (1967). Curriculum theory and the concept of educational milieu. *High School Journal, 51,* 132–146.

+ ———. (1969). Instructional and expressive educational objectives: Their formulation and use in curriculum. In W. J. Popham, E. W. Eisner, H. J. Sullivan, and L. L. Tyler, *Instructional objectives.* Chicago: Rand McNally.

√ ———. (1972). *Educating artistic vision.* New York: Macmillan.

+ ———. (1977). On the uses of educational connoisseurship and criticism for evaluating classroom life. *Teachers College Record, 78,* 345–358.

o+ ———. (1985). *The educational imagination,* 2d ed. New York: Macmillan.

√ Geertz, C. (1973). *The interpretation of cultures.* New York: Basic Books.

√ Greene, M. (1967). Higher dignity. *Teachers College Record, 69,* 271–276.

√ ———. (1968). Art, technique, and the indifferent gods. *Teachers College Record, 70,* 256–261.

+ Huebner, D. (1966). Curricular language and classroom meanings. In J. B. Macdonald and R. R. Leeper (Eds.), *Language and Meaning.* Washington, D.C.: Association for Supervision and Curriculum Development.

√ Jackson, P. W. (1966). *Life in classrooms.* New York: Holt, Rinehart and Winston.

+ Kelly, E. F. (1975). Curriculum evaluation and literacy criticism. *Curriculum Theory Network, 5,* 87–106.

√ Kozloff, M. (1968). *Renderings: Critical essays on a century of modern art.* New York: Simon and Schuster.

√ Langer, S. (1951). *Philosophy in a new key.* New York: Mentor Books.

√ ———. (1957). *Problems in art.* New York: Scribner's.

○+ McCutcheon, G. (1979). Educational criticism: Methods and application. *Journal of Curriculum Theorizing, 1*(2), 5–25.

+ Mann, J. S. (1966). Functions of curriculum research. *Educational Leadership, 24,* 77–85.

○ ———. (1968). A discipline of curriculum theory. *School Review, 76,* 359–78.

○ ———. (1969). Curriculum criticism. *Teachers College Record, 71,* 27–40.

√ Meager, R. (1963). The uniqueness of a work of art. In M. Levich (Ed.), *Aesthetics and the philosophy of criticism.* New York: Random House.

○ Munby, A. H. (1979). Philosophy for children: An example of curriculum review and criticism. *Curriculum Inquiry, 9,* 229–249.

√ Osborne, H. (1955). *Aesthetics and criticism.* London: Routledge & Kegan Paul.

√ Pepper, S. C. (1945). *The basis of criticism in the arts.* Cambridge: Harvard University Press.

√ Rader, M. (1960). *A modern book of aesthetics.* New York: Holt, Rinehart and Winston.

√ Rosenberg, H. (1966). *The anxious object: Art today and its audience.* New York: New American Library, Mentor Books.

○ Ross, D. D. (1981). Ms. Shores' classroom: A curriculum criticism. Paper presented at the annual meeting of the American Educational Research Association, Los Angeles.

○ ———. (1984). An introduction to curriculum criticism. *Journal of Thought, 19,* 47–60.

√ Smith, R. A. (Ed.) (1966). *Aesthetics and criticism in art education.* Chicago: Rand McNally.

√ Sparshott, F. E. (1966). The case for aesthetics. In R. A. Smith (Ed.), *Aesthetics and criticism in art education.* Chicago: Rand McNally.

√ Stolnitz, J. (1970). The artistic and the aesthetic. In H. E. Kiefer & M. K. Munitz (Eds.), *Perspectives in education, religion, and the arts.* Albany: State University of New York Press.

√ Tomas, V. (1963). Aesthetic vision. In M. Levich (Ed.), *Aesthetics and the philosophy of criticism.* New York: Random House.

o   Vallance, E. (1977). The landscape of "The Great Plains Experience": An application of curriculum criticism. *Curriculum Inquiry, 7,* 87 – 105.

+   ———. (1981). Focus on students in curriculum knowledge: A critique of curriculum criticism. Paper invited as part of symposium entitled, "A Second-Generation of Alternative Research Methodologies," at annual meeting of the American Educational Research Association, Los Angeles.

+   Walker, D. F. (1971). A naturalistic model for curriculum development. *School Review, 80,* 51 – 65.

√   Waller, W. (1932). *The sociology of teaching.* New York: Wiley.

√   Weitz, M. (1966). The role of theory in aesthetics. In R. A. Smith (Ed.), *Aesthetics and criticism in art education.* Chicago: Rand McNally.

9

Phenomenological Inquiry:
Life-World Perceptions

——— *George Willis*

Until the artist is satisfied in perception with what he is doing, he continues shaping and reshaping. The making comes to an end when its result is experienced as good — and that experience comes not by mere intellectual and outside judgment but in direct perception. An artist, in comparison with his fellows, is one who is not only especially gifted in powers of execution but in unusual sensitivity to the qualities of things. This sensitivity also directs his doings and makings (Dewey 1958:49).

What is Phenomenological Inquiry?

Although phenomenological inquiry is correctly classified as a form of interpretive inquiry, it is that form of interpretive inquiry which focuses on human perceptions, particularly on the aesthetic qualities of human experience. As such, it is that form of interpretive inquiry that comes closest to artistic inquiry, and it can be represented metaphorically as a visual process, even though perception includes other senses as well as the visual. Attention falls on perception itself and the immediate feelings it evokes. What is it that the individual sees in life? Other forms of interpretive inquiry are primarily concerned with meaning and so can be represented metaphorically as aural processes. In them attention falls on cognition and linguistic interpretation of experience. What is the meaning of what the individual hears life say? In forms of practical inquiry attention falls on acting, and practical inquiry can be represented metaphorically as kinesthetic, even though the acting considered by such inquiry is rational. What is it that the individual is urged by life to do? Human experience, of course, inevitably includes perceiving, thinking, and acting inextricably connected in certain ways, but it all begins with perceptions, and in this sense phenomenological inquiry is inquiry into what is primary in human experience. In its most basic form, phenomenological inquiry investigates the distinctively human perceptions of individual people and results in descriptions of such perceptions which appeal directly to the perceptions of other people.

The quality of the experiences which human beings undergo is what most distinctively sets humans apart from all other animals. In all animals, experiencing consists of the three interrelated processes of perceiving, thinking, and acting. Although these processes can sometimes be separated chronologically, how they are or are not connected in other, more important ways largely determines the kind of experience undergone and the quality of experience.

In the lowest order animals, perceiving is little more than rude tactile sensations, thinking is little more than simple nerve impulses, and acting is little more than random motions. These processes are so underdeveloped that the word "experiencing" hardly seems applicable. In higher order animals, which have well developed brains and other specialized organs, perceiving is ordinarily through several potentially acute senses, thinking involves extremely complicated organizing of nerve impulses, and acting appears teleological, at least to the extent that it seems purposefully directed at maintaining the animal's biological well being. Here the word "experiencing" seems far better to apply, for what the animal undergoes involves learning of a kind which begins to approximate human learning. However, even in animals such as chimpanzees and dolphins, which display the closest approximations to human intelligence, something still seems lacking in their experience, for there is little evidence to indicate that such animals develop a distinct consciousness of their perceptions, thoughts, or actions.

Only humans appear to have the capacity for fully experiencing their own experiences. Individual human beings may, therefore, have highly developed inner life-worlds in which they self-consciously think through the meanings of their perceptions and weigh alternative courses of action. Meanings and actions thus self-consciously considered become autonomous and result in new circumstances in both the world external to the individual and in the inner life-world. These altered circumstances must be constantly reperceived and reconsidered anew, and such self-consciousness about consciousness is what seems to make human experience unique. Human experiencing thus involves an ongoing, cyclical relationship among the processes of perceiving, thinking, and acting in which the deepening and refining of one process helps further deepen and refine the others. Human learning is thus more rich than the learning which can be experienced by any other animal, and it is the potential richness of learning which gives human experience its distinctive quality and much of its value.

Human beings can have perceptions of the external world without becoming conscious of them, but our consciousness of external perceptions — our life-worlds — is where each of us lives in the most deeply personal sense. Not only do we feel our perceptions more acutely when we become consciously aware of them within our life-worlds, but we begin autonomously to consider what we can do about them. Put another way, our initial human consciousness of external perceptions can be considered our perceptions of our perceptions, and it is what the individual life-world begins with. Again, however, perceiving precedes making meaning or acting. We simply feel inwardly in certain ways about the external world we perceive before we can consider what our feelings mean or before we can consciously attempt to change anything. These personal and inwardly perceptual portions of individual life-worlds are where our distinctively human experience begins. Everything flows from them. In this sense they are nothing less than the basic curricula of our individual lives. Although influenced by the external world, they are inward and autonomous. They are what phenomenological inquiry investigates.

As the foregoing discussion indicates, phenomenological inquiry is not about the physiology of perception; it is about the course of primary human consciousness in individual lives. It investigates such perceptions through whatever methods are appropriate for discerning individual life-world perceptions and for expanding and refining the perceptions of the inquirer. Thus it includes intuitive scanning of the inquirer's own primary consciousness, empirical scanning of evidence of the primary consciousness of others, and use of some means or medium—such as meditation, painting, poetry, discursive prose — to render metaphorically what the inquirer has perceived about life-world perceptions. In its most basic form its renderings are descriptions of life-world perceptions. In extended form it may consider what individual life-world perceptions do or do not have in common, of how they are influenced by the context in which they occur, and how life-world perceptions provide experience its distinctively human qualities. These extended considerations may also include how such commonalities (or their lack) within life-world perceptions influence human meaning making and acting. None of these extended considerations is primary, however. In fact, the more such commentary and analysis are undertaken, the more the phenomenological descriptions become interpreted; hence, the more the inquiry becomes hermeneutical, narrative, or even practical. Again, basic phenomenological inquiry results in descriptions of individual life-world perceptions. Even when rendered discursively, these descriptions are metaphorical, for they can provide only evidence of life-world experience, not the original primary consciousness itself. Nonetheless, these descriptions are ultimately curricular in and of themselves, for in providing concrete examples of distinctively human experiencing which appeal directly to the perceptions of other human beings, they provide us with powerful invitations to similarly experience the primary experience of others and so change the course of our own life-worlds. This direct communication through examples requires no further hermeneutical interpretation or practical suggestion. Whether or not this understanding of what is at the heart of phenomenological inquiry is ever actually accepted or articulated by the inquirer, it is what the phenomenological inquirer most shares with the artist. Both strive to communicate what is primary within the experience of individual human beings through the best possible examples, examples which appeal directly to what is primary.

As the foregoing discussion also indicates, except in its most basic form (and then only theoretically) phenomenological inquiry cannot be sharply distinguished from hermeneutical inquiry, for human consciousness of perceptions inevitably leads into conscious consideration of what perceptions mean. Nonetheless, the most gifted artists in perceiving and metaphorically representing the world are not necessarily concerned immediately with the meanings of their creations or with how their creations change the world. Therefore, in order to clarify the nature of phenomenological inquiry itself and to identify several of the most purely phenomenological inquiries undertaken to date within the field of curriculum studies, in this chapter I wish to maintain the distinction between phenomenology and hermeneutics, even though in two ways it makes this chapter very much like an exercise in peeling an onion. An onion consists of many discernible layers but with no discernible center beneath; once one has begun peeling, one needs to have some sense of when to stop. There is a similar risk in treating phenomenology and hermeneutics separately. First, since we are humans, there may not be at the center of our life-worlds any pure perceptions or feelings untainted by the meanings we impose upon them. Indeed, our experience would not have many of its distinctly human qualities without meaning making, and meaning making can only rarely be postponed, let alone avoided altogether. Only non-human animals appear to have pure perceptions of the external world, but only humans appear to have inward consciousness of external perceptions. Second, when we look for pure perceptions we run the risk of an infinite regress. I have maintained that phenomenological inquiry focuses on life-world perceptions of perceptions of the external world, but it is also possible to maintain that there are still more inward and pure perceptions (because they may be less tainted by meaning) of "ordinary" life-world perceptions, still further perceptions of those perceptions, and so on. But it is not necessary to keep peeling away the onion until we tearfully find we have nothing left.

How Not to Peel the Onion

If, indeed, phenomenological methods are those which lead to descriptions of individual phenomenological states, the inward, perceptual life-worlds of individuals prior to, or separated as fully as possible from, their making meaning or their taking action, then a fundamental problem is how phenomenological states can be known. We always have immediate experience of our own phenomenologies, but we never have immediate experience of the phenomenologies of other people.

For better or worse, the word "phenomenological," which is now widely used to refer to human consciousness in general, has been borrowed from the writings of the phenomenological philosophers who developed many modern understandings about consciousness. A discussion of the phenomenological tradition and its influence is considerably beyond the scope of this chapter, but despite its numerous contributions, one unhelpful legacy of this tradition for curriculum inquirers is its general approach to how phenomenological states can be known. Within this tradition, phenomenology involves a transcendental search for the "essences" of human experience, invariant structures of thought or consciousness which can be known only intuitively. If one can only set aside all of one's ordinary, taken-for-granted assumptions about perceptions, one can ultimately discover within one's own consciousness the same essential structures which are found within everyone else's consciousness. Two assumptions which support this approach are that all individual phenomenologies are essentially alike and that these essences can be discerned through appropriate intuition of one's own perceptions. This approach thus suggests that if one can appropriately discern one's own perceptual life-world, there is no need to inquire about life-worlds of others; indeed, such inquiry would be futile, since one cannot experience another person's life-world, which, in any case, is essentially like one's own.

Once one has accepted these assumptions from the phenomenological philosophical tradition, efforts to expose the essential center of the onion have begun. Furthermore, there is no way of knowing if or when one has ever reached the center. One's intuitions might or might not be appropriate. One's perceptions might or might not be pure. One's experience might or might not match the experience of someone else. One is supposed to be able to comprehend all of experience by comprehending one's own, but one can never comprehend whether one's own comprehensions are complete or sound. In this way the entire onion inevitably gets peeled away and no essential center found. The difficulty for the curriculum inquirer who has inherited this legacy from the phenomenological philosophic tradition is not in attempting to refine one's intuitions about one's own primary experience, but in using intuition as the only methodological cutting tool. An empirical knife is also necessary. Through its use the separate layers of the onion can be clearly seen and one develops some sense about when to stop peeling. Indeed, one may even slice boldly through the entire onion empirically to discover that is has many different layers but no essential center after all. The perceptive phenomenological inquirer therefore concludes that there is no invariant structure of human consciousness and that the different layers of different individuals' life-world perceptions can be described and valued for their own sake. My own primary experience may or may not have something in common with the primary experience of another person, but that is actually beside the point. First come the gathering and sharing of primary perceptions. Phenomenological inquiry thus includes both intuitive scanning of one's own life-world and empirical, naturalistic gathering of evidence about the life-worlds of others. Phenomenological states are known through direct evidence of one's own primary experience and indirect evidence of the primary experience of others. Phenomenological states are shared with others only metaphorically.

Attempting to Peel the Onion without Tears: Some Examples

Since phenomenological inquiry is at heart an artistic process, its only totally successful practitioners—those who have actually peeled the onion without tears—have been artists, writers, storytellers, or other people who have perceived something real, or true, or valuable about their own or others' life-worlds and who have exemplified their perceptions well in a creative medium which has permitted other individuals to experience them in their own ways. The world has had such outstanding phenomenological inquirers as Shakespeare, Wordsworth, Beethoven, Melville, Monet, and Conrad (to name some of my favorites), but the field of curriculum studies has yet to see their likes. This is not to cast aspersions on curriculum inquirers, for the field of curriculum studies is very young historically—perhaps still in its infancy—and has been so focused on immediately instrumental concerns that more efficacious ways of enhancing human experience have only begun to be investigated. An expanded vision of what is properly curricular has yet to emerge widely. Until it does, the only successful practitioners of phenomenological inquiries which are at heart curricular will continue to be considered artists and storytellers, not curricularists.

Given the relatively narrow way in which the newly born academic field of curriculum studies has developed during the twentieth century and the real difficulties involved in separating phenomenology and hermeneutics, it is hardly surprising that few distinctively phenomenological investigations have yet been carried out within it and that none of its members has yet peeled the onion without any tears. Beginning in the 1970s, however, there have been a few self-conscious efforts actually to do phenomenology within the field of curriculum studies itself. This chapter briefly considers three of the earliest and most original studies which attempt to encounter and to describe perceptual phenomenological states. These studies share certain similarities but have certain differences as well. Each represents an approach to phenomenological inquiry which has yet to be fully followed out. Despite their individual shortcomings, collectively they may come reasonably close to representing what phenomenological inquiry can and should be and may prove indicative of the future of phenomenological inquiry in curriculum. The first study, by Pinar and Grumet (1976), cuts into the onion intuitively but does not sufficiently use the empirical knife when necessary to cut cleanly. The second study, by van Manen (1978 – 1979), quickly and roughly slices empirically through the entire onion, but disregarding what this knife reveals, it then keeps on both empirically and intuitively peeling away the separate halves in search of an essential center. The third study, by Willis and Allen (1978), cuts cleanly into the onion empirically but not sufficiently deeply to reveal much more than can also be revealed by the intuitive knife alone.

Pinar and Grumet have pioneered the first approach to phenomenological inquiry in curriculum. They have developed and refined this approach in many individual writings, but their joint book, *Toward a Poor Curriculum: An Introduction to the Theory and Practice of Currere* (1976), is their fullest elaboration of what they suggest phenomenological inquiry should be. In it they develop a theoretical position, describe their method, provide examples of the method in use, and point out some curricular implications. Although heavily influenced by the phenomenological philosophic tradition and by psychoanalytic theory, the book represents a highly original approach to curriculum studies.

A "poor" curriculum is the individual's life-world considered in its own right, not as an artifact of the external world. "Currere" is the course each individual life-world takes. Therefore, Pinar and Grumet do not consider curriculum in the ordinary terms of planning, schooling, subject matter, course of study, or behavior, but in terms of what happens within the individual's primary experience. They suggest encountering one's primary experience through a four step method. First, engage in free associative remembrance of the past. Second, meditatively ponder the future. Third, analyze past experience and future aspiration in order to gain better intuitive and cognitive understanding. Fourth, in light of the first three steps, choose what to be. The first two of these steps are purely phenomenological, although the last two also include hermeneutical and even practical considerations. Hence

Pinar and Grumet do not make a sharp distinction between phenomenology and hermeneutics, but they do focus more on encountering and describing primary experience than on interpreting it. Their basic method is to intuitively scan their own life-worlds and record the forms of consciousness which these immediate perceptions take. These straightforward, autobiographical descriptions of the course of their own life-worlds are in themselves curricular, for they may presage courses in the life-worlds of others who appropriate these examples in their own ways.[1]

The intuitive scanning of one's own primary experience, which Pinar and Grumet suggest, is borrowed directly from the philosophical phenomenological tradition, although in elaborating it in their own ways appropriate to curriculum studies they have not pursued the traditional philosophic search for universal essences within experience. Certainly, however, perceiving one's perceptions more directly is one time-honored result of intuitive scanning, which has been the general method of the traditional search. But Pinar and Grumet appropriately suggest also using these perceptions to reconstruct one's experience and to offer an example of possible reconstruction to others. The important question, then, is not about the purity of their methods. (For instance, how far do their third and fourth steps actually extend phenomenological methods into hermeneutical and practical concerns?) The important question is why limit offering such examples only to others who might use them in scanning and reconstructing their experiences? If descriptions of primary experience are useful empirical examples to others, then why have Pinar and Grumet not used them extensively in initially scanning their own experience? Certainly, they do not suggest that examples of others' primary experience which they had previously encountered empirically were not valuable to them in intuitively scanning their own experiences, but neither do they emphasize such examples. However valuable, then, may be the four step method of intuitive scanning one's own experience which the study describes in detail, it does not sufficiently emphasize how individuals may make use of empirical evidence of the life-worlds of others. Hence, in emphasizing the use of direct evidence of one's own life-world obtained intuitively, it tends to deemphasize the use of indirect evidence of others' life-worlds obtained empirically.

The second study, by van Manen (1978–1979), is the first of a series of studies in which van Manen develops a somewhat different methodology for phenomenological inquiry in curriculum. This methodology strongly emphasizes the use of empirical evidence of the life-worlds of others. In this sense van Manen's methodology breaks sharply from the phenomenological philosophic tradition in a way which Pinar and Grumet's study does not fully exploit; however, in another sense it does not break from this tradition as fully as Pinar and Grumet do, for in its own way it suggests that phenomenological inquiry remains a search for universal essences within primary human experience.

The methodology van Manen describes is based on the "Utrecht School" of phenomenological pedagogy in the Netherlands. Although the Utrecht School explicitly claims to reject a universal structure of consciousness, it still recognizes intuitive scanning as a means of encountering the perceptual life-world. Its major value for curriculum studies, however, arises from its affirmation that one's own life-world can be known within the common sense world of everyday experience, for this affirmation opens the way for consideration of descriptions of the life-worlds of others. Such descriptions can be found in material "obtained from such sources as existential or phenomenological literature, poetry, novels, diaries, interviews, folk wisdom, observations, and art" (van Manen 1978–1979:58). Thus, any and all sources of descriptions of the perceptual portions of the life-worlds of others which can be encountered empirically are potentially valuable; one does not need to confine inquiry only to one's own primary experience. Although the life-worlds of others cannot be known directly, one can still make reasoned inferences about them from whatever empirical evidence is at hand. The specific methodology which van Manen describes includes three steps. First, gather material from one's own and other's life-worlds. Second, discern the underlying structures in these materials. Third, formulate recommendations and orientations to practical action. Van Manen points out that appropriate thinking and acting arise from exhaustive descriptions of primary perceptions. Considering what one's own experience does and does not have in common with the experience of others provides the grounds for understanding and for a pedagogic competence which results in actions maximizing the possibilities of human autonomy. Nonetheless, first come descriptions of primary perceptions themselves.

The major problems inherent in this methodology arise from its second step. What underlying structures can be found in such life-world materials? What, if anything, do these structures have to do with exhaustive descriptions? To be sure, the underlying structures for which this methodology encourages the search are not the universals of ordinary empirical sciences, nor are they limited to the "deep structures" sought by such constructivist social sciences as ethnography and ethnomethodology, which attempt to uncover how personal meaning is created in social settings and which suggest that such meaning can be known in conventional ways. Van Manen makes such points clear in a subsequent study (van Manen 1979) in which he elaborates his theoretical position more fully, insisting there are still deeper ground structures of life-world experience, or, as he sometimes calls them, "themes" or an underlying "grammar." The life-worlds of all people have some things in common, van Manen believes, and the second step of

his methodology calls on the phenomenological inquirer to attempt to identify these things. Interestingly, despite the new terminology and the inclusion
of empirical means within this methodology for encountering primary experience, these deepest of all possible structures of experience which van
Manen postulates must still ultimately be very much what the phenomenological philosophic tradition postulated as the essences of experience. That,
however, is not a point which van Manen clarifies, instead insisting that the
underlying grammar of primary experience cannot fully be known either intuitively or empirically, but only through its hermeneutical and instrumental
uses. He believes that properly encountering the grammar of phenomenological life-world experience results in understanding and orientations to
action.

Van Manen's approach, therefore, does not sharply differentiate phenomenological inquiry from hermeneutical or even practical inquiry, yet his
reluctance to break fully from that part of the phenomenological philosophic
tradition which pursues essences within human experience has limited how
both intuitive and empirical evidence have been used in his subsequent
work and in similar phenomenological inquiry which he has inspired. For
instance, subsequent studies by van Manen and others self-consciously
using this methodology have artistic qualities, but they seem collectively to
have slipped into a kind of orthodoxy in which straightforward, metaphorical descriptions of phenomenological states, as in autobiography or storytelling, are not deemed sufficient to create appropriate understanding or
orientations to action unless these descriptions are also accompanied by
some direct interpretation of the underlying structures which presumably
they illustrate. This collective reticence to let life-world materials speak directly for themselves is a problem yet to be resolved. The methodology van
Manen's approach is based on explores the depths of primary experience
both intuitively and empirically, but its insistence on finding an underlying
grammar and linking it directly with hermeneutical and practical concerns
is ironical, for it thus seems to leave little room for the straightforward, metaphorical communication of primary experience through a creative medium, which is the heart of phenomenological inquiry itself and among the
most basic of curricular tasks.[2]

The third study, by Willis and Allen (1978), suggests that phenomenological inquiry cannot only take place empirically, but can be directed
simultaneously at the individual life-worlds of a large number of persons.
Although the study begins with a discussion of the phenomenological philosophic tradition and includes the phrase "deep structures of experience,"
it does not postulate anything invariant within experience. Instead, it observes that there seem to be some "commonalities" within the primary experiences of different people and ponders whether the dynamics of individ-

uals' perceptual life-worlds fall into any "patterns." It speculates that one such general pattern may recur repeatedly in much of the philosophical and imaginative literature of Western civilization which describes primary life-world experience, and it sets out to test whether a similar pattern seems to occur individually or collectively among students in two small education courses by asking students at the end of each day's class to meditate briefly on their personal reactions to the class and to record adjectives which most accurately reflect their moods.

The study therefore combines both intuitive scanning and empirical reports of individual life-worlds in both its speculative and its data gathering phases. Examples derived both from intuitive scanning of personal life-worlds by Western writers and from their use of still previous examples inform the perceptions of the authors of the study, and the students provide descriptions (albeit very brief ones) of their own life-worlds each day following their meditative scanning of their primary experience. Emphasis in the study clearly falls, nonetheless, on the empirical reports by the students of what they perceived about their perceptions. The study also maintains reasonably sharp distinctions among the phenomenological, the hermeneutical, and the practical; for aside from its initial speculations, it attempts only seldomly and only tentatively to interpret what the reports of the students mean, and it encourages no specific courses of action, merely suggesting that the reports of the students may stand as examples to others who find themselves in similar circumstances in life. The basic methodology, therefore, is simply to collect as many reports as possible of the phenomenological states of others and let these reports speak for themselves.

The results of the study are, of course, inconclusive, for the reports by the students of their life-worlds were too brief and too variable for any general patterns to emerge clearly. Among the many questions which arise about the study are whether such brief meditations probe deeply enough into life-worlds to be considered phenomenological at all and whether such brief reports accurately reflect the perceptual life-world. To such questions the authors answer simply that each person in some way experiences personal experience, and it is not necessary to confine investigations to whatever elite group may do so most perceptively; and that there is no reason to believe (hence no reason to even raise the question) that brief reports of the perceptions of the many are more or less accurate reflections of personal phenomenologies than are extended reports of the few. There is, however, no attempt by Willis and Allen to relate the dynamics reflected in the self-reports with changes in the students' external world, and the number of students engaged in reporting is simply too small to permit any general patterns in individual phenomenologies to emerge over and above those particular patterns strongly influenced by the specific environment in which the students found themselves. The authors acknowledge the incompleteness of their inquiry on such matters, but they point out that the focus of the study is on collecting and comparing phenomenological reports from a number of people in similar circumstances, not in interpreting them. Beyond all this, the major shortcoming of the study as a piece of phenomenological inquiry is the authors' reporting of individual phenomenologies only in a collective and highly abstract way. There are no detailed, concrete, metaphorical case studies of any individuals' life-worlds. The individuals in this study may speak for themselves, but the authors permit them to do so only extremely briefly. The authors develop no form of artistic reporting through a creative medium, which phenomenological inquiry demands. Although the study suggests much about gathering and using empirical evidence of phenomenological states, its mode of reporting is too literal to reveal all that a more unconstrained piece of phenomenological inquiry should.[3]

What the Onion Means for Curriculum Inquiry

Onions enhance flavor when blended with other foods but are seldom good to eat by themselves. What this seems to mean for curriculum inquiry is that inquirers should keep the phenomenological onion separate from hermeneutical, practical, and other foods when first peeling it in preparation for eating, but the eating is best done in combination with other ingredients. Taste is still another form of perception.

In more literal terms, what this means is that just as there is no single best way to prepare or eat onions, there is no single best methodology for conducting phenomenological inquiry and no single best way of blending it with other forms of inquiry. The methodologies described by Pinar and Grumet, van Manen, and Willis and Allen are all appropriate ways of encountering far more than we in curriculum studies now know about the phenomenologies of students and teachers. We now actually know very little, but we should at least by now know that in the future we are unlikely ever to know much more until we give up the expectation of finding universal structures in primary human experience. Commonalities, themes, or patterns — yes; structures or essences — no. Individual phenomenologies are unique and can be represented to other people only metaphorically. But first we need more and more varied basic descriptions of primary phenomenological states from which better to discern both similarities and differences. Therefore, we now need more intuitive inquiries which probe a few individual phenomenologies deeply, we need more empirical inquiries which probe a lot of individual phenomenologies in a variety of ways, we need to learn more about how metaphorically to describe what we have begun to discern, and we need to learn more about how to blend these descriptions artistically and appropriately with hermeneutical and practical concerns for a variety of curricular uses which promote rather than constrain autonomy.

In short, we now need to develop an extended series of varied but exemplary case studies which focus on phenomenologies themselves. In doing so, we may begin with only a few of our perceptions, but ultimately we are likely to enhance all of our senses.

Notes

1. In *Toward a Poor Curriculum: An Introduction to the Theory and Practice of Currere* the authors not only describe portions of their own life-worlds as they know them intuitively, but — with lesser emphasis — they describe portions of the life-worlds of others as the authors know them through empirical evidence. The book also includes some interpretations of both the authors' and others' life-worlds and offers suggestions about how to encourage others intuitively to scan their own life-worlds. So, despite the specific method which emphasizes the intuitive scanning of one's own primary experience, the book should by no means be considered solely a pure type, one which exemplifies only immediate descriptions of phenomenological states exactly as their experiencer encounters them intuitively. Indeed, the two authors in their separate papers seem to place different degrees of emphasis on the autobiographical. Especially during the 1970s, Pinar has been more inclined than Grumet toward a pure type of autobiographical phenomenological writing and Grumet has been more inclined toward writing which includes descriptions and interpretations of the life-worlds of others.

2. Van Manen has made a major contribution to the field of curriculum studies through his founding in 1983 of *Phenomenology + Pedagogy,* a journal devoted to the kind of phenomenological writing consistent with his methodology, and his editorship of this journal until 1987. *Phenomenology + Pedagogy* has published many high-quality, exemplary pieces of this kind of writing, many of which have been heavily influenced by van Manen's own fullest—and now "classic"— statement of his beliefs about what phenomenological inquiry should be, "Practicing Phenomenological Writing" (van Manen 1984). My criticisms are not with the basic approach nor with the work it has inspired, the best of which I greatly admire, but with its assumption that there are underlying structures of human experience which are best revealed directly. I also fear that van Manen's own good work has proved so pursuasive that much recent phenomenological writing published in *Phenomenology + Pedagogy* now reiterates his themes and style and that this problem of sameness has been exacerbated since van Manen has left the editorship.

3. Willis and Allen have not carried out any subsequent studies which collect self-reports by a large number of people about their phenomenological

states. However, Willis has written two commentaries on how knowledge about individual phenomenologies encountered through the kinds of methods described by Pinar and Grumet, van Manen, and Willis and Allen can be used in curriculum studies (Willis 1979, 1982).

References

(Symbols preceding entries are explained on page 40)

√ Dewey, J. (1958). Having an experience. *Art as experience.* New York: Capricorn Books, G. P. Putnam's (Original 1938).

○+ Pinar, W. F., and Grumet, M. R. (1976). *Toward a poor curriculum: An introduction to the theory and practice of currere.* Dubuque, IA: Kendall-Hunt.

+ van Manen, M. (1978 – 1979). An experiment in educational theorizing: The Utrecht School. *Interchange, 10.* 48 – 66.

○+ ———. (1979). Objective inquiry into structures of subjectivity. *The Journal of Curriculum Theorizing, 1*(1), 44 – 64.

+ ———. (1984). Practicing phenomenological writing. *Phenomenology + Pedagogy, 2*(1), 36 – 69.

+ ———. (1990). *Researching lived experience: Human science for an action sensitive pedagogy.* Albany: State University of New York Press.

+ Willis, G. (1979). Phenomenological methodologies in curriculum. *The Journal of Curriculum Theorizing, 1*(1), 65 – 79.

+ ———. (1982). Creating curriculum knowledge from students' phenomenologies. In W. H. Schubert & A. L. Schubert (Eds.), *Conceptions of curriculum knowledge: Focus on students and teachers* (pp. 45 – 48). University Park, PA: College of Education, The Pennsylvania State University.

○+ Willis, G., and Allen, A. J. (1978). Patterns of phenomenological response to curricula: Implications. In G. Willis (Ed.), *Qualitative evaluation: Concepts and cases in curriculum criticism* (pp. 34 – 71). Berkeley, CA: McCutchan.

10

Hermeneutic Inquiry:
The Hermeneutic Imagination
and the Pedagogic Text

——— *David G. Smith*

At the end of a recent graduate course entitled, "Interpretive Inquiry in Educational Research," a course in which phenomenology, critical theory, semiotics, and post-structuralism were all made topical along with hermeneutics, one student remarked, "But it's all hermeneutics, isn't it?" The comment signalled a sense that whenever we are engaged in the activity of interpreting our lives and the world around us, we are engaging in what the Greeks called "practical philosophy" (Gadamer 1983), an activity linkable to the character of Hermes in the Greek pantheon.[1] Hermes, as well as being the deliverer of messages between the gods and from the gods to mortals on earth, was known for a number of other qualities as well, such as eternal youthfulness, friendliness, prophetic power, and fertility. In a sense, all of these features are at work in the hermeneutic endeavor to this day, as the practice of interpretation attempts to show what is at work in different disciplines and, in the service of human generativity and good faith, is engaged in the mediation of meaning. There is one further aspect of Hermes that may be worth noting, namely his impudence. He once played a trick on the most venerated Greek deity, Apollo, inciting him to great rage. Modern students of hermeneutics should be mindful that their interpretations could lead them into trouble with "authorities."

We might ask why hermeneutics is such an ubiquitous feature of the contemporary intellectual landscape. One finds the term everywhere, not just in the older traditions of philosophy and theology, but more lately in literary criticism. In recent years also, for example, there have appeared texts on the hermeneutics of psychology (Messer, Sass, and Woolfolk 1988) and economics (Market Process 1988). Canada may be distinguished in forming the first society specifically oriented to the exploration of hermeneutics and post-modern thought.[2] The answer to the question of hermeneutics' attractiveness to the times resides, perhaps, in the general state of exhaustion of

what Karl-Otto Apel (1985) has called the "dogmatic-normative" traditions
of epistemology and metaphysics as they functioned foundationally in the
establishment and continuation of contemporary discourse domains from
the eighteenth century Enlightenment to the present day. The critique of
"foundationalism"[3] inherent in the current post-structuralist movements signals what many people already understand intuitively which is that, for Western cultures at least, there is a crisis of value at work that cannot be resolved
simply by appealing to traditional forms of logic and authority. It may be precisely the inability of traditional (Western) forms of discourse to deal single-
handedly with the lived problems of modernity that makes interpretation or
re-interpretation of contemporary paradigms and their institutional embod-
iments necessary. Indeed, Gadamer (1983:100) has so summarized the situation: "Only when our entire culture for the first time saw itself threatened
by radical doubt and critique did hermeneutics become a matter of universal
significance." One might quibble with the right to speak of universals but
not with the link between social trouble and the need for interpretation.

In educational terms, the hermeneutic imagination throws open the
challenge to inquire into what we mean when we use words like curriculum,
research, and pedagogy. We are challenged to ask what makes it possible for
us to speak, think, and act in the ways we do. From the perspective of post-
modern hermeneutics,[4] the project is even more searching; namely, a concern for how we shall proceed pedagogically after we have given up the pre-
sumption of ever being able to define in unequivocal foundational terms all
of the key referents in our professional lexicon. For example, how might we
orient our lives with children when we can no longer take for granted what a
child is in any discrete sense, when we make problematic all of the usual
categories for understanding childhood in our culture (development, cognition, achievement, et cetera) or when we take up the question of the meaning of children as one which is not answerable except self-reflexively, that is
from the question of who I am in-relation-to my children? The new United
Nations' *Convention on the Rights of the Child* underscores how it is that in
spite of enormous public expenditure on formal educational programs for
children and good rhetoric speaking on children's behalf, in actuality children are the most frequently abused and neglected of all the world's citi-
zens, in countries like the United States and Canada as well as in the Third
World.[5] It may be that the meaning and place of children in our lives is the
most important consideration to be taken up in education today, not just because the voice of the young has been translated out of any meaningful involvement with the powers that be,[6] but also because the question of the
young (their conception, care, and nurturance) devolves precisely on so
many of the defining issues of our time, such as the meaning of power, gender relations, and the matter of how we might learn to live more responsibly

within the earthly web of our planetary home. But not only that: Hermes was "a young god always" (Stapleton 1982:141), which means in a sense that the hermeneutic imagination works from a commitment to generativity and rejuvenation and to the question of how we can go on together in the midst of constraints and difficulties that constantly threaten to foreclose on the future. The aim of interpretation, it could be said, is not just another interpretation but human freedom, which finds its light, identity, and dignity in those few brief moments when one's lived burdens can be shown to have their source in too limited a view of things.

Hermeneutics from Aristotle to Gadamer

Hermeneutics has a long history.[7] Aristotle once used the word in the title of one of his works *(Peri Hermenia)*, and there was a school of interpretation in ancient Alexandria. It was not until the Reformation in the sixteenth century however that the question of interpretation itself became problematic. The issue was one which still inheres in contemporary debates, which is whether the authority for the meaning of a given text resides within a traditional interpretive community such as the Church (or now the State), or whether a text has its own internal coherence and integrity which can be recovered by any well-intended individual possessed with the right skills. In 1567 Matthias Flacius Illyricus wrote the first 'methods text' for hermeneutics, the *Arts Critica,* inspired by the need of Protestant theologians to validate their efforts through scriptural interpretations that were independent of Roman Catholic tradition.

In the eighteenth century the question of method assumed full prominence, and this was the case not just for the interpretation of sacred texts but also for the newly emergent understanding of science which characterized the Enlightenment. Johan Martin Chladenius wrote a treatise in 1742 outlining the procedures for the "Correct Interpretation of Reasonable Discourses and Books." The timing is notable for its location in the middle of the foundational texts which have underwritten virtually all economic, political, and philosophical activity in the modern West, such as Descartes' *Discourse on Method,* Mill's *Logic* and Adam Smith's *Wealth of Nations.* The point is that eighteenth century philosophers were full of optimism that life in general could be systematically brought under the control of correct logical procedure. It is *that* assumption, of truth being ultimately a methodological affair, that much of contemporary hermeneutics wishes to challenge.

The most under-appreciated of all hermeneutical thinkers is probably Friedrich Schleiermacher who in the nineteenth century was part of the early Romantic movement inspired by the aesthetics of J. G. Fichte and H. Schelling.[8] From Schleiermacher on, three themes in hermeneutic inquiry have always been present; namely, the inherent creativity of interpretation, the pivotal role of language in human understanding, and the interplay of part and whole in the process of interpretation. That process later became articulated as "the hermeneutic circle" at work in all human understanding.

For Schleiermacher, interpretation and understanding are creative acts, not just technical functions. Texts, works of art, and so on, are expressions of a creative spirit which any interpreter must somehow engage if interpretations are to be made that are faithful to an author's original intention. This process of engagement Scheiermacher termed "divinitory," as distinct from "comparative." The divinitory character of interpretation is the "feminine force in the knowledge of human nature," a knowledge made possible by the deep commonality of all people. The comparative approach on the other hand is "masculine." Depending as it does on the employment of typologies, it is incapable of "yielding a unity." A unity occurs when the singular and the common "permeate each other" by means of "intuiting" or divining what is at work on the part of the original author. In this last formulation can be discerned perhaps the most abiding contribution from Schleiermacher; namely, a pointing to the way in which good interpretation involves a playing back and forth between the specific and the general, the micro and the macro. When this interplay is applied to the understanding of persons, one is inevitably drawn into a consideration of how language both encourages and constrains a person's self-understanding. As Schleiermacher put it, "every discourse depends on earlier thought . . . (and) it follows that every person is on the one hand a locus in which a given language is formed after an individual fashion, and on the other, a speaker who is only able to be understood within the totality of the language." There is foreshadowed here all subsequent attempts to show the articulation between language as general system and language as individual speech and utterance. Ferdinand de Saussure's (1959) characterization of *langue et parole* and Wilhelm von Humboldt's description of *Sprache und Rede* (Sweet 1978–80) are perhaps the two most notable of such attempts. Schleiermacher's emphasis on the creative spirit in any work, that is on the inner driving integrity which gives an interpreter access to its specific aspects, resonates with Julia Kristeva's (1980) recent stress on understanding the "desire" in language and Paulo Freire's challenge to "grasp the human aspiration" of a people's speech and action.[9]

If Schleiermacher's romanticist hermeneutics marked a watershed for the nineteenth century, Wilhelm Dilthey's work showed the way to the twentieth century interests in philosophical hermeneutics and the methodological concerns of the social and historical sciences (Hodges 1952; Makreel 1975; Richman 1976). Dilthey was profoundly influenced by the philosopher of history J. G. Droysen who refined from von Humboldt a distinction still residual today in the so-called quantitative/qualitative debate in educational research, the distinction between the historical sciences and the natural sciences. Droysen designated the term Verstehen to refer to "understanding" as the method appropriate for the historical sciences, while causal "explanation" (Erklarung) was the methodological foundation of the natural sciences. Dilthey later developed this distinction in his efforts to define the human sciences as their own speciality, the Geisteswissenschaften. Pushing away the mechanistic models of explanation which were the order of the day, Dilthey, under the influence of the new phenomenological investigations of Edmund Husserl, began to explore "understanding" as a methodological concept which has its origin in the process of human life itself. Human understanding is a "category of life" (Lebenskategorie) which is manifest daily whenever we find ourselves in situations of which we have to make sense. Furthermore, as human beings we are surrounded by the "expressions of life" (Lebensausserung) in texts, artifacts, gestures, voices, and so forth and we understand them to the degree to which we can show how they emerge from "lived experience" (Erlebnis), that deep sediment and texture of our collective life. Good interpretation shows the connection between experience and expression. There is a strong affinity here with the ideas of the later Wittgenstein who argued that the meaning of words and statements is reflective of specific "forms of life" (Lebensform). We might note, too, that Dilthey was one of the first to suggest that written statements are the most elevated form of human expression, an idea which predated Paul Ricoeur's (1985) later attempt to formulate *textual* interpretation as a foundation for a general hermeneutic, and also Jacques Derrida's (1978) critique of phonocentrism, the Western predisposition to privilege speech over writing.[10]

Any serious consideration of the development of hermeneutics must inevitably point to Edmund Husserl as the most significant shaper of all of the interpretive streams of human science which have flourished since the turn of the century. Not only did Husserl introduce the notion of the "life-world" (Lebenswelt) to characterize our sense of the world as it is there for us before we say or do anything about it, but he also laid the ground for those later phenomenologies of human social behavior such as Alfred Schutz's (1970) interpretive sociology and Harold Garfinkle's (1967) ethnomethodological studies. Most important of all, however, was Husserl's massive project of overturning the Enlightenment ideal of objective reason. Through his theory of *intentionality* Husserl showed that we never think or interpret "in general" as a rhetorical activity that bears no necessary connection to the world at large. Rather, thinking and interpreting are always and everywhere precisely about the world. I cannot abstract thinking itself out from what it is that I am thinking about. A clear split between subjective thinking and objective thinking is ridiculous because my subjectivity gets its bearings from the very world that I take as my object. Furthermore, the world is always a world I share with others with whom I communicate, so my descriptions of the world are always subject to modification on the basis of what I share communicatively.

From Husserl on, words like "understanding," "interpretation," and "meaningfulness" are rooted, hermeneutically speaking, in a sense of the dialogical, intersubjective, and conversational nature of human experience. Husserl forged the possibility of a new unity between Self and Other, and, I suspect, inaugurated a foundation for a more friendly relation between human beings and the earthly habitat. The political, social, and economic implications of the Husserlian revolution have never been adequately worked out. One of the poverties of post-modern formulations may be shown, for example, in the evidence of what happens when a liberation from objective reason is not linked to a recovered sense of the Other. Interpretation easily lapses into a dalliance of interpretations rather than leads to a renewed embrace of the Other and the world in the service of a fuller appreciation of the human prospect.

Husserl's student Martin Heidegger gave a radically new meaning to the term hermeneutics by incorporating it into his unique re-writing of the Western philosophical tradition around the question of Being. After Heidegger, hermeneutics is no longer a particular domain of metaphysics or a special school of speculative philosophy; rather it is *the* foundational practice of Being itself. Interpretation is the means by which the nature of Being and human be-ing is disclosed. Interpretation is the primordial condition of human self-understanding so that a phenomenology of Being reveals its fundamental mode to be precisely hermeneutical. As Heidegger (1962:62) expressed it in *Being and Time,* "The phenomenology of Being (Dasein) is a hermeneutic in the primordial signification of this word, where it designates this business of interpreting."

Heidegger's casting of interpretation as the primordial mode of human existence (he later [1977] allied the notion of interpretation to the Greek sense of "thinking") put Dilthey's project of a method for the human sciences into crisis because thereafter *method* could never attain a status independent of the project of thinking itself. Method could never achieve a kind of solitary stable state ready for universal application, because indeed it bore the same character and quality as that to which it sought access. This was the point taken up more fully by Heidegger's student Hans-Georg Gadamer, who in his landmark work *Truth and Method* (1979) argued that the appropriate method for interpreting any phenomena could only be disclosed by the phenomena itself through a kind of Socratic dialogical engagement between question and phenomenon.

There is not room here to explore other key themes in Heidegger's hermeneutics of existence except to highlight two aspects which Gadamer later developed in his own work; namely, the historico-temporal quality of human experience and the linguisticality of understanding. According to Heidegger, human experience of the world takes place within a horizon of past, present, and future. Understanding that which confronts us as new is made possible in the "now" by virtue of the forestructure of understanding which is already in us through past experience. Gadamer pursued this idea in two important respects. The first was to reinstate in a positive way the manner in which pre-judgment is a necessary requirement of all understanding. This he emphasized as a counter to the objectivist thrust of the natural sciences and its claim that knowledge could be free from human interest. For Gadamer, prejudice (pre-judgment) is not a swear word, but rather a sign that we can only make sense of the world from within a particular "horizon" which provides the starting point for our thoughts and actions. Understanding between persons is possible only to the degree that people can initiate a conversation between themselves and bring about a "fusion" of their different horizons into a new understanding which they then hold in common. Putting the matter in a slightly different way, it could be said that Gadamerian hermeneutics validated a new appreciation of tradition as the received life-stream out of which it is possible to say or do anything at all. For Gadamer, tradition is not sclerotic, nostalgic, or antiquarian; rather it opens out into the future to engage what comes to meet it as new. This understanding of our temporal nature Gadamer called "effective historical consciousness" (wirkungs-geschichlisches bewusstsein), and its character is revealed most pristinely in the structure and function of language. Inevitably I speak within the language into which I was born, but my language already contains within itself in a sedimentary way the evidence of its own malleability and evolution, reflective of the political, economic, and social changes in which my forebearers engaged through the course of their personal and collective lives. My language contains within it the evidence not just of the openness of my life, but, in a deep and subtle way, its anticipation of being transformed in the face of new lived realities. How I will be transformed depends upon my orientation and attitude toward what comes to meet me as new; whether I simply try to subsume or repress it within prevailing dispensations (a possible prelude to war or hostilities) or whether I engage it creatively in an effort to create a new common, shared reality.

In this so-called post-modern era, Gadamer might be described as the last writer of a hermeneutics of continuity, a hermeneutics which attempts to hold the structure of understanding together within a language of understanding. As such, his hermeneutics supports all of the recent work in the study of narrative and story (Gergin and Gergin 1983; Polkinghorne 1988; Sarbin 1986), which proceeds from an affirmation of the traceably constitutive nature of human understanding and its roots in recollection and memory. Indeed, it could also be argued that, since Gadamer, as a result of the ascendent post-structuralist interpretive movements and even the neo-Marxist critical traditions which work from a vision of radical rupture and separation rather than conversation, the question of continuity has assumed a status of vital importance. Of great pedagogical and curricular significance, it devolves on the question of whether understanding is, say, a necessarily cumulative, evolutionary work in progress, linear and sequential, or whether it is a more complex clustered affair with occasional bursts of illumination but not working on a plane of any sort nor in any particular direction. It may be fair to say that Gadamer stands as a link between the totalizing proclivities of hermeneutics up till the last quarter of the twentieth century, and the contemporary hermeneutics of "play" and "desire" signified in post-modern writers like Derrida and Kristeva.[11] Indeed, in many important ways, Gadamer prefigures post-modern hermeneutics. His description of play as the basic modus of understanding, his articulation of the way in which within everything said there is something unsaid, and his working through of a theory of the relationship between speech and writing—these matters are all central in the interpretive activity of the present time. Whether or not such activity is formally called "hermeneutics" seems almost beside the point now, except that no contemporary writer in the human sciences can proceed without eventually acknowledging a debt to those figures referred to in this section who all at one time or another were preoccupied with the question of the nature and character of our subject. Of course in these Derridean days, the very impulse to know what something like hermeneutics "is" in its essential nature, that impulse or desire with its imperial masculine, "logocentric" overtones is what is now thrown into question. But logocentrism or the metaphysics of pressure can only be deconstructed because deconstruction itself is an interpretive hermeneutical activity.[12]

The Nature of Hermeneutic Inquiry

Reviews and summaries like the foregoing are inevitably incomplete and because of that, like all forms of writing they contain a certain violence. But it remains for us now to ask how the hermeneutic tradition can inform the interests of curriculum, research, and pedagogy. We have seen that hermeneutics is not just 'one thing' nameable and applicable in some vulgar instrumental sense. Rather it refers to a whole range of topics and questions which had their internal legitimacy within a context of German and European philosophy. That context might be seen as something which inevitably constrains or even devalues the potentiality of the interpretive project, located as it is within an undeniably Eurocentric origin and nexus. Quite notable, however, is the way in which the hermeneutic imagination has the capacity to reach across national and cultural boundaries to enable dialogue between people and traditions superficially at odds. Hermeneutics is able to shake loose dogmatic notions of tradition to show how all traditions open up onto a broader world which can be engaged from within the language of one's own space. Impressive interpretive work in this kind of cross-cultural mediation has been undertaken by such scholars as Zhang Longxi (1985, 1988) in the Chinese context, Oh Mahn Sang (1986) in Korea, and Cynthia Chambers (1989) with North American aboriginal peoples. All three draw specifically on hermeneutic formulations to problematize the hegemony of dominant culture in order to engage it transformatively. These three examples also provide excellent models of a kind of interpretive research that curriculum developers of the future will require as they face the challenge of mediating meaning in the midst of cultural difference. Given that teachers throughout the Western world are now working in classrooms increasingly cosmopolitan in makeup, curriculum and pedagogy cast in frames and conceptions which do not address the new realities of global intercourse will be severely impoverished. The hermeneutic insistence on the articulation between whole and part in the development of understanding invites new considerations of what we mean by a "world," a challenge currently being taken up in the work of the World Order Studies movement.[13] Later we will briefly discuss the implications of this for interpretive life-world research.

Is there such a thing as "the hermeneutic method" of inquiry that can be applied to concerns in curriculum, research, and pedagogy? The answer to this question is perhaps best answered not directly but contextually. We saw briefly in the previous section how the matter of method has been dealt with within the hermeneutic tradition itself, showing our contemporary preoccupation with it to be a modern construct linked to the sciences of control. Here it may be most helpful to show the hermeneutic imagination in relation to the two other most currently dominant traditions of educational theorizing in the West, the critical tradition and, so we might call it, the tradition of consciousness. Then we can ask for the unique contribution of hermeneutics in a more practical sense.

By the tradition of consciousness is meant the long journey of Western culture to establish the mind as the locale and arbiter of knowledge and experience. Rooted in Aristotle's logic and systems of classification, Cartesian dualism, and Kantian idealism, the tradition of consciousness valorizes the work of perception as the means by which the human subject grasps reality then anchors it as reality through the legitimating codes of the times embedded in users' language. The tradition of consciousness shapes curriculum decision-making as fundamentally a form of arbitration over the correctness or appropriateness of ideas, that is as a judgment of the degree to which they "re-present" reality,[14] and the truth of things is defined according to standards of orthodoxy such as science or communal tradition. The modus of the tradition of consciousness is argumentation and dispute so that winners can be declared. Given that maturity is measured by the degree of an individual's subjective appropriation of the so-called objective world, personal autonomy is the most celebrated social quality, with loneliness and anomie the most common personal complaints. Fundamentally conservative in the tone and gesture, the tradition of consciousness proceeds on an assumption that once things are arbitrated as true, they are true once and for all, storable or transmittable as needs arise at any given moment. Pedagogy is most basically an act of cultural reproduction and transmission. Research involves getting the facts of a particular case right and conveying them accurately.

The critical tradition shares with the tradition of consciousness a common lineage through Kantian idealism and the determination that the nature of reality can be decided in advance of a full experience of it (Jardine 1989). When categories such as class, labor, or surplus value, for example, are taken as ultimately fixable determinants of social reality, instead of being simply interpretive frameworks which themselves can be interpreted, then as categories they can be used as conceptual weapons by which to browbeat others and the world into a preordained recognizable form. This accounts for how the implementation of critical pedagogy programs in the name of equality and justice sometimes seems to do violence to the very people the programs are designed to assist (Ellsworth 1989). Dialogue in the critical sense becomes dialogue with a hidden agenda: I speak *to* you to inform you of your victimization and oppression rather than *with* you in order that together we create a world which does justice to both of us. The interest of the critical tradition is not just persuasion but a predetermination to shape the social order in fixed directions; it requires material evidence of ideas translated into practice. The curricular agenda of the critical has the character of a blueprint operating in the name of justice. Pedagogy is concerned with mobilizing the social conscience of students into acts of naming and eradicating the evils of the times. The social end in view is utopian (Greek u-topos, no place), a community of ideal speech and life-order free of distortion, inequity, and duplicity.

The frustration of the critical vision resides precisely in the very ambiguity and complexity of language which hermeneutics tries to uphold.[15] That is to say, all programs and practices have to be mediated linguistically (we have to talk together about what is to be done, write memos, policies, and so on), and the only way this can be carried on without violating the participants concerned is to ensure that there is a genuine meeting of the different horizons of our understanding. The fact that rectitude is not always decidable in any clear sense presents a profound difficulty for the critical tradition, leaving the necessity of frequently suspending judgment on the actions of others if basic trust in human relations is not to be undermined.

It is not difficult to see how and why the tradition of consciousness and the critical tradition are constantly at war in educational 'circles,' each finding its identity as the binary opposite of the other. The one seeks stability and the solidification of culture, the other repudiation and a new world. Not only do they compete as siblings within the same grand Western epistemic tradition, but as the post-structuralists (especially Derrida) have helped us to understand, that tradition itself is predicated on the desire to put interpretation to rest. Call that desire the predisposition to theologize, and call theology the war over the true name and nature of things. Both the tradition of consciousness and the critical tradition begin by wanting to get things *right,* which means there will always be a war over whose interpretations can be taken as being so. In the face of resistance, the pedagogical practice of the tradition of consciousness leads to metaphysical tantrums; the critical tradition leads to physical exhaustion. But Hermes is neither concerned to make a word mean one thing and one thing only, nor is only one preconceived way of doing things the only way. The hermeneutic imagination constantly asks for what is at work in particular ways of speaking and acting in order to facilitate an ever-deepening appreciation of that wholeness and integrity of the world which must be present for thought and action to be possible at all. As a child, I am born into a world that "seems" complete. But I learn the language of my community only to find holes and difficulties which point to the limits of our collective understanding. Those borders and boundaries which serve to secure our life together and give us an identity are permeable. As Paulo Freire (1971) has put it, reality is always "hinged." Reality is always reality-for-us but it always opens out into a broader world which serves or can serve to enrich our understanding of who we are. Again, for us as educators this requires a consideration of what we mean by "world" when we speak of the world of curriculum, research, and pedagogy. This is a profound hermeneutic requirement, given the way in which the hermeneutic tradition has shown that all understanding takes place within an articulation of whole and part.

One of the most important contributions hermeneutics makes to all contemporary social theory and practice, then, not just to curriculum and pedagogy, is in showing the way in which the meaning of anything is always arrived at referentially and relationally rather than (for want of a better word) absolutely. The final authority of concepts, constructs, or categories does not reside in the concepts themselves but within the dialogically arrived at agreement of people to consent to them. The hermeneutic deflection of absolutism in favor of relationism does not elevate the relational as the new absolute except in the sense of supporting the view that relationality (living together creatively on the planet) requires a new set of conditions for pedagogy and the procedures of inquiry. In the terms elaborated by Gadamer (1979) and Rorty (1979),[16] the hermeneutic modus has more the character of conversation than, say, of analysis and the trumpeting of truth claims. When one is engaged in a good conversation, there is a certain quality of self-forgetfulness as one gives oneself over to the conversation itself, so that the truth that is realized in the conversation is never the possession of any one of the speakers or camps, but rather is something that all concerned realize they share in together. This is a point well stated by Thomas Merton: (1961). "If I give you my truth but do not receive your truth in return, then there can be no truth between us." The conversational quality of hermeneutic truth points to the requirement that any study carried on in the name of hermeneutics should provide a report of the researcher's own transformations undergone in the process of the inquiry; a showing of the dialogical journey, we might call it. Underscored here is a profoundly ethical aspect to hermeneutic inquiry in a life-world sense; namely, a requirement that a researcher be prepared to deepen her or his own self-understanding in the course of the research. Other people are not simply to be treated as objects upon whom to try out one's methodological frameworks. We might note briefly, too, that another aspect of conversation is that it is never finished. As in good improvisational jazz, one thing leads to another, but success has one foundational, definitional requirement which is that group members be committed to staying 'with' each other, constantly listening to subtle nuances of tempo and melody, with one person never stealing the show for the entire session. Hermeneutic pedagogy, for example, requires a giving of oneself over to conversation with young people and building a common shared reality in a spirit of self-forgetfulness, a forgetfulness which is also a form of finding oneself in relation to others.

Requirements of the Hermeneutic Imagination

In his working through of a hermeneutical position for our contemporary situation, Gadamer (1977, 1979, 1985) has suggested that it is not possible, in genuine inquiry, to establish correct method for inquiry independently of what it is one is inquiring into. This is because *what* is being investigated itself holds part of the answer concerning *how* it should be investigated. Genuine inquiry always has much more the character of a kind of dialogical messing about, in tune with what the Greeks simply called "thinking." Schleiermacher (1979) called hermeneutics a "commonsense endeavour." There are, however, a number of requirements that must be attended to by those who find hermeneutical formulations fruitful for new lines of research in the human sciences. The first is to develop a deep attentiveness to language itself, to notice how one uses it and how others use it. It is important to gain a sense of the etymological traces carried in words to see what they point to historically. Every hermeneutical scholar should have a good etymological dictionary at their side. The loss of philology as a core subject in modern universities is a great loss, a sign perhaps of the eclipse of a genuinely historical consciousness in favor of the more efficient proclivities of a technical age. But gaining a sense of how one's collective language works, what drives it, what are its predispositions in terms of metaphor, analogy, and structure, and so on, such understanding is quite essential for the work of the interpretive imagination, because in a deep sense our language contains the story of who we are as a people (Michaels and Ricks 1980).[17] It is reflective of our desires, our regrets and our dreams; in its silences it even tells us of what we would forget.

A second requirement for hermeneutical explorations of the human lifeworld is a deepening of one's sense of the basic *interpretability* of life itself. This is a matter of taking up the interpretive task for oneself rather than simply receiving the delivered goods as bearing the final word. This sounds trivial, perhaps, but we live in a world with many 'heavy' interpretations: ideologies and fundamentalisms masquerade as forms of truth lying beyond the reach of interpretation itself. Indeed in a time when the very act of thinking has become a target of intense commercial and political manipulation, the need is great for persons who can meaningfully deconstruct what is going on and propose alternative, more creative ways of thinking and acting. In the graduate Interpretive Inquiry seminar at the University of Lethbridge, we have been experimenting for a number of years with different ways of shaking loose our own dogmatic (culturally predetermined) ways of interpreting the details of our daily experience, trying to deepen our sense of what is implicated in the specifics of our thought and actions. Of course, as the hermeneutic tradition always reminds us, *how* we interpret details is very much related to our macro-frames, so we struggle continuously and contingently to extend our sense of what is at work, relying not only on the more conventional perhaps-on-the-verge-of-exhaustion grand narratives of marxism, psychoanalysis, or critical analysis, but also, importantly, on the more suffocated narratives of our time, such as those concerning spirituality (eastern, western, and aboriginal), feminism, and the new discourses about north-south relations and global interdependence.[18] In orienting (interesting word) ourselves this way, we also affirm the hermeneutic insight that good interpretation is a creative act on the side of sharpening identity within the play of differences, and we thereby give voice to and show features of our lives ordinarily suppressed under the weight of the dominant economic, political, and pedagogical fundamentalisms of the times. This is all in the service of that deeper etymological sense of what it means to be fundamental; namely, showing a connection to the earth (Latin, *fundus* land). Living as we do as inheritors of the Enlightenment principles of abstraction, we are discovering that so many of our modern pains issue from a cultural determination to refute or refuse the interconnectedness of everything.

The interpretational activities of the seminar are not just focused on texts per se, but on the deep texture of our lives. So we engage in Icon Studies, using semiotics theory to interpret the iconic character of the educational world revealed in signs, pictures, and photographs as well as in simple everyday things that we explore as "artefacts."[19] In Sound Studies we examine the relationship between sound structure and social structure, investigating the sonic environment of pedagogy. Here we draw particularly on the theoretical work of Canadian musicologist R. Murray Schafer (1977) in his studies concerned with the "tuning of the world," and the field studies of Steven Feld (1984) from the University of Texas at Austin.

Conversation Windows is an activity involved with the deconstruction of conversation fragments taken from street corners, coffee shops, hallways, and so on, undertaken in an attempt to hear what people are saying about their lives before a microphone is pushed into their faces or an interview schedule predetermines what should be of interest. We pay careful attention to the tone, mood, and context of the speech as well as to its tropes, spaces, and structure. Time Studies invite seminar students, many of whom are practicing teachers during the day, to reconstruct in as great detail as possible certain time frames of their professional day. This is done to try to recover a sense of how professional practices are constructed through the "minutiae" of day-to-day events, through responses made to certain students in their classroom, through staff interactions, through interruptions, and so forth. All of these activities help to give our lives a sense of text which we can then interpret; discovering what is at work in practices we once engaged in dogmatically, that is, as if there was nothing more to be said about them.

Citing these activities points to a third important aspect of hermeneutical research, which is that hermeneutics is not really concerned with hermeneutics per se; that is, with its character as another self-defining imploding discourse within a universe of other discourses. Far more important is its overall *interest* which is in the question of human meaning and of how we might make sense of our lives in such a way that life can go on. As such, the hermeneutic imagination works to rescue the specificities of our lives from the burden of their everydayness to show how they reverberate within grander schemes of things. Hermeneutics is about finding ourselves, which also, curiously enough, is about losing ourselves; that is, giving up the precious "fundamentalist" logocentric impulse in the name of a greater freedom and dignity. Constantly engaged in the practice of interpretation, the hermeneutic imagination is not limited in its conceptual resources to the texts of the hermeneutic tradition itself but is liberated by them to bring to bear any conceptualities that can assist in deepening our understanding of what it is we are investigating. This means that the mark of good interpretative research is not in the degree to which it follows a specified methodological agenda, but in the degree to which it can show understanding of what it is that is being investigated. And "understanding" here is itself not a fixable category but rather it stands for a deep sense that something has been profoundly heard in our present circumstances. Similarly, "hearing something in the present" does not just mean simply being aware of vibrations on the eardrums, but a registering of them within the deep web of sounds and voices that make up the structure of one's consciousness as language, memory, and hope. This means that hermeneutical consciousness is always and everywhere a historical consciousness, a way of thinking and acting that is acutely aware of the storied nature of human experience. We find ourselves, hermeneutically speaking, always in the middle of stories, and good hermeneutical research shows an ability to read those stories from inside out and outside in. Hermeneutical research is a multidimensional enterprise, not just a vertical (theological) one or horizontal (empirical) one. Weak research is concerned only with surfaces, whether in the name of statistics or psychologism. Pedagogically, the highest priority is in having children and young people gain precisely a sense of the human world as being a narrative construction that can be entered and engaged creatively; to have a sense that received understanding *can* be interpreted or re-interpreted and that human responsibility is fulfilled in precisely a taking up of this task.

A fourth aspect of hermeneutical inquiry implicit in all of the others suggested so far has to do with its inherent creativity. Hermeneutics is about creating meaning, not simply reporting on it. This distinguishes the hermeneutic effort from, say, ethnographic and grounded theory formulations wherein the task is to try to give an account of people's thoughts and actions strictly from their own point of view (Dobbert 1982; Glaser and Strauss 1967). Hermeneutically we understand how impossible such a task is, given that I always interpret others from within the frame of our common language and experience so that whatever I say about you is also a saying about myself. Within the hermeneutic agenda, however, the purpose is not to translate my subjectivity out of the picture but to take it up with a new sense of responsibility—to make proposals about the world we share with the aim of deepening our collective understanding of it. This involves what Gadamer has referred to as "the art of hermeneutic writing" which necessarily has the character of a certain exaggeration requiring for its completion the voice of an other. Good hermeneutic writing is "strong," to use the word in the meaning of social philosopher Alan Blum (1984); its desire is to provoke new ways of seeing and thinking within a deep sense of tradition, bringing about new forms of engagement and dialogue about the world we face together.

It is precisely the hermeneutical suggestion that the full truth of things can never be the conscious property of any one person or group that incites the fulminating Apollonian rage on the part of those who would wish to have the foundations of knowledge secured before proceeding with an engagement with the world as such. And given that the "foundationalist" view is the one that has underwritten most pedagogic practices today and is responsible for the artificial distinction between thinking and doing (the theory/practice split) which haunts the modern destruction of the world in the name of science, given all of this, what is the shape and texture of the world that the hermeneutic tradition itself must presume in order to make the claims that it does? Perhaps the most important point to affirm here is that there is an integrity to the world that somehow must be preserved even at the same time as we inquire into how best to alleviate our pains while living in it. Gadamer's (1987:349) question, "Does what already supports us require any grounding?" at once makes relative all parochial logocentric attempts to have the last word about defining the unshakable foundations of things, at the same time as it invites us deep into the hermeneutic project of articulating a more full sense of the world which affirms local identities. Instead of the imperial, triumphal, subsuming, and distinctly masculine languages which have characterized the self-descriptions of the Western tradition to this point,[20] the hermeneutic way points to how meaning is always "webbed," challenging us to speak about our life together in a way that is both ecological and ecumenical, two terms derived from the Greek word for "household" (oikos). The task is one of "understanding," the character of which the hermeneutic tradition has been at great pains to elucidate, not just because "understanding" is now one more thing co-optible by the human sciences but because without an ongoing search for understanding we are reduced to terror, xenophobia, or the kind of isolation that breeds complacency, hubris, and self-contempt.

All writing is in a sense autobiographical, and as I have worked through the ideas of this chapter, many times I have wondered about my own interest in the subject of hermeneutics. How is it that Hermes and I found each other? I think the matter has partly to do with the fact that my pre-adult years were all spent in different parts of the world (particularly Africa and Asia). Wherever we went, not only was I always acutely aware of being different, but in every place too I witnessed how the question of difference seemed to inhere in virtually all of the historical, politico-economic, and pedagogical struggles at work in those locations. Everywhere there seemed to be a need for a language of "understanding" that could take up "difference" not as a problem to be solved but as an invitation to consider the boundaries and limits of one's own understanding. Hermes and I found each other, I suspect, because of a mutual recognition that identity means nothing without a set of relations, and that the real work of our time may be defined by an ability to mediate meaning across boundaries and differences, whether those boundaries and differences be concerned with gender, race, or ideas. And somehow it seems to me that the hermeneutic imagination has an important contribution to make to that task, not to settle everything once and for all by assigning people and things to their (so it might be thought) "essential" places, but for the profound pedagogical purpose of affirming the way in which present arrangements always border on and open onto the space of an Other whose existence contains part of the story of our shared future. And whether there will be a future indeed depends on the full power of creative interpretation. Hermeneutics for everyone?

Notes

1. Information here concerning the character of Hermes has been drawn entirely from Stapleton (1982).

2. The Canadian Society for Hermeneutics and Postmodern Thought, inaugurated in May 1985, made the following "Statement of Purpose" in its publication, *Bulletin* (1988), *3*(3), 15: "(The society) was created to serve as a forum for interdisciplinary conversation. It is committed to the goal of opening up new and much needed channels of communication between the various human disciplines. For the success that these disciplines have enjoyed in defining their boundaries has not been without attendant negative consequences. The more precisely each discipline has defined its own terrain, the more difficult the effort of communication between or across disciplines has become. The society does not propose to tear down fences. It would be more appropriate to think of conversations *over* fences, as one might converse with one's neighbours. What make our particular conversations possible is an emphasis on methodological self-reflection, and the realization that the so-called facts that one discovers are already the product of many levels of interpretation. Interpretation is an activity common to all the human disciplines (in the humanities as well as in the social sciences, from the analysis of texts to the study of peoples and cultures), and hermeneutics is the study of this activity." Those interested in membership in the society should write to CSH/SCH, Department of Philosophy, McMaster University, Hamilton, Ontario, Canada L8S 4K1.

3. In English the most comprehensive working out of the anti-foundationalist case is Rorty (1979).

4. Whether or not there is such a thing as "post-modern hermeneutics" is a topic of debate. Here I simply prefer to say that all of the conversations about post-modernism are interpretive, hermeneutic endeavors. See the debate between the two primary players, Hans-Georg Gadamer and Jacques Derrida (1989). John Caputo (1987) attempts to show the articulation between hermeneutics and post-modernism/deconstructionism.

5. United Nations, *Convention on the Rights of the Child* (New York: Unesco, forthcoming). See also reports such as that of economist Leonard Silk: "The United States has the highest child poverty rate of any industrialized country." Reported in *The International Herald Tribune* (May 13–14, 1989), 9.

6. David Kennedy has recently completed an important study tracing the development of concepts of childhood in Western culture. He argues that under the Enlightenment rationality of the modern era the child has been reduced to child-as-object, a turn which undermines the ontological place of the child in the adult-child relation. See David Kennedy, "Young Children's Thinking: An Interpretation from Phenomenology." Ph.D. diss., University of Kentucky, 1986. Reviewed in *Phenomenology + Pedagogy* (1988), *6*(2), 109–113.

7. The best general survey is still, in my view, Palmer (1967). There is a good introduction in Wachterhauser (1986). For this paper I was greatly assisted by the historical survey of Kurt Mueller–Vollmer (1985).

8. In English, the two most important documents of Schleiermacher's hermeneutics are Kimmerle (1977) and Schleiermacher (1978). All of the quotations that follow are from Schleiermacher (1978).

9. Paulo Freire discusses this theme in a film documenting experiments using his praxis model. See "Starting from Nina: The Politics of Learning." (Toronto: Development Education Centre, 1978).

10. Students looking for an accessible introduction to Derrida would find helpful Richard Kearney's interview with him in Kearney (1984).

11. Play and desire are central themes throughout the work of both Derrida and Kristeva. See Derrida (1978:278–294) and Kristeva (1983).

12. See note 4 above.

13. I have in mind here a wide range of writing and inquiry that may be referred to generically as World Order Studies. Key figures include Ali Mazrui, Immanuel Wallerstein, Andre Gunder Frank, Ashis Nandy, Rajni Kothari, Richard Falk, R. B. J. Walker, Saul Mendelovitz, and many others. The Centre for the Study of Developing Societies in Delhi, India, and the World Order Models Project, United Nations Plaza, New York, publish an important journal called *Alternatives*. A good introductory text is Walker (1984). Major themes addressed in this field of discourse include North-South Relations, Peace and Disarmament, Colonialism and Post-Colonialism, and the future global habitat.

14. "Representationalism" as a basic gesture of Western Thinking is well discussed by Rorty (1979). Madison (1988) discusses the critique of representationalism as a feature of post-modern philosophy.

15. This position on a hermeneutic understanding of the tradition of ideology critique has been well worked out by Paul Ricoeur (1973).

16. Gadamer (1979) elaborates on the conversational mode of inquiry in Part III. Rorty (1979) deals with it explicitly. In a curriculum research context, see Carson (1986).

17. See the film series by Robert McNeil, "The Story of Language," for a good introduction to this topic.

18. The World Order Studies movement has crystallized in its work many of these themes (see note 13 above for the names of significant writers). Ashis Nandy (1983, 1987) has written eloquently and profoundly on all of these topics from a non-Western point of view. Nandy is also a frequent contributor to the journal *Alternatives*.

19. A useful introduction to semiotics in Berger (1984). See also Silverman (1983).

20. I am thinking particularly here of Gregory Ulmer's description of the "imperial dispensation" of the logocentric tradition of the West, in "Textshop for Post(e) pedagogy," in Atkins and Johnson (1985). Ashis Nandy (1983:100) has written of the culture of the West as one of "hyper-masculinity, adulthood, historicism, objectivism, and hypernormality."

References

(Symbols preceding entries are explained on page 40)

√ Apel, K. (1985). Scientistics, hermeneutics, critique of ideology: An outline of a theory of science from an epistemological-anthropological point of view. In K. Mueller-Vollmer (Ed.), *The hermeneutics reader* (pp. 321–345). New York: Continuum.

+ Atkins, E. (1988). Reframing curriculum theory in terms of interpretation and practice: A hermeneutical approach. *Journal of Curriculum Studies, 20*(5), 437–448.

√ Atkins, G. D., and Johnson, M. (Eds.) (1985). *Writing and reading differently.* Laurance, KS: University Press of Kansas.

√ Berger, A. A. (1984). *Signs in contemporary culture.* New York: Longmans.

√ Blum, A. (1984). *Self-reflection in the arts and sciences.* Atlantic Highlands, NJ: Humanities Press.

+ Bredo, E., and Feinberg, W. (1982). The interpretive approach to social and educational research. In E. Bredo and W. Feinberg (Eds.), *Knowledge and values in social and educational research* (pp. 115 – 128). Philadelphia: Temple University Press.

√ Caputo, J. (1987). *Radical hermeneutics: Repetition, deconstruction, and the hermeneutic project.* Bloomington, IN: Indiana University Press.

√ Carson, T. R. (1986). Closing the gap between research and practice: Conversation as a mode of research. *Phenomenology + Pedagogy, 4*(2), 73–85.

√ Chambers, C. M. (1989). *For our children's children: An educator's interpretation of Dene testimony to the Mackenzie Valley pipeline inquiry.* Ph.D. dissertation, University of Victoria, British Columbia.

√ Cherryholmes, C. H. (1988). *Power and criticism: Poststructural investigations in education.* New York: Teachers College Press.

○ Daignault, J. (1989). Curriculum as composition: Who is the composer? Paper delivered at the Eleventh Annual Conference of the *Journal of Curriculum Theorizing,* Bergamo Center, Dayton, Ohio, October 18–22.

√ Derrida, J. (1978). *Writing and difference* (A. Bass, trans.). Chicago: The University of Chicago Press.

√ de Saussure, F. (1959). *Course in general linguistics* (eds., C. Bally and A. Sechehaye; trans., W. Baskin). New York: Philosophical Library.

√ Dobbert, M. L. (1982). *Ethnographic research: Theory and application for modern schools and society.* New York: Praeger.

√ Ellsworth, E. (1989). Why doesn't this feel empowering? Working through the repressive myths of critical pedagogy. *Harvard Educational Review, 59*(3), 299–324.

√ Freire, P. (1971). *Pedagogy of the oppressed,* trans., M. B. Ramos. New York: Herder & Herder.

√ Gadamer, H. (1977). *Philosophical hermeneutics,* trans., D. E. Linge. Berkeley: University of California Press.

√ ———. (1979). *Truth and method* (W. Glen-Doepel, trans.). London: Sheed and Ward.

√ ———. (1983). Hermeneutics as practical philosophy. In F. G. Lawrence (trans.)., *Reason in the age of science* (pp. 88–138). Cambridge: The MIT Press.

√ ———. (1985). On the origins of philosophical hermeneutics. In *Philosophical Apprenticeships.* Cambridge: MIT Press.

√ ———. (1987). Foreword to the second edition of *Truth and Method.* In K. Baynes, J. Bohman, and T. McCarthy (Eds.), *After philosophy: End or transformation.* Cambridge: MIT Press.

√ Gadamer, H., and Derrida, J. (1989). *Dialogue and deconstructionism: The Gadamer-Derrida encounter.* Albany: SUNY Press.

√ Garfinkle, H. (1967). *Studies in ethnomethodology.* Englewood Cliffs: Prentice Hall.

+ Garman, N. B. (1990). Theories embedded in the events of clinical supervision: A hermeneutic approach. *Journal of Curriculum and Supervision,* 5(3), 201–211.

o Garman, N. B., and Holland P. (1989). Of imaginative compact: Curriculum theory and the mythopoetic. Paper delivered at the Eleventh Annual Conference of the *Journal of Curriculum Theorizing,* Bergamo Center, Dayton, Ohio, October 18–22.

√ Gergin, K. J., and Gergin, M. M. (1983). Narratives of the self. In T. R. Sarbin and K. E. Schiebe (Eds.), *Studies in social identity* (pp. 254–273). New York: Praeger.

o Gitlin, A., and Goldstein, S. (1987). A dialogical approach to understanding: Horizontal evaluation. *Educational Theory,* 37(1), 17–27.

√ Glaser, B. C., and Strauss, A. (1967). *The discovery of grounded theory: Strategies for qualitative research.* Chicago: Aldine.

√ Heidegger, M. (1962). Being and time (J. Maquarrie and E. Robinson, trans.). New York: Harper and Row.

√ ———. (1977). The end of philosophy and the task of thinking. In D. Krall (Ed.), *Martin Heidegger: Basic writings* (pp. 369–392). New York: Harper and Row.

√ Hodges, H. A. (1952). *The philosophy of Wilhelm Dilthy.* Boston: Routledge & Kegan Paul.

o Jardine, D. (1989). A bell ringing in an empty sky. Paper delivered at the Eleventh Annual Conference of the *Journal of Curriculum Theorizing,* Bergamo Center, Dayton, Ohio, October 18–22.

√ Kearney, R. (Ed.) (1984). *Dialogues with contemporary continental thinkers* (pp. 105–126). Manchester, England: Manchester University Press.

√ Kimmerle, H. (Ed.) (1977). *Hermeneutics: The handwritten manuscripts of Friedrich Schleiermacher* (trans., J. Duke and J. Frostman). Missoula, MT: Scholars Press.

√ Kristeva, J. (1980). *Desire in language.* New York: Columbia University Press.

√ ————. (1983). Psychoanalysis and the polis. In W. J. T. Mitchell (Ed.), *The politics of interpretation* (pp. 75–98). Chicago: The University of Chicago Press.

√ Longxi, Z. (1985). The Tao and the Logos: Notes on Derrida's critique of logocentrism. *Critical Inquiry, 11*(3), 385–398.

√ ————. (1988). The myth of the other: China in the eyes of the west. *Critical Inquiry, 15*(1), 108–131.

+ Macdonald, J. (1988). Theory-practice and the hermeneutic circle. In W. F. Pinar (Ed.), *Contemporary curriculum discourses* (pp. 101–113). Scottsdale, AZ: Gorsuch Scarisbrick.

√ Madison, G. B. (1988). Postmodern philosophy? *Critical Review, 2*(2/3), 166–182.

√ Makreel, R. (1975). *Dilthy: Philosopher of the human sciences*. Princeton: Princeton University Press.

√ *Market Process* (1988), *6*(1), entire issue.

√ Merton, T. (1961). A letter to Pablo Antonio Cuadra concerning giants. In *Emblems of a season of fury* (pp. 70–89). Norfolk: New Directions.

√ Messer, S. B., Sass, L. A., and Woolfolk, B. L. (Eds.) (1988). *Hermeneutics and psychological theory*. New Brunswick, NJ: Rutgers University Press.

√ Mueller-Vollmer, K. (1985). Language, mind, and artifact: An outline of hermeneutic theory since the enlightenment. In K. Mueller-Vollmer (Ed.), *The hermeneutic reader* (pp. 1–53). New York: Continuum.

√ Nandy, A. (1983). *The intimate enemy: Loss and recovery of self under colonialism*. Delhi: Oxford University Press.

√ ————. (1987). *Traditions, tyranny, and utopias: Essays in the politics of awareness*. Delhi: Oxford University Press.

√ Palmer, R. (1967). *Hermeneutics*. Evanston: Northwestern University Press.

√ Polkinghorne, D. E. (1988). *Narrative knowing and the human sciences*. Albany: SUNY Press.

o Reynolds, W. M. (1989). *Reading curriculum theory: The development of a new hermeneutic*. New York: Peter Lang.

√ Rickman, H. P. (Ed.) (1976). *Wilhelm Dilthy: Selected writings*. New York: Cambridge University Press.

√ Ricoeur, P. (1973). Ethics and culture. *Philosophy Today, 17*(2/4), 153–165.

√ ————. (1985). The model of the text: Meaningful action considered as a text. In J. B. Thompson. (Ed. & Trans.), *Hermeneutics and the human sciences* (pp. 197–221). New York: Cambridge University Press.

√ Rorty, R. (1979). *Philosophy and the mirror of nature.* Princeton: Princeton University Press.

√ Sang, O. M. (1986). *The meaning of moral education: An interpretive study of moral education curriculum in Korea.* Ph.D. dissertation, University of Alberta.

√ Sarbin, T. R. (Ed.) (1986). *Narrative psychology: The storied nature of human conduct.* New York: Praeger.

√ Schleiermacher, F. D. E. (1978). Outline of the 1819 Lectures. *New Literacy History, 10*(1), 1–16.

√ Schutz, A. (1970). *On phenomenology and social relations.* Chicago: The University of Chicago Press.

√ Silverman, K. (1983). *The subject of semiotics.* New York: Oxford University Press.

○ Smith, D. G. (1988). Brighter than a thousand suns: Facing pedagogy in the nuclear shadow. In T. R. Carson (Ed.), *Toward a renaissance of humanity* (pp. 275–285). Edmonton: Faculty of Education, University of Alberta.

√ Stapleton, M. (1982). Hermes. In *The Hamlyn concise dictionary of Greek and Roman mythology* (pp. 140–142). London: Hamlyn.

√ Sweet, P. (1978–80). *Wilhelm von Humboldt: A biography* (2 volumes). Columbus: Ohio State University Press.

√ Walker, R. B. J. (Ed.) (1984). *Culture, ideology, and world order.* Boulder, CO: Westview Press.

√ Wachterhauser, B. R. (Ed.) (1986). *Hermeneutics and modern philosophy.* Albany: SUNY Press.

11

Theoretical Inquiry:
Components and Structure

——— Richard W. Grove
and Edmund C. Short

The purpose of theoretical inquiry in curriculum is to create and critique conceptual schemes by which the essential nature and structure of curricular phenomena and processes can be made intelligible. When developing a curriculum, we necessarily adopt and employ some conceptual scheme and some specialized vocabulary and language. We utilize these to think about and communicate what we mean when we address or propose curriculum. Likewise, when doing inquiry related to curriculum, we necessarily adopt and employ some conceptual scheme. How are such conceptual schemes formulated and how do we know which of these is more valid and efficacious than another? These are questions this chpater on theoretical inquiry in curriculum attempts to answer.

A conceptual scheme defines an entity's constitutive elements and the relationships among those elements. In creating a conceptual scheme, two kinds of concepts are usually stipulated: constitutive concepts and structural concepts. The elements or components identified as constituting the entity are conceived and defined through constitutive concepts. The relationships identified among those elements are conceived and defined through structural concepts. The whole array of concepts, both constitutive and structural, produces a language system or a conceptual scheme by which we can think and talk about the entity.

Conceptual schemes are not givens in any field of thought or practice; they must be created. This is as true in curriculum thought and practice as in any other field. Many different conceptual schemes in curriculum compete for attention and use. It is the business of theoretical inquiry in curriculum to create and critique conceptual schemes related to curriculum phenomena and processes and thereby enable curriculum thought and practice to distinguish between vital, fruitful language and reified, stifling language. It also helps curriculum practitioners and researchers to continue to clarify the essential nature of curriculum.

Theoretical inquiry is the most fundamental of all the practical, inter-disciplinary forms of inquiry that can be undertaken in curriculum studies. Other forms of practical inquiry, such as, normative, critical, evaluative, integrative, and action inquiry, generate essential knowledge that helps inform curriculum decisions and activity. But theoretical inquiry related to curriculum provides the conceptual tools with which all other kinds of practical inquiry and ordinary curriculum activities are comprehended and articulated. If theoretical inquiry is limited or poorly done, other curriculum thought is weakend or hampered.

Theoretical inquiry is a form of curriculum inquiry that has attracted a large number of curriculum scholars. A variety of conceptual schemes related to curriculum have been generated and can be found in the literature. Many of these schemes have prompted heated debate over their merits and usefulness; others remain largely unrecognized and uncritiqued. To illustrate the kind of work done in theoretical inquiry, we will sketch some examples of conceptual schemes that have been created by this form of inquiry. In this way, the general purposes served and the kind of knowledge produced by theoretical inquiry in curriculum can be identified in concrete terms and understood more clearly.

Examples of Theoretical Inquiry in Curriculum

Tyler. Certainly the most familiar example is one formulated by Ralph Tyler in the 1940s (Tyler 1949). It posits four elements: purposes, learning experiences, organization of learning experiences, and evaluation. *Purposes* are explicated as objectives, the form of which is shaped according to desired student behaviors and course content. *Learning experiences* are defined as interactions between the learner and the external conditions in the environment; thus, learning is perceived as taking place through active behavior. *Organization of learning experiences* should efficiently produce a cumulative effect according to the criteria of continuity, sequence, and integration; these criteria address the need for developing the vertical and horizontal dimensions of the curriculum. *Evaluation* is conducted by examining changes in students' behavioral outcomes via pretesting and post-testing instrumentation; long-term follow-up is also suggested.

The *objective* is the structural concept of the scheme in that it provides the criteria for selecting and relating all other elements. The majority of the criticism leveled at the scheme has decried the shortcomings of objectives determined prior to instruction, especially those behavioral in nature. Essentially, this was a criticism of the scheme's technical perspective. Tyler justified predetermined objectives on the basis of their providing consistent criteria for selecting the particulars of the other three elements, i.e., content and materials, methods of instruction, and testing procedures. In doing so, he was emphasizing the importance they play in knitting together the constitutive elements of his conceptual scheme and the curriculum that is generated from it. The focus on student behavior was justified by Tyler on the basis of its being readily identifiable as evidence of learning.

For all of the debate Tyler's scheme has generated, its interactively deliberative nature has often been overlooked. He thought the four elements should be addressed in a staff dialogue and expects the answers to vary by grade level and school. In addition, he specifies a deliberative process for the organization of learning experiences in planning a unit of instruction.

Duncan and Frymier. One of the most elaborate conceptual schemes presented in the curriculum literature is one created by James Duncan and Jack Frymier in 1966 (Duncan and Frymier 1967). They explicate three primary elements: actors, artifacts, and operations. *Actors* are the people directly involved with or "inside" the curriculum. Thus, a boundary is established between participants in the enacted curriculum and those who indirectly participate (e.g., administrators) and those who do not participate at all (e.g., some community members). *Artifacts* are educational products, particularly subject matter or content. Educational products are not viewed as materials but, rather, the ideas that beget and are embedded in materials. *Operations* are processes involving modifications in elements or relationships between elements.

The structural concept is the *curriculum event.* A curriculum event has the potential for restructuring and reorganizing human experience; it has three dimensions: structure, process, and value. The relationship between actors and artifacts determines the structure of a curriculum event. Temporal modifications determine the process or operations of a curriculum event. Values associated with elements and their relationships determine the value of a curriculum event.

The curriculum event and the scheme's elements and their relationships are then utilized to define and discuss curriculum molecule, curriculum, curriculum development, instruction, the learning act, and other related concepts. A curriculum molecule consists of a specific combination of actors, artifacts, and operations; the curriculum event is conceived as one type of molecule. The curriculum is viewed as a set of events in time that has the potential for reconstructing human experience. Curriculum development is the process of selcting appropriate curriculum events. Instruction is those acts of a teacher in a curriculum event that have the potential (in a specific instructional setting) for influencing the reconstruction of experience. A learning act is a set of sequential behaviors that evolve in stages, effecting a reconstruction of the learner's experience.

One characteristic of this scheme is the focus on the enactment of curriculum implied by the three elements as they are integrated in the curriculum event; this gives rise to the interactional perspective of the scheme. Commensurate with this is the view of learning as the active reconstruction of experience. Thus, the scheme moves the focus of concern away from planning or preenactment, although Duncan and Frymier deem planning important, to a concern for the emergent curriculum of classroom interaction. However, the scheme becomes so complex that some logical discontinuities develop in its elements and their relationships.

Macdonald. Another scheme was conceptualized by James Macdonald in 1970 (Macdonald 1986). It is like Duncan and Frymier's scheme in that Macdonald defines curriculum as what is learned and, thus, focuses on enactment instead of planning. There are four elements: the boundaries of curriculum, units of discourse, the relationship of variables, and the ethical and/or moral dimension of curriculum. *The boundaries of curriculum* are determined by people acting in the setting of a specific school system; there are five subsystems: administrative, curriculum development, instructional, staff personality, and student personality. Curriculum is described and understood by looking at events and their outcomes in these five subsystems. The *units of discourse* are acts and events; acts are observable or inferable from observation and events are patterns of action in time. In establishing *the relationship of variables* as an element, Macdonald transforms a structural concept into a constitutive one; this concept is discussed below as structural in keeping with the organization of this analysis. *The ethical perspective* on actual curriculum events is deemed necessary by Macdonald. This perspective is based on the idea that curriculum actors must regard decisions and actions during the curriculum enactment process as ethical obligations based on what is best for one another in the situation. Thus, decisions and actions cannot be determined prior to enactment and be considered ethical.

The structural concept is that of *emergent structure,* a term consistent with Macdonald's views although not his precise words. Structure emerges from interactions and, as is suggested above, cannot be defined ahead of time. This notion is consonant with the interactional perspective of Duncan and Frymier. According to Macdonald's thinking, however, any actor in curriculum is done an ethical injustice when not afforded the opportunity to engage freely in a discourse of her/his choosing.

Unique features of this scheme include the conceptions of system and subsystems, inferring from observation, and the need for the ethical perspective. Although Duncan and Frymier as well as Tyler conceived of people as actors or participants in the process of curriculum development, neither differentiated nor specified transacting systems and subsystems to the degree that Macdonald did. Also, though both previous schemes regard the description of behavior as primary evidence for evaluation, Macdonald's scheme gives equal status to the inference of behavior. Finally, the most well-known feature is the argument for the primacy of the ethical perspective in regard to the acting out of curriculum events. Not only is the perspective radically different in meaning from Tyler's, but it is also different in explicitness; Macdonald explicates his perspective as an element of his scheme. The result is his basing the validity of the interactional perspective in the realm of the ethical.

Walker. In 1970, Decker Walker put forth a conceptual scheme that has been frequently adopted in thinking about curriculum decision-making (Walker 1971). His "naturalistic" scheme is derived from observing actual curriculum development projects and consists of three major elements: platform, deliberation, and design; there are two subelements: data and policy. A curriculum *platform* is the system of beliefs an educator brings to the development process; components of the belief system are conceptions, theories, aims, images, and procedures, all either dealing with what exists, what is possible, or what is desirable. *Deliberation* is the process of dialogue, argumentation and/or debate, most commonly in a group setting, during which beliefs and *data* are utilized as tools of persuasion. The main operations in deliberation are formulating decision points, devising alternative choices at the decision points considering arguments for and against decision points and alternatives, and choosing the most defensible alternative. Thus, the validity of the decision-making process rests with the defensibility or justifiability of decisions, based on circumstances and/or "natural and conventional" principles. Out of deliberation arise decisions that set precedents and, thus, *policy.* These precedents are cited during debate in lieu of platform principles in order to persuade. A curriculum *design* is a set of abstract relationships embodied in a design object or materials-in-use; designs may be explicit or implicit. The theoretically most interesting output of the naturalistic scheme is the set of design decisions generated by the deliberative individual or group.

The structural concept is the *systems model;* as with Macdonald, we again must use a term that the author of the scheme did not use. The concepts of input, processing of data, and output are arguably implicit in the articulation of the scheme. Specifically, individual platforms and the data at hand represent input; deliberation represents the processing of information in the form of data and beliefs; and output is represented as design decisions based on past deliberation (policy) or current deliberation.

Walker focuses on preenactment, as does Tyler; however, he deals primarily with the process of curriculum decision-making instead of its products, giving rise to his naturalistic or process-oriented perspective. As in the

216 Richard W. Grove and Edmund C. Short

schemes of Duncan and Frymier and Macdonald, the interacting of curriculum participants lies at the heart of Walker's scheme. The unique features of
the scheme are the conception of platform as a source of input and the conception of design decision as outcome. In identifying platform, Walker drew
a focus on the individual curriculum developer and her/his function in the
decision-making process. The focus on design decisions as the natural outcome of curriculum development drew the focus away from the classroom
and broke the previously unassailed link between the design process and
student learning. Thus, Walker's real world focus is tighter than the foci of
the previous authors, the world of curriculum development becoming an object of study unto itself.

Goodlad. John Goodlad and his associates formulated a conceptual
scheme that defines curriculum decision-making more comprehensively
than does Walker's (Goodlad 1979). Three major elements are posited: substantive, political-social, and technical-professional. *Substantive* elements
deal with what is learned and are related to all domains, i.e., the societal,
institutional, personal/experiential, and ideological; Tyler's scheme is cited
as an example containing solely substantive elements. Therefore, substantive elements, i.e., purposes, experiences, organization of experiences, and
evaluation, are considered commonplaces and must be addressed in every
curriculum development project. Goodlad adds the ideological to his list of
commonplaces, indicating that values and interests are part of the make-up
of all humans and, thus, are present in all curriculum design decisions. *Political-social* elements consist of groups and individuals affecting curriculum decision-making; Goodlad terms this total group the "sanctioning
body." *Technical-professional* elements are relevant knowledge and skills as
well as useful professional lore. These elements are considered integral
parts of all elements in all domains.

Process is the structural concept of the scheme. The processes utilized
to deal with substantive elements are translation and interpretation. These
processes focus on the making of substantive curriculum decisions based
on the values and interests people bring to a curriculum decision-making
situation. Political-social elements are dealt with via the process of trans-
action. This process is represented by activity within and among domains,
groups, and individuals.

This scheme is similar to Tyler's in that commonplaces of curriculum
development are understood to be substantive elements. It is similar to Walker's scheme in that decisions and decision points are considered to be outcomes. It is also similar to Macdonald's in its inclusion of social systems
and subsystems, although very different in expanding its focus beyond the
school only. In fact, its broad view of social and political elements is arguably its most unique feature. Thus, its perspective is eclectic, attempting to
integrate substantive, sociopolitical, and technical/professional elements

as well as various domains and their milieus. The result is a complex conceptual scheme that is difficult to comprehend in its entirety.

Other Examples and Comments

In looking at the above conceptual schemes in total, some guarded statements about theoretical inquiry in curriculum to-date can be made. In general, perspectives vary among most of the schemes as necessarily do their constitutive and structural concepts. Thus, each theory of inquiry made manifest by its unique conceptual scheme is marked by its own particular ideology or arrangement of concepts, as suggested by Goodlad.

More specifically, there has been a shift away from the purely technical perspective of Tyler to humanistic perspectives, i.e., values, beliefs, and ethics have gained increased prominence in the dialogue on curriculum theorizing. The same cannot be said, however, for curriculum practice. The challenge and dilemma for curriculum theorists has been and will continue to be the conceiving of humanistic conceptual schemes that can function efficaciously as part of a larger and more encompassing reform or restructuring effort. The likelihood of such schemes emerging requires not only a major upheaval in the educational community but also, on the part of curriculum theorists, an acute sense of timing and commitment and top-notch conceptual abilities steeped in the history of theoretical inquiry in curriculum. These conditions are not impossible to meet during the late twentieth and early twenty-first centuries; but they are indeed fraught with social and personal difficulties.

Theoretical inquiry in curriculum need not focus on generating the sort of comprehensive conceptual schemes illustrated here; it may also focus on a more limited range of curriculum dimensions, even a single element. Examples of theoretical work of this kind are cited in Table 1.

Examples of studies that critique the work of earlier theoretical inquiry are those of Kliebard (1970), Botel and Botel (1975), Wise (1976), and Macdonald (1986).

The label *curriculum theory* is often used in the literature to refer to the knowledge generated by the process of theoretical inquiry. This was especially true in the 1950s and 1960s when scholars were beginning to define the focus, boundaries, and dimensions of the field of study called *curriculum*. However, it should be noted that in the 1970s and 1980s the term *curriculum theory* was more often used to refer to the normative positions embedded in curriculum. In this sense, curriculum theory has more to do with the results of normative or critical inquiry in curriculum, which are the topics of discussion in the next two chapters.

Table 1

Theoretical Studies on Curricular Components

1. *Curriculum development strategies:* Gay 1985; Klein 1989; Lewy 1977; Short 1983; Skilbeck 1982; Steller 1983; Tamir 1985.

2. *Curriculum content selection and design:* Goodlad 1963; Herrick 1965; Klein 1985; 1986; Schwab 1978; Short 1986; 1987; Vallance 1985.

3. *Curriculum materials development:* Frymier 1986; Kantor, Anderson, and Armbruster 1983; Kennedy and McDonald 1986; Tyler, Klein, and Michael 1971.

4. *Establishing educational objectives:* Raths 1971; Schutz, Baker, and Gerlack 1971; Tyler 1949.

5. *Defining curriculum:* Beauchamp 1981; English 1983; Johnson 1967; Macdonald 1967; Vallance 1983.

6. *Formulating and communicating curriculum plans and/or guides:* Donmoyer 1989; Harris 1985; Payne 1969; Short 1987; Westbury 1983.

7. *Curriculum policy development:* Anderson 1982; Berman 1988; Bonser and Grundy 1988; Kirst and Walker 1971; Maxwell 1985; Westbury 1977; Tanner 1988.

8. *Creating curriculum theory:* Macdonald 1982; McCutcheon 1982; Pinar and Grumet 1988; Walker 1982.

9. *Defining curriculum research questions:* Chipley 1989; Foshay 1987; Kimpston and Rogers 1986; Posner 1989; Short 1985; Short 1991.

10. *Conducting curriculum inquiry:* Aoki 1979; Berman 1988; Beyer 1986; Clandinin and Connelly 1987; Haggerson 1988; King 1981; Short 1991.

Guidelines for Conducting Theoretical Inquiry in Curriculum

Little has been written on how to do theoretical inquiry in curriculum. Nevertheless, it is clear that it is an interdisciplinary, creative, and conjunctive enterprise. There is an empirical dimension that requires knowledge of the real world of curriculum, obtained by scientific, ethnographic, phenomenological, or other appropriate forms of inquiry. There is a philosophical dimension that requires knowledge of speculative, analytic, and ampliative concepts and processes in curriculum. There is a compositional or artistic design dimension that requires knowledge of potential forms and structures framed by the contingencies of time, space, resources, human interactions, and media in particular curriculum settings.

Prior to beginning formal theoretical inquiry, the theoretician must also have had wide experience with various curricular phenomena, processes, and problems in order to appreciate what is to be conceptualized. This immersion in curricular realities informs one's perceptions and forms the basis for judgment as to what aspects are fundamental and what perspectives are central to making curriculum intelligible.

There is no escaping favoring certain concepts and ways of thinking over others in choosing how to formulate a conceptual scheme pertaining to curriculum. This is to be expected and not to be resisted because of some thought of creating a scheme that is value-free or generic. The very language and concepts that make up and underlie conceptual schemes actually represent choices among many possibilities. Choice is inevitable in the context of theoretical curriculum inquiry as much as it is in practical curriculum decision-making (Huebner 1966). Any truly consistent system of concepts and language, whether chosen or created, is capable of communicating only one dominant value perspective. The virtue of any viable scheme lies in its conceptual clarity, its perceived fit with reality, and the compellingness of its structure and justification. The worth of a conceptual scheme lies not in the supposed correctness of its choice of concepts and language but in its utility and efficacy, which can only be judged in practice.

The basic procedures, therefore, utilized in doing theoretical inquiry in curriculum can be formulated as four fundamental guidelines.

Guideline 1. The first step in doing theoretical inquiry in curriculum is to settle on the scope and boundaries of the curricular phenomenon or process one intends to conceptualize. This may be as broad as all that curriculum might encompass or as limited as a single, constitutive element. However, if one chooses to deal with a limited focus, one must assume a larger configuration of concepts of which this is a part. This approach risks the possibility that the results may be later judged as unrelatable to any larger conceptual framework. Much work on curriculum objectives suffers from this failure. Nevertheless, conceptualizing the whole of curriculum with all of its fundamental elements and interrelationships is a gigantic task and not many who undertake it fully complete it.

Guideline 2. The curriculum theoretician then proceeds to discern phenomenologically the key elements and their relationships which together are to be used to define the whole curriculum or the whole process on which the inquiry is focused. These elements and their configuration are then conceptualized by adopting and defining constitutive and structural concepts that articulate the nature of the curricular phenomenon or process.

Skills of perception, analysis, creativity, imaginative synthesis, explanation, and justification are used in creating the array of vocabulary and language that constitutes the conceptual scheme. Data, insight, the focal aim, and one's theoretical perspective all enter into the process (Gotshalk 1969:

42 – 46). It is not enough to simply assert and configure a scheme; it must also be justified. That is, coherent arguments must be given for why each element is identified and labeled as it is. Formal criteria for doing this task include not only clarity, consistency, and completeness but also persuasiveness and fit with reality.

Guideline 3. A conceptual scheme that is generated and set forth by this process must ultimately be useful in everyday curriculum work or in curriculum research. If a scheme requires transformation into a level of discourse commensurate with the locus of its use, then the theoretician must engage in this transformation from the level of discourse in which it was originally presented into a level of discourse appropriate to its use in a specific context. Harris (1985) has discussed the goals and processes for achieving this kind of transformation in both theoretical and normative curriculum inquiry.

Guideline 4. Finally, the most telling step in theoretical inquiry curriculum comes in the effort to critique and evaluate the conceptual scheme that has been created. Besides assessing whether the formal criteria mentioned above have been met, the validity and efficacy of the formulation must also be assessed. Some of this can be accomplished by examining the formulation itself by the methods of ampliative philosophical criticism. But much of it must await the accumulation of case studies of situations in which the conceptual scheme was employed. Practical criteria can be applied to these case data regarding the problems and/or successes encountered in using the scheme for curriculum practice or research. Evidence of how well the scheme facilitates accomplishing these tasks can be used to judge the degree of validity and efficacy it possesses. A scheme that appears to be too complex or troublesome to use after several cases have been evaluated may suggest that users should drop it and adopt some other conceptual scheme. It is quite possible that any technically adequate conceptual scheme can be useful for some purpose, but it needs to be determined through careful critique and evaluation just what purposes and situations it best serves or whether its value and usefulness are so questionable that it had best be replaced by a more valid and efficacious scheme.

The need for competent theoretical inquiry in curriculum is quite apparent when one looks at work of this kind that has been attempted to date. The full range of interdisciplinary studies that have been suggested here needs to be conducted on every theoretical and conceptual dimension of curriculum that is selected for inquiry. Frequently, some of these phases have been omitted and the relevance and value of what has been done remains in question. In addition, it is also important to pull together whatever theoretical studies have been done in curriculum on similar or related topics and, using the methods of integrative inquiry described later in this book, provide syntheses of existing theoretical work which then may be used to inform further theoretical inquiry in curriculum.

References

(Symbols preceding entries are explained on page 40)

o Anderson, D. C. (1982). Research as a basis for curriculum policy-making: A cautionary note. *Journal of Curriculum Studies, 14,* 69–78.

o Aoki, T. T. (1979). Toward curriculum inquiry in new key. Occasional paper No. 2. Edmonton, Alberta: Faculty of Education, University of Alberta.

o Beauchamp, G. A. (1981). *Curriculum theory,* 4th Ed. Itasca, IL: F. E. Peacock.

o Berman, L. M. (1988). Problematic curriculum development: Normative inquiry in curriculum. *Journal of Curriculum and Supervision, 3,* 271–295.

o Beyer, L. E. (1986). The parameters of educational inquiry. *Curriculum Inquiry, 16,* 87–114.

o Bonser, S. A., and Grundy, S. J. (1988). Reflective deliberation in the formulation of a school curriculum policy. *Journal of Curriculum Studies, 20,* 35–45.

o Botel, M., and Botel, N. (1975). *Critical analysis of the taxonomy of educational objectives.* Washington, D.C.: Curriculum Development Associates.

o Chipley, D. R. (1989). Making sense out of curriculum: Some formative notes and an exploratory model. *Journal of Curriculum and Supervision, 5,* 70–80.

o Clandinin, D. J., and Connelly, F. M. (1987). Inquiry into schooling: Diverse perspectives. *Journal of Curriculum and Supervision, 2,* 295–313.

o Donmoyer, R. (1989). A policy statement approach to curriculum design. Paper given at Professors of Curriculum, Orlando.

o Duncan, J. K., and Frymier, J. R. (1967). Explorations in the systematic study of curriculum. *Theory into Practice, 6,* 180–199.

o English, F. W. (1983). Contemporary curriculum circumstances. In F. W. English (Ed.), *Fundamental curriculum decisions.* 1983 ASCD Yearbook (pp. 1–17). Alexandria, VA: Association for Supervision and Curriculum Development.

o Foshay, A. W. (1987). The curriculum matrix. *The Educational Forum, 51,* 341–353.

o Frymier, J. R. (1986). After thirty years of thinking about curriculum. *Theory into Practice, 25,* 58–63.

o Gay, G. (1985). Curriculum development. In T. Husen and T. N. Postlethwaite (Eds.), *International Encyclopedia of Education* (pp. 1170–1179). New York: Pergamon Press.

o   Goodlad, J. I. (1963). *Planning and organizing for teaching.* Washington, D.C.: National Education Association.

o   ———. (1979). The conceptual system for curriculum revisited. In J. I. Goodlad and Associates, *Curriculum inquiry: The study of curriculum practice* (pp. 343–364). New York: McGraw-Hill.

√   Gotshalk, D. W. (1969). *The structure of awareness.* Urbana, IL: University of Illinois Press.

o   Haggerson, N. L. (1988). Reconceptualizing inquiry in curriculum: Using multiple research paradigms to enhance the study of curriculum. *Journal of Curriculum Theorizing, 8,* 81–102.

o   Harris, I. B. (1985). An exploration of the role of theories in communication for guiding practitioners. *Journal of Curriculum and Supervision, 1,* 27–55.

o   Herrick, V. E. (1965). Concept of curriculum design. In J. B. Macdonald, D. W. Anderson, and F. B. May (Eds.), *Strategies of curriculum development* (pp. 17–38). Columbus, OH: Charles E. Merrill.

+   Huebner, D. (1966). Curriculum language and classroom meanings. In J. B. Macdonald and R. R. Leeper (Eds.), *Language and meaning* (pp. 8–26), Washington, D.C.: Association for Supervision and Curriculum Development.

o   Johnson, M. (1967). Definitions and models in curriculum theory. *Educational Theory, 17,* 127–140.

o   Kantor, R. N., Anderson, T. H., and Armbruster, B. B. (1983). How inconsiderate are children's textbooks? *Journal of Curriculum Studies, 15,* 61–72.

o   Kennedy, K. J., and McDonald, G. (1986). Designing curriculum materials for multicultural education: Lessons from an Australian development project. *Curriculum Inquiry, 16,* 312–326.

o   Kimpston, R. D., and Rogers, K. B. (1986). A framework for curriculum research. *Curriculum Inquiry, 16,* 463–474.

o   King, J. A. (1981). Methodological pluralism and curriculum inquiry. *Curriculum Inquiry, 11,* 167–174.

o   Kirst, M. W., and Walker, D. F. (1971). An analysis of curriculum policy-making. *Review of Educational Research, 41,* 479—509.

o   Klein, M. F. (1985). Curriculum design. In T. Husen and T. N. Postlethwaite (Eds.), *International Encyclopedia of Education* (pp. 1163 – 1170). New York: Pergamon Press.

o   ———. (1986). Alternative curriculum conceptions and designs. *Theory into Practice, 25,* 31–40.

o   ———. (1989). *Curriculum reform in the elementary school: Creating your own agenda.* New York: Teachers College Press.

o Kliebard, H. M. (1970). Reappraisal: The Tyler rationale. *School Review, 78*, 259–270.

o Lewy, A. (Ed.) (1977). *Handbook of curriculum evaluation*. New York: Longman.

o Macdonald, J. B. (1967). An example of disciplined curriculum thinking. *Theory into Practice, 6*, 166–171.

o ———. (1982). How literal is curriculum theory? *Theory into Practice, 21*, 55–61.

o ———. (1986). The domain of curriculum. *Journal of Curriculum and Supervision, 1*, 205–214.

o Maxwell, T. (1985). The illumination of situational analysis by frame factor theory. *Curriculum Perspectives, 5*, 46–52.

o McCutcheon, G. (1982). What in the world is curriculum theory? *Theory into Practice, 21*, 18–22.

o Payne, A. (1969). The study of curriculum plans. Washington, D.C.: National Educational Association.

o Pinar, W. F., and Grumet, M. R. (1988). Socratic *Caesura* and the theory practice relationship. In W. F. Pinar (Ed.), *Curriculum discourses*. Scottsdale, AZ: Gorsuch Scarisbrick.

o Posner, G. J. (1989). Making sense of diversity: The current state of curriculum research. *Journal of Curriculum and Supervision, 4*, 340–361.

o Raths, J. D. (1971). Teaching without specific objectives. *Educational Leadership, 28*, 714–720.

o Schutz, R. E., Baker, R. L., and Gerlack, V. S. (1971). Stating educational outcomes. In R. L. Baker and R. E. Schutz (Eds.), *Instructional product development* (pp. 1–21). New York: Van Nostrand Reinhold.

o Schwab, J. J. (1978). The practical: Translation into curriculum. In I. Westbury and N. J. Wilkof (Eds.), *Science, curriculum, and liberal education: Selected essays by Joseph J. Schwab* (pp. 365–383). Chicago: The University of Chicago Press.

o Short, E. C. (1983). The forms and uses of alternative curriculum development strategies: Policy implications. *Curriculum Inquiry, 13*, 43–64.

o ———. (1985). Organizing what we know about curriculum. *Curriculum Inquiry, 15*, 237–243.

o ———. (1986). A historical look at curriculum design. *Theory into Practice, 25*, 3–9.

o+ ———. (1987). Curriculum decision making in teacher education: Policies, program development, and design. *Journal of Teacher Education, 38,* 2–12.

o Short, E. C. (Ed.) (1991). *Forms of curriculum inquiry.* Albany: State University of New York Press.

o Skilbeck, M. (1982). School-based curriculum development. In V. Lee and D. Zeldin (Eds.), *Planning in the curriculum* (pp. 18–34). London: Hodder and Stroughton.

o Steller, A. W. (1983). Curriculum planning. In F. W. English (Ed.), *Fundamental curriculum decisions.* 1983 ASCD Yearbook (pp. 68–89). Alexandria, VA: Association for Supervision and Curriculum Development.

o Tamir, P. (Ed.) (1985). *The role of evaluation in curriculum development.* London: Croom Helm.

o Tanner, L. N. (Ed.) (1988). *Critical issues in curriculum.* 87th Yearbook of the National Society for the Study of Education, Part 1. Chicago: The University of Chicago Press.

o Tyler, L. L., Klein, M. F., and Michael, W. B. (1971). *Recommendations for curriculum and instructional materials.* Los Angeles: Tyl Press.

o Tyler, R. W. (1949). *Basic principles of curriculum and instruction.* Chicago: The University of Chicago Press.

o Vallance, E. (1983). Curriculum as a field of practice. In F. W. English (Ed.), *Fundamental curriculum decisions.* 1983 ASCD Yearbook (pp. 154–164). Alexandria, VA: Association for Supervision and Curriculum Development.

o ———. (1985). Ways of knowing and curricular conceptions: Implications for program planning. In E. W. Eisner (Ed.), *Learning and teaching the ways of knowing.* 84th Yearbook of the National Society for the Study of Education, Part II (pp. 199–217). Chicago: The University of Chicago Press.

o Walker, D. F. (1971). A naturalistic model for curriculum development. *School Review, 80,* 51–65.

o ———. (1982). Curriculum theory is many things to many people. *Theory in Practice, 21,* 62–65.

o Westbury, I. (1977). Educational policy-making in new contexts: The contribution of curriculum studies. *Curriculum Inquiry, 7,* 3–18.

o ———. (1983). How can curriculum guides guide teaching? *Journal of Curriculum Studies, 15,* 1–45.

o Wise, R. I. (1976). The use of objectives in curriculum planning: A critique of planning by objectives. *Curriculum Theory Network, 5,* 43–47.

12

Normative Inquiry:
Dimensions and Stances

——————— *Louise M. Berman*

Persons living in a democracy live with tensions. Whose values or norms are honored? What norms or values shape groups? What issues surface when the norms of groups and individuals intersect or collide? Within shifting, dynamic settings concepts of justice, decision-making, compassion, equity, and goodness interact, come into conflict, and are frequently modified.

Questions such as the following may be asked: Whose notions of goodness prevail? How is compassion exemplified? What are just behaviors in situations in which justice may not be valued? Living out the basic tenets of democracy in any context is not easy.

In educational institutions, establishing settings where democratic ways of thinking and living flourish may be even more baffling. Democracy involves processes of opening up, uncovering the hidden, uplifting, dealing with oppression. Confounding dilemmas may surface when normative issues inherent in the democratic process become the basis of curriculum development.

Nonetheless, democracy's schools at any level must consider as an ongoing task the delineating, creating, uncovering, and sustaining of viable norms if educational institutions are to prepare persons for life in a democratic system. In terms of the realities of schooling, then, those responsible for the nurturing and educating of students must look at curriculum development in terms of its norms, values, judgments, and decisions.

Educational institutions have long given attention to knowledge, activities, teaching strategies, and evaluation procedures. To cull the norms which are governing the processes of schooling, to be aware of conflicting values, and to create new norms when such seems appropriate appear to be difficult and subtle processes.

The purpose of this chapter, then, is to delineate processes by which educators: (1) develop planning documents in curriculum in which value issues are highlighted, and consistency characterizes the integration of the parts of the curriculum based upon the designated norms and values; and (2) suggest means by which planning documents become reality in terms of a particular class or group of students. In other words, consideration is given to: (1) the identification and creation of norms which might characterize schooling in a democracy and (2) the pre-teaching reflections of the teacher upon the application and negotiation of the values predominant in the classroom with the norms of the potential curriculum including those in planning documents. Although an obvious third step would be the identification of norms and values in the actual teaching situation, such consideration is beyond the scope of this discussion.

The remainder of this chapter deals with seven topics: the need to engage in curriculum planning that gives attention to norms and values; the purpose of normative curriculum development; the kinds of questions which normative curriculum development answers; background of normative curriculum inquiry; definitions of terms; places to look when engaging in normative planning; and practical application.[1]

Need

Educators are most human when they are dealing with the meaning of schooling in all its diversity and in all its possibility. The task of the curriculum developer, whether that person be a teacher, a principal, or someone else charged with curricular responsibilities, is to uncover, create, or sustain norms that account for the individual both as unique and as community member. I believe the heart of the curriculum development process is inquiry into norms, values, judgments, and decisions. What is being suggested is not new, for curriculum developers can hardly do their jobs thoughtfully without giving attention to curriculum purposes.

Still the recent spate of national and state tests, the perceived obligation of schools to respond to various pressure groups, and the increasing blandness of textbooks designed to offend no one (and so to challenge neither) necessitate a reconsideration of the curriculum development process. One way to proceed is to conduct inquiry into forms of normative curriculum expression. In other words, attention is given to curricula that have clear interrelationships among the parts of the curriculum and that are based upon designs which evidence integrity and worthwhileness in ethical orientation.

The Purpose

Curriculum inquiry can take many forms. Inquiry can be conducted into a number of practical curriculum issues including, for example, selec-

tion of content, learning activities or experiences, and evaluative procedures. In this chapter we are proposing inquiry into the norms or values inherent in curriculum planning. Here we are considering curriculum
planning at two levels: (1) the general plan as developed by a school or
school system, or by a curriculum author who establishes a plan, and (2)
the pre-thinking and planning that a teacher does based upon knowledge of
the plan and his/her knowledge of self and the class or group of students for
which the teacher is responsible. The purpose, then, of normative curriculum inquiry is to study curriculum development in terms of the integration
and interrelationship among the parts of the curriculum so that integrity,
consistency, and congruity based on considered values characterize the curriculum. Such inquiry takes place when curriculum developers put together
a plan. It also takes place when teachers search for a match between the plan
and their own settings composed of teachers, learners, content, and milieu.

In a different vein the purpose of normative inquiry can be seen as consciousness raising. Although match, integrity, and fit are important to normative inquiry, more critical reasons have to do with the search for more apt
ways to ascertain and deal with the "good." Elevation of the spirit, tran-
scendence of mundaneness, and stimulation of the imagination are also
purposes. Those interested in normative inquiry are concerned about opening up rather than constricting, synthesis rather than only analysis, and
movement of the field rather than criticism.

Normative inquiry

- evokes new images.
- provides new life and direction to the curriculum field.
- possesses the potential for suggesting new ways to deal with old components of the field or to find new ways to teach the fresh.
- uses metaphor, allusion, and myth to assist people in shifting perspectives
  and dealing with the world in unique ways.
- provides insights on irrelevancies and injustices in curriculum.
- uncovers ethical and moral dilemmas necessitating major curricular revision.
- searches for a fragile balance between the logical and the imaginative.
- breaks old structures and builds new relationships in the forsaking of out-
  worn questions and the creation of more powerful ones.
- allows for the unpredictable, the unexplainable, the possible, and the
  promising.
- assumes a dialectic with the real world and the world yet to be discovered
  and recovered.

Normative curriculum inquiry takes a searching look at the curriculum
field in a spirit of graciousness, gentleness, and wholeness. The purpose is

the creation of newness, but newness ensconced in the tradition of moral inquiry.

Questions Addressed by Normative Curriculum Inquiry

Normative curriculum inquiry addresses questions having to do with the values and norms underlying curriculum and their application to the various components of curriculum. In this chapter Schwab's (1983) common-places (content, teacher, students, and milieu) are useful in thinking about components. Persons might, however, use other components in defining the curriculum.

The questions grow out of the curriculum development process which takes place at two stages: (1) development of the overall plan, and (2) the pre-thinking that takes place prior to teaching in a classroom.

Questions growing out of the first stage include but are not limited to:

1. What are the major norms or values which are central to the curriculum?

2. On what basis are the norms or values judged as adequate?

3. How are the norms and values reflected in the curriculum plan? Is consistency and interrelationship among the parts of the curriculum evident? How is possible conflict among norms or values handled?

A second set of questions arises in the pre-thinking and planning of the teacher in terms of the implementation of the curriculum:

1. What values and norms does the teacher bring which resonate with or conflict with the norms of the stated curriculum?

2. How would the teacher describe the norms and values of the group, individual, or class to be taught in terms of the norms of the stated curriculum? What are the points of commonality and dissonance?

3. What is the meaning of the answers to the above questions for what takes place in the actual teaching situation?

Background of Normative Curriculum Inquiry

Curriculum texts through the years have given attention to the development process. The spelling out of objectives and the relating of such objectives to the selection and organization content, activities, and evaluation procedures have been common ways of deliberating about curriculum. Much curriculum development work conducted within the above framework has used content as the central organizer.

Another body of curriculum literature provides guidance in determining the scope of the factors that must be considered in reality-oriented curriculum development. Such texts focus on the roles and functions of the community and professional persons. Attention to group dynamics, lines of authority, and relationships among the various levels of state and local groups characterize much of this literature (Beane et al. 1986; McNeil 1985; Miller and Seller 1986; Ornstein and Hunkins 1988).

A third group focuses upon the knowledge of teachers. Although variety of perspectives characterize this group of writers, the common element is the assistance to teachers in making visible the bases for their decisions. The worthwhileness of teachers' decisions underlies much of this writing, although the interrelationships between the planned curriculum and teacher decisions may not be of major concern (Wittrock 1986).

Because of current emphasis upon school-based curriculum development, teacher empowerment, and teacher knowledge as integral to what happens in classrooms, it is critical to develop those kinds of curriculum documents which both enhance and delimit what happens in classrooms and which encourage uniqueness within a democratic community.

A number of efforts have been made to engage in what might be called normative curriculum inquiry. For example, in *New Priorities in the Curriculum,* values guiding the curriculum proposal were laid out in terms of a statement on the nature of a process-oriented person (Berman 1968). What followed in terms of the substance and activities of schooling focused on eight processes related to the process-oriented person. Similarly, in *Curriculum: Teaching the What, How, and Why of Living* attention was given to the norms governing the proposed curriculum with a large section of the work devoted to acquiring understanding as to what was happening in the educational setting (Berman and Roderick 1977). Miel and Brogan in *More than Social Studies* (1957) built a case for the schools educating for democracy and interrelated curricular components with their understanding of the meaning of democracy. Other works that illustrate normative curriculum inquiry include Atkinson and Murray (1983), Egan (1978); Foshay (1987), Hohmann et al. (1979), Kreigh and Perko (1983), and Stratemeyer et al. (1957).

Among the challenges in laying out the blueprint is presenting the case so that the curriculum inquirer's result may be "choice worthy" (Gadamer 1981), possess the potential for situating itself in reality, introduce the possibility of developing more meaningful norms or values, and invite participation, a genuine sharing in an event, an attitude of being present.

Although examples can be found of rather clear statements which encourage normative curriculum inquiry, little work exists on the intermediate steps between the development of the planning document whether done by a group or an individual and the reflective experience of the teacher prior to entering the classroom, the stage where the planning document is applied to the local situation.

Before proceeding further, a brief look is given to the meaning of certain terms.

Problems of Definition

Using a language of norms and values as a basis for curriculum inquiry presents problems. First, persons do not ordinarily define themselves in terms of values (Bellah et al. 1985). Individualism, instrumentalism, and context-specific kinds of behaviors are endemic to American life obliterating in many instances commitment to shared values which are necessary in the formation of community. Communities have shared traditions, shared memories, and a desire to connect with others. Bellah writes about communities of memory which have a history and communities of hope which allow persons to connect personal aspirations with the aspirations of a larger whole.

Bellah's analysis of the current status of the American people indicates much greater ambiguity on value issues than a statement published by the Educational Policies Commission in 1951. Its table of contents indicates, "The American People are Agreed on Certain Values: Human Personality— The Basic Value; Moral Responsibility; Institutions as the Servants of Men; Common Consent; Devotion to Truth; Respect for Excellence; Moral Equality; Brotherhood; The Pursuit of Happiness; Spiritual Enrichment" (Educational Policy Commission 1951).

In the absence of clearly shared values, such as the writers of the Educational Policies Committee credited to the American people, one avenue which is possible in arriving at norms or values is careful attention to the meaning of goodness within particular situations. Lightfoot has discussed goodness in terms of making imperfections visible and working on them (Lightfoot 1983: 309). Perhaps such a stance is feasible in dealing with normative inquiry in curriculum.

Normative inquiry in curriculum deals with moral, ethical, and value issues with all their ambiguities. On the other hand, normative inquiry assumes that values implicit in a setting can be teased out, that values can be treated.

An educational system is remiss that ignores normative issues. In community curriculum planning, therefore, sustained attention might be given to the norms and values which are seen to be central to the curriculum. At the reflective stage of the individual teacher, attention might be focused upon the norms and values of the specific context and the process by which the stipulated values of the planning document are negotiated within the classroom setting.

According to Frankena, a normative philosophy of education contains "statements and recommendations of a normative kind about the ends, principles, means, methods, and subject matter of education or statements about the ends that are *desirable* or *good,* the principles that *should* be followed, the means that *ought* to be used" (Frankena 1965: 6). Normative inquiry is difficult, for normative presumes standards; these standards may be discovered, unearthed, or created. They need not be merely regulative or prescriptive; on the other hand, the norms may be enduring ones such as justice or caring. A tension is created between dealing with norms found in the context or situation while developing norms that allow for new understandings, vision, and ethical behavior to emerge.

In brief, normative curriculum inquiry possesses a focus. Values and norms fall out from the focus. Congruency and consistency with the focus and values help determine the substance, milieu, and evaluation procedures in proposed curricula.

Normative Inquiry: The Development Stage

As mentioned earlier, normative inquiry can take place at several stages. This chapter is concerned about the planning stage in terms of an overall vision, whether that vision be developed by an author, by a group of professional persons with a school system or a school building. In other words, normative inquiry is appropriate for the larger community. Indeed, plans developed by the larger community provide certain guidelines for the pre-teaching thinking of the teacher.

The concern at the development stage is to design curricula that possess simultaneously visionary yet potentially situationally oriented elements, generic and yet possibly contextually relevant ideas. The development statement ordinarily accounts for the realities of the educative process, such as the substance of the curriculum, the teaching of the designated content, possible modes of organizing, and plans for evaluating and researching the process. Within the development statement is a set of guidelines for adapting the curricula to a given set of students.

Thus the development stage may be characterized by the following:

1. Normative inquiry is based upon a set of values, norms, or moral statements that are consistent and pervade the various components of the proposal. The values and standards may transcend what is and provide a vision of what might be. On the other hand, normative inquiry is not so utopian in perspective that it cannot be linked in some way with prevailing norms.

2. After an analysis of the ethical or normative issues that seem critical, persons interested in normative curriculum inquiry may seek to develop curricular proposals in which a fit exists between the norms and curricular components. Components ordinarily include substance of the curriculum, aspects of the setting or milieu, the disposition of resources, and evaluative

procedures. For example, if interdependence is valued as a norm, the content, the activities, and the organization of the milieu build upon that norm. Although some solitary events may be planned, a major thrust of the curriculum may be upon engagements in which person-person relationships are highlighted.

3. Normative inquiry deals with conflicts in value orientations which may emerge as the match is sought among the components of the curriculum. Such inquiry also provides guidance for the adaptation of the normative stance to the local situation. Although attention is given to attaining consistency and congruency among the parts of the curriculum, attention is also given to incongruities, questions, and issues for which no easy answers exist.

4. Normative inquiry is designed in such a way that educators in the local situation may take into account the emerging and developing knowledge of students. This point is illustrated later in the chapter.

5. Normative curricular inquiry lends itself to various modes of research. Studies might be descriptive, interpretive, historical, or any combination of research methodologies depending on how the mode of inquiry takes shape.

Normative Inquiry: The Pre-Teaching Stage

Assuming that a proposal is in place and that a teacher is about to embark on teaching, having at her disposal the preestablished proposal, what are some of the issues to which she must give consideration? The researcher in an attempt to find out how a teacher deals with the stated curriculum might investigate with the teacher prior to her teaching such matters as the following:

Intentionality

In the teacher's adaptation of the curriculum, where does the intentionality reside? In the objectives of the pre-determined curriculum? Within the students? Within the teacher? How intentionality is determined is important, for if neither students nor teachers attend to the matter directly, then both teachers and students can be burdened with a lethargic approach to classroom interaction with the human drive of intentionality being ignored.

Intention can be treated directly as when objectives are clearly defined, or intention can be seen as emergent as when students have opportunities within contexts to build upon past learnings and thus let objectives emerge (Eisner 1985: 120 – 122). In such cases researchers may need to plan to videotape the classroom and extract from the tape or a transcription matters of intention. Whose intentions are honored? What is the significance of intention in the curriculum? What are the levels of consciousness of intention? What degree of initiation of intention does the student anticipate? In any event in preplanning, matters relative to intention need to surface for examination.

Freedom

Like intention, researchers may study how teachers plan for freedom. In certain types of curriculum organization, freedom is a major consideration. In other types, developers may not see it as a major concern. How do teachers plan for thinking about the individual within the community? How does one maintain the tension between individual choice and community cohesion?

Values

Even as freedom is a condition for values to flourish, so values are the glue that holds the parts of the puzzle or the realities of the classroom together. Values enable a match between the various parts of the curriculum.

It is beyond the scope of this chapter to consider the various configurations of values which might be taught. Consequently attention is directed toward the derivation of values considered in the classroom. Are they elected from the students? Or are they predetermined and planned for without consideration to the given group of students. In normative curriculum inquiry, ordinarily a value stance underlies the curricular orientation but such values may not be directly taught. However, the stance of the curriculum proposal might be that values are elicited from students. Figure 1 shows possible stances that might be considered as the teacher plans.

Consider the dilemmas posed for the teacher in her preplanning as she looks at each of the quadrants.

Quadrant A. The curriculum teaches a core body of values that students accept. Congruency between the student and the curriculum is evident here. However, the student may not develop the critical skills necessary to deal with value dilemmas or situations in which a fit may not exist between the values of the student and those evident in a situation.

Quadrant B. Here the curriculum is designed to help students deal with value dilemmas; however, the students unquestioningly accept the values they have been taught. Students have not developed critical skills necessary for dealing with value dilemmas (Alschuler 1982). Students may be frustrated by the lack of perceived core values in the curriculum and lack skills to deal with problematic situations. A mismatch exists between the students

Figure 1. Teacher Consideration of Values
STUDENT
Accepts Core Values

CURRICULUM

Curriculum includes core body of values accepted by students. Congruency between student and curriculum.	Curriculum designed to elicit values, but students lack critical criteria to deal with values.
(A)	(B)

Core of Values Taught (C) (D) **Student Values Elicited and Critiqued**

Curriculum includes core body of values. Students concerned about their own values, which may or may not be congruent with core values.	Curriculum designed to elicit values from students who are attuned to dealing with value issues.

Deals With and Examines Own Values

and the curriculum designed for them. The curriculum may need to be adjusted to where the students are, for students may move in gradual steps rather than in big leaps in their moral and ethical development (Knefelkamp et al. 1978; Perry 1970).

Quadrant C. Here students are used to examining and dealing with their own values; however, the curriculum is designed to teach selected core values. Thus, a dysfunction may exist between students and the curriculum.

Quadrant D. The curriculum is designed to help students deal with their own values. The students are attuned to dealing with value positions. Congruence exists between the curriculum and the students undergoing it. The outcomes of Quadrant D may be students able to deal with multiple value perspectives.

Congruency between student and curriculum relative to perspectives on values is possible in Quadrant A, although a dysfunction may occur if the students' core values are different from the core values of the curriculum. In Quadrant D, the possibility of a fit also exists. Here caution needs to be exercised that the curriculum and the students develop critical skills so that a possibility exists for the development of community values as well as individual values.

Significance of the Lived Experience

Related to the concept of values is the issue of the significance of the lived experience. Does the curriculum proposal invite the teacher to take into account the lived experience, and if so, how is such experience handled?

Figure 2 offers some possible ways of thinking about the lived worlds of students and the relationship to the proposed curriculum. Although Figure 2 overly simplifies the considerations relative to the significance of the lived experience, it draws attention to the fact that students are not clean slates. Decisions to deal with or ignore the experiential worlds of students are intentional.

Figure 2. Possible Orientations Toward the Lived Experience of Students

STUDENT

Lived World of Students Significant to Them

Curriculum invites sharing of inner knowledge. Lived world of students significant. Congruency between curriculum and students.	Curriculum imposes "outsiders'" knowledge. Students wish to deal with lived world. Incongruency between expectations of students and demands of curriculum.
(A)	(B)
Lived World of Students Evoked (C)	(D) **Knowledge Imposed— Lived World of Little Significance**
Curriculum designed to evoke lived experience. Students not used to dealing with lived experience. Incongruency between expectations of students and curriculum.	Curriculum deals primarily with experts' knowledge. Students expect to deal with "outsiders'" knowledge. Congruency between expectations of students and curriculum.

CURRICULUM

Students Not Used to Dealing with Own Experiences— Accept "Outsiders' " Knowledge

Quadrant A. Here a congruency exists between the purpose of the curriculum and the lived worlds of the learners. The lived worlds of students are seen as significant to them. Students wish to deal with their own realities, to engage in dialogue. They are interested in constructing their own histories and in sharing their inner knowledge. The curriculum is designed to evoke their ideas and to assist them in negotiating their thinking with outsiders' thinking.

Quadrant B. Here an incongruency exists between the intent of the students and the purposes of the curriculum. Students are used to dealing with their own inner dynamics, with disclosing their own meanings, with raising their own questions. The curriculum, however, is designed to "teach" outsiders' generalizations and principles.

Quadrant C. Incongruency again exists, this time because the curriculum is designed to help students address and act on their own personal knowledge but students are not equipped to do so. Their tendencies, for whatever reasons, are toward the imposition of knowledge.

Quadrant D. Congruency exists here. The curriculum is designed to teach outsiders' knowledge, and students are attuned to dealing with others' knowledge rather than with the dialogical process in which others' knowledge is made personal.

In dealing with the lived worlds of students, we are not dealing with black-and-white issues. Students are more or less used to dealing with the dialogical process in constructing knowledge. Curriculums may be designed on a continuum in terms of dealing with the dialogical, transformative, reconstructive processes.

Practical Application

Attention is now directed toward concepts and questions that might guide the individual interested in developing and/or implementing normative curriculum inquiry. These questions might be asked by the person(s) involved in development, or the questions might be asked by researchers setting out to study and interpret what is happening.

The concepts treated are curricular focus, language, substance, perspectives on students, perspectives on teachers, setting, and evaluation. Each of these concepts is briefly considered. Parallel columns are used to show how the topics interrelate in terms of the development process and the pre-thinking on the part of teachers. The purpose of considering development and pre-thinking in this way is to encourage the development of community while at the same time stimulating teacher and student creativity within that community. The development which takes place in the broader context is referred to as community curriculum development, indicated that the planning is for a larger group than an individual classroom. The reflective thinking and planning that a teacher does in trying to make sense of the community curriculum development, her own ideas and questionings, and her perceptions of the students whom she teaches are called pre-teaching planning.

Focus

Community Curriculum Development	*Pre-teaching Planning*
What appears to be the center or the organizing concept that delineates what will be emphasized in the curriculum?	What meaning does the proposed organizing center have for the teacher?
Is the focus a philosophical stance, a view of persons, a view of society?	What meaning does the stance have for the teacher?
How does the focus play itself out in terms of what is highlighted, included, and excluded from the curriculum?	What does the focus suggest for what will be highlighted, included, or excluded for a particular group of students?
How generative and compelling is the focus in terms of encouraging teacher creativity?	What are the teacher's responses to the focus? Does the focus evoke a creative response?
How enduring is the focus?	Does the focus invite the teacher to deal with enduring concepts?
Does the focus invite attention to norms and values central to democratic living?	What norms and values seem to grow out of focus that have meaning for a particular class?
What conflicting perspectives might be evoked through this focus?	How shall conflicting perspectives be handled with this group of students?

Language

What attention is given to the multiple meanings students bring to language?	How shall the teacher plan for the multiple perspectives on language which her students bring?

Is attention primarily in the structural use of language or on the inner meanings of persons?

To what degree does classroom interaction focus upon meanings of students as opposed to the structural uses of language?

How is the focus played out in language?

What kinds of language and meanings might students bring to the focus?

Substance

What substance or knowledge is recommended to treat the focus?

What is the meaning of any specified knowledge to the teacher?

Is major attention focused on the inner knowledge which students develop or the knowledge found in text?

What is the meaning of the specified knowledge in terms of a particular group of students?

What knowledge is most central to the focus?

Is the knowledge recommended as central appropriate for a given group of students?

How does the knowledge or substance recommended incorporate the values growing out of the focus?

What knowledge or substance seems most appropriate for this class in light of the focus and the values which grow out of it?

What encouragement is given for locally and personally generated knowledge?

How can I generate knowledge with students that helps to clarify the focus?

Does the substance derive from a multiplicity of sources traditions, and substance selected primarily from one tradition?

What can be learned from the various traditions and cultural sources represented in the classroom?

How does the substance represent the norms and values growing out of the focus?

Does the substance enable the dealing with the norms and values growing out of the focus?

What substance is necessary for survival? for a satisfying existence?

What substance is necessary to this group of students for survival? for a satisfying existence?

Students

What values for students grow out of the focus?

How do the values growing out of the focus mesh with the values of the group of students for whom curriculum is being designed?

At what points is opportunity made for student decision-making relative to the curriculum?

Are the decision points for students in the curriculum appropriate for a given group of students?

What assumptions are made about students?

Are the assumptions about students congruent with the given group of students? How will incongruencies be handled?

Teachers

What assumptions are made about the role of the teacher in curriculum planning?

Are the assumptions made about the teachers congruent with the perspective of the teacher designing curriculum for a specific group of students? If not, how are differences handled?

Does the teacher's task in curriculum development and implementation seem congruent with the norms reflected in the curriculum?

Does the teacher see incongruity in the norms in the curriculum?

Setting

Do the norms within the curriculum take into account variations in settings relative to choices of activities, available materials, or persons in setting?

How does the curriculum lend itself to the norms within the specific setting?

What opportunities are given for the creation of norms appropriate to a given setting?

What norms need to be created within the particular setting?

Evaluation

Are the assumptions inherent in the evaluation made explicit?

Do the assumptions about the evaluation process seem relevant to the particular situation?

Do proposed evaluation procedures match with the focus of the curriculum?

Do evaluation procedures exist which are congruent with the focus of the curriculum but are more pertinent to the local situation?

Does the evaluation process invite creative approaches on the part of the local staff?

What evaluation procedures might be created that are in line with the focus but are also pertinent to the local situation?

| How is competence defined? (Short 1984) | How does the teacher's meaning of competence influence how curriculum is developed in the local setting? |
| How is competence linked to the norms integral to the curriculum? | How is competence defined in a situation in which the norms may differ from those in the proposal? |

In conclusion, normative inquiry raises tough questions. Yet, the time has come to deal with the tough problems encountered when teachers, students, and communities are empowered. Normative inquiry enables educational leaders to keep a steadfast eye on norms and values being implemented, studied, created, and changed. This form of inquiry enables one to constantly question the norms guiding our democracy.

Note

1. Certain topics in this chapter have also been treated in Berman (1988).

References

(Symbols preceding entries are explained on page 40)

○ Alschuler, A. S. (Ed.) (1982). *Values concepts and techniques,* Revised Ed. Washington, D.C.: National Education Association.

○ Atkinson, L. D., and Murray, M. E. (1983). *Understanding the nursing process,* 2d Ed. New York: Macmillan.

✓+ Beane, J. A., Toepfer, C. F., Jr., and Alessi, S. J., Jr. (1986). *Curriculum planning and development.* Boston: Allyn & Bacon.

✓ Bellah, R. N., Madsen, R., Sullivan, W. M., Swidler, A., and Tipton, S. M. (1985). *Habits of the heart: Individualism and commitment in American life.* New York: Harper & Row.

○ Berman, L. M. (1968). *New priorities in the curriculum.* Columbus, OH: Charles E. Merrill.

+ ———. (1988). Problematic curriculum development: Normative inquiry in curriculum. *Journal of Curriculum and Supervision, 3,* 271–294.

○ Berman, L. M., and Roderick, J. A. (1977). *Curriculum: Teaching the what, how, and why of living.* Columbus, OH: Charles E. Merrill.

○ Educational Policy Commission (1951). *Moral and spiritual values in the public schools.* Washington, D.C.: National Education Association.

o Egan, K. (1978). Some presuppositions that determine curriculum decisions. *Journal of Curriculum Studies, 10,* 123–133.

+ Eisner, E. W. (1985). *The educational imagination: On the design and evaluation of school programs,* 2d Ed. New York: Macmillan.

o Foshay, A. W. (1987). The curriculum matrix. *Educational Forum, 51,* 341–353.

+ Frankena, W. K. (1965). *Philosophy of education.* New York: Macmillan.

√ Gadamer, H. (1981). *Reason in an age of science.* (Trans. F. G. Lawrence). Cambridge, MA: MIT Press.

o Hohmann, M., Banet, B., and Weikard, D. P. (1979). *Young children in action: A manual for preschool educators.* Ypsilanti, MI: High/Scope Press.

o Knefelkamp, L., Widick, C. A., and Parker, C. A. (Eds.) (1978). *Applying new developmental findings: New directions for student services, No. 4.* San Francisco: Jossey-Bass.

o Kreigh, H. Z., and Perko, J. E. (1983). *Psychiatric and mental health nursing: A commitment to care and concern,* 2d Ed. Reston, VA: Reston.

o Lightfoot, S. L. (1983). *The good high school: Portraits of character and culture.* New York: Basic Books.

√+ McNeil, J. D. (1985). *Curriculum: A comprehensive introduction,* 3rd Ed. Boston: Little, Brown.

o Miel, A., and Brogan, P. (1957). *More than social studies: A view of social learning in the elementary school.* Englewood Cliffs, NJ: Prentice-Hall.

√+ Miller, J. P., and Seller, W. (1986). *Curriculum: Perspectives and practice.* New York: Longman.

√+ Ornstein, A. C., and Hunkins, F. P. (1988). *Curriculum: Foundations, principles, and issues.* Englewood Cliffs, NJ: Prentice-Hall.

√ Perry, W. G., Jr. (1970). *Forms of intellectual and ethical development in the college years: A scheme.* New York: Holt, Rinehart and Winston.

+ Schwab, J. J. (1983). The practical 4: Something for curriculum professors to do. *Curriculum Inquiry, 13,* 239–265.

√ Short, E. C. (Ed.) (1984). *Competence: Inquiries into its meaning and acquisition in educational settings.* Lanham, MD: University Press of America.

o Stratemeyer, F. B., Forkner, H. L., McKim, M. G., and Passow, A. H. (1957). *Developing a curriculum for modern living,* 2d Revised Ed. New York: Bureau of Publications, Teachers College, Columbia University.

+ Wittrock, M. C. (Ed.) (1986). *Handbook of research on teaching,* 3rd Ed. New York: Macmillan.

13

Critical Inquiry:
A Paradigm for Praxis

———— Kenneth A. Sirotnik

When we talk of curriculum inquiry, into what are we inquiring? I share with others such as Goodlad (1979) and Eisner (1985), the notion that curriculum is a very comprehensive body of content and activities that have both implicit and explicit consequences for learners, educators, families, and society. Curriculum includes the purposes and functions of schools and schooling and the ways in which schools and the delivery of education are organized. Curriculum includes not only the content of subject matters, but how knowledge is organized, how teachers teach, how learners learn, and how the whole is evaluated. And curriculum includes the ways in which educational resources—knowledge, time, expertise, money—are distributed.

Taking this broad view of *curriculum* and, consequently, the scope of *curriculum inquiry,* some persistent and, I think, significant questions come to mind: What are public schools for, what *should* they be for, and for whom? Should they serve the expressed wishes of the individual family, the desires of special interest groups within the community, the consensus of opinion district-wide, the views of the state that might be inferred from legislated reform, the aggregate ideology of a nation, and/or the needs of an increasingly interdependent world? How do philosophical, historical, psychological, sociological, political, and economic analyses come together to determine the functions of schooling in our society and the goals of a common curriculum? Should there even be a *common* curriculum? Are there moral and ethical imperatives that derive from the relationship between those who teach and those who are taught? If so, what are the implications for learning, teaching, and the education of educators?

Moving on to related aspects of curriculum like how schools are structured and what goes on in schools in terms of teaching and learning: How are excellence and equity—quality education and equal access to, and receipt of, quality education—simultaneously achieved for all students? (Of course, this question and many to follow beg answers to those raised in the opening paragraph.) When we talk about individual differences in "ability" among students, are we talking about some sort of fixed, immutable construct like tradtional notions of "intelligence," or do we have in mind dynamic concepts like readiness to learn, potential, or, in Scheffler's (1985) terms, the capacity and propensity *to become*. How, then, are individual differences "handled" from an instructional point of view? Are they to be minimized using sorting and stratification processes (like homogeneous grouping and tracking), or are they to be accepted using heterogeneous grouping and a variety of teaching and learning strategies (like individualization, peer tutoring, and cooperative learning)?

And what should be taught and how should it be organized? To what extent are the ways of knowing disciplinary-based and/or interdisciplinary? To what extent should learning, teaching, and teachers become subject specialized at the elementary levels? What virtue is there in teaching and learning subjects placed in one-to-one correspondence with 40 – 55 minute chunks of time at the secondary level? Should a culturally pluralistic society find its primary sources of knowledge in the classics of Western thought, or can more contemporary literature and thinking make up a substantial part of course syllabi? Should knowledge be conceived of primarily as a body of facts or ideas?

Further, how do we evaluate what goes on in schools? What use do teachers make of standardized test score results? What meanings are attached to these scores by teachers, administrators, parents, students, legislators, corporate executives, and others? Are facets of human potential and achievement adequately represented in a bell-shaped curve? In appraising a school program, what are the relative weights to be assigned to assessments of basic skills, verbal communication, written communication, critical thinking (from deductive problem-solving to dialectical discourse), divergent thinking and creativity, and so forth? How are meaningful assessments of this array of learnings conducted and communicated to relevant constituencies? How is the theory and practice of accountability functional and/or dysfunctional in public education at school, district, state and national levels?

This chapter is not about any one of these questions or any of the rest of the iceberg of curricular queries. This sample of questions has been posed, rather, to make a point: Curriculum inquiry is not about trivial issues. It is about important issues, and important issues have at their core, fundamental beliefs, values, and human interests at stake. Ideological content is latent, if not manifest, in virtually every important question concerning schooling, and, therefore, curriculum.

What, then, of *inquiry?* Can we seek answers to important questions such as these by recourse only to epistemologies and methodologies that purport to be value-free? Are there really value-free philosophies and technologies of inquiry in the first place? *Critical* inquiry begins with the answer "No!" and continues with a process of *informed reflection and action guided by explicit, normative considerations*. Moreover, since *critical* inquiry is basically *dialectical* in nature, its methodology can be seen as embodying these same normative considerations.

In the remainder of this chapter, I will try to unpack the concepts squeezed into the preceding paragraph. First, the use of "critical" as an adjective describing inquiry will be clarified as will, necessarily, the notion of "normative considerations." Second, "dialectical" methodology will be discussed as it plays out, or should play out, in competent, human discourse and action. I should warn the reader that others more steeped in the philosophy of critical theory and radical pedagogy may have alternative interpretations and usages of the term "critical inquiry." My particular construction is based upon a body of work attempting to bring some of the concepts of critical theory to the level of critical practice in public schooling, such that educators become consciously and actively involved in their own processes of school improvement and evaluation (Sirotnik 1987, 1989b; Sirotnik and Oakes 1982a).

Making Inquiry Critical

Critical inquiry is at once empirical, explanatory, interpretive, deliberative, reflective, instrumental, and action-oriented in many of the ways that have been described in other chapters. But it is more. To be *critical*, an inquiry must also challenge directly underlying human interests and ideologies. This challenge is based explicitly on *normative* considerations. It is based upon a commitment to *social justice*—to the ideals of justice as *fairness* (Rawls 1971; 1985) and to the simple yet enduring morality that underlies the Golden Rule (and its obverse): "Do unto others as you would have them do unto you" (and "Do *not* do unto others as you would *not* have them do unto you").[1]

This ethical stance is entirely compatible with the intent, if not always the actions, of our constitutional democracy in the United States of America. Moreover, when we, as a nation, pledge "liberty and justice for all," I, and I hope educators in general, take it seriously. It does not mean liberty and justice for some at the expense of liberty and justice for others. It is *not* an ethical stance compatible with racial determinism, hedonism, and nihilism, for example. Most importantly, *it is an ethical stance*. Notwithstanding our curious propensity for embracing the relativity of values, we have, to our ever lasting credit, a governing document, including a bill of *rights*, that enables ethically-based argument rooted in social justice. Since inquiry *about* hu-

man affairs in the hope of *improving* human affairs is inquiry *into* human
affairs, considerations of justice are paramount. The idea of *improvement*
suggests immediately that judgments of goodness are being (and will be)
made. Such inquiry cannot be considered apart from its consequences for
human beings, and it is evaluative by its very nature (Sirotnik, in press). Values, beliefs, and human interests are always at stake.

Yet traditional forms of inquiry, whether of the positivist/post-positivist
or phenomenological persuasions, attempt to position knowers apart from
ideology and human interests. Positivist/post-positivist approaches (experimental and quasi-experimental studies, correlational studies, survey studies, and the like) go even further: they attempt to position knowers apart
from what is to be known, principally through the techniques of operational
definition and measurement. Phenomenological approaches (like ethnography, ethnomethodology, and symbolic interactionism), on the other hand,
eschew attempts to objectify knowledge and rely more on the intersubjectiv-
ity inherent in humans trying to understand affairs that are human.

Other chapters in this book describe in more detail the epistemologies
and methodologies of these and other traditions of inquiry. All of these traditions can produce useful knowledge, but they do not provide a sufficient
epistemology or methodology for *using* knowledge. Only when knowledge is
subjected to a normative critique, wherein underlying ideologies become
manifest, can it come to be both understood and acted upon with clearer
consequences for human beings. Values, beliefs, and human interests, at
best, are only objects *of* study in traditional inquiry paradigms. In a critical
inquiry, they are guideposts *for* study *and* action. In a critical inquiry, knowledge is speculative and heuristic. No matter how carefully generated, knowledge may well be rejected when sifted through normative screens that ask,
not about the size and significance of correlation coefficients, but rather
about fundamental assumptions concerning moral and ethical responsibilities.

And as argued above, considerations of justice provide a normative
framework suited well to the ideals of our democratic system. James March's
discussion of the biases inherent in building knowledge-based models for
social action are insightful:

> Independent of its truth value, a model has justice value. Different mod-
> els suggest different actions, and the attractiveness of the social and
> moral consequences of those actions do not depend entirely on the de-
> gree to which the models are correct. Nor is this problem solved in any
> significant way by producing a more correct model. Since two equally
> correct models may have radically different action implications and rad-
> ically different moral force, we can easily imagine a circumstance in
> which we would be willing to forego some truth in order to achieve some
> justice (March 1972:414).

For example, "Children learn best when sorted into homogeneous 'ability' groups" is a standard part of the conventional wisdom of many practicing educators, and a body of research exists to support this view. "Children learn best in heterogeneous, cooperative learning groups" is an alternative proposition that is enjoying increasing support from the research literature and the practices of a number of educators. When acted upon, these alternative propositions have radically different consequences for teaching and learning, and for teachers and students, illustrating nicely the point being made above by March.

Doing Critical Inquiry

Critical inquiry is dialectical, dialogical, and deliberate. It is not something that happens serendipitously or casually. It has to be worked at with rigor and continuity. By its very nature, it is not something that comes to an end; rather, it is a way of professional life. Indeed, it is what I would argue ought to be the basis of professionalism and the professionalization of educational practice.

Using the word "dialectic" or "dialectical" is not exactly commonplace in ordinary parlance. Yet as unfamiliar as we are with the words, we engage in the processes almost daily as we consider, and reconsider, the various decisions of daily life. To be sure, there is a range of meanings and formality in the definition and use of dialectical methods—from the Socratic dialogues in Plato where arguments are constructed through ordinary conversation using a series of questions and answers, to the more formal Hegelian constructions that pose a thesis, an antithesis, a synthesis (a new thesis), a new antithesis and synthesis, and so on. If we interpret dialectical methodology broadly as a knowledge-*building* process where what is presumably known is continually reknown through questioning, arguing, counter arguing, reflecting, challenging, contradicting, reconciling, modifying, revising, and so forth, then we can acknowledge and celebrate more formally what educators already do—and could do even better—as they use and generate knowledge in the context of practice.

Critical inquiry is also dialogical. To be sure, one can engage in this process by oneself, through a kind of inner, dialectical monologue. However, we are concerned here less with a collection of individual "reflective practitioners" and more with a reflective *collective* of practitioners. Educators, for example, work in complex organizations like schools, school districts, and colleges of education. Inquiry into complex questions and issues like those suggested above is not only an individual affair. Decisions made or not made and interests served or not served transcend any one human being. Critical inquiry as a process for understanding and improving schools and schooling must therefore be dialogical — a process of competent communication between and among communities of educators.

Competent Communication

Communication — moreover, *competent* communication — is the hallmark of a critical inquiry and, therefore, probably the greatest stumbling block in critical inquiry. We (educators, Americans, society in general) do not have a good track record, in my opinion, of communicating well with one another, even at the lowest level of competence — comprehension — let alone the highest level — challenging constructively beliefs, values, and human interests. Let us consider further these and other features that might characterize a more competently communicative setting.

Among the many who have written on the subject, the critical theory of communication developed by Jurgen Habermas is particularly relevant.[2] First, there are *conditions* for competent communication to enable what Habermas would call an "ideal speech situation." In practice, of course, these are conditions to be *approximated* thereby increasing the potential for, in Habermas' words, a "justified consensus" among stakeholders. Four conditions ought to obtain:

1. *Comprehensibility*. Utterances must be understood; misunderstandings must be clarified, exemplified, illuminated, etc., before further competent communication can take place.

2. *Sincerity*. The speaker must be honest and the hearer must trust the intentions of the speaker; both parties must show good faith through their actions.

3. *Fidelity*. All available and mutually recognized pertinent information must support the truth of utterances. Inquiry methods will not be limited to traditional empirical techniques, but will be expanded to include the variety of phenomenological methods and, importantly, the critical evaluation of all information.

4. *Justifiability*. Utterances must be recognized by all parties as not only appropriate or legitimate for the speaker but, more importantly, appropriate in relation to explicit moral and ethical commitments. Critical inquiry is thereby explicitly normative and focuses on underlying values, beliefs, interests, intentions, etc.

Second, these conditions must be facilitated by a process that embodies the essence of social justice, i.e., fairness, in the rules for discourse and dialectical methodology. Toward this end, Habermas argues that all participants must have (and believe they have) equal opportunities to:

1. initiate and/or enter the discourse;

2. refute or call into question the comprehensibility, sincerity, fidelity, and/or justifiability of the utterances by others;

3. express their values, beliefs, attitudes, sentiments, intentions, interests, etc.; and

4. regulate (i.e., command, oppose, permit, forbid, etc.) the discourse.

In a nutshell, competent communication will only occur in an environment characterized by *mutual trust*—trust not only between people, but also trust in the ideas, facts, values, and interests that people share and upon which they act.

With these criteria in mind, I once again note the difficulty of undertaking a critical inquiry. The above conditions — ideals to be approximated, hopefully more than less—make clear the importance of inspired and sustained leadership and facilitation. Space does not permit exploring the existing conditions and circumstances of schooling that interfere with competent communication and the transformations required to make more competent communication possible. Fundamental changes will neccesarily involve redistributing power among stakeholders in educational decision-making, revising the concepts and practices of educational accountability, and reconstructing the insular conditions within which educators work (Clark and Meloy 1989; Sirotnik 1989b).

Substance

But conditions and processes alone do not make a critical inquiry. There has to be something to inquire about. And as the sampler of queries opening this chapter were intended to suggest, we are certainly not without substantive issues in the world of public schooling. The trick here is to pose a project of critical inquiry that builds conditions, process, and substance into a dialectical web of inquiry in action. A number of writers in the tradition of critical theory and inquiry have proposed questions and/or issues to help guide or frame critical discourse.

For example, Berlak and Berlak (1981:22–23) develop a "dilemma language" organized around perennial schooling tensions regarding control relationships between teachers and students, curriculum views, on the nature of knowledge, learners, and learning, and societal issues such as justice, equity, and the distribution of resources. Illustrative dilemmas in the control, curriculum and societal domains are, respectively: teacher vs. child control of time, knowledge as content vs. knowledge as process, and equal allocation of resources vs. differential allocation of resources.

A critical evaluation of knowledge itself can serve as the basis for a critical inquiry into schooling (and curriculum). For example, building on the work of Young (1971), critical educators such as Aronowitz and Giroux (1985:145) and Bates (1980:9) have proposed the following questions: What counts as school knowledge? How is school knowledge organized? What are the underlying codes that structure such knowledge? How is what counts as school knowledge transmitted? How is access to such knowledge determined? What kind of cultural system does school knowledge legitimate? What are the processes of control? Whose interests are served by the production and legitimation of school knowledge? What ideological appeals justify the system?

A Generic Process

The work of Paulo Freire, of course, is seminal for these and other educators who have begun to make the transition from critical theory to critical *practice*.[3] Although this work and the dilemmas and questions above are oriented primarily to developing a critical pedagogy at the classroom level, they are equally relevant (with minor translations) to the organizational levels of schooling as well. In my own work, for example, Freire's concepts of problematization, dialogical communication, and the use of information to provoke consideration of underlying moral, ethical, and political themes have been most influential.

Space does not permit a more detailed analysis of Freire's pedagogy. But as my colleagues and I have worked through these concepts and translated them for use by educators in public schools, we have found that five generic questions are usually sufficient to maintain a dialectical tension between substantive issues, history, old and new knowledge, ideology and human interests, and action.

First, problems have to be identified and understood in their present context. Whatever the issue — student assessment, using time effectively, grouping students for instruction, staff communication, administrator leadership, etc.—participants in a critical inquiry must come to recognize that a problem exists and come to share a common perception of the problem. The generic question is simply *"What are we doing now?"* In order to minimize the common phenomenon of people talking past one another, time is well-spent simply by clarifying what appears to be problematic in schools.

Second, problems do not happen overnight; they have a history as well as a current context. *"How did it come to be this way?"* is the question to frame this part of the inquiry. By viewing problems historically, participants set the stage for a more critical discussion in which social, political and economic features of the issues become evident. In this way, and through the several steps to follow, what appears to be problematic on the surface suggests a deeper core of more fundamental dilemmas. For example: problems in student assessment may reflect deeper concerns about issues of accountability and the purposes of schooling; concerns about using time effectively may be symptomatic of more fundamental questions regarding the nature and organization of knowledge; and difficulties in staff communication and administrator leadership may suggest basic issues around the distribution of power and the professional rights and responsibilities of educators, whether teachers or administrators.

Third, to be, indeed, *critical,* participants must confront the political reality of significant educational issues and recognize and contend with embedded values, beliefs, and human interests. Making inquiry critical has already been discussed in the previous section. In short, the operant question here is *"Whose interests are, and are not, being served by the way things are?"* The dialectic is set in motion by an "up-front," moral commitment to social justice and ethical responsibilities that follow from this commitment — for example, guaranteeing equal access to, and receipt of, educational excellence for *all* children in our democratic society. Such commitment in no way closes off conversation; indeed, it helps to clarify how action oriented inquiry is normative and, given the complexity of significant educational issues, how far from settled are the questions that we face. For example: If we track kids, then why? ... Who benefits? ... Who doesn't? ... Is this practice consistent with what we think public schools should be for? ... Is this practice consistent with what we know about good instructional practices? What about standardized testing ... what for? ... Whose interests are being served? ... What conceptions of human learning potential underlie norm referenced assessment? ... Do these conceptions make educational sense? ...

Fourth, the critique of knowledge requires knowledge to critique. Critical inquiry demands of participants that they inform the inquiry, that they bring knowledge of all types to bear upon the issues under discussion. Knowledge derives from all the methods considered in this book. Knowledge derives not only from the domain we label "education," but from other disciplinary and interdisciplinary sources as well (literature, history, the Arts, business, economics, political science, and so on). Knowledge includes the results of research studies (correlational, experimental, ethnographic, participant-observational, etc.) typically presented in books, journals, and unpublished reports. It also includes the educational innovations in curriculum and instruction and in organizational leadership and development that are typically disseminated by consultants through association-sponsored and in-service workshops. The results of inquiries conducted by local education agencies and the experiential accounts of the participants themselves form part of the knowledge base as well. Moreover, information can be deliberately generated as part of the inquiry process through the use of surveys, interviews, observations (teachers observing one another, for example), and reviews of documents such as curriculum plans, textbooks, and evaluation instruments. The question to keep in mind here is *"What information and knowledge do we have (or need to get) that bear upon the issues?"*

And fifth, critical inquiry must both inform and be informed by action. This, of course, is the idea of *praxis* — the idea of bringing critical knowledge to bear upon practice while at the same time recognizing the contribution of practice to furthering critical knowledge. To be sure, there is not nearly enough dialogue currently among educators in schools to even understand significant problems in their current and historical contexts. But extending the dialogue is not enough, as if, by doing so, the ever-illusive "closure" will somehow be attained. Complex organizations, like districts and schools, are *ambiguous*. Waiting around for "answers" in such places is inconsistent with the very idea of organizational change and school improvement.[4] The notion of deriving answers to complex problems fits well with conventional research paradigms where knowledge is produced one place (e.g., research universities, laboratories or centers) and then exported to other places (e.g., schools). It fits well with thinking about educators as objects to be changed rather than as subjects who are engaged in change.

The principles and procedures of critical inquiry, however, eschew dichotomies between researcher and practitioner, theory and practice, objects and subjects, and the like. Instead, participants in a critical inquiry are themselves knowers; and they must come to know and reknow in the context of their daily work. Notwithstanding the ever-present uncertainty in educational organizations, actions can and must be taken, reviewed, revised, retaken, and reviewed, revised and retaken again and again. The generic questions to be asked at every opportunity are *"is this the way we want things to be?"* and *"What are we going to do about it?"* Critical inquiry never really ends. In essence, it is the process of organizational *renewal* itself.

Critical Inquiry In Action

I know of no educational organizations—schools, districts, colleges of education, for example—where critical inquiry as I have described it is the norm, where professional roles and expectations are built around critical, reflective and collaborative practice, where, in short, critical inquiry is intrinsic to the culture of the organizational workplace. However, I have had enough experiences with groups of educators working at the margins of a critical inquiry to suggest that the paradigm offers realistic guidelines for more authentic communication, decision-making, action-taking, and evaluation by people who are genuinely and actively seeking a more democratic vision of schooling.

Currently, several activities underway in the Puget Sound Educational Consortium are beginning to resemble critical inquiries involving educators from the public schools and school districts and the College of Education at the University of Washington.[5] For example, a study group is in its third year of working through the implications of normative assumptions about educational equity and excellence; issues include reconceptualizing the curriculum, altering structures and processes of leadership, accountability, and change, and expanding and revising methods of evaluation (Sirotnik, 1989a). Another group has formed to consider restructuring several middle schools into innovative and exemplary preservice and inservice educational centers; this group has decided to conduct their inquiry as a dialectic using the five generic questions discussed in the previous section (Gehrke 1989).

Of course, there are many examples of individuals undertaking discrete projects of critical inquiry as a mode of study.[6] These efforts have critiqued many aspects of curriculum and, more generally, schooling: purposes and functions of schools in society; content and texts; pedagogical relationship between teacher and learner; grouping, sorting, and stratification of students; teacher education; clinical supervision; role of technology; leadership and administration; power, control, accountability and evaluation; and more.

Concluding Comment

It is a crucial mistake for educators to believe, and act on the belief, that they are not without a *rhetoric of inquiry* no matter what their ontological, epistemological, and methodological persuasions.[7] By "rhetoric of inquiry," I mean the gestalt created through considerations of how rational human beings generate knowledge, communicate it, and act with it. This gestalt includes our methods of sense-making, our metaphors and other figures of speech, and our ethical, moral and political interests (Nelson 1987). To believe that somehow human inquiry is anti-rhetorical, is to separate knowing and acting in ways that sever the connection between being human and knowing about human being. And if the aim of our inquiries is the betterment of the human condition, then "what is better" had better be intrinsic to the arguments.

In this sense, then, this chapter, like the others in this book, is rhetorical and necessarily so. But it would be another crucial mistake to conclude, therefore, that all is relative—that when it comes to modes of inquiry, each to his/her own, one is just as good as another. What is Good is precisely the question. And regardless of relative conceptions of goodness from Plato to Hitler to Habermas, we are not without a contemporary consensus of values, historically grounded, that rises above the special interests of individuals and groups.[8] Justice, I would argue, is at the core of these values, and, since human inquiry is of consequence to human beings, justice is at the core of our inquiries as well.

Notes

1. In addition to Rawls's work have been other significant inquiries into the nature and implications of social justice. See, for example, Gewirth (1978) and Phillips (1986). Related work specifically in the field of education is also relevant. See, for example, Strike (1982) and Goodlad, Soder, and Sirotnik (1990). It should be noted as well that others have challenged moral frameworks based upon social justice. Although space does not permit a discussion of these critiques, they represent important alternative (but not incompatible) positions. See, in particular, Noddings (1984).

2. What follows is taken from Habermas's (1970a; 1970b; 1979) writings and, in particular, the interpretations of these writings by McCarthy (1973; 1978).

3. Among his many writings, see, in particular, Freire (1973; 1977; 1985). For an application of Freirian pedagogy, see Shor (1987).

4. I am making reference here to a very large body of literature on organizational theory and decision-making, a sample of which includes Benson (1977); March and Olsen (1976); and Weick (1979).

5. The Puget Sound Educational Consortium is a partnership of fifteen equal members that includes fourteen school districts (and their schools) in the greater Puget Sound area and the College of Education, University of Washington. A description of this partnership can be found in Keating and Clark (1988).

6. Just a sample of this body of work that has not already been referenced includes: Anyon (1979); Apple (1979); Apple and Weis (1983); Bredo and Feinberg (1982); Bullough et al. (1984); Beyer (1988); Carr and Kemmis (1986); Cornbleth (1982); Foster (1980); Giroux (1983; 1988); Karabel and Halsey (1977); Oakes (1985); McNeil (1986); Popkewitz (1987); Sirotnik and Oakes (1986b); Smyth (1985); Whitty (1985); and Zeichner (1983).

7. For a provocative discussion of the importance of considering *rhetoric* in any consideration of *inquiry*, see Nelson, Megill, and McCloskey (1987).

8. This concept of commitment in an ever-changing world can be grounded in arguments such as that offered by Rorty (1987). See also Bernstein (1985).

References

(Symbols preceding entries are explained on page 40)

○ Anyon, J. (1979). Ideology and United States history textbooks. *Harvard Educational Review, 49,* 36 1–386.

○+ Apple, M. W. (1979). *Ideology and curriculum*. Boston: Routledge & Kegan Paul.

○ Apple, M. W., and Weir, L. (Eds.) (1983). *Ideology and practice in schooling*. Philadelphia: Temple University Press.

 + Aronowitz, S., and Giroux, H. A. (1985). *Education under siege: The conservative, liberal, and radical debate over schooling*. South Hadley, MA: Bergin & Garvey.

√ Bates, R. J. (1980). Educational administration, the sociology of science, and the management of knowledge. *Educational Administration Quarterly, 16*(2), 1–20.

√ Benson, J. K. (1977). Organizations: A dialectical view. *Administrative Science Quarterly, 22,* 1–21.

○+ Berlack, A., and Berlack, H. (1981). *Dilemmas of schooling: Teaching and social change*. New York: Methuen.

√ Bernstein, R. J. (1985). *Beyond objectivism and relativism: Science, hermeneutics, and praxis*. Philadelphia: University of Pennsylvania Press.

○ Beyer, L. E. (1988). *Knowing and acting: Inquiry, ideology, and educational studies*. Philadelphia: The Falmer Press.

√ Bredo, E., and Feinberg, W. (Ed.) (1982). *Knowledge and values in social and educational research*. Philadelphia: Temple University Press.

○ Bullough, R. V., Jr., Goldstein, S. L., and Holt, L. (1984). *Human interests in the curriculum: Teaching and learning in a technological society*. New York: Teachers College Press.

○+ Carr, W., and Kemmis, S. (1986). *Becoming critical: Education, knowledge, and action research*. Philadelphia: The Falmer Press.

√ Clark, D. L., and Meloy, J. M. (1989). Renouncing bureaucracy: A democratic structure for leadership in schools (pp. 272–294). In T. J. Sergiovanni and J. H. Moore (Eds.), *Schooling for tomorrow: Directing reforms to issues that count*. Boston: Allyn & Bacon.

○ Cornbleth, C. (1982). Reconsidering social studies curriculum. *Theory and Research in Social Education, 13*, 31–45.

+ Eisner, E. W. (1985). *The Educational Imagination: On the Design and Evaluation of School Programs*, 2d Ed. New York: Macmillan.

○ Foster, W. P. (1980). Administration and the crisis of legitimacy: A review of Habermasian thought. *Harvard Educational Review, 50*, 496–505.

+ Freire, P. (1973). *Pedagogy of the oppressed*. New York: Seabury Press.

+ ———. (1977). *Education for critical consciousness*. New York: Seabury Press.

+ ———. (1985). *The politics of education: Culture, power, and liberation*. South Hadley, MA: Bergin & Garvey.

○ Gehrke, N. (January 1989). Personal communication. University of Washington.

√ Gewirth, A. (1978). *Reason and Morality*. Chicago: The University of Chicago Press.

+ Giroux, H. A. (1983). *Theory and resistance in education: A pedagogy for the opposition*. South Hadley, MA: Bergin & Garvey.

○ ———. (1988). *Schooling and the struggle for public life: Critical pedagogy in the modern age*. Minneapolis: University of Minnesota Press.

+ Goodlad, J. T., and Associates (1979). *Curriculum inquiry: The study of curriculum practice*. New York: McGraw-Hill.

√ Goodlad, J. I., Soder, R., and Sirotnik, K. A. (Eds.) (1990). *The moral dimension of teaching*. San Francisco: Jossey-Bass.

√ Habermas, J. (1970a). On systematically distorted communication. *Inquiry, 13*, 205–218.

√ ———. (1970b). Towards a theory of communicative competence. *Inquiry, 13*, 360–375.

√ ———. (1979). *Communication and the evolution of society*. Boston: Beacon Press.

√ Karabel, J., and Halsey, A. H. (Eds.) (1977). *Power and ideology in education*. New York: Oxford University Press.

o   Keating, P. J., and Clark, R. W. (1988). Accent on leadership: The Puget Sound Educational Consortium. In K. A. Sirotnik and J. I. Goodlad (Eds.), *School-university partnerships in action: Concepts, cases, and concerns* (pp. 148–166). New York: Teachers College Press.

√   March, J. G. (1972). Model bias in social action. *Review of Educational Research, 42,* 413–429.

√   March, J. G., and Olsen, J. P. (1976). *Ambiguity and choice in organizations.* Oslo, Norway: Universitetsforlaget.

√   McCarthy, T. (1973). A theory of communicative competence. *Philosophy of Social Science, 3,* 135–156.

√   ———. (1978). *The critical theory of Jurgen Habermas.* Cambridge, MA: MIT Press.

o   McNeil, L. M. (1986). *Contradictions of control: School structure and school knowledge.* Boston: Routledge & Kegan Paul.

√   Nelson, J. S. (1987). Seven rhetorics of inquiry: A provocation. In J. S. Nelson, A. Megill, and D. N. McCloskey (Eds.), *The rhetoric of the human sciences: Language and argument in scholarship and public affairs* (pp. 407–433). Madison, WI: University of Wisconsin Press.

√   Nelson, J. S., Megill, A., and McCloskey, D. N. (Eds.) (1987). *The rhetoric of the human sciences: Language and argument in scholarship and public affairs.* Madison, WI: University of Wisconsin Press.

√   Noddings, N. (1984). *Caring: A feminine approach to ethics and moral education.* Berkeley: University of California Press.

o   Oakes, J. (1985). *Keeping track: How schools structure inequality.* New Haven, CT: Yale University Press.

√   Phillips, D. L. (1986). *Toward a Just Social Order.* Princeton: Princeton University Press.

o   Popkewitz, T. S. (Ed.) (1987). *The formation of school subjects: The struggle for creating an American institution.* Philadelphia: The Falmer Press.

√   Rawls, J. (1971). *A theory of justice.* Cambridge, MA: Harvard University Press.

√   ———. (1985). Justice as fairness: Political not metaphysical. *Philosophy and Public Affairs, 14*(3), 223–251.

√   Rorty, R. (1987). Science as solidarity. In J. S. Nelson, A. Megill, and D. N. McCloskey (Eds.), *The rhetoric of the human sciences: Language and argument in scholarship and public affairs* (pp. 38–52). Madison, WI: University of Wisconsin Press.

√ Scheffler, I. (1985). *Of human potential: An essay in the philosophy of education*. Boston: Routledge & Kegan Paul.

+ Shor, I. (1987). *Critical teaching and everyday life*. Chicago: The University of Chicago Press.

+ Shor, I., and Freire, P. (1987). *A pedagogy for liberation: Dialogues on transforming education*. South Hadley, MA: Bergin & Garvey.

○ Sirotnik, K. A. (1987). Evaluation in the ecology of schooling: The process of school renewal. In J. I. Goodlad (Ed.), *The ecology of school renewal*. 86th Yearbook of the Society for the Study of Education, Part I (pp. 41–62). Chicago: The University of Chicago Press.

○ ———. (1989a). Equal access to quality in public schooling: Issues in the assessment of equity and excellence. In J. I. Goodlad and P. J. Keating (Eds.), *Access to knowledge: An agenda for the nation's schools* (pp. 159–185). New York: The College Board.

○ ———. (1989b). The school as the center of change. In T. J. Sergiovanni and J. H. Moore (Eds.), *Schooling for tomorrow: Directing reforms to issues that count* (pp. 89–113). Boston: Allyn & Bacon.

○ ———. (Ed.) (In press). *Evaluation and social justice: Issues in public education*. New directions in program evaluation. San Francisco: Jossey-Bass.

+ Sirotnik, K. A., and Oakes, J. (1986a). Critical inquiry for school renewal: Liberating theory and practice. In K. A. Sirotnik and J. Oakes (Eds.), *Critical perspectives on the organization and improvement of schooling* (pp. 3–93). Boston: Kluwer-Nijhoff.

○ Sirotnik, K. A., and Oakes, J. (Eds.) (1986b). *Critical perspectives on the organization and improvement of schooling*. Boston: Kluwer-Nijhoff.

○ Smyth, W. J. (1985). Developing a critical practice of clinical supervision. *Journal of Curriculum Studies, 17,* 1–15.

√ Strike, K. A. (1982). *Educational policy and the just society*. Urbana, IL: University of Illinois Press.

√ Weick, K. E. (1979). *The social psychology of organizing*. New York: Random House.

○ Whitty, G. (1985). *Sociology and school knowledge: Curriculum theory, research, and politics*. New York: Methuen.

√ Young, M. F. D. (Ed.) (1971). *Knowledge and control*. London: Collier-Macmillan.

○ Zeichner, K. M. (1983). Alternative paradigms of teacher education. *Journal of Teacher Education, 34*(3), 3–9.

14

Evaluative Inquiry:
Situational Assessment

——————Jean A. King

    Curriculum evaluation is as old as education itself. It began when a teacher wondered for the first time what was happening to his students as a result of instruction and intuitively looked for information that would help him decide what to change the next time around. Since program evaluation's heyday in the post-Sputnik era, educators have developed and expanded such intuitive notions, but the basic need for collecting data with which to make thoughtful decisions about curriculum has not changed. The focus of this chapter is the evaluation of curriculum practice, an idea sufficiently broad to encompass a variety of evaluative activities that have as a common concern the examination of a curriculum *in situ* to assess what is happening and to decide what—if anything—to do about it.

    What characterizes curriculum evaluation? It can best be described in terms of its multiple purposes, strategic approaches, and applications for real world teaching and learning. First, it is a concept that allows for multiple definitions of *curriculum* and that therefore offers up a broad range of curricular activities for evaluation. As Johnson (1977) points out, the evaluation of curriculum practice potentially includes the assessment of numerous items, including both processes (goal setting, objective writing, instructional planning, etc.) and their products (goals, objectives, instructional plans, etc.). In practical terms, this assessment can target something as specific as the development and use of a single curricular document (e.g., a local or state curriculum guide or a published curriculum like *Man, a Course of Study*); as general as an assessment of an overall approach to teaching (e.g., cooperative learning or progressive education); as personal as an individual's response to years of traditional schooling or as typical as standard practice at a given site ("We've always done it this way at Beauregard").

    Second, because of its encompassing nature, the evaluation of curriculum practice also allows for multiple philosophical and methodological approaches, ranging from the strictly quantitative to the strictly qualitative, each with differing assumptions about knowledge and reality. The traditional empiricist can assign students randomly to curricular "treatments," collect data throughout the instructional process, then evaluate outcomes at the end of instruction to "prove" or "disprove" predetermined hypotheses. Railing against this quantitative approach, a curriculum ethnographer might instead move into a school for a time to record the living curriculum as seen through the eyes of those who experience it — its student participants. Or, using a phenomenological approach, a curriculum reconceptualist might reflect evaluatively on her own experience in schools. A critical inquirer might dialogue with practitioners over the presence or absence of certain normative ideals in curriculum practice, and engage in action necessary to remove contradictions. All of these approaches are delineated elsewhere in this book and may be drawn upon as appropriate. Whatever their philosophical orientation, those who evaluate curriculum practice have available to them an array of methodological options, including document analysis, formal observation, interviews, and questionnaires.

Third, and most important, the evaluation of curriculum practice must relate directly to an actual curriculum, i.e., a curriculum that teachers and students have used, are using, or will use either at schools or other sites. Distinct from forms of curriculum research that generate material for *theoretical* discussion, curriculum evaluation provides information for people who must make *practical* decisions based on the information available to them. Evaluation information is information that someone, somewhere will *use.* Possible studies differ on several variables, creating a range of options: they can be formative or summative; formal or informal; small-scale or multinational; quantitative or qualitative; past, present, or future-oriented. They may be demanded as signals of implementation by outside funding agencies (King and Pechman 1984), or they may be generated from a burning question in a practitioner's mind. But, whatever its nature, an evaluation makes information available to people in hopes of illuminating practice. It is this decision orientation that distinguishes the evaluation of curriculum practice from other forms of curriculum inquiry. Even if results gather dust, unused in a file drawer, their potential for affecting decisions remains.

Traditional approaches. A brief look at the history of curriculum evaluation suggests that the field has changed dramatically in recent years, moving beyond two traditional approaches: rational goal attainment; and the curriculum horserace. In the first approach — stated explicitly in the Tyler Rationale — evaluative information is collected for predetermined curriculum goals and objectives to assess which of these have been achieved successfully. Such information is clearly helpful for gauging the extent to which a curriculum did what it set out to do, and the approach is rational in that there is a logical matching of intent with actual outcomes. However, problems may stem from a failure to document the implementation process (Tyler 1949) or from ignoring critical outcomes, whether good and bad, that were unintended (Scriven 1967; Patton 1986). In a certain sense, this approach is "quasi-evaluation" in that it focuses on a limited set of questions rather than an overall determination of the curriculum's value (Stufflebeam and Welch 1986).

The other traditional approach — the curriculum horserace — is a second form of quasi-evaluation that thrived during the 1960s when major federal curriculum projects created new curricula to compete with traditional courses. The notion of a horserace correctly suggests two curricula running neck and neck toward the homestretch in June when students take a test to determine which curriculum is "better." The limitation of this approach is implicit in the question, "Better for what?" Not surprisingly, research suggests that students learn best what they have been taught (Walker and Schaffarzick 1974), so that rather than focusing on the race itself, the more important evaluation questions focus on issues like what the racetrack looks like and where the horses end up. Labelling one curriculum "good" and another "bad" after an uncertain competition in the classroom provides little information on which to base decisions.

The rational goal attainment model and the curriculum horserace have their place in the repertoire of a curriculum evaluator. What limits these approaches, however, is a tendency to focus on selected observable end-products at the expense of measures of the ongoing implementation process and other outcomes. In recent years the notion of implementation evaluation has evolved to include two distinct activities: first, the documentation of what actually takes place during implementation (process); and second, the outcomes of these curricular activities (products). To evaluate curriculum practice, both should be included where appropriate.

Guidelines for Evaluation

How, then, is an evaluation study framed? The following guidelines provide rules of thumb for conducting evaluations, but, as such, are purposefully general. More specific information about evaluation methods can be found in the citations at the end of this chapter.

Deciding a purpose. The first step in conducting a curriculum evaluation is to decide the overall purpose or goal for the evaluation. Those who will participate should agree on the reasons for conducting such a study so that energies may be focused on what will assist the evaluation process, rather than on activities unrelated to the overall goal. Given the often limited resources available for evaluation, such agreement may be essential to the timely and effective completion of the project. The following examples suggest the diversity of possible evaluation goals:

- Concerned that too few individuals control the formal curriculum, a superintendent initiates a study of the curriculum development process in her district;
- the end of a grant period is near, and the funding agency's project officer wants evidence that an expensive program funded across the country has made a difference;
- a school system has rewritten its ninth grade mathematics curriculum and after two years the school board wants to see if students are learning and achieving more;
- a group of teachers in an elementary school have worked on integrating computers into their instruction and are now interested in knowing what has happened in their classrooms as a result; or
- a fifteen-year veteran of the classroom, sensing impending burnout, wants to explore his personal curriculum practice.

In each case, a general awareness of what the evaluation will be about should enable those involved to use time and other resources wisely in order to proceed rationally. In the case of a new curriculum, the earlier in the development process that the evaluation goal is determined, the better.

Asking the relevant questions. The next guideline involves framing specific questions that the evaluation study will answer. While it is important to generate questions from everyone with a stake in the evaluation results, an attempt to answer too many questions can diffuse the evaluation and end in what has become all too typical in evaluation studies: vague results that are of limited value. Any overall goal can generate questions too numerous for a single study to answer, and it is important to emphasize only those questions that may make a difference in future actions.

Several factors may help to determine these questions. First, because of its real world orientation, the evaluation of curriculum practice requires questions that have practical answers, rather than questions of a theoretical nature. As Patton (1986) notes, evaluation questions must be empirical, i.e., they must require information that someone in the field can provide. Second, questions should be categorized as process- or product-oriented and a check made that if an outcome will be studied, the process leading to it can be documented. Similarly, if the focus of the study will be on a process, a check to examine potential outcomes is in order. Third, it usually makes sense to choose questions whose answers may result in change. Evaluation outcomes that suggest potential modifications in curriculum practice can have a positive effect; those that make clear why the glass must remain half empty may be of limited value.

Making the human connection. Next, the questions selected must be meaningful to someone. Research on evaluation use has suggested consistently that people use results that are important to them (King 1988), so in identifying questions for a study, it makes sense to target those that make a difference to the individuals who can follow through on recommended actions. The procedural guideline implicit here is to locate individuals in the evaluation setting who care enough to become involved in the evaluation process and then encourage and assist them in guiding the evaluation. The person who commissions the evaluation may or may not be willing to play that role, but in any event must be an important audience.

For example, consider the case previously cited of the superintendent whose overall evaluation goal is to learn about the curriculum development process in her district. Numerous questions immediately come to mind, indeed, more questions than one study could easily answer, for example:

- What is the formal curriculum in the system?
- Who in the system is charged with the curriculum development process that creates this formal curriculum?
- What is the process currently used to generate curriculum documents? Who is involved? Who controls final decisions about content?
- What voice do classroom teachers have in the development process?
- How is the locally developed curriculum related to state curriculum guides?
- What philosophical orientation does the curriculum have? Is this orientation consistent across subjects and years?
- How is the formal curriculum presented to teachers? Do they use it or store it in their desk drawers?
- How is the political process played out in curriculum development in the district, i.e., how do school board members, parents, funding agencies, special interest gruops, etc. exert influence?
- How has the curriculum development process evolved over the years? It is different in different subject areas? Has it been affected by major national trends?
- Is this district's process similar to those of neighboring districts? Is it better or worse?
- How does the curriculum development process in this system relate to the current state of curriculum theory?

The list could go on, but obviously many questions exist from which an evaluator could select specific questions for study.

How would these be determined? All require information from the field in their answers, and the focus is clearly on a process. Remembering that the superintendent has requested this study, the evaluator would be wise to visit with her and discuss both what she wants to know and how much she might be willing to alter in the curriculum development process depending on the outcomes of the evaluation. If the curriculum development process itself were open to change, the superintendent might want information suggesting how to broaden the involvement of teachers or how to move toward building-level curriculum work apart from centralized control. Knowing this, the evaluator could then meet with significant others involved in the curriculum development process to explore their questions, interests, and willingness to change. Based on these conversations, appropriate and useful questions could evolve so that the evaluative effort might eventually have an effect.

One might predict that curriculum supervisors, textbook representatives, and state department personnel in this district would have rather different interests. From even this relatively straightforward example, then, the weighty role of organizational politics in the evaluation process should be self-evident (House 1973). The evaluation process may bring information to light that has the potential to disrupt the status quo and, as such, can have a destabilizing effect even when everyone is operating in the best of faith.

Developing an appropriate methodology. Once the specific questions for the evaluation are identified, the evaluator's role becomes one of selecting appropriate and feasible methods for collecting information to answer them. Many practitioners are intimidated by curriculum evaluation because they have a minimal background in research design and statistical methods. Lacking a white lab coat and unable to discuss ANOVA, factor analysis, and multiple regression in casual conversation, they fear that what their intuition tells them is evaluation will not pass in the scientific world. Such a mindset, however, may well be counterproductive to the improvement of practice. The experimental approach of the quantitative study is only one of many evaluation approaches, and, depending on the curricular context, it may be neither appropriate nor correct. Rather than assuming one research orientation is always *the* approach to take, the choice of methodology should stem directly from the type of issues under examination. In this sense, evaluation is instrumental; it is curriculum inquiry conducted using any appropriate methods as a means to an end—to providing useful information to someone about an important question.

For example, in the case of our superintendent, an examination of the curriculum development process would almost necessarily require case studies of several curriculum projects in the system, including on-site observations of the deliberation process, interviews with curriculum specialists, principals, and teachers, analysis of the documents produced, and so on. Creating a traditional, tightly controlled experimental design to answer the superintendent's questions would radically alter the existing process, rendering the experiment's outcomes meaningless. In this case, such a study would be counterproductive and fail to answer the superintendent's central questions.

Regardless of an individual's commitment to certain methodology, then, the evaluation of curriculum practice requires *appropriate* methods chosen to answer specific questions. In any event, evaluators should be certain to examine, as needed, both the process and the product of the implementation in question and to analyze the data so that the people most interested in the results will have as much information as possible as they consider the outcomes.

Maintaining the flow of information. Another guideline relates to reporting. In an individual project or small-scale evaluation, everyone will know on a day-to-day basis how the evaluation is proceeding and who is generating what information. This model is appropriate regardless of the size of the project. Throughout the process of any evaluation, people involved should continually receive information about it. In some sense, an ideal evaluation is an ongoing collaborative effort between someone with a question in a particular setting and an evaluator who will help him answer it. As the evaluation unfolds, the evaluator routinely informs interested parties of what is happening.

In practice, this exchange may not happen if people lack time or interest in such collaboration. Whatever the level of involvement, however, evaluation use does not wait until the production of a formal report. It is a dynamic process, beginning as soon as any information is available to those whose questions are under study. This suggests the merit of using multiple report formats in addition to the more traditional final report: informal conversations; memos; progress reports; formal presentations at meetings; multimedia reporting; and executive summaries. While the danger of misuse stemming from inadequate information is clear, the natural tendency of people to act on information as it is received makes it incumbent on the evaluator to provide the best information he or she has as it becomes available.

In the example of the superintendent, the evaluator should plan to meet with her on a monthly basis to discuss where the project stands and the current information available about the curriculum development process in the system. Memos or short status reports to those directly involved might help to alleviate anxieties about the final outcome of the study. In addition, the evaluator might make himself available for phone calls or interviews from any concerned parties.

Judging the judging. The practical, context-specific nature of curriculum evaluation suggests one final guideline. The final step of any evaluation should be its own evaluation, an assessment of how well the study answered the questions raised, how well it met the needs of those individuals who asked the questions, and the extent to which it made appropriate suggestions for change. If it fails in any of these areas—if it does not meet the overall need or answer the specific questions; if those who were interested are not satisfied with the process; or if individuals are left not knowing how to proceed — then the evaluator needs to look carefully at what went wrong. The political nature of the evaluation process can produce lose-lose situations where failure is predetermined; the question is how to learn from those experiences to produce more positive experiences in future projects.

Evaluation Examples

As should be clear by now, curriculum practitioners can address a wide range of questions in differing ways through evaluation studies. As a matter of fact, under the right circumstances *any* curriculum or curricular practice —past, present, or future — can be the subject of a meaningful evaluation. Three specific examples from very different contexts help to make this point. The first example comes from a classroom setting where Ms. MacCallum, an experienced teacher, teaches two advanced sections of seventh grade English in a highly traditional school.

> Despite the faculty's belief in the merits of 19th century school grammar, Ms. MacCallum was motivated by a summer linguistics course to write an experimental curriculum based on the concepts of structural and generative grammar. Knowing that the students were more or less randomly assigned to her first or second period class, Ms. MacCallum used the new curriculum with one class and her traditional approach with the other. During the course of the year, she routinely monitored the difficulties students had with specific grammatical ideas. In June the scores of the experimental class on the grammar section of the standard departmental final surprised her. She checked to see if the topics that students struggled most with were those where they missed the most test items. (They were.) However, even though the class had spent significantly less time on drill and practice, overall their tests suggested they understood the concepts better than their second period peers. When other teachers heard about the test scores, they were interested in learning more about MacCallum's linguistics approach, and the department chair asked her to present the curriculum in an August inservice session.

While it is true that graduate students in a research seminar could fault Ms. MacCallum's evaluation design on numerous counts, the fact remains that she had an overall goal, specific questions, and a real interest in the outcomes. She used the evaluation process to monitor an important instructional change and to see if the change warranted continuation.

Such evaluation can also work at the system level for a major curriculum reform. Consider an evaluation to determine the continuation or modification of a million-dollar curriculum improvement program (King and Pechman 1982).

> Well aware of a dramatic drop in achievement as students attended high school, a large urban system inaugurated a major curricular innovation that used special objectives, targeted instruction, computerized testing, and continuous monitoring of progress. The superintendent brought in a nationally known scholar as kick-off speaker and consultant, and the school board made a substantial, longterm financial commitment to the project. Teachers were systematically "in-serviced" for two weeks each at a central staff development facility, many becoming enthusiastic converts to an approach they sensed could work with difficult students and potential dropouts. Others were less enthusiastic, particularly when the computerized scoring became cumbersome and slow. After two years and a change of administration, many individuals increasingly questioned the commitment of so much money to the program, and the new superintendent commissioned a fullscale evaluation to determine what parts of it — if any — were working. An evaluation team designed a formal study that would, among other things, compare students whose teachers were highly committed to the program with those whose teachers had not received any training. Based on an interim evaluation report six months later, the assistant superintendent responsible for curriculum eliminated the program *per se* while maintaining the components that seemed to work. He also reassigned the staff development specialists and launched his own curricular initiative.

The evaluation study conducted for this million-dollar program was far more systematic than that of Ms. MacCallum, as well it should have been. But, even in this larger arena, the notion of an overall purpose, specific questions, and someone who cares about the results is the same.

The third example, a case study sponsored by a national organization (Bresler and Stake 1989), demonstrates an even broader evaluation context.

> A detailed case study, the evaluation report documents actual activities in art and music in several elementary classrooms, suggesting the dirth of meaningful instruction in these subjects. Using a qualitative approach, the evaluator spent a substantial amount of time with teachers and students in their classes, recording the number of minutes devoted to the arts, examples of standardized cut-outs, colored dittos, and, only occasionally, an allowed flight of fancy. Interviews with teachers revealed their discomfort and lack of preparation for instruction in the arts, as well as their sense that these subjects differed dramatically from the "basics" in importance, content, and instructional methods. In one instance, the evaluation process itself—the mere fact that the evaluator had interviewed her—inspired a teacher to include examples of poetry and art in her teaching.

In this case, the notion of curriculum is written large; the evaluation uses the
few observed classrooms to suggest an answer to a general question about
instruction in the arts. The audience for this evaluation is a broad one, going
well beyond the individual teachers and even their school system. The implications for action apply at a national level to everyone concerned about
the future of the arts in the United States.

Other examples of the kinds of problems for which curriculum evaluation is appropriate surely exist, but these three suggest the range of possibilities — from a single teacher, to a large urban system, to a national community of interested individuals; from a comparison of a traditional with an
innovative curriculum, to an assessment of the implementation of a major
curriculum change project, to the documentation of the status quo in a specific subject area; from an intuitive approach, to a formal quantitative study,
to a formal qualitative study. Each study contained implications for future
practice and the expectation that someone would act on them. The evaluation of curriculum practice, then, can engender thoughtful decisions about
the curriculum, however defined, and it is this ability, finally, that establishes
evaluation's importance among the forms of curriculum inquiry.

References

(Symbols preceding entries are explained on page 40)

+ Ariav, S. T. (1986). Curriculum analysis and curriculum evaluation: A contrast.
      Studies in Educational Evaluation, 12, 139–147.

+ Barham, I., and Prosser, M. (1985). Review and redesign: Beyond course eval-
      uation. *Higher education, 14,* 297–306.

√ Beer, V., and Bloomer, A. C. (1986). Levels of evaluation. *Educational Evalua-
      tion and Policy Analysis, 8,* 335–345.

○ Bresler, L. E., and Stake, R. E. (1989). Discrepancies in teacher belief in class-
      room practice in the arts: Institutional values and the pressure toward ac-
      ademics. Paper presented at the Annual Meeting of the American Educa-
      tional Research Association, San Francisco.

○ Byrd-Bredbenner, C., O'Connell, L. H., Shannon, B., and Eddy, J. M. (1984). A
      nutrition curriculum for health education: Its effect on students' knowl-
      edge, attitude, and behavior. *Journal of School Health, 54,* 385–388.

○ Carter, K. R. (1986). A cognitive-outcomes study to evaluate curriculum for the
      gifted. *Journal for the Education of the Gifted, 10,* 41–55.

√ Cooley, W., and Bickel, W. (1986). *Decision-oriented educational research.* Boston: Kluwer-Nijhoff.

+ Dreyfus, A. (1986). Step by step formative curriculum evaluation in science education. *Studies in educational evaluation, 12,* 139–147.

○ Eggen, T. J. H. M., Pelgun, W. J., and Plomp, T. (1987). The implemented and attained mathematics curriculum: Some results of the Second International Mathematics Study in the Netherlands. *Studies in Educational Evaluation, 13,* 119–135.

√ Fetterman, D. (Ed.) (1988). *Qualitative approaches to evaluation in education.* New York: Praeger.

+ Fraser, B. J., with Houghton, K. (1982). *Bibliography of curriculum evaluation literature.* Tel Aviv: Israel Curriculum Centre, Ministry of Education and Culture.

√ Herman, J. L. (Ed.) (1987). *Program evaluation kit,* 2nd Ed. Newbury Park, CA: Sage.

+ Hill, J. (1985). Curriculum evaluation: Practical approaches to dealing with the pitfalls. *NASSP Bulletin, 69* (478), 1–6.

+ House, E. R. (Ed.) (1973). *School evaluation: Politics and process.* Berkeley: CA: McCutchan.

√ ———. (Ed.) (1986). *New directions in educational evaluation.* Philadelphia: The Falmer Press.

○ Howitz, E. K. (1985). Formative evaluation of an experimental foreign-language class. *Canadian Modern Language Review, 42,* 83–90.

+ Johnson, M., Jr. (1977). *Intentionality in education.* Albany, NY: Center for Curriculum Research and Services.

√ Joint Committee for Standards on Educational Evaluation (1981) *Standards for evaluation of educational programs, projects, and materials.* New York: McGraw-Hill.

√ Joint Committee for Standards on Educational Evaluation (1988). *The personnel evaluation standards.* Newbury Park, CA: Sage.

√ Kidder, L. H., and Fine, M. (1987). Qualitative and quantitative methods: When stories converge. In M. M. Mark and R. L. Shotland (Eds.), *Multiple methods in program evaluation.* New Directions for Program Evaluation, No. 35 (pp. 57–85). San Francisco: Jossey-Bass.

+ King, J. A. (1988). Research on evaluation use and its implications for evaluation research practice. *Studies in Educational Evaluation, 14,* 285–299.

○+ King, J. A., and Pechman, E. M. (1982). *The process of evaluation use in local school settings,* Final Report of NIE Grant 81–0900. New Orleans, LA: Orleans Parish School Board. ED 233 037.

270   *Jean A. King*

+ ————. (1984). Pinning a wave to the shore: Conceptualizing evaluation use in school systems. *Educational Evaluation and Policy, 6*, 241–251.

+ Lewy, A. (1977). *Handbook of curriculum evaluation.* New York: Longman.

+ McCormick, R., and James, M. (1983). *Curriculum evaluation in schools.* London: Croom Helm.

+ Patton, M. Q. (1986). *Utilization-focused evaluation,* 2nd Ed. Beverly Hills, CA: Sage.

+ Scriven, M. (1967). The methodology of evaluation. In R. W. Tyler, R. M. Gagne, and M. Scriven, *Perspectives on curriculum evaluation* (pp. 39–83). Chicago: Rand McNally.

√ Stake, R. E. (1986). An evolutionary view of educational improvement. In E. R. House (Ed.), *New directions in educational evaluation* (pp. 89–102). Philadelphia: The Falmer Press.

+ Stufflebeam, D. L., and Welch, W. L. (1986). Review of research on program evaluation in United States school districts. *Educational Administration Quarterly, 22,* 150–170.

○ Sugranes, M. R., and Neal, J. A. (1983). Evaluation of a self-paced bibliographic instruction course. *College and Research Libraries, 44,* 444–457.

+ Talmage, H. (1985). Evaluating the curriculum: What, why, and how. *NASSP Bulletin, 69* (481), 1–8.

+ Tamir, P. (Ed.) (1984). *The role of evaluators in curriculum development.* London: Croom Helm.

+ Tyler, R. W. (1949). *Basic principles of curriculum and instruction.* Chicago: The University of Chicago Press.

√ ————. (1986). Changing concepts of educational evaluation. *International Journal of Educational Research, 10,* 1–113.

○+ Walker, D. F., and Schaffarzick, J. (1974). Comparing curricula. *Review of Educational Research, 44,* 83–111.

○ Wesdorp, H. (1984). The evaluation of traditional grammar curriculum in the Netherlands. *Studies in Educational Evaluation, 10,* 283–297.

○ Wierstra, R. (1984). A study on classroom environment and on cognitive and effective outcomes of the PLON-Curriculum. *Studies in Educational Evaluation, 10,* 273–282.

+ Willis, G. (1988). The human problems and possibilities of curriculum evaluation. In L. E. Beyer and M. W. Apple (Eds.), *The curriculum: problems, politics, and possibilities.* Albany, NY: State University of New York Press.

√ Worthen, B. R., and Sanders, J. R. (1987). *Educational evaluation: Alternative approaches and practical guidelines.* New York: Longman.

15

Integrative Inquiry:
The Research Synthesis

——————— *Colin J. Marsh*

Knowledge is an essential ingredient of all decision-making. In planning educative actions and in deciding what the curriculum shall be for a particular set of students, knowledge of many kinds is called for. Some of this knowledge may be about the way the curriculum is presently being carried out and about its impact (evaluative knowledge). Some of this knowledge may be about how the ethical ideals espoused for the curriculum are embedded in various organizational, curricular, and instructional practices (critical knowledge). Some may pertain to the array of norms and values that are intended to guide and permeate curricular choices on a number of practical dimensions (normative knowledge). Some may pertain to the ways that the elements of the curriculum are conceptualized and related in an integral structure such that it may be understood and enacted in the real world (theoretical knowledge). Some of the other kinds of knowledge that may be needed in educational decision-making are philosophical, historical, scientific, ethnographic, narrative, aesthetic, phenomenological, or hermeneutic in character. These may be derived through the fundamental processes of inquiry associated with each of these disciplines. Both interdisciplinary and disciplinary knowledge are needed to inform deliberations about educational goals and about appropriate courses of action to be taken in reaching these goals.

Prior to and during the activities of curriculum deliberation and/or enactment, the requisite knowledge must be sought out and brought together in a form useful for reaching the decisions that need to be made. Here is the place for a form of inquiry that yields integrative knowledge, that is, the type of knowledge that brings together what is known from various, perhaps disparate studies, that may be relevant to the particular needs of practice. Through integrative inquiry, ongoing or previously done studies are screened and synthesized for the kinds of knowledge that will help address those problems which are at hand and about which planning or action decisions must be made.

Knowledge that already exists in individual studies and reports is not usually in an appropriate form for direct use in decision-making. This knowledge needs to be related to knowledge generated in other relevant studies, and the whole body of knowledge needs to be assessed, reorganized, and interpreted in terms dictated by the existing need for knowledge. In other words, it must be transformed into synthesized knowledge if it is to be useful and appropriate for dealing with practical educational decisions. Thus, integrative inquiry is one of the most important and complex forms of practical inquiry that can be undertaken. Its value lies in matching knowledge to need and in the skillfulness with which the process of synthesis is accomplished.

Synthesis refers, according to the dictionary, to a process whereby some set of parts is combined or integrated into a whole (Strike and Posner 1983b: 346). It is more than just assembling sets of information. The emphasis is upon integrating diverse material into a particular conceptual framework so that some new perspectives or relationships are introduced.

Ward provides four criteria for determining the adequacy of knowledge generated through the process of synthesizing research. It must:

- address significant variables and interactions (inclusiveness),
- use terms which avoid equivocal meanings (unequivocalness),
- provide guidance for practice (practicality),
- represent a consensus so as to be acceptable and relevant to researchers and practitioners (consensus) Ward 1983b: 32–33).

From these definitions and goals of synthesis it is evident that both intellectual and communication skills are needed by researchers in doing integrative inquiry: intellectual skills to sort, explore, group, and synthesize knowledge and communication skills so that practitioners and researchers can reach a consensus on what information is needed, how it is to be presented, and in what format. Experts on knowledge synthesis and transfer, such as Rich and Goldhar, emphasize the client/audience focus of all integrative inquiry efforts. They state that the process of knowledge collation, analysis, and transformation should include:

- needs sensing,
- the collation of knowledge on the basis of these needs,
- the actual transfer of knowledge to the intended audience (Roberts 1983: 428).

Integrative knowledge can be presented in a number of different formats depending upon the needs of the intended audience. For example, a five-page document, a published article or book, a report, resource packet, or brochure, a slide-tape presentation, a chart, or research bulletins can all be used to convey the results of integrative inquiry (Roberts 1983: 431–432).

Several specific approaches to synthesizing and integrating research knowledge have gained favor in the literature. Among these are meta-analysis (Glass 1977; Glass et al. 1981), reiterative conferencing (Glaser 1978), and the comprehensive research review/summary (Cooper 1984; Light and Pillemer 1984). These authorities and others prescribe various steps in their approaches — some in more detail than others. Roberts has identified the following elements common to most integrative inquiry approaches:

- recognition of a system of motivation, of intelligence and creativity, or cognitive structure, of perceived relevance of information inputs and uses of information output;
- formulation of a framework for the purpose of organizing knowledge;
- analysis and repackaging of information which will be readily usable by the clientele — summarizing, condensing, and making judgments about what is of value and what is not (Roberts 1983: 430).

The need for integrative inquiry is not difficult to recognize. Individual research reports make knowledge claims which need to be examined, first of all, to see whether internally they are validly arrived at and are cogently argued. If they survive this kind of critical review, they need also to be examined in relation to the results of other similar or related studies. They may support or contradict the results of other work. The user of research usually wants to know what all the relevant studies add up to, what the current state of knowledge on the subject is, and what it means for the user's practical activities. While complete knowledge may be lacking in many instances, a user of research knowledge needs to know what is available and how much confidence can be placed in it. Thus, the researcher who is able to conduct integrative inquiry performs an important function in bringing together individual studies, assessing their merits, relating them in to some relevant structured and understandable whole, and communicating the substance and meaning of this body of research to an individual or group of clients needing this particular knowledge (Short 1985).

Many users of research knowledge are not in a position to do this for themselves. They may not know how and where to locate the relevant studies. Even if they can do this, they may not be competent enough to evaluate and synthesize them appropriately into a usable form that will serve their particular purposes. Thus, those who are especially trained in conducting integrative inquiry are called upon to provide needed syntheses on behalf of those who need this kind of knowledge. In some cases, because of the large numbers of research studies in a particular domain, the process of adequately integrating this work may require extended exploration of the research literature and months or years of analysis and synthesis simply to prepare a single report. This certainly is the case with articles presented in research reviews, handbooks, and encyclopedias published at five, ten, or twenty year intervals. (Jackson forthcoming; Jenkins 1985; Short, 1982; Tanner 1982; Walker 1976). The same is true to a lesser extent for reports commissioned by a school faculty, for a research team, or in preparation for writing a journal article (Feldhusen 1989; Fraser 1989; Short 1983). Integrative inquiry cannot be done well in haste in any circumstance.

Integrative studies may be of three different types. The simplest type of integrative inquiry involves taking a set of research studies, all of which address exactly the same research question, and reporting how the combined inquiries answer that particular question. For example, Fullan and Pomfret (1977: 375 – 382), within a larger review of research on implementation of curriculum and instruction, analyze and integrate several studies on the relationship between participation in the innovative process and implementation outcomes. Where there is confirmation of the same results among several studies, that is noted; where there is disparity, that is also noted.

A second type of integrative study takes all studies related to a specific topic, reviews them one-by-one, organizes them in ways that distinguish and contrast work on different but related questions, and analyzes or draws implications about what is known and what still needs to be studied. The larger review by Fullan and Pomfret (1977) is an example of this type of integrative inquiry. Fullan's (1982) systematic review of the causes and processes of implementation and their relationship to the outcomes of the change process is another example of an exhaustive review of fifteen factors that were studied in dozens of related studies. Marsh (1986) did an analysis of thirty studies of curriculum implementation in Australia 1973 – 1983. More elaborate analysis and discussion of the limits and uses of this body of literature are possible and necessary with this second type of integrative inquiry. Such reviews become archival resources to which interested persons may turn as these syntheses may be relevant to their needs.

A third type of integrative study is more focused on a specific need for particular knowledge by a specific user or group of users. For example, Marsh (1988) developed a summary of research in Australia related to the use of the Concern-Based Adoptation Model (CBAM) and the instruments associated with the model (Hall and Hord 1987) in teachers' implementation of innovative curriculum materials. This focus on a relatively limited topic of interest to persons using or contemplating using the CBAM for a similar purpose does not allow readers of this research synthesis to know about all the related factors affecting implementation (as does Fullan's review) nor about a single limited question (as the Fullan and Pomfret example does), but it does allow them to gain knowledge specific to their need to make decisions as to whether they will use the CBAM instruments in their own situations. This synthesis of the research is succinct and to the point (thirteen pages). Simple charts convey much information, and careful organization, analysis, and discussion make the report easy to follow even for those not familiar with the individual research studies being summarized. The Hall and Hord volume (1987) is an example of an integrative summary developed for those interested in facilitating change in schools. It synthesizes and organizes all that is known about the CBAM in a completely user-friendly mode. One is scarcely aware that this book is an integrative research summary, but so it is.

A researcher attempting to integrate a series of individual studies into any one of these three types of integrative syntheses, confronts a number of technical and epistemological problems. Among these, Strike and Posner (1983a) note the problem of incommensurability among concepts, conceptual frameworks, theories, and disciplines that sometimes originate under different sets of assumptions. Rich (1983) notes the importance (and difficulty) of understanding the problem-solving processes employed by various users of synthesized knowledge such that an appropriate framework for interpretation of integrated knowledge can be provided to users. Strike and Posner (1983a) and Ward (1983b) note the problem of criteria and standards for preparing and evaluating "good" syntheses.

The art of doing integrative inquiry has only recently received concerted methodological attention (Cooper 1986; Hauser-Cram 1983; Hedges 1986; Hedges and Olkin; Hunter et al. 1982; Jackson 1980; Rosenthal 1984; Slavin 1986; Ward and Reed 1983; Wolf 1986). One of the primary issues confronting the integrative researcher is the matter of how to interpret a series of studies where the "preponderance of evidence" is not clear-cut; some highly technical procedures have been developed to cope with this issue (Ladas 1980; Glass et al. 1981; Hedges 1986).

It is my personal observation that many researchers doing integrative inquiry on various curriculum topics have had limited success in meeting the four criteria (mentioned earlier) set forth by Ward (1983b) and in confronting the technical and epistemological problems involved in carrying out this form of inquiry. There are some notable exceptions (Walker 1976; Weiss 1980). However, in synthesizing empirical/evaluative studies comparing various U.S. curriculum projects between 1957 and 1972, Walker and Schaffarzick (1974) found it difficult to produce a comprehensive synthesis because the types of evaluative instruments and research designs were often dissimilar in the different studies. Cornbleth (1980) concluded from examining five multistate surveys of U.S. social studies curriculum projects that they had had some, but not overwhelming, impact upon teachers and schools, but because of the nature of the indices used to assess impact, such findings warranted very cautious interpretation in any attempt to synthesize the surveys. Steadman, Parsons, and Salter (1980) attempted to synthesize survey findings about 144 curriculum projects in the United Kingdom, but found that evidence reported was limited to "levels of awareness" and "familiarity and use," thus making a summary of findings of rather limited use. The same sort of limited-data problem hampered Nicoll's (1982) attempt to synthesize knowledge about curriculum dissemination procedures across eighty-two Schools Council projects in the United Kingdom.

In synthesizing empirical/historical studies, Kliebard (1986) and Goodson (1983) appear to have addressed significant variables in their attempts to be inclusive, but it is not clear that they have addressed particular needs of practitioners for historical knowledge in determining their selection, organization, and interpretation of relevant studies. In pulling together work of various curriculum theorists, Pinar (1978) employed an innovative conceptual scheme by which to distinguish and interpret their work. Reid (1981) took issue with Pinar's scheme, claiming it used concepts that are too transient and not enduring enough for them to be useful over long periods of time and with diverse theorists. Reid then proposed his own scheme for distinguishing and interpreting curriculum theorists' work.

These kinds of difficulties encountered by integrative researches do not minimize the value of their work or the need for such practice-oriented syntheses. They only demonstrate the tenuousness with which integrative knowledge claims often have to be made and the careful interpretation that necessarily must accompany them if they are not to be taken with too much certainty. In fact, one of the valuable contributions that integrative inquiry makes is to point up the gaps in available knowledge which researchers still need to fill.

Given the current state-of-the-art concerning how integrative inquiry should be conducted, only rather general guidelines can be offered with any degree of confidence. Details of procedure will vary with the type of synthesis attempted. Hurd (1983) has written the only published guidelines for doing synthesis in curriculum inquiry; it is geared specifically to developing a conceptual framework and synthesis for curriculum in biology and may not suffice for other kinds of integrative purposes. Hurd's phases in the synthesis process are indicative, however, of the more general statements to be found on the literature on doing integrative inquiry. He identifies eight interactive phases:

- identification of primary information sources,
- review and conceptual analysis of critical elements,

- identification of informational or conceptual clusters based on patterns derived from the previous analysis,
- synthesis of information in each conceptual cluster,
- continuing reanalysis/synthesis leading to validation of the clusters and refinement of summary statements,
- arrangement of statements in categories appropriate for intended use, and
- interpretation of the synthesis (Hurd 1983: 654–655).

Ward (1983b) has presented a tentative model that includes four phases:

- development of a framework,
- development of detail and implications,
- review of literature and interaction with experts, and
- building a consensus for the synthesis among expert reviewers.

Perhaps the most thorough general treatment of what is involved in doing integrative inquiry has been written by Roberts (1983). Her six primary activities in the synthesis/interpretation process will be stated here and used as rubrics for mentioning some procedural sources relevant to each of her activities and for commenting upon them.

1. *Identify need/request, conduct preliminary search, clarify request.*

This type of activity sets the purpose, focus, and constraints for a particular study involving knowledge synthesis. Roberts found from surveys of both users and providers of syntheses that needs assessments and direct client requests were the most common forms of establishing and clarifying the focus of projected syntheses. She also obtained data on the most frequently used clarification questions researchers asked of clients as well as those facilitative behaviors they used with clients.

Cooper (1984: 19–36) discusses selected procedures in choosing how to formulate a particular problem or empirical hypothesis for guiding an integrative review. Light and Pillemer (1984: 12–49) have a chapter on organizing a review strategy that includes how to formulate a precise focal question and deal with related issues. Roberts (1983: 428) speaks of the need for consensus between knowledge producers and knowledge users on the nature of the knowledge synthesis needed. Ward (1983a: 557, 561–562) reports general planning activities used in a synthesis project leading to clarify the task.

Curriculum problems are frequently complex and involve inputs from various sources. The delineation of the problem typically involves an analysis of classroom sites, the behaviors of students and teachers in formal and informal settings. Users of synthesis reports are typically administrators and senior officials, but also classroom teachers. Their special needs have to be taken into consideration in devising the scope and direction of a synthesis study. Producers of a synthesis need to have the requisite skills of analysis in collecting together relevant data, but they also must have well developed interpersonal skills and be able to communicate effectively with the clients/ users of the synthesis.

2. *Conduct the search for and retrieval of studies.*

Even with the availability of computerized data bases (Batty 1983), the search for relevant sources can pose numerous problems: references that descriptors won't detect, work not yet shared through publications or formal indexes, forgetting to check certain information services and key researchers.

3. *Selecting, screening, and organizing studies.*

Judgments with respect to what studies are relevant to a particular client's knowledge requirements are not easy to make. Here experience in both the client's world and the researcher's world is essential for the integrative researcher. Criteria for selecting and classifying studies have to be established. Scanning them to check whether they meet the criteria or pertain to the established topics takes great expertise and cannot be left to a computer or to a novice. Of course, the central task in this whole process is reviewing and analyzing the contents of these studies. Technical assistance is given by Cooper (1984; 1986) on methods of locating and screening studies, by Cooper (1984), Glass (1983), and Light and Pillmer (1984) on organizing, analyzing, and evaluating studies, and by Glass (1983) and Roberts (1983) on the process of recording the results of analysis.

4. *Determining the conceptual framework and fitting it to the information from the analysis.*

Both the form and the constructs used to convey integrative knowledge are crucial to its use. Dervin (1983) and Holzner (1983) give help on how to interpret user constructs and subsequently design a matching framework around which knowledge can be synthesized.

The conceptual framework which is developed must reflect the parameters and duration of the synthesis study as agreed upon by the producers and users. As the information collected increases in amount, the likely categories for the framework will begin to emerge. Some categories may develop which will require the seeking out of additional data. Judgments have to be made about the desirability of obtaining additional data in terms of the importance of a particular category versus the time constraints of completing the synthesis on schedule.

The synthesis process requires various skills by the producers. They need to analyze the data systematically to produce appropriate categories. In addition, they need to use their creative/intuitive skills to conceptualize groupings which are innovatory — "to isolate unique harmonies that can logically be inferred" (Hurd 1983: 660). Ideally, early attempts at synthesizing and the production of new categories should be communicated to users so that an ongoing, formative dialogue can be maintained to sharpen and refine the conceptual framework.

5. *Developing the synthesis and interpretation into a material product.*

A report of the results of integrative inquiry can take many forms, as noted earlier. The overriding concern with the product of synthetic inquiry must be its utility to users. The format of the synthesis, especially the type of language used, the graphics included, and the range and type of quantitative data incorporated are all crucial considerations. Users can make decisions more effectively if a synthesis presents comparative data so that they can relate present practices with recommendations for change. Ultimately, both integration and interpretation must be included in the material product reporting the synthesis. Information recited but unintegrated and uninterpreted in light of a focal client need is next to useless to a reader of the report. Both Cooper (1984) and Landesman and Reed (1983) have chapters on how to write an integrative report for public presentation.

6. *Delivering the results of synthesis.*

Stand-alone documents and media presentations have their limitations. Knowledge-building with users of synthesized knowledge is an ongoing process, and in-person delivery, interpretation, and trouble-shooting are preferable to delivery by print or other media by themselves. In fact, continued interaction with users may prompt revising and updating integrative knowledge on a continuing basis. Fortunate is the client/user who has an information analyst or knowledge synthesizer on a continuous basis.

In summary, Ward makes four statements about the potential and the limitations of the current state-of-the-art of doing integrative inquiry. He says:

- Only very limited efforts in synthesis can be successful because of inherent incompatibility among competing forms of knowledge.
- With appropriate processes, synthesis can be done in spite of incommensurability.
- A given synthesis cannot be useful to a broad audience because of the specificity of user situations and needs.
- With appropriate knowledge structures, a synthesis document can be useful (Ward and Reed 1983: 13–14).

Concluding Comments

The curriculum field already depends upon integrative inquiry to a very large extent. Integrative inquiry involving empirical/historical/interdisciplinary approaches demonstrates moderate levels of success in bringing together important concepts from diverse sources.

Not all integrative inquiry studies have been successful, nor are they undertaken at a high level of sophistication. In fact, it is far from clear which criteria might be used in distinguishing quality integrative studies. It might be argued that quality synthesis must clarify and resolve previously ill-defined issues; that they result in a progressive problem shift; and that they satisfy standards of good theories such as consistency, parsimony, and elegance (Strike and Posner 1983: 357). However, these are assertions which might be hotly disputed. This form of inquiry is not yet at a level of sophistication where issues of criteria have been resolved. All that can be stated with some certainty is that integrative inquiry is likely to be a major tool for curriculum researchers to develop and refine over ensuing decades.

References

(Symbols preceding entries are explained on page 40)

√ Batty, D. (1983). Information science and techniques as an approach to synthesis and interpretation. In S. A. Ward and L. J. Reed (Eds.), *Knowledge structure and use: Implications for synthesis and interpretation* (pp. 315–341). Philadelphia: Temple University Press.

√ Cooper, H. M. (1982). Scientific guidelines for conducting integrative research reviews. *Review of Educational Research 52*, 291–302.

√ ——. (1984). *The integrative research review: A systematic approach*. Beverley Hills, CA: Sage.

√ ——. (1986). Literature-searching strategies of integrative research reviews. *Knowledge: Creation, Diffusion, Utilization, 8*. 372–383.

○ Cornbleth, C. (1980). An examination of the impact of social studies curriculum project materials. *Journal of Social Studies Research, 4*, 28–33.

√ Dervin, B. (1983). Information as a user construct. In S. A. Ward and L. J. Reed (Eds.), *Knowledge structure and use: Implications for synthesis and interpretation*. Philadelphia: Temple University Press.

○ Feldhusen, J. F. (1989). Synthesis of research on gifted youth. *Educational Leadership, 46*(6), 6–11.

○ Fraser, B. J. (1989). Twenty years of classroom climate work: Progress and prospect. *Journal of Curriculum Studies, 21*, 307–327.

o Fullan, M. (1982). Causes/processes of implementation and continuance. In *The meaning of educational change* (pp. 54–80). New York: Teachers College Press.

o Fullan, M., and Pomfret, A. (1977). Research on curriculum and instruction implementation. *Review of Educational Research, 47,* 335–397.

√ Glaser, E. M. (1978). Development of a knowledge base that represents current state-of-the-art in a given field. Paper prepared for the National Institute of Education, Washington, D.C.

√ Glass, G. V. (1977). Integrating findings: The meta-analysis of research. *Review of Research in Education, 5,* 351–379.

√ Glass, G. V., McGaw, B., and Smith, M. L. (1981). *Meta-analysis in social research.* Beverley Hills, CA: Sage.

o Goodson, I. (1983). *School subjects and curriculum change.* London: Croom Helm.

o Hall, G. E., and Hord, S. M. (1987). *Change in schools: Facilitating the process.* Albany, NY: State University of New York Press.

√ Hauser-Cram, P. (1983). Some cautions in synthesizing research studies. *Educational Evaluation and Policy Analysis, 51,* 155–162.

√ Hedges, L. V. (1986). Issues in meta-analysis. *Review of Research in Education, 13,* 353–398.

√ Hedges, L. V., and Olkin, I. (1986). Meta analysis: A review and a new view. *Educational Researcher, 15*(8), 14–21.

√ Holzner, B. (1983). Social processes and knowledge synthesis. In S. A. Ward and L. J. Reed (Eds.), *Knowledge structure and use: Implications for synthesis and interpretation.* Philadelphia: Temple University Press.

√ Hunter, J. E., Schmidt, F. L. and Jackson, G. B. (1982). *Meta-analysis: Cumulating research findings across studies.* Beverly Hills, CA: Sage.

+ Hurd, P. De H. (1983). Synthesis processes in curriculum development. In S. A. Ward and L. J. Reed (Eds.), *Knowledge structure and use: Implication for synthesis and interpretation* (pp. 645–670). Philadelphia: Temple University Press.

√ Jackson, G. B. (1980). Methods for integrative reviews. *Review of Educational Research, 50,* 438–460.

o Jackson, P. W. (forthcoming). *Handbook of research on curriculum.* New York: Macmillan.

o Jenkins, D. (1985). Curriculum research. In T. Husen and T. N. Postlethwaite (Eds.). *The international encyclopedia of education* (pp. 1257–1263). London: Pergamon.

√ Klein, S. S. (1989). Research and practice: Implications for knowledge synthesis in education. *Knowledge: Creation, Diffusion, Utilization, 11,* 58–78.

○ Kliebard, H. M. (1986). *The struggle for the American curriculum: 1890–1958.*
   Boston: Routledge & Kegan Paul.

√ Ladas, H. (1980). Summarizing research: A case study. *Review of Educational
   Research, 50,* 597–624.

√ Landesman, J., and Reed, L. J. (1983). How to write a synthesis document for
   educational practitioners. In S. A. Ward and L. J. Reed (Eds.), *Knowledge
   structure and use: Implications for synthesis and interpretation* (pp. 575–
   607). Philadelphia: Temple University Press.

√ Light, R. J., and Pillemer, D. B. (1984). *Summing up: The science of reviewing
   research.* Cambridge, MA: Harvard University Press.

○ Marsh, C. J. (1986). Curriculum implementation: An analysis of Australian research studies—1973–1983. *Curriculum Perspectives, 6*(1), 11–21.

○ ———. (1988). Curriculum implementation: An analysis of the use of the
   Concerns-Based Adoption Model (CBAM) in Australia, 1981–87. *Curriculum Perspectives, 8*(2), 30–42.

○ Nicoll, J. (1982). *Patterns of project dissemination.* London: Schools Council.

○ Pinar, W. F. (1978). Notes on the curriculum field. *Educational Researcher,
   7*(8), 5–12.

○ Reid, W. A. (1981). The deliberative approach to the study of the curriculum
   and its relation to critical pluralism. In M. Lawn and L. Barton (Eds.), *Rethinking curriculum studies.* London: Croom Helm.

√ Rich, R. F. (1983). Knowledge synthesis and problem-solving. In S. A. Ward
   and L. J. Reed (Eds.), *Knowledge structure and use: Implications for synthesis and interpretation* (pp. 287–312). Philadelphia: Temple University
   Press.

√ Roberts, J. M. E. (1983). Quick turnaround synthesis/interpretation for prac-
   titioners. In S. A. Ward and L. J. Reed (Eds.). *Knowledge structure and use:
   Implications for synthesis and interpretation* (pp. 425–485). Philadelphia:
   Temple University Press.

√ Rosenthal, R. (1984). *Meta-analytic procedures for social science research.*
   Beverly Hills, CA: Sage.

○ Short, E. C. (1982). Curriculum development and organization. In H. E. Mitzel
   (Ed.), *Encyclopedia of educational research,* 5th ed., Vol. 1 (pp. 405–412).
   New York: The Free Press of Macmillan.

○ ———. (1983). The forms and uses of alternative curriculum development
   strategies. *Curriculum Inquiry, 13,* 43–64.

+ ———. (1985). Organizing what we know about curriculum. *Curriculum Inquiry, 15,* 237–243.

√ Slavin, R. E. (1986). Best-evidence synthesis: An alternative to meta-analysis and traditional reviews. *Educational Researcher, 15* 5–11.

○ Steadman, S. D., Parsons, C., and Salter, B. G. (1980). *Impact and take-up project: An enquiry into the impact and take-up of Schools' Council funded activities.* London: Schools Council.

+ Strike, K. A., and Posner, G. (1983a). Epistemological problems in organizing social science knowledge for application. In S. A. Ward and L. J. Reed (Eds.), *Knowledge structure and use: Implications for synthesis and interpretation* (pp. 47–83). Philadelphia: Temple University Press.

√ Strike, K. A., and Posner, G. (1983b). Types of synthesis and their criteria. In S. A. Ward and L. J. Reed (Eds.), *Knowing structure and use: Implications for synthesis and interpretation* (pp. 343–362). Philadelphia: Temple University Press.

○ Tanner, D. (1982). Curriculum history. In H. E. Mitzel (Ed.), *Encyclopedia of educational research,* 5th ed., Vol. 1 (pp. 412–420). New York: The Free Press of Macmillan.

○ Walker, D. F. (1976). Toward comprehension of curricular realities. *Review of Research in Education, 4,* 268–308.

○ Walker, D. F., and Schaffarzich, J. (1974). Comparing curricular. *Review of Educational Research, 44,* 83–111.

√ Ward, S. A. (1983a). Documentation of a consensus building approach to knowledge synthesis. In S. A. Ward and L. J. Reed (Eds.). *Knowledge structure and use: Implications for synthesis and interpretation* (pp. 551–574). Philadelphia: Temple University Press.

√ ———. (1983b). Knowledge structure and knowledge synthesis. In S. A. Ward and L. J. Reed (Eds.). *Knowledge structure and use: Implications for synthesis and interpretation* (pp. 19–44). Philadelphia: Temple University Press.

√ Ward, S. A., and Reed, L. J. (1983). (Eds.). *Knowledge structure and use: Implications for synthesis and interpretation.* Philadelphia: Temple University Press.

○ Weiss, J. (1980). Assessing nonconventional outcomes of schooling. *Review of Research in Education, 8,* 405–454.

√ Wolf, F. M. (1986). *Meta-analysis: Quantitative methods for research synthesis.* Beverly Hills, CA: Sage.

16

Deliberative Inquiry:
The Arts of Planning

―――――― *Ilene Harris*

This chapter serves a special role in this book, because deliberative inquiry is a policy and action-oriented form of inquiry which links the interrelated tasks of doing practical curriculum activity with conducting formal curriculum inquiry, through a systematic structure of deliberation about curriculum decisions. Deliberative inquiry is a formal process of inquiry about curriculum policy, program development, and other curriculum activity in specific situations of practice, which is informed by asking and answering subsidiary questions, through the multiple forms of inquiry characterized in the other chapters, as well as forms of inquiry outside of the field of curriculum studies.

Generally it is possible, and indeed viewed as desirable, to distinguish the interrelated tasks of doing practical curriculum activity and conducting formal curriculum inquiry. Conducting formal curriculum inquiry is typically characterized by identifying particular curriculum questions amenable to inquiry, for which definite answers or knowledge can be obtained, and addressing those questions through appropriate forms of rigorous, disciplined intellectual processes. It is generally acknowledged that theorists interpretively represent a complex reality by generalization from a plethora of particulars and by selection of areas and principles of inquiry; the consequence is that any theory presents only a partial view of reality (Schwab 1978/1971).

Doing practical curriculum activity is typically characterized by making choices in conceiving, expressing, justifying, and taking action toward desired states of affairs, in specific situations viewed as integral wholes. The judgments, decisions, and commitments relate to policy questions about what should be taught, to whom, and under what guidelines of instruction; ideally they are based on thoughtful examination of alternatives, in the context of values and knowledge. Therefore, practical curriculum activity should be, and often is, informed by the results of formal curriculum inquiry, namely research. Since practical curriculum activity is embedded in specific situations which are integral wholes, and given the fact that any one theory is inherently limited, curriculum judgment and action must be informed by multiple research approaches, sources of knowledge, theories, and principles.

In deliberate inquiry, the tasks of doing practical curriculum activity and conducting formal curriculum inquiry become virtually indistinguishable. Deliberative inquiry is embedded within an important alternative paradigm for the field of curriculum, formulated by Schwab in three landmark papers (1978/1969, 1978/1971, 1978/1973). Schwab argued that curriculum problems are fundamentally "practical problems" about choice and action, which should be addressed by methods appropriate to issues of choice and action, namely "deliberation." His arguments have stimulated a body of exegesis, analysis, extension, and application. This literature has yielded the characterization of a genre of curriculum inquiry — deliberative inquiry — recommended for use in doing practical curriculum activity, to coordinate deliberation about defensible action in particular situations. Deliberative inquiry is a rigorous, disciplined, intellectual process, akin to other types of formal curriculum inquiry; moreover, it provides a framework for applying to actual curriculum problems the results of other forms of inquiry through various "eclectic" arts which are used to apply multiple disciplinary and theoretical perspectives in addressing curriculum problems.

In this chapter, we will first characterize deliberative inquiry, provide an overview of its lineage and its applications in doing curriculum work, and discuss its linkages with related inquiry and research. Then we will focus on the purposes of deliberative inquiry, the types of research questions addressed, and the processes and logic employed in arriving at knowledge claims. It is important to note that the questions addressed are not research questions, as generally understood, but rather questions about what to do in specific situations; the claims reached are not claims for general knowledge, but rather plans of action, grounded by justifications. Then, we will formulate guidelines for conducting and for studying deliberative inquiry; and concurrently illustrate these guidelines in the context of inquiry reported in the field of curriculum studies.

Deliberative Inquiry: An Overview

Over two decades ago, Joseph Schwab enjoined a paradigm shift on the field of curriculum with his now legendary statement: "The field of curriculum is moribund. It is unable, by its present methods and principles, to continue its work and contribute significantly to the advancement of education"

(Schwab 1978/1973: 287). He argued that the field of curriculum should divert its energies from theoretical pursuits aimed at knowledge generation, and focus its attention instead on practical disciplines emphasizing choice and action. The heart and lineage of this argument is Schwab's use of the Aristotelean distinctions between "theoretical" disciplines directed toward knowledge generation and "practical" disciplines directed toward choice and action. Schwab developed these themes in complex characterizations of a discipline of the "practical" and its associated method of "deliberation" (Schwab 1978/1969, 1978/1971, 1978/1973, 1983). In turn, "deliberative inquiry," a term coined by Reid (1982), is embedded in a coherent philosophy of curriculum study, research, and action, which has its lineage in Schwab's thinking and writing beginning in the early fifties (Westbury and Wilkof 1978).

In the "practical" papers, Schwab is asking: What kinds of problems are curriculum problems? What forms of principles and methods are needed to address such problems? What constitutes defensible curriculum action? In response, he argues that the field of curriculum has misconstrued the character of its root problems. He argues that its problems are practical problems about choice and action in specific situations; they are not theoretical problems about what is the case. He argues that these practical problems should be addressed by methods appropriate to issues of choice and action, namely "deliberation" and associated arts of the "practical," the "quasi-practical" (disciplined deliberation about action in hypothetical or general situations), and the "eclectic."

Schwab characterizes two kinds of "practical" arts: arts of perception and arts of problemation. These arts, according to Schwab, begin with the requirement that existing institutions and practices be "preserved and altered piecemeal not dismantled." They begin with sensed "frictions and failures in the machine" and "inadequacies evidenced in felt shortcomings of its products," which suggest "problem situations." The arts of perception, labeled "immediate perception" and "deliberately irrelevant scanning" (observing situations through a succession of lenses), enable us to see and make use of the particularities of practical situations in identifying problems and generating alternative solutions (Schwab 1978/1969; 309–310). Schwab (1964), Pereira (1984), and Roby (1985) suggest that these arts can be enhanced in curriculum deliberation by factoring in four "commonplaces" of education (elements in every education situation) — student, teacher, subject-matter and milieu—in each phase of deliberation. The arts of problemation are those by which one generates alternative formulations of a problem situation and alternative solutions, and acts upon the best one, *not* the right one, all things considered (Schwab 1978/1971: 326, 1978/1969: 291).

Schwab formulates an important role for theory in deliberative inquiry, through use of "eclectic" arts (using multiple theoretical and disciplinary perspectives) and "polyfocal conspectus" (seeing a problem through a succession of lenses). The eclectic arts are rooted in a view of the nature of theorizing and resultant theories. Theorists must distill from a plethora of particulars certain general aspects of reality, but thereby omit many particulars that lend meaning to that reality. They must select areas and principles for inquiry. The consequence is that any theory presents a partial view of educational reality. The problem in using theory to guide practice is that practitioners may perceive any particular theory as covering the whole of reality and see reality and alternatives of education only in its light. As a remedy, Schwab recommends use of eclectic arts. These are arts by which we uncover the inevitable distortions and limitations of any theory, determine which combinations and portions of sciences and theories shed useful light on specific curriculum problems, and thereby render them useful for practice (Schwab 1978/1973; Fox 1985). The arts of the "practical" and of the "eclectic" commingle. Schwab states that "Collectively ... these arts are concerned with bringing a principle to its case ... by mutual accommodation. The principle [theory] must be selected and adapted to the case. But the case becomes a case of [an instance of] this theory or another only as it is made to do so ... " (Schwab 1978/1971: 331).

Schwab's work has stimulated a body of exegesis, analysis, extension, criticism, and application which have made significant contributions to the characterization of deliberative inquiry. There was an initial flurry of general commentary (e.g., Connelly 1972; Fox 1972; Westbury 1972a and 1972b, Wick 1972). Reid has provided the most sustained analysis of deliberative inquiry (1978, 1979, 1981, 1982, 1988). In other general analyses, Fox (1985) explored the role of theories and eclectic arts in deliberative inquiry and in Schwab's corpus of writing. Harris (1986) explored issues related to the communication, articulation, and codification of the concept and practice of "curriculum deliberation"; and in the process, provided a review of the literature of deliberative inquiry.

In *Thinking about the Curriculum* (1978) and subsequent writing, Reid explored the implications of Schwab's ideas for curriculum work and a discipline of curriculum studies. Following Gauthier's (1963) and Vickers's (1965) conceptions of practical reasoning, he characterized curriculum problems as among a wider class of "uncertain practical problems," involving prudential, moral, and ethical considerations; and discussed how 'deliberative' methods are used to solve such problems in everyday life, in issues of public policy, and in turn, in issues related to education and curriculum policy and practice. Most recently, Reid has argued for the importance of considering institutional and political contexts in conducting deliberations (1988).

Reid (1978) argued for the need to elaborate and refine a tradition of curriculum deliberation to help individuals improve their powers of practical reasoning, and to create contexts in which these powers can best be deployed. He observed that traditions of practical reasoning are developed in other practical disciplines, such as Law, by refining criteria for justifying actions and by showing how these criteria are to be weighed in practical situations, through collation and discussion of examples of practice. He referred to work conducted specifically in curriculum decision-making which contributes to development of a tradition of practical reasoning and deliberation. Scheffler (1958), for example, presented a philosophical analysis of processes used in justification of curriculum decisions.

The implication of Reid's argument for developing a tradition of curriculum deliberation is that interpretive descriptive studies of deliberations are needed; and there is an increasing body of such work. In an exemplar study, Walker (1971a and Reid and Walker 1975) reported an empirical analysis of the deliberations of three university-based subject-matter-oriented curriculum development projects. His aim was to explicate the processes by which such groups determine the form and substance of the curriculum plans and materials they create, with a view towards establishing principles and methods for effective deliberation. The study involved design of a content analysis system, based in part on Gauthier's characterizations of "deliberative" moves, and the application of this system to transcripts of discourse. In related work (1971b) Walker formulated a "naturalistic" model of curriculum development which included processes of deliberation and practical reasoning as central features.

In *College Curriculum and Student Protest*, Schwab (1969) exemplifies deliberation in locating the sources of student unrest in the sixties in deficiencies of liberal education. Fox (1972) used Schwab's concepts to describe the deliberations of a science curriculum committee about a problem in teaching botany to middle-class children in the eighth grade in Israel. Siegel (1975) reports a single person deliberation about teaching *Hamlet* to a hypothetical group of students. Roby (1978) summarized an individual deliberation concerning development of a remedial program for black students in an inner-city community college in the late sixties. Orpwood (1983) reported a comprehensive study, conducted within the general framework of deliberative inquiry, designed to identify new directions for science education in Canadian elementary and secondary schools. Atkins (1986) reported a study of the deliberations of a five-member humanities team, at the Community College of Philadelphia, in constructing an interdisciplinary twelve-credit program intended to enhance transfer opportunities for predominantly poor minority students.

Westbury (1972b), like Reid, expressed concern about Schwab's view of "deliberation" as *the* method for addressing curriculum questions, stating that it is a complex method "necessarily without guide or rule." Westbury argued that elaboration of a roster of methods, namely a syntax-in-use of deliberation, was an important task facing curriculum.

There have been reports of methods and hueristics for structuring deliberations. Hegarty (1971) describes use of Nominal Group Technique, a structured group process approach developed in management sciences, as an approach for expeditiously conducting the problem-identification and solution phases of deliberation. She grounds her work in principles and approaches from the field of decision-making in management sciences (Delbecq et al. 1975; Van de Ven and Delbecq 1971). Bonser and Grundy (1988) outline a structured process of deliberation, which includes practitioner/researcher joint reflection, linked with group reflection. Tamir (1989) describes a process of preliminary data-gathering, labeled Pre-Planning Evaluation, which is intended to facilitate all phases of deliberation; and reports an empirical study attesting to its effectiveness. Pereira (1981) and Townsend (1981) report approaches for teaching education students to conduct deliberative inquiry. Schwab, in "The Practical 2: Arts of Eclectic" (1978/ 1973), used examples from personality theory to illustrate the arts of eclectic and how they may be taught. Schwab (1978/1973) and others (Bonser and Grundy 1988, Hegarty 1971, Fox 1985) have argued for the important role of group deliberation in curriculum decision-making; and discussed guidelines for group membership, leadership, and processes for promoting effective curriculum deliberation.

Reid (1978), and others, have argued that effective curriculum deliberation, whatever heuristics of method and structure may be devised, depends ultimately on powers and experience in deliberators — a broad liberal education to inform judgment; knowledge of pertinent research, theories, and principles; experience with particular situations that are the subjects of deliberation; and habits and propensities needed to effectively participate in deliberation. There have been analyses of habits and impulses in deliberators which facilitate or impede deliberation. Pereira (1984) refers to our tendencies of "tunnel vision" and suggests how the practical arts of perception can be enhanced by systematic use of educational "commonplaces." Roby (1985) and Knitter (1985) suggest approaches for modifying habits and impulses which impede effective use of arts of problem formulation and of the "eclectic," respectively. More recently, Knitter (1988) elucidates the concept of 'character' and outlines attributes of individuals and institutions which would constitute virtues, privations, or vices relative to the activity of deliberation.

Discourse about deliberative inquiry has been grounded primarily in philosophical analysis and practical wisdom. Studies are beginning to be reported which assess whether use of the recommended arts of deliberation increase our understanding of curriculum problems and demonstrably affect the outcomes of curriculum planning processes. For example, Tamir (1989) described and empirically demonstrated the effectiveness of a pre-planning evaluation process to facilitate deliberation about curricula for electricians in technical high schools in Israel. Frey (1989) reported an empirical study which assessed the effects of different design processes, including a deliberative inquiry approach, on the actual designs of mathematics curricula at the School of Engineering in Zug, Switzerland.

We have characterized deliberative inquiry as embedded in a coherent philosophy of curriculum study, research, and action; and provided an overview of some of its extensions and applications in curriculum work. In characterizing deliberative inquiry, it is also important to understand its sources outside of the field of curriculum studies and its linkages with related inquiry and research.

Deliberative inquiry has its most important sources in the domains of philosophy and public policy. It is grounded in Aristotle's distinctions between "theoretical" and "practical" disciplines — their starting points, methods, and forms of conclusions — formulated in the *Ethics;* and in work of the pragmatic philosophers, particularly Dewey's theories of thinking, problem-solving, inquiry, and the scientific method (1910, 1916, 1929, 1938).

Deliberative inquiry is also firmly grounded in theories of practical reasoning related to politics and ethics, which provide standards for justification of arguments developed to support decisions and action (Gauthier 1963, Vickers 1965, Toulmin 1958, Baier 1958). These theories of practical reasoning have fundamental similarities. They concern formulation of practical arguments, namely arguments by which decisions are justified for uncertain practical problems. Although these theorists use some different terms, they generally view practical arguments as comprised of premises involving reality judgments, value judgments, and prudential, moral, and ethical considerations, which are weighed in a process of deliberation to justify judgments, decisions, and action. Vickers focuses particularly on how we in fact deal with practical questions at the national policy-making level. Toulmin focuses particularly on the nature of warrants or value judgments used in different fields of activity.

Deliberative inquiry is associated with assumptions about the role of practitioners in curriculum work which lends it a family affinity with other important work in education. A fundamental assumption of deliberative inquiry is that the root problems of curriculum are practical problems about choice and action in specific situations, which should be addressed by practitioners through deliberative processes. This means that schools and classrooms are sites of significant curriculum planning, policy development, and evaluation, by teachers and administrators. Practitioners in schools are assumed to develop a repertoire of experience in their situations which helps them to be sensitive to curriculum problems; to generate imaginative alternative possibilities for action; and to assess the educative and moral consequences of the curricula they create. Consequently, Schon's (1983, 1987) work on "reflection in action" and the exegeses it has spawned (Grimmet and Erickson 1988), discourse about "reflective supervision" (e.g., Garman 1986), and research on teacher thinking and 'practical knowledge' (Clandinin and Connelly 1985) are closely related to deliberative inquiry.

Deliberative inquiry is also closely linked with some of the other forms of inquiry characterized in this book. It has much in common with action inquiry discussed (on pages 309–326) by McKernan. It has in common the same root assumptions about the "practical" and action-oriented nature of curriculum problems and the important role of practitioners in curriculum deliberation. Deliberative inquiry, on the one hand, focuses on the coordinated disciplined processes of deliberation and practical reasoning, involving both reality and value judgments, to make decisions about curriculum policy and action in specific situations, all things considered. Action inquiry, on the other hand, focuses on the importance of doing research in practice to address practical problems, and on the importance of practitioners' involvement in conducting such research as full partners. The particular modes of inquiry and research linked with action inquiry are diverse, ranging from hypothesis testing to hermeneutic styles of inquiry, depending on the questions that arise in practice and dominant research paradigms. Consequently, deliberative inquiry may serve as a framework to incorporate the results of action inquiry in curriculum decision-making.

In turn, although the results of each form of inquiry characterized in this book may inform curriculum deliberation, some are particularly useful. Conceptual and ampliative philosophical inquiry—which focus on logical, normative, or empirical errors or errors in formulating premises in reasoning and in reaching conclusions—is clearly integral to deliberative inquiry; so also is normative inquiry, which focuses on systematic justification of the values and norms associated with curricula. Critical practical inquiry, which focuses on the relationships between the norms and designs expressed in the rhetoric of curriculum policies and their reflection in actual practice, is also integral to deliberative inquiry. Aesthetic inquiry and qualitative evaluation within evaluative inquiry yield vivid portrayals and aesthetic interpretations of specific education situations. These portrayals contribute to deliberative inquiry by helping participants become better connoisseurs of education situations. Evaluation inquiry also yields data which may stimulate a deliberative process; moreover, it yields data which may inform deliberators during each phase of deliberation. Integrative inquiry which synthesizes and translates knowledge from some domain of inquiry may also be used in deliberative inquiry. Finally, phenomenological inquiry and hermeneutic inquiry, which focus on personal perspectives and meanings associated with particular situations, also help participants in deliberations to increase their "appreciation" (understanding) of education situations.

Deliberative Inquiry: Purposes, Types of Questions, Processes and Logic

We now focus on the purposes of deliberative inquiry, the kinds of questions or problems in curriculum for which it is appropriate, and the processes and logic employed in arriving at conclusions. In contrast to other forms of curriculum inquiry, the questions addressed are not research questions, as generally understood, but rather questions about policy and action in specific situations; the conclusions reached are not claims for general knowledge, but rather plans for action, grounded by justifications.

Deliberative inquiry (like action inquiry) is directed toward curriculum decision-making and action in specific situations. By contrast, other forms of curriculum inquiry are directed either toward development of generally applicable knowledge, such as doctrines, explanatory theories, applied theories, or practice theories (Harris 1986); or toward understanding and illuminating curriculum-related phenomena. The fundamental *purpose* of deliberative inquiry is to reach justified decisions about curricular action in particular contexts—decisions about what and how to teach these students based on due consideration of the problematic character of a particular situation. The concept of "particular situation" is relative; deliberative inquiry may focus on curriculum policies and guidelines for a classroom, a school, a district, a state, or a nation.

Deliberative inquiry has other fundamentally important purposes related to its action orientation. Its goal is not merely to reach justified decisions, but also to implement those decisions, which are by their nature public policy decisions, in social and typically institutional contexts, with development of materials and strategies for their use. Therefore, deliberative inquiry is directed toward a product: codified policies and guidelines for use in selection of curriculum content and instructional strategies and materials (Kirst and Walker 1971; Walker 1971). Moreover, deliberative inquiry is intended to be educative for participants (Dewey 1929; Schwab 1978/1969, 1978/1971, 1978/1973; Vickers 1965). In systematically analyzing problem situations and generating alternative solutions, either individually or in groups, participants gain competence in deliberation and reflection on situations; they gain insights and new perspectives about particular situations; they experience personal growth. Thereby, they increase their capacity to act morally and effectively in pedagogical situations. For example, in a report of the deliberations of a curriculum group about teaching botany, Fox (1972) demonstrates how the concepts of a subject-matter specialist and a psychologist are modified and enriched as they interact about conceptions of subject-matter and learners. Equally important, deliberative inquiry, ideally conducted in groups constituted to include important "stakeholders" in decisions, is intended to secure personal and group commitment to policies (Orpwood 1985); it is intended to have persuasive and political force.

The kinds of questions or problems in curriculum for which deliberative inquiry is appropriate are uncertain practical problems—namely questions about action, about what *ought to be done,* all things considered— which involve both reality judgments and value judgments. Reid (1978: 42) characterized "uncertain practical problems" as posing questions that have to be answered (even if the answer is to do nothing), on uncertain grounds, related to a specific context and desired ends, taking into account an existing state of affairs, involving adjudication among conflicting goals and values, and with unpredictable outcomes.

Therefore, the questions addressed by deliberative inquiry are questions about policies and plans for curricula in specific situations, in forms such as: Should we change our curriculum policies *or* what should our new policies be (e.g., with respect to goals, curriculum organization and design, or resource allocation) for [subject matter]? Should we change our curriculum plans and guidelines *or* what specific changes should be made in our curriculum plans and guidelines (e.g., with respect to content and sequence) for [subject-matter])? For example, Atkins (1986) reported the deliberations of a humanities team in a community college, which was addressing the question: What should our plans and guidelines be, with respect to content, curriculum organization, and instructional strategies, for implementing a new curriculum to enhance transfer opportunities for our predominantly poor, mostly minority students; given the assumptions that the curriculum will be interdisciplinary, team taught, and directed toward "initiating students into the larger intellectual community?" Orpwood (1983) reported a large-scale study, conducted within the tradition of deliberative inquiry, sponsored by the Science Council of Canada, designed to address the question: What policies and guidelines should be adopted for the content and instructional strategies for science education in the elementary and secondary schools of Canada?

The questions addressed in deliberative inquiry also relate to the appropriate conduct of deliberations, and the implementation of curricula in specific situations, in forms such as: How shall we manage and carry out our policy deliberation (or program development) process? How shall we manage and carry out the enactment of the prescribed program changes? The questions addressed in deliberative inquiry also involve critical reflection about a specific process of deliberation, in forms such as: Were problem formulations sufficiently numerous and varied to do justice to the situation? Were the commonplaces of education treated in a balanced way so that none was slighted? These types of questions about the structure and conduct of specific deliberations are raised in most reports of deliberations.

Finally, deliberative inquiry has, itself, been the subject of empirical and analytical inquiry by curriculum theorists, who ask questions of the form: What processes do curriculum development groups actually use to formulate policies? What is the relationship between use of curriculum design processes, such as deliberation, and the resulting curricula? For example, Walker addressed questions of the former type in his study of the deliberations of three university-based subject-matter-oriented curriculum development project groups (Walker 1971a and Reid and Walker 1975); as did Atkins (1986), in her report of the deliberations of a humanities teaching team. Tamir (1989) addressed questions of the latter type, in his empirical study of the effectiveness of a pre-planning evaluation process to facilitate deliberation about curricula for electricians in technical high schools in Israel; as did Frey (1989) in his empirical study of the effects of different design processes, including a deliberative inquiry approach, on the actual designs of mathematics curricula at the School of Engineering in Zug, Switzerland.

What processes and logic are employed in arriving at conclusions in deliberative inquiry? It should be emphasized that given the purposes of deliberative inquiry and the questions it addresses, its conclusions are not claims for general knowledge, but rather decisions about plans for action. Such decisions need to be justified. If it is asked: Why do you teach that?, the decision is justified not by a formal proof, or an outline of procedures, or experimental results, alone. The decision is justified by demonstrating that it is the outcome of a rational consideration of a range of possibilities.

The fundamental process for arriving at conclusions in deliberative curriculum inquiry is a structure for "deliberation": a systematic method for individuals, groups, or institutions to formulate and entertain an adequate variety of alternatives — alternative perceptions and formulations of problems in situations and alternative solutions — directed toward decisions about what and how to teach particular students in a particular context. Schwab (1978/1969, 1978/1971, 1978/1973), and other writers in the deliberative tradition (e.g., Reid 1982), argue that deliberation in properly constituted groups is essential to curriculum decision-making — for bringing together diverse sources of evidence and expertise, for education of participants through discovery of diverse perspectives, and for achieving commitment to decisions. Given the purposes of deliberative curriculum inquiry—to make decisions significant for public policy relative to a given context—it follows that the most important curriculum deliberation takes place at local sites, conducted by those who 'live in' the education setting. Schwab (1983), for example, recommends that the "curriculum group" should be comprised of the principal, community representatives, teachers, students, and a chairperson skilled in processes of deliberation.

The logic employed in deliberative inquiry is grounded in theories of practical reasoning (Gauthier 1963, Vickers 1965, Toulmin 1958, Baier 1958), which provide standards for assessment of arguments by which decisions are justified for uncertain practical problems. Theories of practical reasoning generally view practical arguments as comprised of premises involving reality and value judgments, which are weighed in a process of deliberation to justify judgments, decisions, and action.

Central to the conduct of deliberation and practical reasoning is the characteristics of deliberators. Whatever heuristics may be devised for structuring deliberations, and formulating practical arguments, these inquiry methods ultimately relate to the powers and capacities of participants in deliberation. Do they have a broad liberal education to inform judgment? What qualities of character and experience do they bring to the process of deliberation? What is the nature of their experience with education generally? What is their level of connoisseurship of education situations? What is the extent of their direct experience with the specific situation which is the subject of the deliberation? And so on. The results of other forms of curriculum inquiry are assessed primarily by standards applied to the process and the products of inquiry, by canons related to validity, reliability, generalizability, parsimony, coherence, and so on. The results of deliberative inquiry, which are grounded in the choices and the value and reality judgments of deliberators, are assessed also by reference to the wisdom, judgment, character, experience, and knowledge of the deliberators.

The basic structure for deliberation has been characterized in some detail by Schwab (1978/1969, 1978/1971, 1978/1973), and others, as arts of the practical, the quasi-practical, and the eclectic. The practical arts begin with the requirement that existing institutions and practices be preserved and altered piecemeal, not dismantled. These arts are initiated with detection of a problematic situation, with sensing frictions and failures "in the machine," and inadequacies evidenced in felt shortcomings of its products. Without such dissatisfaction, the situation would not be problematic and there would be no need for deliberation. These sensed frictions and shortcomings suggest "problem situations." Schwab notes that 'problem situations present themselves to consciousness, but the character of the problem, its formulation, does not. The character of the problem depends on the discerning eye of the beholder' (Schwab 1978/1969: 316). The problems in the situation are seldom clear from the start. People have widely different perceptions about what the problem "really" is and about the situation in which the problem is located.

Problem situations, sensed problems, are explored and "solved" through a process of deliberation in its most general form: perceiving the relevant details in a situation, generating alternative formulations of the problem(s), generating alternative solutions, and acting upon the best one, not the right one, all things considered. Schwab succinctly characterizes the deliberative process, in terms of arts and competencies of deliberators as follows. He states, "Arts of problemation ... are arts by which we assign various possible meanings to perceived detail and group them in different ways ... to perceive and shape different formulations of 'the' problem posed by the displeasing situation (Schwab 1978/1971: 326). He adds, "There are arts for weighing alternative formulations of a problem ... and for choosing one to follow further ... arts for generating alternative possible solutions ... arts for tracing each alternative solution to its probable consequences, arts for weighing and choosing among them ... reflexive arts for determining when the deliberation should be terminated and action undertaken" (Ibid.). The basic deliberative process, of generating and choosing formulations of problems and solutions, is informed by arts of perception; by systematic use of "commonplaces" of education; by observation and data collection; and by use of eclectic arts in tailoring, adapting, and combining theoretical and disciplinary perspectives to address specific curriculum problems.

Schwab (1978/1971) distinguishes two arts of perception—immediate perception and "deliberately irrelevant scanning" (systematically scanning a situation through multiple lenses, some of which may initially appear irrelevant) — used in generating alternative formulations of a problem situation. These are arts by which one "sees," discriminates, and gives meaning to the rich and varied particulars of a dissatisfying situation, in order to diagnose the sources of the difficulties.

In using the arts of perception, one encounters a longstanding philosophical problem; namely, the search for systematic and general ways to deal with uniqueness. This problem was formulated and addressed for curriculum studies by Westbury (1972b), in his recommendation of a tool from this tradition, the systematic use of "commonplaces" which function like a coordinate system to provide general terms to guide inquiry. Schwab (1964, 1978/1969, 1978/1971, 1978/1973) has characterized commonplaces for curriculum; use of these commonplaces have become part of the tradition of deliberative inquiry. He proposed that situations which give rise to curriculum problems invariably involve four "commonplaces." Someone (a teacher) is teaching something (subject matter) to someone else (students) in a network of social and cultural contexts (milieux). These four common-places — student, teacher, subject-matter and milieu — serve as a checklist for the topics and interrelationships which must be considered throughout the deliberative process of formulating, assessing, and choosing among problem formulations and among solutions. The art of perception, rendered systematic through the use of commonplaces, typically requires observations of particular situations, and data collection to refine and guide perception and observation.

Overall, the deliberative process is spiral, rather than linear or circular; and involves backtracking and revision, with an intricate interplay of ends and means; problem, data and solution. For example, selection of a problem formulation does not preclude a return to other formulations at a later stage of deliberation. Solutions may reveal new problems, such as of limited resources. The deliberative process is also reflective. Participants are enjoined to explore their values, preconceptions, predispositions, and prejudices pertaining to formulations of problems and solutions — a process intended to be both educative and productive in yielding more appropriate analyses of problem situations and more appropriate solutions.

The intended outcome of deliberative inquiry is a decision for action, developed through a process designed to educate participants and to obtain their support. In addition, the method may yield a codification of the process and its conclusions — a coherent argument in support of action, which details the alternatives considered and the rationales for choices — which may provide guidance in implementing the decision(s) in changing and unforeseen circumstances.

Guidelines for Conducting Deliberative Inquiry

The task of formulating guidelines for deliberative curriculum inquiry is a difficult one. As discussed, it is a disciplined process for generating, considering, and choosing alternative formulations of problems and solutions relative to a specific context, embedded within an important paradigm for curriculum research, policy, and action. It is a complex process, involving both reality and value judgments, negotiated among morally engaged individuals interacting in the setting of social institutions. Whatever principles, approaches, prescriptions, or heuristics may be devised and codified for deliberative inquiry, the process ultimately depends on the capacities and judgment of deliberators, embedded in their character, their general education, their connoisseurship of education situations generally, and their knowledge of the particular situation which is the subject of inquiry. Yet, a roster of approaches and heuristics is being developed which provide helpful guidelines for deliberative inquiry in areas which are likely to be difficult. These guidelines relate to: the use of group processes; structuring the process of problem formulation; use of education commonplaces; use of data collection strategies; use of eclectic arts; and development and analysis of solutions.

Although deliberative inquiry may be conducted by individuals, ideally it is conducted in properly constituted groups — in order to bring together the diverse sources of evidence and expertise needed for judgmental processes; to educate participants; and to achieve commitment to policy decisions which must be implemented. As Schwab comments: "The desirability of each alternative must be felt out, 'rehearsed,' by a representative variety of all those who must live with the consequences of the chosen action. And a similar variety must deal with the identification of problems as well as with their solution" (1978/1969: 319).

Schwab (1978/1969, 1983), and others, have discussed the appropriate constitution of groups for purposes of deliberative inquiry. He recommends that there should be representation of knowledge and expertise for four commonplaces of curriculum: subject matter (e.g., familiarity with scholarly materials under treatment and the discipline from which they come); learners (e.g., abilities, learning styles, attitudes, aspirations); milieus (e.g., characteristics of communities, socioeconomic background, future employment); and teachers (e.g., background, attitudes, approaches to teaching, willingness to try new methods). He recommends, also, that the group should include expertise in the processes of curriculum deliberation and of "curriculum-making." He recommends, in addition, that the group should include expertise in curriculum evaluation, because evaluation data serves an important role in deliberative inquiry; it may provide the stimulus for curriculum review, and it provides evidence and feedback in all phases of deliberation. It does not follow that the group should be comprised of six persons. Two or more of these bodies of experience may be found in one person. In turn, more than one person may be needed to fully represent some bodies of experience. Fox (1972) observes that the "eclectic" approach recommended for deliberative inquiry requires that no one theory or school of thought about a commonplace, such as subject matter, dominate or blind participants to alternatives.

Approaches have also been recommended for leadership of deliberations. Fox (1972) provides a description, and vivid illustrations of the "curriculum specialist" as leader of deliberation, in a group considering problems in teaching botany. The paper includes what Fox labels "protocols" of the deliberation: transcripts printed in a half-page left-hand column, linked with analyses and summaries of the argument and rationales for the leaders' strategies printed in the right-hand column. The protocols are used by participants to reflect on the direction of the deliberation, to reconsider hastily made decisions, to review the strategies of the leader, and so on. The protocols also help to prepare leaders of deliberative inquiry by illustrating their roles and strategies. For example, Fox' protocols demonstrate that the leader: maintained balance among four commonplaces of education; decided when to support and when to restrict introduction of further complexity; frequently articulated summaries of arguments, commitments and reasons for commitments; decided when to terminate a line of argument; and decided when to suspend deliberation in favor of data-collection, research, individual study, or appointment of subcommittees. Atkins' transcript of a portion of the deliberations of a humanities curriculum development team (1986) also vividly illustrates the role of the leader in: articulating broad goals; maintaining balance in consideration of commonplaces; and articulating periodic syntheses, summaries, and directives, to maintain the flow of deliberation from formulation, weighing and choosing formulations of the problem through to formulation, weighing and choosing solutions.

Developing, weighing, and choosing among alternative formulations of the problems in a situation is a fundamentally important aspect of deliberative inquiry, particularly in group settings. Deliberation begins with dissatisfactions or symptoms of problems in concrete situations. The essence of methodic inquiry during the first stage of deliberation is to initiate and sustain a process through which the nature of a problem is exposed through a careful analysis of the relevant details of the specific situation. If this stage is short-circuited — if solutions address the wrong problem or just a fraction of many separate or interrelated problems — the original dissatisfactions and demands for change will remain, accompanied by considerable frustration and waste of resources, time, and effort.

Two general approaches have been described for structuring the process of problem formulation in curriculum deliberation (Hegarty 1971, Bonser and Grundy 1988); although described primarily in terms of problem formulation, these approaches are also useful in generating solutions. Hegarty describes the use of a structured group process approach labeled Nominal Group Process (NGP), developed by Van de Ven and Delbecq in management sciences (Delbecq et al. 1975), in the problem identification phase of reviewing the microbiology curriculum for senior science students at the University of New South Wales.

In NGP, members are selected so that the group has representation of knowledge and experience related to four commonplaces of education; students, teachers, subject-matter, and milieu. NGP begins by setting a task which each member works on in silence for twenty minutes. For example, the microbiology curriculum review group was asked to: "List problems which you have encountered in connection with the goals, objectives, learning programme and outcomes of the microbiology course for final year science students at this university. All types of problems are appropriate to list." Then, each member is asked to read one problem which is written on a chalk board, round-robin style, until there are no new problems. In this way, problems are effectively divorced from their proponents, thereby controlling unproductive group dynamics and promoting group acceptance of the list of problems. The group reviews the list, to define and clarify the meaning of items. Then, each member privately selects and rank orders the five items viewed as most important; the yield is a prioritized list of problems in the situation viewed as important by the group. This is followed by a second round of discussion for clarification, and voting. The list, with appropriate documentation, is submitted to the group responsible for generating solutions to problems.

Hegarty refers to studies showing the effectiveness of NGP, as compared with other group process approaches (Delbecq et al. 1975 and Van de Ven and Delbecq 1971), with respect to the number of problems identified, identification of all aspects of a problem, determination of priorities, the quality of ideas, and the acceptability of ideas to group members. She outlines aspects of the process which help to account for its effectiveness: the task orientation which achieves efficient use of group and individual time and effort; the structure, which promotes open expression of diverse ideas; the equal status of members, which helps to offset inequalities of status and power; and the production of written products, which involves each member in the group task and promotes greater commitment to the group's work and its outcomes.

Bonser and Grundy (1988) describe a structured process for deliberation labeled "reflective deliberation," involving practitioner and researcher collaboration, in the context of deliberation about a particular school's policy for computer education. They view "reflective deliberation" as more consistent than NGP with the view of deliberative inquiry as a rational art, involving "spiral discovery of meaning, critical reflection, back-tracking, review and revision." "Reflective deliberation" proceeds through four cycles. In Phase I, pairs of "practitioners" and "researchers" produce jointly authored written statements about the problems in a situation, based on initial audio-recorded and transcribed semi-structured interviews and reflection on the initial interview. In Phase II, groups of four or five, who participated in Phase I, review each other's written statements and produce a written summary for their group. In Phase III, a larger group comprised of participants in Phases I and II, review the summary statements of each small group to discern and categorize major problems and issues related to the subject of the inquiry. In Phase IV, the whole group produces and confirms a policy statement.

In whatever structure deliberative inquiry is conducted, it fundamentally involves analysis of the details of complex particular situations to generate, weigh, and choose among formulations of problems and solutions. The use of education commonplaces has been recommended as a tool—a heuristic — to systematically analyze particular situations (Pereira 1984, Schwab 1978/1969, 1978/1971, 1978/1973, Westbury 1972a). This means that throughout a deliberation, whatever its starting point, participants should consider important aspects of every education situation and the complexities of their interrelationships, i.e., commonplaces: student, teacher, subject-matter, milieu. The commonplaces are akin to a coordinate system and serve multiple functions during deliberations. They serve as a checklist to guide perception; they provide categories and terms which help to locate details in a situation and determine their significance; they provide criteria for consideration of alternative problem formulations and solutions; they serve as reminders of what aspects of a situation need to be explored in depth and what aspects need to be weighed in the balance in policy choices. In turn their use helps to avoid tunnel vision and guard against one-sided arguments. Pereira (1984) presents extended analyses and examples of the use of commonplaces in deliberative inquiry; Fox (1972) and Atkins (1986) provide excellent illustrations of the use of commonplaces in actual deliberations.

Deliberative inquiry is informed by the knowledge and experience of participants. In addition, effective analysis of problem situations often requires data collection and/or research. Tamir (1989) describes an approach to data collection called Pre-Planning Evaluation (PPE), and reports an empirical study of its effectiveness in reviewing curricula for electricians in technical high schools in Israel. Questionnaires were designed, based on the commonplaces and an extensive review of the literature, to elicit baseline data and viewpoints from samples representing pertinent sources of information, e.g., students, graduates, teachers, employers; data related to each commonplace were summarized. Five independent planning committees each received different levels of PPE information just prior to their deliberations: no information; full information; full information, except for data on learners; full information, except for data on teachers; and full information, except for data on milieus. Based on observations during deliberations and analyses of policy proposals, Tamir concluded that PPE information, when provided, has a significant and positive effect on the process and product of curriculum development committees. It results in identification of a greater proportion of curriculum problems in a situation, more balanced consideration of commonplaces, reduction of the time needed for formulation of problems, and an increase of time devoted to productive discussion of solutions.

Orpwood (1983) describes a combination of multiple imaginative approaches to analysis of a problem situation ("a wave of criticism") in a major study of science education in Canadian Schools, sponsored by the Science Council of Canada. These approaches included: sponsorship of a series of papers, representing different views of goals in science for the 'educated person'; analysis of science curriculum policies and teaching approaches by science teaching specialists reflected in school curriculum guides and science textbooks; surveys of science teachers, to elicit their views about goals and instructional strategies; case studies of science education at eight sites across Canada to identify actual aims, instructional strategies and institutional contexts; an analysis of historical trends; and compilation of statistical data for science enrollment. This data served as background for workshops and deliberative conferences in school districts across Canada.

Deliberative inquiry is also informed by multiple disciplinary and theoretical perspectives, through the use of "eclectic arts" — to determine which combinations and portions of sciences and theories shed useful light on particular curricular problems. Schwab (1978/1971) provides an outstanding analysis of the use of eclectic arts, with examples from personality theory to illustrate these arts and how they may be taught. Fundamentally, however, use of eclectic arts depends on the disciplinary and theoretical knowledge of deliberators.

Formulation of problems in a situation relies primarily on arts of perception and analysis; while formulation of solutions relies to a greater extent on arts of invention. Most of the heuristics discussed above for problem formulation apply as well to generation of solutions: use of group process; structured group process approaches; use of education commonplaces; observation and data collection; and use of eclectic arts. In addition, formulation and consideration of solutions benefits from development of materials and teaching strategies, a particularization in examples to assess the feasibility and consequences of policy statements. Schwab (1978/1973) provides a general description of this process. Atkins (1986), Fox (1972), and Reid and Walker (1975) provide excellent examples.

Summary and Needed Work

In this chapter, we have characterized deliberative inquiry; given an overview of its lineage and its application in doing curriculum work; discussed its linkages with related inquiry and research; outlined its purposes, the questions it addresses, and the processes and logic used in reaching conclusions; and discussed some approaches, devices, and heuristics for conducting deliberative inquiry. The advancement of deliberative inquiry in curriculum studies depends on developing traditions of deliberation, through conducting, reporting, and analyzing actual deliberations, as exemplified in work reported by Walker (1971a) and Atkins (1986). It depends also on assessing the effectiveness of approaches to deliberation, recommended and based on practical wisdom. Such assessment may involve the effectiveness of empirical studies with respect to deliberation processes and outcomes, as exemplified in work reported by Frey (1989) and Tamir (1989). Or, to be entirely consistent with the epistemology associated with deliberative inquiry, such assessments may involve rigorous processes of deliberative reflection.

References

(Symbols preceding entries are explained on page 40)

o Atkins, E. (1986). The deliberative process: An analysis from three perspectives. *Journal of Curriculum and Supervision, 1,* 265–293.

√ Baier, K. (1958). *The moral point of view.* Ithaca, N.Y.: Cornell University Press.

+ Bonser, S. A., and Grundy, S. J. (1988). Reflective deliberation in the formulation of a school curriculum policy. *Journal of Curriculum Studies, 20,* 35–45.

+ Clandinin, D. J., and Connelly, F. M. (1985). Personal practical knowledge and modes of knowing: Relevance for teaching and learning. In E. W. Eisner (Ed.), *Learning and teaching the ways of knowing.* 84th Yearbook of the National Society for the Study of Education, Part II, pp. 174–198. Chicago: The University of Chicago Press.

+ Connelly, F. M. (1972). The functions of curriculum development. *Interchange, 3,* 161–177.

√ Delbecq, A. et al. (1975). *Group techniques for program planning: A guide to nominal group and delphi processes.* Glenview, IL: Scott, Foresman and Company.

√ Dewey, J. (1910). *How we think.* New York: D. C. Heath.

√ ———. (1916). *Democracy and education.* New York: Macmillan.

√ ———. (1929). *The sources of a science of education.* New York: Liverright.

√ ———. (1938). *Logic: The theory of inquiry.* New York: Holt, Rinehart & Winston.

o+ Fox, S. (1972). The practical image of the 'practical.' *Curriculum Theory Network, 10,* 45–57.

+ ———. (1985). Dialogue: The vitality of theory in Schwab's conception of practice. *Curriculum Inquiry, 15,* 63–89.

o Frey, K. (1989). Do curriculum development models really influence the curriculum? Paper presented at the annual meeting of the American Educational Research Association, San Francisco.

√ Gauthier, D. P. (1963). *Practical reasoning: The structure and foundations of prudential and moral arguments and their exemplifications in discourse.* London: Oxford University Press.

o+ Grimmett, P. and Erickson, G. (Eds.) (1988). *Reflection in teacher education.* New York: Teachers College Press.

+ Garman, N. (1986). Reflection, the heart of clinical supervision: A modern rationale for practice. *Journal of Curriculum and Supervision, 2,* 1–24.

+ Harris, I. B. (1986). Communicating the character of 'deliberation.' *Journal of Curriculum Studies, 18,* 115–132.

+ Hegarty, E. (1971). The problem identification phase of curriculum deliberation: Use of the nominal group technique. *Journal of Curriculum Studies, 9,* 31–41.

o+ Kirst, M. W., and Walker, D. F. (1971). An analysis of curriculum policy-making. *Review of Educational Research, 41,* 479–509.

+ Knitter, W. (1985). Curriculum deliberation: Pluralism and the practical. *Journal of Curriculum Studies, 17,* 383–395.

+ ———. (1988). The informing vision of the practical: Variations on a theme of Prometheus. *Curriculum Inquiry, 14,* 165–182.

o Orpwood, G. W. F. (1983). Deliberative inquiry: The study of politics and practice in Canadian science education. Paper presented at the annual meeting of the American Educational Research Association, Montreal.

o ———. (1985). The reflective deliberator: A case study of curriculum policy-making. *Journal of Curriculum Studies, 17,* 293–304.

+ Pereira, P. (1981). Curriculum students and their discontents. Paper presented at the annual meeting of the American Educational Research Association, Los Angeles. ERIC: ED 201 635.

+ ———. (1984). Perception and the practical arts. *Journal of Curriculum Studies, 16,* 347–366.

+ Reid, W. A. (1978). *Thinking about the curriculum: The nature and treatment of curriculum problems.* Boston: Routledge & Kegan Paul.

+ ———. (1979). Practical reasoning and curriculum theory: In search of a new paradigm. *Curriculum Inquiry, 9,* 187–207.

+ ———. (1981). The deliberative approach to the study of curriculum and its relation to critical pluralism. In M. Lawn and L. Barton, *Rethinking curriculum studies,* pp. 160–187. London: Croom Helm.

+ ———. (1982). Deliberative curriculum theory: A manifesto. Paper presented at the annual meeting of the American Educational Research Association, New York City.

+ ———. (1988). A research agenda: The institutional context of curriculum deliberation, *Journal of Curriculum and Supervision, 4,* 3–16.

○ Reid, W. A., and Walker, D. (Eds.) (1975). *Case studies in curriculum change.* London: Routledge & Kegan Paul.

○ Roby, T. W. (1978). Problem situations and curriculum resources at Central College: An exemplification of curricular arts. *Curriculum Inquiry, 8,* 95–117.

+ Roby, T. (1985). Habits impeding deliberation. *Journal of Curriculum Studies, 17,* 17–35.

+ Scheffler, I. (1958). Justifying curriculum decisions. *School Review, 56,* 461–472.

√ Schon, D. A. (1983). *The reflective practitioner: How professionals think in action.* New York: Basic Books.

√ ———. (1987). *Educating the reflective practitioner: Toward a new design for teaching and learning in the professions.* San Francisco: Jossey-Bass.

√ Schwab, J. J. (1964). The teaching of science as inquiry. In P. F. Brandwein (Ed.), *The teaching of science.* Cambridge: Harvard University Press.

○+ ———. (1969). *College curriculum and student protest.* Chicago: The University of Chicago Press.

+ ———. (1978). The practical: A language for curriculum. In I. Westbury & N. J. Wilkof (Eds.), *Science, curriculum, and liberal education.* Chicago: University of Chicago Press, pp. 287–321. The paper was first published in 1969.

+ ———. (1978). The practical 2: Arts of eclectic. In I. Westbury & N. J. Wilkof (Eds.), *Science, curriculum, and liberal education.* Chicago: University of Chicago Press, pp. 322–364. The paper was first published in 1971.

+ ———. (1978). The practical 3: Translation into curriculum. I. Westbury and N. J. Wilkof (Eds.), *Science, curriculum, and liberal education.* Chicago: The University of Chicago Press, pp. 365–383. The paper was first published in 1973.

+ ———. (1983). The practical 4: Something for curriculum professors to do. *Curriculum Inquiry, 13,* 239–265.

o   Siegel, J. S. (1975). Curricular deliberation about Hamlet: An exercise in the practical. Ph.D. dissertation, University of Chicago.

o+ Tamir, P. (1989). *Effects of different curriculum process models on the outcomes.* Paper presented at the annual meeting of the American Educational Research Association, San Francisco.

+   Townsend, R. (1981). Administrators and their problems. Paper presented at the annual meeting of the American Educational Research Association, Los Angeles.

√   Toulmin, S. (1958). *The uses of argument.* Cambridge, England: Cambridge University Press.

√   Van de Ven, A. and Delbecq, A. (1971). Nominal versus interacting group processes for committee decision-making effectiveness. *Academy of Management Journal, 14,* 203–212.

√   Vickers, G. (1965). *The art of judgment: A study of policy-making.* London: Chapman & Hall.

o   Walker, D. F. (1971a). A study of deliberation in three curriculum projects. *Curriculum Theory Network, 7,* 118–134.

o   ———. (1971b). A naturalistic model for curriculum development. *School Review, 80,* 151–165.

+   Westbury, I. (1972a). The Aristotelian 'art' of rhetoric and the 'art' of curriculum. *Philosophy of Education, 28,* 126–136.

+   ———. (1972b). The character of a curriculum for a 'practical' curriculum. *Curriculum Theory Network, 10,* 37–44.

+   Westbury, I., and Wilkof, N. (Eds.) (1978). *Science, curriculum, and liberal education: Selected essays.* Chicago: The University of Chicago Press.

+   Wick, W. (1972). Knowledge and action: The theory and practice of the 'practical.' *Curriculum Theory Network, 10,* 37–44.

17

Action Inquiry:
Studied Enactment

———— *Jim McKernan*

Educational action researchers argue that curriculum inquiry and theory should deal with practice, with classrooms and other curricular settings, and should be done by practitioners (Corey 1953; Elliott 1985; Stenhouse 1975, 1981; Carr and Kemmis (1986). The purpose of this chapter is to explain and interpret this assertion. I will first define the concept of *action research*, then discuss alternative varieties or styles of curriculum action research, and finally outline the principles of procedure for doing curriculum action research or *studied enactment.*

Definitions and Varieties of Action Research

Definitions of action research will not equip one with the skills of *studied enactment*, but they may provide spectacles for understanding conflicting conceptions of this dynamic research and professional development process. There are three mainstream approaches to action research corresponding to what I have elsewhere called *scientific, practical, and critical* action research (McKernan 1988). Here I will describe the distinctive features of each of these forms of action inquiry, as well as the linkages among them, and I will illustrate by way of specific examples, how action research can be employed in curriculum improvement.

Scientific Action Research

Early action research, and other forms of teacher research (Buckingham 1926; Lippitt and Radke 1946; Lewin 1946, 1947; Chien, Cook, and Harding 1948; Corey 1953; Taba and Noel 1957), placed a premium on the use of the scientific method. These studies were highly quantitative in their view of data analysis and were rooted in the science-in-education movement and the work of measurement-minded psychologists of the late nineteenth and early twentieth centuries. Corey (1953:141) defined action research as "research undertaken by practitioners in order that they may improve their practices." Typical of these studies was a desire to "hypothesize or predict that certain results will follow from what appear to be better practices" (Corey 1953:27). Borg and Gall (1979:37) stress that "action research involves the application of the steps of the scientific method to classroom problems." Indeed, the concern to use statistical tests and designs in many experiments has continued down to the present day (Borg 1981). Scientific action research in the USA tends to be viewed as a "less rigorous small scale version of experimental research, using statistical methods to test a hypothesis so as to inform a subsequent practical decision" (Wallace 1987:104).

Kurt Lewin (1946, 1947) and his colleagues attempted to study numerous social problems scientifically and to improve the quality of human relations as a result of their researches into action. For Lewin (1947:333) the process was one of action ideation, planning, fact-finding, execution, and monitoring of results of actions taken. Lewin, regarded by many as the "father" of action research, was foremost an experimentalist (Marrow 1969). Underlining Lewin's scientific approach, Edward C. Tolman remarked:

> Freud the clinician and Lewin the experimentalist — these are the two men whose names will stand out before all others in the history of our psychological era. For it is their contrasting but complementary insights which first made psychology a *science* applicable to real human beings and to real human society (Marrow 1969:ix).

Lippitt and Radke (1946) argued for the construction of "scientific research instruments" to aid in the process of data gathering. Taba and Noel (1957) provided a model for the scientific mode of action research applied to curriculum problems: (1) identify problems (2) analyze problems (3) formulate ideas or hypotheses (4) gather and interpret data (5) formulate action (6) evaluate the results of action.

The Southern Study (1946) was an early example of scientific curriculum problem solving by practicing teachers. In this study teachers used curriculum-development workshops and professional collaboration to identify problems and practical solutions in constructing and field testing pilot curriculum units. Taba used scientific action research in a variety of projects centering around problems of intergroup education and prejudice in schools (Taba, Brady, and Robinson 1952; Taba and Noel 1957).

The interactive R D & D model (research, development, and dissemination) has found support through various projects linking schools with external change agents (Tikunoff, Ward, and Griffin 1979; Griffin, Lieberman, and Jacullo-Noto 1983). This collaborative style is arguably within a "sci-

entific" camp insofar as it lays emphasis upon external social science research "experts" and internal practitioners, needs assessments and surveys, and the application of social scientific approaches and methods to the
solution of educational difficulties.

Collaborative action research studies of staff development (Hovda and
Kyle 1987; Oja and Smulyan 1989) might be described as "R, D, & D +
Teachers." The scale and scope of external and internal participation in
these projects have often demanded support by large funding agencies such
as the National Institute of Education.

A recent example of scientific action research, reported by Bowes
(1986), used an experimental design to study single sex science teaching
and a route to unbiased choices for third year science pupils. The problem
was to help find ways to allow pupils more choice in choosing science as a
specialism in 4th and 5th year in a British comprehensive school. A variety
of strategies were studied: developing careers advice systems; upgrading
counseling; developing syllabi; single sex teaching in science. Pupils were
assigned to control and experimental groups and were studied over a three
year period (1982–1985). Pupils were interviewed. Teachers kept diaries and
met frequently. At the end of the first year, using a chi-square test, it was
found that significant differences in choosing science occurred ($p > .01$), indicating sex bias in 1982 and 1984 despite the trreatment (action research
solutions). Nevertheless, the researchers argue that they approve of the
single sex provision because girls receive positive discrimination at a
vital stage in their school career. Girls also appeared to match boys in
achievement. Boys resented the single sex classes and seemed lost
without the girls.

A number of tightly controlled experimental action research studies are
reported by Gregory (1988) in his studies of social disadvantage/reading
failure, withdrawal classes for remedial pupils, truancy, etc., in a British local education authority. Gregory tests hypotheses and attempts to measure
changes. He argues that schools can change practice on the basis of tightly
controlled studies. Borg (1981:248–279) offers practical designs for scientific action research.

Practical Action Research

Curriculum reform has often been cast as practical concern as opposed
to a technical-scientific one, especially when it is tied closely to the human
and practical problems of deliberation and reflection (Schwab 1969, 1971,
1973, 1983; Reid 1978; Stenhouse 1975). Oakeshott (1967) has described deliberation as "reflection related to choice." Action research is a form of practical reflection related to curriculum choice. It would seem that the aim here

is to develop the practitioner's personal interpretive account of professional practice and theory. In short, action research aims at an epistemology of practice (Strike 1979) for the practitioner while contributing a utilitarian or use function to the solution of social practice problems.

John Elliott has defined action research as "the study of a social situation with a view to improving the quality of action within it" (Elliott 1981:1). For Elliott, curriculum research and development is essentially a practical rather than a theoretical business:

> It aims to feed practical judgment in concrete situations, and the validity of the "theories" it generates depends not so much on "scientific" tests of truth, as on their usefulness in helping people to act more intelligently and skillfully. In action research "theories" are not validated independently and applied to practice. They are validated through practice (Elliott 1981:1).

In this view, action research is a process initiated by teachers and other educational practitioners in response to a practical problem confronting them. Key to Elliott's analysis is the idea that the action researcher builds up a personal interpretive understanding of the work. However, given that the thrust of inquiry is devoted to teachers' practical difficulties, there is implicit in this approach linkage with scientific action research, particularly Elliott's model building, which is based upon Lewinian ideas of spiralling cycles of planning, hypothesizing, fact-finding, and evaluation. One of the chief features of the *Ford Teaching Project*, directed by Elliott, and based upon the study of teachers' ability to implement inquiry-discovery methods in fostering pupils' independent reasoning, was the avowed aim of testing experimental hypotheses. For example, the main premise, or hypothesis, upon which the project was founded was stated in propositional form as "the more able teachers are at self-monitoring in their classroom practice, the more likely they are at bringing about fundamental changes in it" (Elliott 1988:49). In an earlier publication (Elliott 1976) some thirteen hypotheses were stated for Ford Project teachers to test.

A major source of support and inspiration for practical action research came from Lawrence Stenhouse (1975, 1981) and his experimental work on a process model of curriculum development. Through the integrated Humanities Curriculum Project in Britain (Schools Council, 1970), Stenhouse argued that the teacher must adopt a research role towards his or her teaching. Stenhouse defined research as "systematic and sustained inquiry, planned and self-critical, which is subjected to public criticism and to empirical tests where these are appropriate" (Stenhouse 1981:113). The basic tenet of Stenhouse's argument can be briefly stated: teachers are in charge of classrooms and classrooms are the ideal laboratories for testing educational ideas. Moreover the teacher is a participant observer in a naturalistic setting in which each observation and research opportunities present themselves. Theories, furthermore, demand situational verification.

Other notable examples of practical teacher action research are found in Elliott and Ebbutt (1986), Gregory (1988), Hustler, Cassidy, and Cuff (1986), Nixon (1981), and Winter (1987). Typical and memorable is the work of Armstrong (1981) where all the ingredients of teacher diary, ethnography, and literary criticism come together to chart the progress of children's thinking. Enright (1981) discusses the use of the diary as a tool for action research. Thompson (1986) and Kelly, Whyte, and Smail (1984) report some of the effects of Girls Into Science and Technology (GIST), an externally funded large-scale action research project aimed at improving girls' attitudes toward science curriculum and at increasing participation of girls in crafts and science subjects in the U.K.

Several recent examples of classroom action research are contained in Hovda and Kyle (1987). They have gathered an international selection of action research projects in two special issues of the *Peabody Journal of Education*. Among them is Aubrey's (1987) kindergarten study which investigated writing and acceptance of children's natural expression. Another is Richard's (1987) study, "The Bums of 8 H," an action project focusing on the problem of motivating students to learn.

Critical Action Research

It is not my intention to suggest that action research cannot have critical, or indeed, scientific dimensions as well as practical and deliberative dimensions. Indeed, Stenhouse believed that for any inquiry to count as research it must have critical dimensions as well as empirical dimensions. However, to distinguish practical from critical action research, the latter must have a strong affiliation with critical theory, such as the work of the Frankfurt School, especially that of Habermas (1974).

Perhaps the distinction between practical and critical action research is best understood in connection with Elliott's preference for Aristotelian practical philosophy and the work of Gadamer (1975) rather that the work of Habermas. Elliott believes that theoretical understanding is constitutive of practical action and discourse (Elliott 1987:157), whereas on Habermas' account, actions must be subjected to an emancipatory-theoretical critique. That is, for Elliott and Gadamer, actions precede discourse while critical theorists would argue that discourse precipitates action. Gadamer has claimed that forms of understanding that hold persons as their object yield up moral knowledge which serves to guide choice in particular practical situations.

Thus those who hold that critical discourse should precede action would fall into the camp of critical action researchers rather than that of practical action researchers.

Carr and Kemmis (1986) are the principal advocates of critical educational action research. These authors eschew the positivistic-scientific variety of educational research in favor of an activist-interpretive critical philosophy, strongly located in the philosophy of critical theorists such as Habermas, with aspects of Freire's liberation pedagogy and Marxist conceptions added. For Carr and Kemmis

> action research is simply a form of self-reflective inquiry undertaken by participants in social situations in order to improve the rationality and justice of their own practices, their understanding of these practices, and the situations in which the practices are carried out (Carr and Kemmis 1986:164).

Critical educational action researchers seem determined to expose the unjust constraints which thwart teachers' work and impede rational action and equality in schools. Yet the model is not original in conception; it carries much of the baggage of both the scientific and practical conceptions. From the scientific model they borrow heavily from the theoretical spiral model of Kurt Lewin: planning, acting, observing, and, reflecting. This model conceives of the process as a series of reflective spirals in which a general plan is developed, actions and observation of that action ensues, and then reflection on that action is undertaken (Kemmis & McTaggart 1988). Then the spiral is repeated with a new plan and more reflection. Thus the trading off of retrospective understanding and the potential of future action is directly out of the Lewin theory of action research (Lewin 1947). The critical model includes a synthesis of scientific and the practical. From the scientific they lean on the inductive process of scientific problem solving, a la Lewin. From the practical they seek advances in improvement and involvement. Carr and Kemmis argue:

> Action research aims at improvements in three areas: firstly, the improvement of a *practice;* secondly, the improvement of the *understanding* of the practice by its practitioners; and thirdly, the improvement of the *situation* in which the practice takes place (1986:165).

Exponents of critical action research are largely associated with the "Deakin School" of action research at Deakin University in Australia (Carr and Kemmis 1986; Grundy 1987; Kemmis and McTaggart 1987, 1988; Kemmis and Di Chiro 1987). Several case studies of critical curriculum action research are beginning to appear in the literature. A study by Reid (1988) examines the use of writing as a tool to negotiate and understand children's understanding of curriculum. Di Chiro, Robottom, and Tinning (1988) provide an account of action research in a college setting concerning the development of an innovative Biosocial Studies course at Deakin University. In this setting, following dissatisfaction with the organization of the course, changes in course language, organization, and practice were imposed. Tutors were asked to assess these changes. The problem of assessing the changes was subjected to the four dimensions of the action research cycle: planning, acting, observing, and, reflecting. In the first cycle, it became evident that notions like "teacher as researcher" were not engaged or understood by students. Students perceived a gulf between "teaching" and "research." A second cycle, dealing directly with language, organization, and practice caused the team, upon reflection, to conclude that formal assessment had negative effects on course outcomes. This led to action to reorganize the assessment components of the Biosocial Studies course.

Procedures in Curriculum Action Research

In general terms, the procedures for conducting curriculum action research include the following: (1) defining and clarifying the problem, (2) conducting a situational review/needs assessment, (3) formulating hypothesis/ideas for solution, (4) developing an action plan, (5) implementing the action plan, (6) researching-evaluating the effects of action taken, (7) taking decisions — reflecting, explaining, and understanding action taken, (8) recording and disseminating the procedures and results, and (9) if a solution is not evident, this cycle is begun anew; that is, the problem is redefined. Elsewhere, I have described in some detail a model of the action research process as a *series* of action-reflection cycles (McKernan 1988:195).

I will comment upon each of these procedures briefly and illustrate them from an actual study undertaken in Northern Ireland high schools at which I served as an action research facilitator (McKernan et al. 1978).

1. Recognition, Definition, and Clarification of the Problem

One should be clear that action research does not necessarily mean small projects. Skilbeck (1984:99) suggests "what defines action research is not scale, or teacher involvement, but the construction of action programs to solve problems or meet defined practical needs." Action inquiry begins with the recognition that some difficulty or satisfactory practical problem exists. It may be a single or a complex problem. In the School Cultural Studies Project (SCSP) in Northern Ireland teachers had expressed considerable difficulty in getting effective discussion going in connection with implementing a trial set of materials focusing on a multi-site intercultural social studies course for high school studies. The premise advanced in the project was that discussion was the best teaching-learning strategy for developing pupil understanding of contentious value-moral issues. Project teachers commented that discussion was a difficult but desirable teaching strategy for this purpose. The problem in this situation, at least the "general idea" as Elliott (1981) calls it, was to employ discussion as a teaching strategy, improve participation of pupils, and thereby enhance pupil understanding. An important first step was to acknowledge that this difficulty existed across the project schools and that some practical action needed to be taken.

One of the first tasks we undertook was to become clear about the various dimensions of the problem.

- How much talking to pupils do in the classroom?
- How much talking does the teacher do?
- Is teacher talk instructional, question-posing, etc?
- What pupils fail to get involved in discussion?
- What do pupils do when they are not discussing?
- Why do pupils fail to discuss?
- Are the same pupils always opting out of discussion?
- What time of day are discussions held?
- Is the teacher cast in role of expert? Socratic/devil's advocate? Facilitator? Neutral on value issues?
- Does the teacher help to involve pupils?

By asking such questions, we began to clarify the dimensions of the discussion problem and learn new facts pertinent to our inquiry. We were indebted to the work of the Humanities Curriculum Project (Schools Council 1970) for insights into procedures for handling controversial issues through discussion.

The action research problem, as it gradually emerged and became clarified, was formulated as follows: How does a practicing teacher mount effective discussion work in the classroom?

A caveat should be issued at this stage: one should not attempt to tackle problems that are not practical and about which little can be done. Manageability and possibility are key concepts in action research. Pupil participation in discussion may also be related to some larger and deeper problem. For example, it may be the case that pupil's life histories of curriculum and pedagogical experience will show that a particular pedagogy was fostered, such as some authoritative-didactic teaching style, leaving pupils with the belief that discussion and open dialogue is in violation of the school's rules of engagement. Thus, the action research may have to be revised in light of exhuming such constraints on human action.

2. Needs Assessment/Situational Analysis

This step coincides with gathering the answers to the questions posed above and each project teacher reflecting carefully upon where he or she is now and where each would ideally like to be at some future stage of discussion work. The author functioned as a classroom observer/second order facilitator at this stage. By sitting in on classes and keeping field notes, tape recording discussion work, conducting interaction analysis, gathering accounts of practice from the perspectives of both teacher, researcher, and students, I was able to provide a fairly accurate picture of what was actually going on (McKernan 1978). Teachers also answered questionnaires and offered open-ended commentaries in extended interviews on the nature of their discussion work.

3. Action Hypotheses/Ideas/Practical Solutions

On the heel of this fact-finding, or "reconnaissance," certain hypothetical action responses were elicited from project teachers. Teachers decided to test new ideas to improve discussion work. These were formulated formally as hypotheses at bimonthly social studies workshops:

1. Pupil participation will increase if dicussion groups are arranged so that participants are in a face-to-face situation. (Teachers experimented with different furniture rearrangements.)

2. Pupil participation and depth of understanding is related to group size—discussion groups should not be larger than fifteen pupils.

3. The teacher needs to function not as a moral expert, but as a "chairperson" who has responsibility for supporting and encouraging pupil participation/understanding and who follows an agenda working as an "equal" in the group (McKernan et al. 1978).

4. Pupils will more readily agree to participate and consequently develop their understanding, if they agree with the rules laid down for group discussion procedure.

These and a number of other hypotheses were tested by individual teachers in their own classrooms. Progress and difficulties were reported at workshop meetings. Thus, the notion of the "self-monitoring" teacher was sown as part of the professional work ethic of the teachers who saw them-

selves as mounting individual case-studies of their own practice. The net effect was a multi-site attack on common problems by project teachers.

4. Development of the Action Plan

On the basis of the reconnaissance and broad action hypotheses,
teachers and central team staff worked out a set of practical guidelines
for teaching through discussion which modified the role of the teacher
(McKernan et al. 1978).

5. Implementation of the Action Plan

The concern here is to answer the question, "What should be done?
Once an action plan is hatched, the crucial thing is to put it into practice.
This is the essence of studied enactment in action inquiry; it is the stage of
trying things out. Things will work out differently for different teachers. This
is a usual response and should be expected. Modification is almost certain.
Two dozen teachers from twelve project schools experimented with the strategy and evidence of their progress was collected by themselves and central
project staff. Part of the plan was to use the bimonthly workshop meetings
to plan future classes and to gather accounts of teacher experimentation
with the new pedagogical role of discussion. In addition a handbook was
drafted giving precise guidelines for experimentation and monitoring; it was
a do-it-yourself guide to discussion work for teachers (McKernan et al. 1978).

6. Researching and Evaluating the Action Plan

Of paramount importance is the task of observing the effects of the new
action in practice. What are the effects of the revised actions? Emphasis was
placed upon teachers as researchers of their classrooms, a role which was
difficult for many. Teachers were encouraged to keep diaries, logs, anecdotal
records, tape recordings, etc., of their classrooms. They often required the
assistance of an outside non-participant observer who would organize data
collection through audio-video records, field notes, interviews with students
and teachers. Methods of data gathering and analysis for action research are
discussed in Elliott (1976; 1981), Hopkins (1985), Kemmis and McTaggart
(1988), Nixon (1981), and Walker (1985).

Evaluation is about both content and process. That is, new materials
and other forms of "evidence" became the subject of teachers' formative
evaluation as well as teachers' use of the strategy in handling discussion.
Some effort and resources were directed to helping teachers to research
their practice through keeping records, diaries, etc. This led to the identification of a whole range of practical constraints on teachers-as-researchers,

most notably the lack of time and research skills to do research (McKernan 1982, 1989a).

7. Reflecting, Explaining, and Understanding the Action Taken

At this stage the researcher must stop and reflect upon what has transpired. One must unearth the effects of the actions taken and seek to explain these within the context of the project. Here the group has an opportunity to use action research as a way of learning (Shumsky 1958) in terms of reviewing achievements and failures and forging a consensus from the myriad accounts. One should ask "What have we learned thus far?" A simple tabulating of successes and the obvious constraints is required.

In the SCSP project, the essential aspect of dealing with controversial issues is that since they involved value judgments they could not be settled immediately by resource to data. This idea seemed to act as a support to pupils who wished to share their views with others — ironically support in the form of ethical relativity many pupils felt their own beliefs were as good as others! As one pupil commented, "Social studies is a place where you can say those things you are not allowed to say at home."

But teachers are the key reflective actors. At workshop meetings both transcripts and audio/video tapes of teacher-pupil actions were analyzed in an attempt to arrive at rational explanations of the actions. The group in analyzing one classroom discussion noticed that a teacher had not used appropriate questioning techniques to follow-up a pupil's comments when he stated that the hostilities in Northern Ireland caused Catholics and Protestants to hate each other, even though he gave no reasons for this conclusion. Lack of teachers' providing evidence for understanding controversial issues was another point that surfaced from the group's analysis. Another was the difficulty noted in sustaining any coherent theme throughout the discussion. All these analyses provided clues to subsequent actions that they decided should be undertaken.

8. Recording and Disseminating Results

For it to count as research, there is an obligation to keep written records and to record the results of one's inquiry. Both writing and audio/video recording provides the opportunity to reflect when drafting a plan, during the project, and especially at the end of a cycle of work. It is not necessary to publish the account but it should be written to state what has been learned.

A useful technique for recording action inquiry is the short case report. This allows for a concise report to be drafted without the onerous task of writing the more lengthy case study. A brief report will be welcomed by busy teachers and can be used as the stimulus for whole-project team reflection.

9. Revision of Problem: Implementing the Second Action Cycle

Workshop teachers agree that there were problems not noticed at the outset. The real problem was not that of getting discussion of value issues but rather the problems created for teachers as a result of teaching controversial issues. Initially, the problem was cast in pupil terms: getting pupils to discuss. Yet the reflective group more and more began to see a set of problems confronting teachers themselves. In particular, they recognized the problem of getting teachers to reflect upon and research the effects of teaching about controversial issues. This was seen as the key to understanding how pupils can develop their understanding.

The reflective group of action researchers decided as a result of their ongoing work with discussion in the classroom to develop a coherent set of fifteen guidelines, to function as a "code of practice," or set of operational principles of procedure governing discussion. I present four of these guidelines by way of illustration:

- When possible, the teacher, functioning in the role of group discussion leader, should seize the opportunity to develop reflective problem-solving skills: identifying problems, offering hypothetical solutions, testing hypotheses, gathering data, analyzing data, formulating conclusions.
- The teacher-leader should not be seen to dominate discussion or to count as an expert.
- The teacher-leader, not just the pupils, is responsible for introducing new ideas, evidence, facts, resources to fuel the inquiry.
- The teacher-leader should not press for group consensus but elicit a variety of responses and alternative views.

These guidelines functioned as hypotheses which the project teachers continued to test in their work with discussion-based teaching.

Researching Action Inquiry

Smulyan (1987) has pointed out that few researchers have examined the actual collaborative process experienced by a team of project action researchers. However, several researchers (Burton 1986, McKernan 1989b, Ross 1987, Oberg & McCutcheon 1987, Sirotnik 1988) are beginning to focus upon the process of teachers "doing" action research and to describe the constraints on this activity. They note the lack of documentation available from such projects that might shed some light on the types of problems faced. The use of action research in pre-service teacher training (Ross 1987,

Rudduck 1989) is another area of renewed interest for those researching action inquiry.

This chapter has attempted to set forth an understanding of action inquiry as a process of studied enactment. It has argued that action research seeks to inquire into practical problems experienced by practitioners which are problematic and unacceptable, yet within the scope of an acceptable solution. Scientific, practical, and critical conceptions of action research are evident in this form of curriculum inquiry. All these conceptions of action research embody a series of spiralling cycles of planning, acting, observing, and reflecting on the action, and involve the persons experiencing the problem directly in the research process. Moreover, curriculum action research seeks to describe, usually by case study/storytelling, what is happening from the point of view of the teachers, the pupils, and the second-order action researcher (if any); furthermore, these actions are made intelligible by reference to the subjective situated accounts of participants. There is a requirement to observe and provide written accounts of one's experimentation. Research is viewed as systematic self-critical inquiry made public. Participants must observe ethical principles in the conduct of action research; these will include negotiation of access; accounts; respecting confidentiality; obtaining authorization—in short, negotiating a research contract. The language and theories of studied action enactment must be cast in the discourse of the practical language and concepts of the practitioners. Action enactment involves unconstrained dialogue between all actors in the setting. The problem of action research is now one of inducting teachers into the research and deliberation process of curriculum problem-solving. Action research is an invitation to inquiry and self-development. As such, it counts as an authentic form of curriculum inquiry (Schubert 1980, 1986).

References

(Symbols preceding entries are explained on page 40)

o Armstrong, M. (1981). The case of Louise and the painting of landscape. In J. Nixon (Ed.), *A teachers' guide to action research* (pp. 15–36). London: Grant McIntyre.

o Aubrey, M. J. (1987). A teacher's action research study of writing in the kindergarten: Accepting the natural expression of children. *Peabody Journal of Education, 64*(2), 33–64.

√ Borg, W. (1981). *Applying educational research: A practical guide for teachers.* New York: Longman.

√ Borg, W., and Gall, M. (1979). *Educational research: An introduction,* 3rd Ed. New York: Longman.

○ Bowes, D. (1986). Single sex science teaching: A route to bias free choices for third year pupils. In D. Hustler, A. Cassidy, and E. C. Cuff (Eds.). *Action research in classrooms and schools* (pp. 160–165). London: Allen & Unwin.

√ Buckingham, B. R. (1926). *Research for teachers.* New York: Silver Burdett.

+ Burton, F. (1986). A teacher's conception of the action research process. *Language Arts, 63,* 718–723.

○+ Carr, W., and Kemmis, S. (1986). *Becoming critical: Education, knowledge, and action research.* Philadelphia: The Falmer Press.

√ Chein, I., Cook, S., and Harding, J. (1948). The field of action research. *American Psychologist, 3,* 43–50.

○+ Corey, S. M. (1953). *Action research to improve school practices.* New York: Bureau of Publications, Teachers College, Columbia University.

○ Di Chiro, G., Robottom, I., and Tinning, R. (1988). An account of action research in a tertiary context. In S. Kemmis and R. McTaggart (Eds.). *The action research planner,* 3rd Ed. (pp. 132–143). Geelong, Victoria: Deakin University Press.

+ Elliott, J. (1976). Developing hypotheses about classrooms from teachers' practical constructs. *Interchange,* 76(2), 2–22.

+ ———. (1981). Action research: A framework for self-evaluation in schools. Schools Council Programme 2: Teacher Pupil Interaction and the Quality of Learning (TIQL). Working paper No. 1 (pp. 1–28). Norwich: Centre for Applied Research in Education, University of East Anglia.

+ ———. (1985). Educational action research. In J. Nisbet and S. Nisbet (Eds.). *World yearbook of education, 1985: Research, policy, and practice* (pp. 231–250). New York: Kogan Page.

+ ———. (1987). Educational theory, practical philosophy, and action research. *British Journal of Educational Studies,* 35, 149—169.

○ ———. (1988). Teachers as researchers: Implications for supervision and teacher education. Paper given at the Annual Meeting of the American Educational Research Association, New Orleans.

○ Elliott, J., and Ebbutt, D. (Eds.) (1986). *Case studies in teaching for understanding.* Cambridge, UK: Cambridge Institute of Education.

○+ Enright, L. (1981). The diary of a classroom. In J. Nixon (Ed.), *A teachers' guide to action research* (pp. 37–51). London: Grant McIntyre.

√ Gadamer, H. G. (1975). *Truth and method*. London: Sheed and Ward.

○ Gregory, R. (1988). *Action research in the secondary school*. London: Routledge, Chapman, & Hall.

√ Griffin, G. A., Lieberman, A., and Jacullo-Noto, J. (1983). *Executive summary of the final report on interactive research and development on schools*. Austin: University of Texas, Research and Development Center for Teacher Education.

+ Grundy, S. (1987). Critical curriculum practice: Developing curriculum praxis. In *Curriculum: Product or Praxis* (pp. 121–160). Philadelphia: The Falmer Press.

√ Habermas, J. (1974). *Theory and practice*. Trans. by J. Veirtel. London: Heinemann.

+ Hopkins, D. (1985). *A teacher's guide to classroom research*. Philadelphia: Open University Press.

○+ Hovda, R., and Kyle, D. (Issue Eds.) (1987). The potential and practice·of action research, Parts I & II. *Peabody Journal of Education, 64*(2) & *64*(3).

○ Hustler, D., Cassidy, A., and Cuff, E. C. (Eds.) (1986). *Action research in classrooms and schools*. London: Allen & Unwin.

○ Kelly, A., Whyte, J., and Smail, B. (1984). *Girls into science and technology: Final Report*. Manchester, UK: Department of Sociology, Manchester University.

+ Kemmis, S., and Di Chiro, G. (1987). Emerging and evolving issues of action research praxis: An Australian perspective. *Peabody Journal of Education, 64*(3), 101–130.

○ Kemmis S., and McTaggart, R. (Eds.) (1987). *The action research reader*. Geelong, Victoria: Deakin University Press.

○+ ———. (Eds.) (1988). *The action research planner,* 3rd Ed. Geelong, Victoria: Deakin University Press.

√ Lewin, K. (1946). Action research and minority problems. *Journal of Social Issues, 2,* 34–46.

√ ———. (1947). Group decision and social change. In G. E. Swanson, T. Newcomb, and E. Hartley (Eds.). *Readings in social psychology* (pp. 330–344). New York: Henry Holt.

√ Lippitt, R., and Radke, M. (1946). New trends in the investigation of prejudice. *Annals of the American Academy of Political and Social Science, 244,* 167–176.

√ Marrow, A. J. (1969). *The practical theorist: The life and work of Kurt Lewin.*
New York: Basic Books.

○ McKernan, J. (1978). *Teaching controversial issues.* Unpublished Doctor of
Philosophy thesis. Coleraine, NI: University of Ulster.

○ ———. (1982). Constraints on the handling of controversial issues in Northern Ireland post-primary schools. *British Educational Research Journal,*
8(2), 57–71.

+ ———. (1988). The countenance of curriculum action research: Traditional,
collaborative, and emancipatory-critical conceptions. *Journal of Curriculum and Supervision, 3,* 173–200.

+ ———. (1989a). Constraints on curriculum action research. Paper presented
at the Annual Meeting of the American Educational Research Association,
San Francisco.

+ ———. (1989b). Varieties of curriculum action research: Constraints and typologies in Anglo-Irish and American projects. Paper presented at the Annual Meeting of the American Educational Research Association, San
Francisco.

○ McKernan, J., Haire, A., & Patton, J. (1978). *Discussion as a teaching strategy.*
Handbook No. 1, Schools Cultural Studies Project. Coleraine, NI: Education Center, University of Ulster.

○+ Nixon, J. (Ed.) (1981). *A teacher's guide to action research.* London: Grant
McIntyre.

√ Oakeshott, M. (1967). Rational conduct. In *Rationalism in politics.* London:
Methuen.

+ Oberg, A. A., and McCutcheon, G. (1987). Teachers' experience doing action
research. *Peabody Journal of Education, 64*(2), 116–127.

○+ Oja, S. N., and Smulyan, L. (1989). *Collaborative action research: A developmental process.* Philadelphia: The Falmer Press.

○ Reid, J. (1988). Negotiating education. In S. Kemmis and R. McTaggart (Eds.).
The action research planner, 3rd Ed. (pp. 111 – 132). Geelong, Victoria:
Deakin University Press.

+ Reid, W. A. (1978). *Thinking about the curriculum: The nature and treatment
of curriculum problems.* Boston: Routledge & Kegan Paul.

○ Richards, M. (1987). A teacher's action research study: The bums of 8 H. *Peabody Journal of Education, 64*(2), 65–79.

+ Ross, D. (1987). Action research for pre-service teachers: A description of why
and how. *Peabody Journal of Education, 64*(3), 131–150.

+ Rudduck, J. (1989). Critical thinking and practitioner research: Have they a place in initial teacher training? Paper presented at the Annual Meeting of the American Educational Research Association, San Francisco.

√ Schools Council/Nuffield Foundation (U.K.) (1970). *The humanities curriculum project: An introduction.* London: Heinemann.

+ Schubert, W. H. (1980). Recalibrating educational research: Toward a focus on practice. *Educational Researcher, 9*(1), 17–24, 31.

+ ———. (1986). Curriculum research controversy: A special case of a general problem. *Journal of Curriculum and Supervision, 1,* 132–147.

+ Schwab, J. J. (1969). The practical: A language for curriculum. *School Review, 78,* 1–23.

+ ———. (1971). The practical: Arts of eclectic. *School Review, 79,* 493–542.

+ ———. (1973). The practical 3: Translation into curriculum. *School review, 81,* 501–522.

+ ———. (1983). The practical 4: Something for curriculum professors to do. *Curriculum Inquiry, 13,* 239–265.

+ Shumsky, A. (1958). *The action research way of learning.* New York: Bureau of Publications, Teachers College, Columbia University.

+ Sirotnik, K. A. (1988). The meaning and conduct of inquiry in school-university partnerships. In K. A. Sirotnik and J. I. Goodlad (Eds.). *School-university partnerships in action: Concepts, cases, and concerns.* New York: Teachers College Press.

+ Skilbeck, M. (1984). *School-based curriculum development.* London: Harper.

+ Smulyan, L. (1987). Collaborative action research: A critical analysis. *Peabody Journal of Education, 64*(3), 57–70.

+ Stenhouse, L. (1975). *An introduction to curriculum research and development.* London: Heinemann.

+ ———. (1981). What counts as research? *British Journal of Educational Studies, 29,* 103–114.

+ Strike, K. A. (1979). An epistemology of practical research. *Educational Researcher, 8*(1), 10–16.

o Taba, H., and Noel, E. (1957). *Action research: A case study.* Washington, D.C.: Association for Supervision and Curriculum Development.

o Taba, H., Brady, E. H., and Robinson, J. (1952). *Intergroup education in public schools.* Washington, D.C.: American Council on Education.

o The Southern Study (1946). *Cooperative study for the improvement of education.* A Staff Report of the Southern Association Study prepared by F. Jenkins, D. C. Kent, V. M. Sims, and E. A. Waters. In *Southern Association Quarterly, 10,* February-August.

o Thompson, J. (1986). Some unseen efforts of GIST. In D. Hustler, A. Cassidy, and E. C. Cuff (Eds.), *Action research in classrooms and schools* (pp. 147–155). London: Allen & Unwin.

√ Tikunoff, W. J., Ward, B., and Griffin, G. A. (1979). *Interactive research and development on teaching study,* Final Report. San Francisco, CA: Far West Laboratory for Educational Research and Development.

+ Walker, R. (1985). *Doing research: A handbook for teachers.* London: Methuen.

√ Wallace, M. (1987). A historical review of action research: Some implications for the education of teachers in their managerial role. *Journal of Education for Teaching, 13,* 97–115.

o Winter, R. (1987). *Action research and the nature of social inquiry: Professional innovation and educational work.* Aldershot, Hants: Gower.

Afterword:
Closing Reflections

—— *Edmund C. Short*

The authors of the preceding chapters have sought to articulate the essential processes and rationales associated with the use of various forms of curriculum inquiry. It is now appropriate to reflect upon the value and significance of their work, to raise some issues suggested by the volume as a whole, and to appraise the current status of curriculum inquiry on the basis of what has been presented here.

Significance and Value

Viewed as a whole, the work of these writers demonstrates the extraordinary breadth and vitality of the contemporary enterprise in curriculum inquiry. New forms of curriculum inquiry have entered the field and gained legitimacy. In terms of their utility and acceptability they have gained status among curriculum researchers; in terms of their methodological and epistemological soundness they have met the test of critical scholarship. Both the conventional and the newer forms of curriculum inquiry are extensively explained and grounded in the more general literature on these forms of inquiry and are able to withstand the arguments of those who would discount any of them as ill-conceived or as inept ways of creating knowledge. While no codified research methodology is entirely free of criticism, the basic legitimacy of these forms of inquiry is no longer really being questioned. Their place within the repertoire of legitimate forms of curriculum inquiry is assured. Arguments over the best form of curriculum inquiry or over which is and which is not legitimate are virtually ended.

Another matter of significance is apparent in the chapters toward the end of the book: the central place of interdisciplinary inquiry in curriculum research. A number of distinguishable interdisciplinary forms of inquiry have emerged and have been increasingly used to address practice-oriented

327

questions in curriculum. Their relevance to this task is now more broadly understood. Because many curriculum questions are so complex, they require interdisciplinary approaches. If it was not previously understood that there are several different kinds of interdisciplinary inquiry, the last seven chapters in the book make this fact quite clear. While these forms of inquiry differ in purpose and process from one another, all use a selected set of disciplinary or transdisciplinary forms of inquiry in conjunction with their own special focus and methodology.

Beyond their usefulness in interdisciplinary research, the various forms of disciplinary inquiry have important independent uses in curriculum inquiry as well. They can address questions that only disciplinary forms of inquiry can address. The importance of these forms of inquiry in curriculum research is well illustrated in the several chapters at the beginning of the book. The entire book argues implicitly that both disciplinary and interdisciplinary forms of inquiry are essential if the whole range of curriculum research questions is to be dealt with adequately.

It is obvious from the examples of curriculum studies cited throughout the book that a greater range and variety of curriculum topics and questions are now being studied than was possible in the past when a somewhat limited set of research approaches was being recognized and used. These expanded approaches have increased the capability of addressing more and different kinds of curriculum research questions. For this reason, the chances of providing curriculum practitioners and others with more of the kind of knowledge they need to deal intelligently with their day-to-day problems and decisions have increased considerably. This is indeed a significant development.

One of the most valuable revelations of this book is how the language used in curriculum inquiry has been transformed from a narrower, limited language of two or three decades ago to the rich and highly diversified language of today. The appropriation of new forms of inquiry into curriculum research has brought not simply an alternative language to the earlier scientific and theoretical language but many alternative languages as well.

Dwayne Huebner, to whom this book is dedicated, wrote a paper in 1963 entitled, "Notes Toward a Framework for Curriculum Inquiry," in which he sought to expand the range of inquiry that might be undertaken within the field of curriculum studies. He focused on two kinds of language: *theoretical language* — "language used by an observer of curricular events which is intended for the description, explanation, and prediction of occurrences of these curricular events;" and *ideological language* — "language used by an actor within a curricular event, which is intended to facilitate the identification of alternative courses of action available to the actor, the selection of one alternative, and the legitimation of his decisions and actions prior to or after the decision and act" (Huebner 1963:2). On the basis of this perspective, Huebner projected a program of curriculum inquiry, developed suitable concepts and language systems for this program, and offered forms of inquiry ranging from the analytic to the critical, from the anticipatory to the legitimating, from the aesthetic to the imaginative, and from the philosophical to the political.

In so doing, Huebner foreshadowed the expansion of curriculum inquiry to include a variety of forms of inquiry and thereby stressed the significance of creating new language in curriculum research. The choice of vocabulary matched with the inquiry tools of the various forms of inquiry is at the heart of the research enterprise. It provides a new way of seeing something or of seeing something from a different perspective. In a 1966 article entitled, "Curriculum Language and Classroom Meanings," Huebner cast these same views into a case for recognizing diverse systems of rationality that can guide curriculum research and practice. He identified scientific, aesthetic, technical, ethical, and political rationalities, each of which carry with them the use of a specific language system. In the chapters in this book there is ample evidence that the specialized vocabularies associated with the various forms of inquiry have brought new vision and new power to the research going on in curriculum studies.

Issues

One of the issues this book raises is the question of how best to conceive and distinguish various forms of inquiry. A case was made in the introduction to this volume for the way in which this book addressed and dealt with this issue. Nevertheless, a critical reading of the chapters is bound to raise questions about possible overlaps, subdivisions, or omissions among the forms of inquiry presented. To stimulate further thought regarding one of these questions, the possibility of overlaps among several of these forms of inquiry, consider the problems posed by the terms "critical" or "criticism" appearing in the titles of three different chapters.

The chapters on ampliative criticism, aesthetic criticism, and critical praxis are presented as quite different forms of inquiry. The first, ampliative criticism, is considered to be philosophical inquiry because its purpose is to correct and amplify a system of curricular thought and argument. The second is artistic because its purpose is to disclose the formal qualities of a curricular work aesthetically. The third is ethical and practical because its purpose is to prompt corrective action where practice and intent are at odds. The sort of criticism operative in each of these forms of inquiry is not the same. In the first it is a logical and semantic criticism. In the second it is a criticism involving connoisseurship. In the third it is a type of practical criticism in which the discrepancy between word and deed is removed.

If there is a similarity among these forms of inquiry, it is in their use of evaluative criteria for making discriminating judgments. In this regard they share this feature with several other very different forms of inquiry, such as conceptual analysis, theoretical inquiry, normative inquiry, evaluative inquiry, integrative inquiry, deliberative inquiry, and action inquiry. So this apparent similarity is not a similarity in form but in process.

There is another set of inquiry approaches where it is possible to observe the presence of apparent similarities in form. In narrative inquiry, phenomenological inquiry, and hermeneutic inquiry there are clear overlaps in method and purpose. The origin of the research data in all these approaches is from within the subject, stated by the subject, and negotiated between the subject and the researcher. Some scholars assert that there is really only one basic form of inquiry here (the interpretive) with three possible emphases — either on the subject's perceptions, on the subject's own statement of personal narrative, or on the negotiated meaning of the statement between researcher and subject.

The view presented in this book is that these are three separate and distinct forms of inquiry because each can address separate research questions and the other two forms are not required to be used to address the pertinent question. All three focus on language as mediator of a subject's meanings, and thus there is another kinship across these forms of inquiry that is not shared by other forms of inquiry. But there the similarities end. Each has its own purpose, logic of procedure, and standards for establishing knowledge claims.

On the other hand, it might be possible to slice these critical and interpretive forms of inquiry in other ways. Much careful taxonomical work needs to be done on this whole matter of identifying and distinguishing various forms of inquiry if the issues involved are to be satisfactorily resolved. Meanwhile, most researchers, curriculum researchers included, will probably go on using or inventing forms of inquiry they find fitting for their particular research programs regardless of how they are labeled or distinguished from other forms of inquiry.

Another issue the book raises concerns the epistemological assumptions underlying the work presented on each form of inquiry. Fuller explication of these assumptions might have been desirable in certain cases. On what grounds can the results of narrative inquiry, for instance, or aesthetic inquiry or action inquiry, be said to be valid knowledge? How are the stated methods of procedure to be justified in relation to these assumptions? These and other related questions, while sometimes addressed in part in some of these chapters, are legitimate questions that should be raised about all of these guidelines for inquiry if we want to assess their authenticity as viable approaches to generating knowledge. While these issues are elaborated upon to some extent in various chapters, most of the writers choose to refer readers to more fundamental treatises where the epistemological bases for the particular form of inquiry are spelled out in greater detail rather than attempt to do this themselves in the limited space available. For a fuller understanding of these matters, it would be well to turn to these treatises and find the necessary elaboration not always stated here in these chapters. Informed criticism might then be pursued (Eisner and Peshkin 1990, Howe and Eisenhart 1990).

Another complaint that might be registered is that several of these writers do not deal with the various orientations that researchers bring to their work that govern the way they perceive and use the same form of inquiry—what is referred to in the opening essay as *theories of inquiry*. It is inevitable that some view of how best to orient the particular form of inquiry might be adopted by a researcher. It may be rationalistic or technical, humanistic or metaphysical, or any one of a number of other value orientations. This is what Huebner identified as systems of rationality. They color the choice of concepts and language that emerge within the inquiry.

Some scholars suggest that research is value-free, relying solely upon the dictates of standard methodologies to produce knowledge. Yet it is evident that among those who use the same form of inquiry there are several "schools of inquiry" which reflect different ways of interpreting the use of the methodology. These differences can be argued but the arguments cannot be settled. In the end one has to adopt an orientation one believes is most valid.

It would be instructive to turn back to the various chapters in this book and note those that explicitly identify some of the commonly held theories or norms of inquiry that are extant in curriculum inquiry. Where these orientations are not acknowledged explicitly, readers might examine the cited studies of that type to determine what orientation the researchers adopted and whether there is convergence among studies toward a single orientation or whether a wide variety of theories of inquiry are being used.

A related issue concerns where all this diversity among forms of curriculum inquiry and in inquiry orientations within each form of inquiry is leading. The implication to be drawn from the book is that these trends are desirable and are to be welcomed. Nevertheless, some curriculum scholars are skeptical that these trends are advantageous. They suggest that curriculum inquiry would be better served by focusing attention on the practical need for certain kinds of curriculum knowledge and using the most promising forms of inquiry to address them with a barrage of studies.

Perhaps the best solution of this issue is not an either-or decision but a both-and decision. The tendency when concentrating on particular needs of the field is for new and diverse approaches to be ignored or forgotten; the tendency when diversity in approach and orientation reigns is for particular knowledge needs to fail to attract enough studies to turn up useful knowledge. Neither of these extremes is advantageous. The field of curriculum inquiry no doubt needs to be open simultaneously to work of both types.

Status

Between the 1960s and the 1990s a considerable shift has taken place in the kind and focus of research being done in the field of curriculum inquiry. In the early 1960s, reviews of curriculum research noted that the emphasis was on developing theories or conceptual systems describing or prescribing curriculum or curriculum planning processes (Goodlad 1960, Elliott and Foshay 1963). This is akin to what is discussed in this book under theoretical inquiry though it was then more narrowly focused and understood than it is today and its methods of inquiry were less well articulated. In the intervening years since the 1960s we have paid less attention to this kind of work and are only now returning seriously to it with renewed interest and with more viable methods of inquiry at our disposal.

Huebner's (1963) work, previously mentioned, first urged the use of multiple forms of inquiry in curriculum studies. Probably because Huebner's paper remained unpublished, its influence was more limited than the work of Joseph Schwab (1970). Schwab reached a wider audience through publications and conference presentations with his admonitions to break away from the search for curriculum theories and to employ the methods of the practical. This is akin to what is described in this book under deliberative and action inquiry. The net result of Huebner's and Schwab's leadership in curriculum inquiry was the gradual appearance of several alternative approaches to the early 1960s reliance on scientific theoretical work.

Historical inquiry was championed by Arno Bellack and subsequent generations of curriculum scholars including Herbert Kliebard, Laurel Tanner, Daniel Tanner, and O. L. Davis, Jr. Others such as James Macdonald (1971), William Pinar (1974), and Elliot Eisner (1979) pioneered in reaching out to philosophy, literature, politics, critical theory, aesthetics, psychoanalysis, and many other fields to embrace their disciplinary forms of inquiry or to appropriate their language or value orientations. State-of-the-art reviews of the status of curriculum research in the 1980s recognized the growth and valuable contribution that all these forms of inquiry were making to the field of curriculum studies (Schubert 1982; Jenkins 1985; Short 1987).

The present volume testifies to two more recent developments in curriculum inquiry beyond acknowledging and demonstrating the accomplishments noted in the 1980s. First, it gives evidence of the rising self-consciousness of those doing curriculum inquiry about the quality and authenticity of the various methods of inquiry that the field has embraced. Researchers are asking and answering questions about how to do these types of inquiry and how to do them well. They are now writing sophisticated guidelines for conducting these forms of inquiry that attempt to ground them in legitimate arguments related to longer traditions of inquiry found elsewhere in disciplinary or practical fields of inquiry. By so doing, they are beginning to take responsibility for educating new generations of curriculum scholars in the arts of doing curriculum inquiry in its various forms. This new development involving the articulation of inquiry approaches and communication of these to would-be researchers cannot help but enhance the quality of inquiry done in the future in the field of curriculum studies. This important new development may mark the advent of an entirely new era in curriculum research.

Second, this book gives evidence that the battles of the 1970s and 1980s waged within the field of curriculum studies over introducing some of the newer forms of curriculum inquiry are for the most part behind us and that now more careful and balanced discourse, with less political and polemic overtones, is the order of the day in the 1990s. There is little evidence in the chapters of this book of the attitude that "my-form-of-inquiry-is-better-than-your-form-of-inquiry." In fact, there is an implicit acceptance of alternative forms of curriculum inquiry by each of the writers, prompted no doubt by the recognition that the forms of inquiry they describe are suited to only certain kinds of curriculum questions and that other kinds of questions are important and need to be addressed by other appropriate forms of inquiry. This development moves the field of curriculum studies a long way beyond the attitudes of the 1960s and, for that matter, beyond those of the 1970s and 1980s.

The work presented in this book is forward-looking and hopeful. It represents a major intellectual accomplishment. While it is difficult to predict where curriculum inquiry will go during the rest of the 1990s, the presentations of the various forms of curriculum inquiry in this book put the field of curriculum studies in a much better position to advance its research and practice goals than at any time in the past.

References

Eisner, E. W. (1979). *The educational imagination: On the design and evaluation of school programs.* New York: Macmillan.

Eisner, E. W., and Peshkin (Eds.) (1990). *Qualitative inquiry in education: The continuing debate.* New York: Teachers College Press.

Elliot, D. L. and Foshay, A. W. (1963). Chart or charter: Recent developments in educational discourse. *Review of Educational Research, 33*(3), 233–244.

Goodlad, J. I. (1960). Curriculum: The state of the field. *Review of Educational Research, 30*(3), 185–245.

Howe, K., and Eisenhart, M. (1990). Standards for qualitative (and quantitative) research: A prolegomenon. *Educational Researcher, 19*(4), 2–9.

Huebner, D. (1963). Notes toward a framework for curriculum inquiry. Unpublished paper. Forthcoming in *Journal of Curriculum and Supervision, 6*(2).

Huebner, D. (1966). Curricular language and classroom meanings. In J. B. Macdonald and R. R. Leeper (Eds.), *Language and meaning*, pp. 8–26. Washington, D.C.: Association for Supervision and Curriculum Development.

Jenkins, D. (1985). Curriculum research. In T. Husen and T. N. Postlethwaite (Eds.), *The international encyclopedia of education*, pp. 1257–1263. London: Pergamon.

Macdonald, J. B. (1971). Curriculum theory. *Journal of Educational Research, 64*(5), 196–200.

Pinar, W. F. (Ed.) (1974). *Heightened consciousness, cultural revolution, and curriculum theory.* Berkeley, CA: McCutchan.

Schubert, W. H. (1982). Curriculum research. In H. E. Mitzel (Ed.), *Encyclopedia of educational research*, 5th Ed., pp. 420–431. New York: Macmillan.

Schwab, J. J. (1970). *The practical: A language for curriculum.* Washington, D.C.: National Education Association.

Short, E. C. (1987). Curriculum research in retrospect. ERIC Document Reproduction Service. ED 282 919.

Contributors

Louise M. Berman is Professor of Education at the University of Maryland.

D. Jean Clandinin is Professor of Education at the University of Alberta.

Jerrold R. Combs is Professor of Education at the University of British Columbia.

F. Michael Connelly is Professor of Education at the Ontario Institute for Studies in Education.

LeRoi Daniels is Professor of Education at the University of British Columbia.

O. L. Davis, Jr., is Professor of Education at the University of Texas at Austin.

Arthur W. Foshay is Professor Emeritus of Education at Teachers College, Columbia University.

Richard W. Grove is Research Associate at Research for Better Schools in Philadelphia.

Nelson L. Haggerson is Professor Emeritus of Education at Arizona State University.

Ilene B. Harris is Associate Professor in the Medical School and Adjunct Associate Professor of Education at the University of Minnesota.

Valerie J. Janesick is Associate Professor of Education at The University of Kansas.

Jean A. King is Associate Professor of Education at the University of Minnesota.

Colin Marsh is with the Secondary Education Authority of Western Australia in Osborne Park.

Jim McKernan is Lecturer in Education at University College Dublin, National University of Ireland.

William H. Schubert is Professor of Education at the University of Illinois at Chicago.

Edmund C. Short is Professor of Education at The Pennsylvania State University.

Kenneth A. Sirotnik is Professor of Education at the University of Washington.

David G. Smith is Associate Professor of Education at the University of Lethbridge.

Elizabeth Vallance is Director of Education at The Saint Louis Art Museum.

George H. Willis is Professor of Education at the University of Rhode Island.

DEMCO 38-296

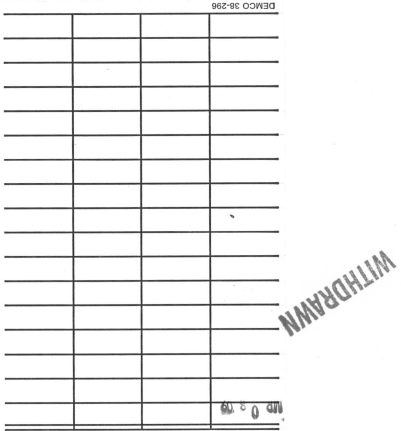

DATE DUE

WITHDRAWN